1 and 2 Timothy, Titus

Good News Commentaries

1 and 2 Timothy, Titus

Gordon D. Fee

A GOOD NEWS COMMENTARY

New Testament Editor

W. Ward Gasque

1817

HARPER & ROW, PUBLISHERS, SAN FRANCISCO

Cambridge, Hagerstown, New York, Philadelphia
London, Mexico City, São Paulo, Singapore, Sydney

for
David M. Scholer
and
J. Ramsey Michaels
fellow servants
and
fellow heirs

1 AND 2 TIMOTHY, TITUS: *A Good News Commentary.*
Copyright © 1984 by Gordon D. Fee. All rights reserved. Printed in the United States of America. No
part of this book may be used or reproduced in any
manner whatsoever without written permission except in the case of brief quotations embodied in critical
articles and reviews. For information address Harper
& Row, Publishers, Inc., 10 East 53rd Street, New
York, NY 10022. Published simultaneously in Canada by Fitzhenry & Whiteside, Limited, Toronto.

FIRST EDITION

Designed by Design Office Bruce Kortebein

**Library of Congress Cataloging in Publication
Data**
Fee, Gordon D.
    1 AND 2 TIMOTHY, TITUS.

    (A Good News Commentary)
    Bibliography: p.
    Includes index.
        1. Bible. N.T. Pastoral Epistles—Commentaries.
I. Bible. N.T. Pastoral Epistles. 1984. II. Title.
III. Title: First and Second Timothy, Titus.
IV. Series.
BS2735.3.F44   1984   227'.83077   83-49061
ISBN 0-06-062338-1

84 85 86 87 88 10 9 8 7 6 5 4 3 2 1

About the Series

This is the first major series to use the popular Good News Bible, which has sold in the millions. Each volume is informed by solid scholarship and the most up-to-date research, yet each is biblically faithful and readily understandable to the general reader. Features include:

Introductory material highlighting authorship, dating, background information, and thematic emphases—plus a map

Full text of each Good News Bible book, with running commentary

Special end notes giving references for key words and concepts and providing suggestions for further reading

Full indexes for Scripture and Subjects/Persons/Places.

Series Editor W. Ward Gasque is Vice-Principal and Professor of New Testament at Regent College in Vancouver. A former editor-at-large for *Christianity Today*, he is the author of numerous articles and books and has edited *In God's Community: Studies in the Church and Its Ministry, Handbook of Biblical Prophecy, Apostolic History and the Gospel,* and *Scripture, Tradition, and Intererpretation.* Dr. Gasque's major involvement is in the provision of theological resources and education for the laity.

Contents

Foreword

The Good News Bible Commentary Series

A lthough it does not appear on the standard best-seller lists, the Bible continues to outsell all other books. And in spite of growing secularism in the West, there are no signs that interest in its message is abating. Quite to the contrary, more and more men and women are turning to its pages for insight and guidance in the midst of the ever-increasing complexity of modern life.

This renewed interest in Scripture is found outside of, as well as in, the church. It is found among people in Asia and Africa as well as in Europe and North America; indeed, as one moves outside of the traditionally Christian countries, interest in the Bible seems to quicken. Believers associated with the traditional Catholic and Protestant churches manifest the same eagerness for the word that is found in the newer evangelical churches and fellowships.

Millions of individuals read the Bible daily for inspiration. Many of these lay Bible students join with others in small study groups in homes, office buildings, factories, and churches to discuss a passage of Scripture on a weekly basis. This small-group movement is one that seems certain to grow even more in the future, since leadership of nearly all churches is encouraging these groups, and they certainly seem to be filling a significant gap in people's lives. In addition, there is renewed concern for biblical preaching throughout the church. Congregations where systematic Bible teaching ranks high on the agenda seem to have no difficulty filling their pews, and "secular" men and women who have no particular interest in joining a church are often quite willing to join a nonthreatening, informal Bible discussion group in their neighborhood or place of work.

We wish to encourage and, indeed, strengthen this worldwide movement of lay Bible study by offering this new commentary series. Although we hope that pastors and teachers will find these volumes helpful in both understanding and communicating the Word of God, we do not write primarily for them. Our aim is, rather, to provide for the benefit of the ordinary Bible reader reliable guides to the books of the Bible, representing the best of contemporary scholarship presented in a form that does not require formal theological education to understand.

The conviction of editors and authors alike is that the Bible belongs to the people and not merely to the academy. The message of the Bible is too important to be locked up in erudite and esoteric essays and monographs written for the eyes of theological specialists. Although exact scholarship has its place in the service of Christ, those who share in the teaching office of the church have a responsibility to make the results of their research accessible to the Christian community at large. Thus, the Bible scholars who join in the presentation of this series write with these broader concerns in view.

A wide range of modern translations is available to the contemporary Bible student. We have chosen to use the Good News Bible (Today's English Version) as the basis of our series for three reasons. First, it has become the most widely used translation, both geographically and ecclesiastically. It is read wherever English is spoken and is immensely popular with people who speak English as a second language and among people who were not brought up in the church. In addition, it is endorsed by nearly every denominational group.

Second, the Good News Bible seeks to do what we are seeking to do in our comments, namely, translate the teaching of the Bible into terms that can be understood by the person who has not had a strong Christian background or formal theological education. Though its idiomatic and sometimes paraphrastic style has occasionally frustrated the scholar who is concerned with a minute examination of the original Greek and Hebrew words, there can be no question but that this translation makes the Scripture more accessible to the ordinary reader than any other English translation currently available.

Third, we wish to encourage group study of the Bible, particularly by people who have not yet become a part of the church but who are interested in investigating for themselves the claims of Christ. We believe that the Good News Bible is by far the best translation for group discussion. It is both accurate and fresh, free from jargon, and, above all, contemporary. No longer does the Bible seem like an ancient book, belonging more to the museum than to the modern metropolis. Rather, it is as comprehensible and up-to-date as the daily newspaper.

We have decided to print the full text of the Good News Bible—and we are grateful for the kind permission of the United Bible Societies to do this—in our commentary series. This takes up valuable space, but we believe that it will prove to be very convenient for those who make use of the commentary, since it will enable them to read it straight through like an ordinary book as well as use it for reference.

Each volume will contain an introductory chapter detailing the background of the book and its author, important themes, and other helpful information. Then, each section of the book will be expounded as a whole, accompanied by a series of notes on items in the text that need further clarification or more detailed explanation. Appended to the end of each volume will be a bibliographical guide for further study.

Our new series is offered with the prayer that it may be an instrument of authentic renewal and advancement in the worldwide Christian community and a means of commending the faith of the people who lived in biblical times and of those who seek to live by the Bible today.

W. WARD GASQUE

Preface

Commentaries are of several kinds. Some interpret the text by carrying on a running dialogue with previous commentaries; others are written as if there had been no previous commentaries. Some are concerned strictly with exegesis (what the text meant to its original recipients); others are more concerned with the here and now, that is, how this word applies for today, but without sufficient regard for what it originally meant (except when they have difficulties to get around!). Since this commentary is purposely of a single kind and has a rather singular point of view, it seemed appropriate at the outset to explain what is intended.

The basic concern throughout is with exegesis, an exposition of Paul's intent in writing these letters to Timothy and Titus in their historical context. But since I am also a committed believer in Scripture as God's Word, it will be clear throughout that more is at stake than merely being informed about the past. However, despite the concern that these letters be heard as God's Word for today, there has been every attempt to remove dogmatic or partisan applications. Hence the reader for the most part has been left on her or his own to "make the applications." For guidelines on these matters, one might consult my *How to Read the Bible for All Its Worth* (co-authored with Douglas Stuart).

What is more important to note is the singular point of view from which this commentary has been written. As will be noted in the Introduction, the crucial matter for writing a commentary on these Epistles is whether or not they are authentic. After teaching these letters several times at the college and seminary level, I grew to have a firm conviction that, despite the linguistic, stylistic, and theological difficulties, one could make more sense of them as having been written by Paul than otherwise. But I was still generally dissatisfied both with my own teaching and with most commentaries that shared my convictions about authorship, because there seemed to be a lack of unifying perspective as to why they were written and what they were all about. It was clear to all that some false teachers lay behind the writing of what was supposed to be the earliest of the letters—1 Timothy. But in general only lip service was paid to that reality; thereafter everything was treated as though what Paul intended were a church manual, to guide the church organizationally through its ongoing years. It was this point of view that I found myself uneasy with, even though much in chapters 2, 3, and 5 seemed to support it.

Then one year I decided to lead a group of seminarians through 1 Timothy by taking 1:3 absolutely seriously—as though that really *were* the reason for the letter, namely, to urge Timothy to stop the false teachers in Ephesus. At every point we asked, How does this, or *may* this, reflect the *ad hoc* situation of the church in Ephesus that was being torn apart by false teachers? The results astonished us. And after a few more times through the PE (Pastoral Episltes) with other classes, I became fully convinced of the correctness of this point of view. It is exactly how one makes the best sense of *all* the earlier letters of Paul, and for me and several generations of seminarians, it has become the key to understanding the PE as well.

I want to thank those many seminarians at Gordon-Conwell who, over several years, have helped shape the thinking that has gone into this commentary, and especially the members of the seminar of Winter Term, 1983, who interacted with the rough draft of this work and helped to make it a better book. Above all I must thank my teaching assistant, Patrick Alexander, who has provided so much help by reading through two full drafts and thus improving the style at many points, by checking primary and secondary references, and by arranging the bibliography. Special thanks to Corinne Languedoc, faculty secretary par excellance, and Connie Gundry and Barbara DeNike, whose combined typing skills made it possible to meet the publisher's deadline.

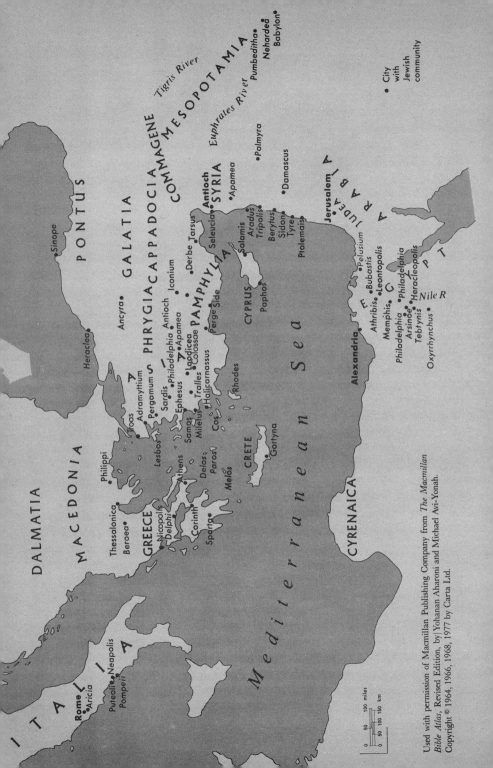

ITALIA
Rome
Aricia
Puteoli
Neapolis
Pompeii

DALMATIA

MACEDONIA
Thessalonica
Beroea
Philippi

GREECE
Nicopolis
Delphi
Corinth
Sparta
Athens
Delos
Paros
Melos

Lesbos
Samos
Miletus
Cos

CRETE
Gortyna

PONTUS
Sinope
Heraclea

GALATIA
Ancyra

PHRYGIA
Troas
Adramyttium
Pergamum
Sardis
Ephesus
Tralles
Philadelphia
Laodicea
Colosse
Halicarnassus
Rhodes

CAPPADOCIA

COMMAGENE

MESOPOTAMIA
Tigris River
Euphrates River
Pumbeditha
Nehardea
Babylon

Palmyra

Antioch
Seleucia
SYRIA
Apamea
Damascus
Apamea
Derbe
Tarsus
Iconium
Antioch

PAMPHYLIA
Perge
Side

CYPRUS
Salamis
Paphos

Aradus
Tripolis
Berytus
Sidon
Tyre
Ptolemais

JUDEA
Jerusalem

ARABIA

EGYPT
Pelusium
Alexandria
Bubastis
Athribis
Leontopolis
Memphis
Philadelphia
Arsinoe
Tebtynis
Oxyrhynchus
Heracleopolis
Nile R

CYRENAICA

Mediterranean Sea

• City
  with
  Jewish
  community

50   100 miles
50 100 150 km

Used with permission of Macmillan Publishing Company from *The Macmillan Bible Atlas*, Revised Edition, by Yohanan Aharoni and Michael Avi-Yonah. Copyright © 1964, 1966, 1968, 1977 by Carta Ltd.

Introduction

Background to the Letters

These three letters (1 and 2 Timothy and Titus), called the Pastoral Epistles (PE) since the eighteenth century, purport to be letters from the Apostle Paul to two of his younger co-workers, whom he has left in charge of the churches in Ephesus and Crete, respectively. Since the early nineteenth century, however, when doubt was first expressed by F. Schleiermacher, a large array of arguments has been forthcoming that have called their authenticity into question, so that at present the large majority of NT (New Testament) scholars worldwide consider them not authored by Paul but by a pseudepigrapher (although a disciple of Paul), around the turn of the first century A.D.

The present commentary has been written from the perspective of Pauline authorship, fully aware of the many difficulties that entails but convinced that theories of pseudepigraphy have even greater historical difficulties.[1] Therefore, although much of what is said in this Introduction indirectly takes the form of conversation with scholarship about authorship, the basic concern is to introduce the reader to the historical data necessary for an intelligent reading of the commentary.

The Recipients

Timothy was a much younger colleague of Paul's, who had become his frequent traveling companion and close friend. According to Acts 16:1–3, Timothy was from Lystra, a Lycaonian town in the Roman province of Galatia in south-central Asia Minor. Paul probably met him for the first time (ca. A.D. 46–48) during his first missionary endeavor in this area (cf. Acts 13:49–14:25 and 2 Tim. 3:11). It is altogether likely that he and his mother and grandmother became converts at this time. During Paul's second visit in this area (ca. A.D. 49–50), on the recommendation of the local believers (Acts 16:2), he decided to take Timothy along on his travels. But because Timothy was of mixed lineage (Jewish mother and pagan father), and so as not to undermine his mission among Diaspora Jews, he had Timothy circumcised.[2] Thus began a lifelong relationship of mutual affection (cf. Phil. 2:19–24).

Paul variously calls Timothy his "beloved and faithful son in the Lord" (1 Cor. 4:17 NAB; cf. Phil. 2:22; 1 Tim. 1:2; 2 Tim. 1:2) and his "fellow worker" in the gospel (Rom. 16:21; cf. 1 Thess. 3:2; 1 Cor. 16:10; Phil. 2:22). As his son, he became Paul's most intimate and enduring companion, who followed him closely (1 Tim. 4:6; 2 Tim. 3:10–11; cf. 2 Tim. 1:13; 2:2), shared his point of view (Phil. 2:20), and could articulate his ways to the churches (1 Thess. 3:2–3; 1 Cor. 4:17). As Paul's fellow worker, Timothy had been entrusted with three previous assignments to churches: to Thessalonica, ca. A.D. 50 (1 Thess. 3:1–10); to Corinth, ca. A.D. 53–54 (1 Cor. 4:16–17; 16:10–11); and to Philippi, ca. A.D. 60–62 (Phil. 2:19–24). He also collaborated in six of Paul's extant letters (1 and 2 Thessalonians, 2 Corinthians, Colossians, Philemon, Philippians; cf. Rom. 16:21). In the present letters he is on yet another assignment, this time a most difficult one. He has been left in Ephesus to stop some false teachers who were in the process of undoing the church as a viable Christian alternative for that city.

Timothy is often pictured as a very young man, somewhat sickly, full of timidity, and lacking in personal forcefulness. Hence in these two letters Paul is frequently viewed as trying to bolster his courage in the face of difficulties. Although there may be some truth to this picture (see 1 Cor. 16:10–11; 2 Tim. 1:6–7), it is probably also a bit overdrawn. He was young by ancient standards (but at least over thirty by the time of 1 Timothy); and apparently had recurring stomach trouble (cf. 1 Tim. 5:23). But a person of his youthfulness who could carry out (apparently alone) the earlier missions to Thessalonica and Corinth was probably not totally lacking in courage. In any case, the exhortations to loyalty and steadfastness in 1 and 2 Timothy are probably the result of two factors: his youthfulness and the strength of the opposition.

Of Titus, much less is known. Curiously, he is not mentioned in Acts. From Paul we learn that he was a Gentile, whose lack of circumcision[3] was a key factor in Paul's securing the right of the Gentiles to a Law-free gospel (Gal. 2:1, 3). He, too, was an early co-worker of Paul's (the event in Gal. 2:1 probably dates ca. A.D. 48–49[4]) who became a trusted compatriot throughout Paul's life. To him Paul had entrusted the ticklish situation in Corinth, which included both the delivery of a very difficult letter (see 2 Cor. 2:3–4, 13; 7:6–16) and the gathering of the Corinthian gift for the poor in Jerusalem (2 Cor. 8:16–24).

According to the letter that bears his name, Titus had been left on Crete, after Paul and he had evangelized the island, to set the churches in order. But he was soon to be replaced by Artemas (see disc. on Titus 3:12) and was to join Paul in Nicopolis. Apparently he had done so, because according to 2 Timothy 4:10 he had gone on to Dalmatia, presumably for ministry.

Although one cannot be certain, Titus was probably older than Timothy (see disc. on Titus 2:15). He also seems to have been of stronger temperament. Paul calls him his "true [legitimate] son," which at least means that his ministry is a legitimate expression of Paul's; most likely it also indicates that he is Paul's convert (cf. 1 Cor. 4:14–15; Philem. 10).

It should be noted that the pictures that emerge in the PE are consonant with what we learn elsewhere. A pseudepigrapher, of course, could have so read Paul's earlier letters and painted his own pictures accordingly. But that would have come very close to his having done research, which is highly unlikely. Moreover, the various movements of Titus (Titus 3:12; 2 Tim. 4:10) are *not* the stuff of pseudepigraphy, which would be expected to have drawn a consistent, easy-to-follow picture of events. These matters about Timothy and Titus, at least, favor the authenticity of the letters.[5]

The Historical Situation of Paul

One of the difficulties of the PE has been to locate them historically in what is otherwise known of the life of Paul. The problem is a combination of several factors.

First, the picture of Paul that emerges from 1 Timothy and Titus portrays him traveling freely in the East. He and Titus have evangelized Crete (Titus 1:5); he has apparently traveled to Ephesus with Timothy and hopes to return (1 Tim. 1:3; 3:14); at some point in all of this he intends to winter in Nicopolis, on the southern Adriatic (Titus 3:12). But in 2 Timothy he is again in prison, this time in close confinement in Rome, where he expects to die (cf. 2 Tim. 1:16–17; 2:9; 4:6–8, 16–18).

The problem arises because this cannot easily be placed in Paul's life as it can be reconstructed from Acts and the earlier letters.[6] To the traditional answer that Paul was released from the imprisonment of Acts 28, returned to the East, and was imprisoned in Rome a second time, it is argued that Paul had intended to travel west from Rome, not east (Rom. 15:23–29), that Luke could hardly have been silent about such an event, and that in any case it would have been highly unlikely for Paul to be either released from a Roman detention or, if released, re-arrested. Since the only evidence we have for such a second imprisonment is from the PE, which are suspect on other grounds as well, such a picture is often viewed as the fabrication of a pseudepigrapher.

But the proponents of the above difficulties simply do not take the historical data seriously enough. If, as most scholars believe,[7] Colossians, Philemon, and Philippians were written from Rome during the imprisonment of Acts 28, then it is clear that Paul had changed his mind about traveling west and now hoped to return to Asia Minor (Philem. 22) and that he himself expected to be released from the first imprisonment (Phil. 1:18–19, 24–26, 2:24).[8] No sound historical grounds exist to think that such did not actually happen. Furthermore, it seems highly unlikely that a pseudepigrapher, writing thirty to forty years later, would have tried to palm off such traditions as Paul's evangelizing Crete,[9] the near capitulation to heresy of the Ephesian church, or a release and second imprisonment of Paul if in fact they had never happened. Again the historical data favor the authenticity of the letters.

But what is still not clear from the evidence of the PE themselves is the actual order of events and the sequence of 1 Timothy and Titus. The most probable solution holds that Paul went to Crete with Titus and (probably) Timothy soon after his release from Roman custody. There they evangelized most of the towns, but they also encountered some opposition from Hellenistic Jews who seemed to be taking a different tack from the struggle over circumcision that had characterized the earlier opposition from Palestinian Judaism (see Galatians 1–2; Acts 15). Paul, therefore, left Titus on the island to regulate things by putting the churches in order.

Meanwhile, Paul and Timothy were on their way to Macedonia by way of Ephesus when the stopover at Ephesus turned out to be a small disaster. Some false teachings similar to those encountered earlier in Colossae, and more recently in Crete, were in the process of totally undermining the church in Ephesus. So Paul excommunicated the two ringleaders of this movement, Hymenaeus and Alexander (1 Tim. 1:19–20); but because he had to press on to Macedonia, he left Timothy in charge of things in Ephesus to stem the tide (1 Tim. 1:3). On his arrival in Macedonia, he wrote letters to both Timothy and Titus. Timothy was to remain in Ephesus, but Titus would be replaced by either Tychicus or Artemas (apparently it turned out to be the latter) and was to join Paul in Nicopolis for the winter (see Titus 3:12). From there (Nicopolis) Paul seems to have been on his way back to Ephesus when he was arrested, probably at Troas at the instigation of Alexander the metalworker (see disc. on 2 Tim. 4:13–15). At what point he touched base at Corinth and Miletus (2 Tim. 4:20) is not so clear.

Eventually he was brought back to Rome, where he had a preliminary hearing before a Roman tribunal (2 Tim. 4:16–18) and was bound over for a full trial. During this time in custody he felt great ambivalence toward him on the part of his friends. Onesiphorus of Ephesus came to Rome, sought him out, and both ministered to his needs and informed him of the situation in Ephesus, which apparently had continued to deteriorate (see 2 Tim. 1:15–18). But others had left him, at least one as a turncoat, but some for legitimate reasons (2 Tim. 4:10–12). In this distress he decided to send Tychicus to replace Timothy at Ephesus (2 Tim. 4:12). With him, Paul sent a letter to Timothy (2 Timothy), urging loyalty to himself and his gospel and requesting, finally, that Timothy should drop everything and make his way to Rome, before winter closed down Mediterranean shipping, he hoped (see disc. on 2 Tim. 4:21).[10]

Occasion and Purpose

In the preceding overview we touched lightly on the occasion of these letters; however, more needs to be said, for this is the crucial matter for understanding. Indeed, this is the crucial matter for the interpretation of all the NT letters, and it is precisely at this point that theories of pseudepigraphy face their greatest difficulties.

Any exegetical analysis of an Epistle presupposes that it is an *ad hoc* document, that is, that it is a piece of correspondence occasioned by a set of specific historical circumstances, either from the recipient's or the author's side—or both. Theories of pseudepigraphy, therefore, must reconstruct a historical situation in the time of the pseudepigrapher, in this case about A.D. 90–110, that accounts for the data of these letters as addressing the "author's" situation while still making them plausible as belonging to the alleged historical situation of the letters themselves. Right here is where the difficulties arise.

The most common reconstruction sees a combination of three factors to have caused an author to write these letters: the waning of Paul's influence in the church; the threat of a "Gnostic" form of false teaching; and the need for organizational structures during the church's transition from an intensely eschatological community with "charismatic" leadership to a people prepared to settle down to a longer life in the world with more "regular" clergy. In most cases scholarship accepts this final item as the ultimate urgency for writing. Thus "the writer, alarmed by the encroachment of alien theories and speculations, seeks to bring the Church back to the genuine Christian teaching, as it had come down from the Apostle Paul. In order that the Pauline tradition may be preserved, he desires that the Church should be rightly organized."[11]

The problems with such a reconstruction, however, are several: It almost totally fails to locate the Epistles into a *specific* identifiable historical context, for example, Ephesus or Crete at the end of the first century.[12]

It therefore tends to see the Epistles as not having genuine logic to their arguments, thus demanding theories of "compositional technique," in which the author is viewed as purposeful in the overall scheme but negligent or without clear reason in the placement of some materials.[13] Furthermore, it must candidly admit that much in these letters does not fit the proposed occasion at all. Most importantly, it never adequately answers the question, Why *three* letters? For example, Why write Titus or 1 Timothy, given one or the other, and why from such a considerably different perspective and historical context? And why 2 Timothy at all, since it fails so badly to fit the proposed reconstruction?[14]

It is proposed here that in contrast to the theories of pseudepigraphy, one can reconstruct the historical setting of these letters so that not only do they fit with other recoverable data from this period but they can also be shown to respond in whole, as well as in all the details, to that historical situation. In the final analysis this is the strongest argument for their authenticity.

1 Timothy   As indicated above, 1 Timothy was occasioned by Paul's having left Timothy in Ephesus as his personal representative in order to stop the influence of some false teachers. This is the one reason that is specifically stated in the letter itself (1:3). Chapters 2 and 3, however, deal with concerns of public worship and the character of the church's leaders and conclude with another statement of purpose: "so that you will know what kind of conduct befits a member of God's household, the church of the living God" (3:15, NAB). Because of this, most scholars, including those who accept Pauline authorship, see the false teachers as the *occasion* of 1 Timothy but argue that "church order as the proper antidote to the false teachers" is the overriding *purpose*. Thus they take the view that 1 Timothy is basically a church manual, and the concern is to set the church in order.[15]

In contrast to that approach, this commentary assumes that everything in the letter has to do with 1:3 ("I want you to stay in Ephesus, just as I urged you. . . . Some people there are teaching false doctrines and you must order them to stop"), and that this expresses both the occasion and the purpose of 1 Timothy. As will be seen in the commentary, this not only makes sense of every detail in the letter, but also helps to explain the nature and content of Titus and 2 Timothy as well. Three questions, therefore, need closer examination: *Who* were the false teachers? *What* was the nature of their teaching? *Why* was 1 Timothy written?

In contrast to Galatia and Corinth, for example, whose problems were basically caused by outsiders ("false brothers" who "had infiltrated our ranks," Gal. 2:4, NIV; cf. 2 Cor. 11:4), in Ephesus as seen in 1 Timothy, there is not a hint that the false teachers came from the outside. To the contrary, not only do they appear to be insiders, but the whole letter makes sense if the prophecy spoken to the elders-overseers of this church recorded in Acts 20:30 had actually been realized: "The time will come when some men *from your own group* will tell lies to lead believers after them."[16] If one takes this seriously, then the difficulty—and urgency—of the situation in Ephesus comes into clear focus. The problem is that *the church is being led astray by some of its own elders.*[17]

Several internal clues support this hypothesis: First, the errorists were clearly teachers (1:3, 7; 6:3), and teaching was the task of the elders (3:2; 5:17). Furthermore, a significant part of the Epistle is allotted to the character, qualifications, and discipline of church leaders (3:1–13; 5:17–25); much of this stands in obvious contrast to what is specifically said of the false teachers. In this regard it is probably also noteworthy that two of the ringleaders of this group are named and excommunicated (1:19–20).

Second, it is clear from 2 Timothy 3:6–9, and further supported by 1 Timothy 2:9–15 and 5:3–16 (esp. vv. 11–15), that these teachers had found a most fruitful field among some women, apparently younger widows, who had opened their homes to them and even helped to spread their teachings (see disc. on 5:13).

Third, the church in Ephesus in all probability was composed of many house-churches (cf. 1 Cor. 16:19; see disc. on 1 Tim. 2:8). If so, then one can envision each of the various house-churches having one or more elders and the problem being not so much a single large gathered assembly being split down the middle as various house-churches capitulating *in toto* to leadership that had gone astray (cf. Titus 1:11). It is this capitulation of some leaders and their followers that forms the ultimate urgency behind everything in the letter.

As with Colossians and Ephesians,[18] the *nature* of the false teaching is difficult to define with precision. Some things are certain. First, it possesses a behavioral as well as a cognitive dimension. The descriptions in 1:3–7 and 6:3–10, plus 3:1–13, show the false teachers to be involved not only in speculations and disputes over words but also in arguments and quarrels of various kinds. They are likewise proud, arrogant, and divisive. The bottom line, however, is greed; they have come to believe that godliness, or religion, is a means to turn a drachma.

Second, on the content side, there are several diverse elements: The false teaching is in some way related to a use of the Old Testament (1:6–10; cf. Titus 1:14–16; 3:9), which in turn partly accounts for its asceticism

(4:3; cf. 5:23; Titus 1:14–16), as well as its "myths and wearisome genealogies" (see disc. on 1:4; cf. 4:7 and Titus 3:9). But there are elements of Hellenism, especially an admixture of Greek dualism (with its dim view of the material world), which also can account for the asceticism, as well as for the assertion that the resurrection (apparently as a spiritual, nonphysical reality) had already taken place (2 Tim. 2:18). What precisely is meant by "so-called knowledge [*gnōsis*]" in 6:20–21 is more difficult to ascertain; in any case, it can be demonstrated to have affinities with the earlier problems in Corinth and Colossae.

Indeed, what is striking about these elements is not so much their affinities with second-century Gnosticism (with which they have far greater differences than similarities) as with the errors that had earlier invaded Corinth (ca. A.D. 53–54) and more recently Asia Minor, especially the Lycus Valley (Colossae and Laodicea). In Corinth the people in the "know" ("gnostics"), who also considered themselves to be the "spiritual" ones, had so imbibed Hellenistic dualism, along with an over-realized eschatology, that they were denying sexual relations within marriage (7:1–7; cf. 1 Tim. 4:3)[19] and a future bodily resurrection (15:12, cf. 2 Tim. 2:18). And in Colossae a form of Hellenistic Judaism had recently begun to syncretize the Christian faith with Jewish and Hellenistic elements that had led to ascetic practices (2:16–23) and an enamorment with wisdom/knowledge (2:3–8) and OT ritual (2:16, 21).[20]

What appears to have happened in the decade of ca. A.D. 54–63 is that Paul had to wrestle on two fronts. On the one hand, a Judaizing faction from the church in Jerusalem, undoubtedly spurred on by conservative elements in the Diaspora, was insisting on the circumcision of Gentiles who had become believers in Jesus. They wanted such people to become full members of Israel as it had been formerly constituted (see Galatians; Phil. 3:2–16). On the other hand, religious syncretism was in the air in the Hellenistic world, and many Hellenistic Jews appear to have been involved in such speculations. When Gentiles were converted, they, too, brought to the faith a lot of foreign baggage, both philosophical and religious, that to them seemed easy enough to absorb within their new faith in Christ. But Paul realized clearly that such foreign elements would ultimately destroy the gospel every bit as much as Judaizing would. He first had to attack some of this in Corinth; a slightly different, and perhaps more subtle brand—due to its distinctively Jewish coloring—had emerged in Asia Minor. Paul had recently addressed these deviations in his letter to Colossae while imprisoned in Rome. On his arrival in Ephesus, he discovered that they had erupted there as well, but now as the "official" line being promulgated by some of the elders. They had to be stopped, and Timothy was left in Ephesus to do it.[21]

The purpose of 1 Timothy, then, arises out of these complexities. The letter betrays evidences everywhere that it was intended for the church itself, not just Timothy. But because of defections in the leadership, Paul does not, as before, write directly to the church, but to the church through Timothy. The reason for this would have been twofold: to encourage Timothy himself to carry out this most difficult task of stopping the erring elders, who had become thoroughly disputatious, and to authorize Timothy before the church to carry out his task. At the same time, of course, the church would be having the false teachers/teachings exposed before them, plus Paul's instructions to Timothy about what he was to do. Thus the letter, though addressed to Timothy, turns out to be all business. As such, it lacks the standard thanksgiving (see disc. on 1:3) and the personal greetings at the end (see disc. on 6:20–21); and such personal words to Timothy as do appear (e.g., 1:18–19; 4:6–16; 6:11–14) are totally subservient to his task of restoring order to the church.

Such an occasion and purpose also helps to explain another phenomenon of the letter, namely, that Paul is forever calling on Timothy to teach "sound" or "healthy" doctrine, but without spelling out the nature or content of such teaching.[22] The reason now becomes obvious. The letter was written to a lifelong companion, who wouldn't have needed such instruction. But the church needed to hear that the deviations were a disease among them and that what Timothy would have to teach would be the words of health (see disc. on 1:10). Just as in 1 Corinthians 4:17, Timothy was there to remind the church of Paul's ways. The letter that would so authorize him would not at the same time need a detailing of those "ways."[23]

Titus   Probably the feature about Titus most noticed by one who has first worked closely with 1 Timothy is how much it resembles that letter. Apart from the situation (1:1–4) and final greetings (3:12–15), only the two semicreedal passages in 2:11–14 and 3:3–7 present material that has no points of correspondence with 1 Timothy. For this reason, Titus has often been viewed as a miniature 1 Timothy and, except for 2:11–14 and 3:3–7, has been treated with benign neglect.

However, closer examination reveals a large number of striking differences from 1 Timothy (and the more striking if this is the work of a pseudepigrapher). The most obvious difference lies with the occasion and Titus' own circumstances. Like Timothy (1 Tim. 1:3), Titus has been *left* on Crete; but unlike Timothy, who was left to reform an established church, Titus has been left behind to set in order what had not yet been accomplished, namely, the *appointing* of elders in the various churches over the whole island (1:5). It seems certain from these data that the churches of Crete were more recent, and that whatever opposition existed had emerged within the church (along with the church itself), especially from Hellenistic Jewish converts (1:9–11).

What one finds in Titus, therefore, is considerably less urgency than in 1 Timothy. False teachers are indeed in evidence (1:10–16; 3:9–11), but the letter as a whole is not dominated by their presence. Titus himself is to rebuke such opponents (1:13), but the appointed elders are ultimately to be responsible to stand against them (1:9). Otherwise there is little of the urgency of 1 Timothy. Titus is not repeatedly urged to "fight the noble fight" (1 Tim. 1:18; cf. 6:12) or to "guard the deposit" (6:20; cf. 6:14) or to give heed to his ministry (4:11–16). Few second person singular imperatives occur—none of the personal, encouraging kind to Titus himself (except perhaps 2:15). There are no mentions of endurance (*hypomonē*) for Titus, no vocatives of direct address or appeal, few appeals to keeping *the* faith or *the* truth, and only one *tauta* imperative ("teach these things," 2:15; cf. 1 Tim. 4:6, 11, 15; 5:7, 21; 6:2, 11). It is not that no urgency lies behind Titus; rather, the urgency is of a different kind, with different emphases.

Since the churches on Crete are newer, the concern in Titus focuses less upon false teachers per se and more upon the church as God's people in the world. The letter, therefore, may be termed both *prophylactic* (serving to warn against false teachings) and *evangelistic* (serving to encourage behavior that will be attractive to the world) in its thrust. Thus, the matter of appointing elders in 1:5–9 has a clear prophylactic concern vis-à-vis the threat of error (1:10–16; cf. 3:9–11). But it also carries with it a concern for the reputation of the gospel in the world (see disc. on 1:6 and 3:8). The dominant theme in Titus, therefore, is *good works* (1:8, 16; 2:7, 14; 3:1, 8, 14), that is, exemplary Christian behavior, and that *for the sake of outsiders* (2:5, 7, 8, 10, 11; 3:1, 8). Christ died precisely to create such a people, who would be zealous for good works (2:14; cf. 3:3–7). Even relationships and attitudes among believers (2:1–10) are to be such that outsiders will not only not reject the gospel (2:5) but might even be attracted to it (2:10).

Why, then, did Paul write such a letter, and *when*? Since it displays a more prophylactic, less urgent, appearance than 1 Timothy, the Epistle to Titus was probably written after the latter. Paul had left Titus in Crete to finish setting the churches in order. After he and Timothy had gone to

Ephesus and found that church in such disarray, Paul left Timothy there to restore order. In Macedonia he wrote back to Ephesus to give Timothy authority for his task there. At the same time he reflected on some similar opposition encountered in Crete while he had been there, so he also wrote to Titus, again to give him authority against these false teachers. But because the situation there lacked the urgency of Ephesus, he encourages Titus to help the people toward exemplary Christian behavior for the sake of the world.

2 Timothy   Even a cursory reading of 2 Timothy after 1 Timothy and Titus reveals both its close relationship to those two letters and its even more significant contrasts. All of the concerns from 1 Timothy have reappeared, but now in a much more urgently personal way.

The key to understanding this letter lies in recognizing Paul's altered circumstances. He is no longer free to pursue his itinerant ministry. Arrested once again (probably in Troas; see disc. on 4:13), he is now in confined imprisonment in Rome (1:16–17; 2:9). He has already undergone a preliminary hearing (4:16–18) and is awaiting his final trial, from which he has little hope of anything except death (4:6–8). His confinement is an obvious hardship for him. Some have ministered to his needs (1:16–18); others have gone out on ministries (4:10, 12); and at least one has abandoned him (4:10). Meanwhile the situation in Ephesus has worsened. Some, from whom Paul had expected better things, have deserted him and his gospel (1:15), and, despite his previous excommunication, Hymenaeus is still at work overthrowing the faith of many (2:17–18).

In the midst of these circumstances Paul sends this second letter to Timothy. It is a letter of many parts. In a sense it is a kind of last will and testament, a "passing on of the mantle." In contrast to 1 Timothy, 2 Timothy is intensely personal, recalling their earliest days together (3:10–11; cf. 1:3–5) and, above all, appealing to Timothy's abiding loyalty—to the gospel, to Paul himself, to his own calling (1:6–14; 2:1–13; 3:10–4:5). In the background stand the false teachers (2:14–3:9); Timothy must resist them and strive to win God's people back. But he is no longer to stay on in Ephesus; rather, he is to entrust that ministry to others who have remained faithful (2:2). Timothy himself is to come to Paul (4:9, 11, 21). In the foreground stands Paul's lifelong concern—the gospel and its ministry: "Fan into flame your gift," Timothy is urged (1:6–7); "guard the deposit" (1:14), "hold fast to the truth" (1:13); and above all, "proclaim the message" (4:2). And Paul's own circumstances, as well as Timothy's, cause him to urge steadfastness even in the face of suffering:

"Do not be ashamed" (1:8, 16); rather, "take your part in suffering" (1:8; 2:3; 3:12; 4:5).

The purpose of the letter seems to be related to these urgencies. It is certainly no "church manual"; nor is it dominated by the false teachers, as is 1 Timothy. The primary reason for writing is simple—to call Timothy to his side. But the larger reason is this appeal to Timothy's loyalty, especially in light of so many defections and Paul's own imprisonment.

Finally, Paul's pervading note of confidence throughout the letter must not be overlooked. Despite his own hardships, the opposition, and the defection of many, Paul recognizes that God's message, the gospel, is not, nor can it be, chained (2:9). Nor will the church go under, for it bears God's seal of ownership: "The Lord knows those who are his" (2:19). Endurance and suffering are called for (1:8; 2:3–7; 3:14; 4:5), but eschatological triumph is assured for those who persevere (2:11–13; 4:8) because God in Christ has already triumphed over death (1:9–10). Therefore, the basic thrust of the letter is an appeal for Timothy to carry on the ministry of the gospel after Paul's death, but even facing death, he is confident that God will see it through (1:5, 8, 14).

The Theology of the Epistles

For those who have difficulty accepting the Pauline authorship of the PE, the problems related to their theology rank with that of language and style (see next section) as decisive against their authenticity. The problem lies not so much with their being non-Pauline in theology—indeed Pauline elements are recognized everywhere—as it does with so much in them that seems un-Pauline, that is, unlike his characteristic way of thinking and speaking as reflected in the earlier letters. Partly this is a matter of language, and partly, shifts of emphasis. Most often these elements are considered to be the more developed concerns of a later time.[24]

However, it seems fair to observe that NT scholarship is sometimes overimpressed with its own judgments about what Paul could, or (especially) could not, have said or done.[25] When one has as little evidence as is available from Paul—and what evidence we do have is occasional, not systematic, in nature—a much larger measure of caution than one usually finds in the literature would seem appropriate. In the final analysis the decision rests upon what impresses one more, the clearly Pauline nature of so much, or the seemingly divergent nature of much. In the following sections we will examine four crucial areas, point out their similarities to Paul, and offer some possible explanations for some of the differences.

The Gospel

One cannot read much of Paul without recognizing that at the heart of everything for him is the gospel, the good news of God's gracious acceptance and forgiveness of sinners, to which the proper response is faith (trusting God that he really does accept sinners) and love toward others. This saving work is totally by God's own initiative, his prior action of grace toward the disobedient, meaning the righteous (whose righteousness is self-righteous, and therefore unrighteousness) as well as the unrighteous. That grace was effected by Christ's death on the cross; it is made effectual in the life of the one who believes by the power of the indwelling Spirit. The believer, therefore, is one who is both forgiven of his or her past sins and indwelt by the Spirit, and thus empowered for loving obedience to God.

Paul employs an extensive language, with a full range of metaphors, to speak of this saving event—justification, redemption, reconciliation, ransom, cleansing, propitiation—but the essence, as just outlined, remains constant. Except in Galatians, followed closely by Romans, where the forensic metaphor of justification has been brought about by the activity of his opponents, no single metaphor predominates. (Note that the *dikai-* ["just, justify"] word group does not appear in the earliest letters [1 and 2 Thessalonians] and appears only as one metaphor among others in 1 and 2 Corinthians [see esp. 1 Cor. 1:30; 6:11]; it disappears again in Colossians, but reappears in Philippians precisely when the Judaizing contingent reasserts itself [3:2–16].)

It will be clear from any careful reading that this concern for the gospel is the driving force behind the PE. Preserving and reaffirming "the Good News that reveals the glory of the blessed God" (1:11) against errors absolutely dominates 1 Timothy, is still a vital concern in Titus, and returns in 2 Timothy as the crux of everything. On that much, most would agree. The problem arises from the *manner* in which this concern is often expressed.

For example, a different language begins to dominate. The gospel is variously equated with "the faith" (1 Tim. 1:19; 3:9; 4:1, 6; 5:8; 6:10, 12; Titus 1:13; 2 Tim. 3:8; 4:7; this is rare in Paul, but see Gal. 1:23; Phil. 1:25, 27), knowing "the truth" (1 Tim. 2:4; 4:3; Titus 1:1; 2 Tim. 2:25; 3:7; but cf. Gal. 5:7; 2 Thess. 2:12), the "deposit" to be guarded (1 Tim. 6:20; 2 Tim 1:14), "sound" or "healthy teaching" (1 Tim. 1:10; 6:3; Titus 1:9; 2:1, 8; 2

Tim. 1:13; 4:3), and "our religion" (*eusebeia*; 1 Tim. 3:16; 4:7–8; 6:3, 5–6; Titus 1:1). The problem, first of all, is that the latter two terms seem to be borrowed from Hellenistic religion and philosophy; and, second, this seems to reduce the gospel from a dynamic proclamation of good news for sinners to a static body of beliefs to be embraced. As an earlier scholar put it, "Paul was inspired, but the Pastor is often only orthodox."[26] Instead of repeating, or re-arguing, the gospel itself, as in Galatians, Romans, Colossians, or Philippians, this author merely appeals to fixed formulas.

Although there is much to be said for this objection (and this Paul does indeed sound different), there are also some other things that must be said: the use of "sound teaching" and *eusebeia*, which do not occur elsewhere in Paul, can nonetheless be shown to fit a Pauline pattern of "appropriation." This is almost certainly a case, as with "wisdom" in 1 Corinthians 1–3 or "justification" in Galatians, in which Paul uses the *language* of the opposition but recharges it with his own content, thus turning it against them.

The basic reason for this kind of "objective" reference to the gospel, however, lies in the nature of these letters in contrast with the others. The other letters (excepting Philemon, of course) were written to churches, to be read aloud and apparently to function as authority as though Paul himself were there. Therefore, it was necessary for him to reiterate the truth that was to correct or stand over against their waywardness. In this case, however, the letters are written to those who themselves both know fully the content of Paul's gospel and are personally to take the place of authority in these churches that his letters had earlier done. This latter phenomenon is totally overlooked in scholarship. It is almost as if the real objection were that Paul should write such letters at all.

Furthermore, the errors at which these letters are directed are not primarily related to the nature of salvation per se, that is, how one receives right-standing before God. Here, as in Colossians, the errors are both more speculative in content and more behavioral in orientation. In such cases one should not be surprised if the gospel is often referred to as a fixed set of beliefs. After all, there has always been a cognitive side to the gospel for Paul.

But beyond that it should be noted that these letters are not totally lacking expressions of the content of the gospel. At several key points, where it serves as contrast to the false teachers, Paul reflects on the gospel itself (1 Tim. 1:12–16; 2:3–6; 3:16; Titus 2:11–14; 3:3–7; 2 Tim. 1:9–10), and in each case the theology, as well as much of the language, is thoroughly Pauline.

Thus in these letters the human condition is that of sinfulness, defined as disobedience or rebellion against God (see 1 Tim. 1:9–10, 13, 15; Titus 3:3; 2 Tim. 3:2–5); the condition is universal in scope and one from which there is no evident escape or human remedy (cf. 1 Tim. 1:13–16; Titus 3:3, 5; 2 Tim. 1:9). For this reason God must intervene with mercy (1 Tim. 1:13–16; Titus 3:3–7; 2 Tim. 1:9–10), and this he has done through the death of Christ, who through his own self-sacrifice secured our redemption (1 Tim. 2:5–6; Titus 2:14) and our justification (Titus 3:7). The scope of this salvation is also universal (1 Tim. 2:3–7; 4:10), including Gentiles as well as Jews (1 Tim. 2:7), but is effectual only for those who believe (1 Tim. 1:16; 4:10; cf. 1:13), and even this faith is God's gift (1 Tim. 1:14). This saving work is effected in the believer's life by the Holy Spirit, who both regenerates and renews (Titus 3:5–6) and enables for life and ministry (2 Tim. 1:6–7, 14). Such grace is to produce obedience in the form of love and other good works (e.g., 1 Tim. 1:5; 2:15b; Titus 2:12, 14; 3:8, 14). Finally, such a life is also lived in hope of promised eternal life (1 Tim. 1:16; 4:8, 10; 6:12; Titus 1:2; 3:7; 2 Tim. 1:10, 12; 2:10, 12a; 4:8, 18), which will be accomplished at Christ's second coming (1 Tim. 6:14; Titus 2:13; 2 Tim. 4:1, 8).

If all of this is not as systematically set forth as some would like, and if some of it appears in slightly different language, there can be no question that the substance is what Paul elsewhere calls "my gospel." And it is precisely this gospel that Timothy has been left in Ephesus to contend for, against the exclusivistic, ascetic, speculative teaching of the wayward elders and the disrepute that their behavior and greed is bringing to the gospel.

Ethics

Closely related to the preceding difficulty is the presentation of Christian ethics in the PE. Instead of the great Christian virtues of love, forgiveness, joy, and so forth, it is alleged, the ethics of these letters are more convention-al, even "bourgeois." This is especially true of the qualifications for church leaders (1 Tim. 3:2–12; Titus 1:6–8); and in Titus 2:12 the Christian life is described in terms of three of the four cardinal virtues of Stoicism. Further-more, in 1 Timothy 6:6–8 godliness seems to be defined in terms of Stoic-Cynic self-sufficiency. Such a view of Christian life, it is maintained, is far removed from the Pauline ideal one finds, for example, in Romans 12–14, Galatians 5–6, or Colossians 3.

Again, there is some obvious validity to this difficulty. At these points the Pastor does indeed sound less like the Paul one is used to quoting. But again, the overall picture is not nearly as cut and dried as this objection tends to view it. Some of the difficulty arises from a partial view of the earlier Paul, some from a distortion of what is actually said in the PE, and some from a different point of view about the occasion and purpose of the letters.

As before, much of the language is very likely that of the opposition, or at least of the environment to which Paul is speaking. There is nothing unusual about Paul's adapting such language to his own purposes. Nothing, for example, is more Stoic-sounding in Paul than Philippians 4:8 or 12. But anyone reading those sentences in the context of Paul recognizes that he means very non-Stoic ideas by them. The same is true here, as is pointed out in the discussion at 1 Timothy 6:6–8 or Titus 2:12.

The lists of qualifications in 1 Timothy 3:2–3 and Titus 1:6–8 are somewhat puzzling and may indeed reflect a well-known schema (see disc. on 1 Tim. 3:1–7). But as is pointed out in the discussion, there are probably two reasons for this: (1) Paul is simply assuming that such people will possess the distinctively Christian virtues; (2) the concern in much of this centers upon the church's reputation before outsiders; therefore, the urgency is not so much with attitudes and relationships within the body of Christ as with blameless, observable behavior.

Furthermore, it is unquestionable throughout the PE that Paul's more distinctively Christian ethic is always expected of believers. The example of Christian lifestyle that Timothy is to set before the church (1 Tim. 4:12) is a thoroughly Pauline list; and other virtue lists are also Pauline (1 Tim. 2:15b; 6:11; Titus 2:2b; 2 Tim. 3:10–11). The motif of Christian life as endurance, even in suffering (2 Tim. 1:8, 11; 2:1, 3, 10–13; 3:12), is also characteristically Pauline.

What needs to be noted, finally, is that, as before, much of what is said about Christian behavior in these letters is a direct reflection of the behavior of the false teachers; and it is likewise their presence that dictates the nature of what is said.

Eschatology

The absolutely essential framework of the self-understanding of primitive Christianity, including Paul, is an eschatological one. Christians had come to believe that, in the event of Christ, the New (Coming) Age had dawned, and that, especially through Christ's death and resurrection and the subsequent gift of the Spirit, God had set the future in motion, to be consummated by yet another coming (Parousia) of Christ. Theirs was therefore an essentially eschatological existence. They lived "between the times" of the beginning and the consummation of the End. Already God had secured their eschatological salvation; already they were the people of the future, living the life of the future in the present age—and enjoying its benefits. But they still awaited the glorious consummation of this salvation. Thus they lived in an essential tension between the "already" and the "not-yet."

This view of Christian existence is thoroughgoing in Paul. Therefore salvation is spoken of as a past event, a present reality, and a future hope. The future is always a certainty. Sometimes, as in 1 Thessalonians 4:13–18 or 1 Corinthians 7:29–31, the hope of the consummation burns more brightly than in other passages. But always the Parousia is the eager expectation that Christians await.

It is sometimes argued that the eschatological perspective of the PE is different from this, that Paul now expects to die before the Parousia (2 Tim. 4:8), and that the letters are written for a church that "must make adjustments for a prolonged stay in the world."[27] The fact that the Coming is now expressed as the *epiphaneia* ("manifestation") of Christ, language similar to that found in Hellenistic religion, also is seen to support this view.

It would seem, however, that much of this objection is the result of a prior commitment to a point of view. For, in reality, the eschatology of these letters is thoroughly Pauline. As in other settings (cf. 2 Thess. 2:3, 7), the present apostasy is seen in terms of the eschatological woes of the End (1 Tim. 4:1; 2 Tim. 3:1). As elsewhere, endurance of suffering and the awaiting of the Coming stand side by side (e.g., 1 Tim. 6:12–14; 2 Tim. 1:12). Salvation, as always, is eschatologically understood as both present and future (1 Tim. 1:16; 4:8; 6:12, 14; Titus 2:12–14; 2 Tim. 1:9–10, 12; 2:3–11). If Paul expects to die in 2 Timothy 4:6–8, he can still speak eagerly of "loving Christ's appearing" (v. 8), a perspective very similar to the ambivalence of Philippians 1:18–26 and 3:12–14, 20–21.

Indeed, it is in 2 Timothy, the letter in which Paul expresses the awareness of his impending death (4:6–7), that he also expresses himself in a most thoroughly eschatological way. In 1 Timothy and Titus salvation is regularly seen as an eschatological phenomenon (1 Tim. 1:16; 4:8–10; 6:12–14; Titus 1:1–2; 2:13; 3:7), very similar to the way it is seen in Romans (5:2–5, 21; 8:17, 18–27; 13:11–12). As in Romans, the future is certain and looked for, but plans are nonetheless made (Titus 3:12; Rom. 15:22–29), and Christian life in the world includes attitudes toward the state and others (Titus 3:1–2; Rom. 13:1–8).

But 2 Timothy seems more self-consciously eschatological, like Philippians. The certainty of the future is guaranteed through Christ, who "has ended the power of death" (1:10). It is the prospect of "that Day" (the Day of Christ's coming) that bolsters Paul (1:12) and is to encourage Timothy and the church toward steadfastness (2:3–13; 4:1, 8). The coming of the Lord will bring with it the eschatological prize (1:12; 2:5–6; 4:8). The present apostasy is evidence of Christ's "coming to rule as king" (4:1), Timothy is urged to remain loyal to his ministry. This scarcely resembles the language of settling in to live for an extended time on planet earth; it is therefore perhaps of more than passing interest that in this letter also, apart from the provision in 2:2, there is no "church order" talk of any kind.

Church Order

In many ways church order is the crucial matter. For many people this is the chief reason for turning to these letters, especially 1 Timothy and Titus; and for others both the concern itself and its content reflect a much later time than Paul's. A standard view suggests that the PE reflect a time like that of Ignatius (ca. A.D. 110–115), when a single bishop (modeled on Timothy and Titus) has primary authority in the church, with elders and deacons under him.[28] An order of women deacons and widows is also argued for, on the basis of 1 Timothy 3:11 and 5:9, respectively.

But as already argued, the idea that the *purpose* of the PE is to offer "a handbook for church leaders" seems to miss their occasion rather widely and simply cannot account for a large amount of the material. The weakness of this view is perhaps also demonstrated by the fact that the entire spectrum of church government, from the hierarchical episcopacy of Roman Catholicism, through the mediating expression of Presbyterianism, to the extreme congregationalism of the Plymouth Brethren, all find support for their polity in these letters. If the Pastor intended with these letters to set the church in order, he seems not to have altogether succeeded.

The reason for such diversity, it is argued in this commentary, is precisely that these letters have quite another purpose; and therefore, as with other such *ad hoc* documents, they *reflect* church structures in the fourth decade of the church as Paul is correcting some theological and behavioral abuses. But church structures as such are not his concern. What, then, can be said with some certainty?

It is a mistaken notion to view Timothy or Titus as model pastors for a local church. The letters simply have no such intent. Although it is true that Timothy and Titus carry full apostolic authority, in both cases they are itinerants on special assignment, there as Paul's apostolic delegates, not as permanent resident pastors. It is a far cry from Timothy's role in Ephesus and Titus' in the churches of Crete to that of Ignatius in Antioch or Polycarp in Smyrna fifty years later.

Timothy, it is true, is called upon to set an example for Christian behavior (4:12), but this is exactly the role Paul had in his churches. They were to learn the "ways" of Christ by following the apostolic model (1 Thess. 1:6; 2:14; 1 Cor. 4:16; 11:1). Both Timothy and Titus are expected to teach, exhort, and rebuke, of course, which would also be the function of the elders after Paul and his itinerant co-workers had left. But these were first of all apostolic functions.

Responsibility for leadership in the local churches (per town or, as is likely in larger cities like Ephesus, per house-church) was from the beginning in the hands of several people, who apparently had been appointed by the apostle and his co-workers (cf. Acts 14:23). In the earliest letters these people are styled *hoi proïstamenoi* (1 Thess. 5:12; Rom. 12:8), language still being used at the time of the PE (1 Tim. 3:5; 5:17). Interestingly, however, despite all the difficulties in some of these churches, none of the letters is ever addressed to these people; nor are they ever given charge to set the church in order or to withstand error. In Philippians 1:1 Paul for the first time addresses both the church and its (plural) leaders (*episkopoi*, "overseers," and *diakonoi*, "deacons"), the identical words used in 1 Timothy 3:2 and 8 (cf. Titus 1:7). Apart from this reference, we would not have otherwise known of their earlier existence; but *because* of such a reference, we may properly assume that other churches also had such plural leadership. It should be finally noted that in none of the earlier letters does the term *elder* (*presbyteros*) appear.

The evidence that emerges in the PE corresponds very closely to this state of affairs. Although some have argued that Timothy and Titus were to appoint a single *episkopos*,[29] under whom there would be a group of deacons, exegesis of the key passages (1 Tim. 3:1–2, 8; 5:17; Titus 1:5–7) and a comparison with Acts 20:17 and 28 indicates otherwise.

In all cases leadership was plural. These leaders are called elders in 1 Timothy 5:17 and Titus 1:5. They were to be appointed in Crete by Titus but had apparently been appointed long ago in Ephesus, probably by Paul himself. The term *elders* is probably a covering term for both overseers and deacons. In any case, the grammar of Titus 1:5 and 7 demands that *elder* and *overseer* are interchangeable terms (as in Acts 20:17 and 28); they are not thereby necessarily co-extensive.

What were the duties of such elders? At this point our information is limited, precisely because this was not Paul's concern. Two things seem certain: that the elders called overseers were responsible for teaching (1

Tim. 3:3; 5:17; Titus 1:9), and that the elders together were responsible for "managing" or "caring for" the local church (see disc. on 1 Tim. 3:4–5; 5:17), whatever that might have involved at that time in its history. Beyond that, everything is speculative.

It is not at all clear that there were "orders" of women's ministries, including widows. The stance taken in this commentary is that there were women who served the church in some capacity, perhaps including leadership (1 Tim. 3:11), but that there was no order of widows who were enrolled and had prescribed duties (see disc. on 1 Tim. 5:3–16).

What seems certain in all of this is that the church order of the PE fits easily with what one finds in the other Pauline letters and Acts; contrariwise, it is unlike the Ignatian epistles both in spirit and in details.

All told, the theology of the PE, despite some differences from the earlier Paul, is more thoroughly Pauline than otherwise; it, too, can be shown to favor authenticity. Moreover, what does emerge further reflects the totally *ad hoc* nature of the Epistles and thus supports the occasion and purpose as outlined.

Authorship

We are led, finally, to some concluding words about authorship, for the critical matters relating specifically to this question have yet to be examined.

External Evidence

The external evidence for the Pauline authorship of the PE is as good as for any other of his letters except Romans and 1 Corinthians. They are first quoted as Pauline by Irenaeus, ca. A.D. 180 (*Against Heresies* 2.14.7; 3.3.3). But they are clearly known much earlier. They are used as early as Polycarp (d. ca. A.D. 135), who "cites" their content (*Philippians* 4:1) in the same eclectic but authoritative way he does the other Pauline letters. They are missing from Marcion's canon (ca. A.D. 150), but Tertullian says Marcion rejected them,[30] which is no wonder, since the content of 1 Timothy 4:1–5 is completely antithetical to Marcionism. By the end of the second century they are firmly fixed in every Christian canon in every part of the empire and are never doubted by anyone until the nineteenth century.[31]

Yet despite this evidence and the fact that they purport to be by Paul and are full of thoroughly Pauline ideas and concerns, it can no longer be merely assumed that Paul wrote them. The chief difficulty, and the one that is ultimately responsible for all the others we have noted, has to do with language and style, but its complexity also makes it the most difficult to present in a brief Introduction like this.

Language and Style

This problem basically has three parts: First, a significant part of the vocabulary is new, in comparison with Paul's earlier letters; and some of this new vocabulary, much of it crucial to the thought of these letters, seems to reflect a great deal more Hellenism than one finds in the earlier letters. Thus, for example, *eusebeia* ("godliness"; often "religion" in GNB) is *the* crucial term to describe the Christian faith (see disc. on 1 Tim. 2:2; 3:16; 4:7–8); *epiphaneia*, rather than *parousia*, is the only term used of Christ's second coming (see disc. on 1 Tim. 6:14; Titus 2:13); the gospel is described by the medical metaphor "sound teaching" (*hygiainousē didaskalia*); God is called *our Savior*; and *sōphrōn* ("sound-minded") and its cognates predominate as virtues. All of these are the language of Hellenism or Hellenistic Judaism.

Second, much of Paul's rich vocabulary, expressing many of his most significant theological ideas, is either missing altogether or is used in some different ways.[32] Thus, for example, *dikaiosynē* ("righteousness") appears only in the sense of "uprightness" and is a virtue to be pursued (1 Tim. 6:11; 2 Tim. 2:22), not a gift of right-standing with God.

Third, a significant number of stylistic features common to these letters (e.g., the use of particles [conjunctions], prepositions, and pronouns, or the use/non-use of the definite article) are considerably different from the earlier letters. By and large, these letters have a more monotonous style, lacking the vigor, the tumbling forth of ideas, that characterize Paul.[33]

Although some of these items can be—and have been—overstated,[34] there can be little question of the correctness of Kelly's observation: "The homogeneity of the Pastorals with one another and their dishomogeneity with the other Paulines must be regarded as an established fact." But he also adds, vigorously: "It cannot be too strongly urged that the inference that the Apostle cannot therefore be their author does not necessarily follow."[35] How, then, shall one evaluate these data?

One answer, of course, is that taken by the majority of scholars, namely, that Paul is not their author. But this answer has its own—for me, insurmountable—difficulties: First, the letters are clearly far more Pauline than otherwise in *all* of their features: language, style, theology. It is difficult to account for this with the hypothesis of pseudepigraphy. An author writing in another's name must be a near genius to be able to imitate so thoroughly. Furthermore, the failure to do so at easily discernible points (e.g., the greeting) and the creating of historical sequences like that noted (earlier) about Titus or that in 2 Timothy 4:9–18 nearly defies reason.

Second, the historical situation of the Ephesian church presupposed in 1 and 2 Timothy, which fits well the period of the 60s, as has been pointed out, scarcely fits what is otherwise known about that church around the turn of the century, the time the pseudepigrapher would have written (see note 12).

Third, and most difficult of all, is to find an adequate reason for such an author to have written these letters and, most significantly, to have written *three* letters. If one can make a good case for 1 Timothy,[36] it is equally difficult to understand why then the author also wrote Titus, and above all why, given the alleged reasons for 1 Timothy, 2 Timothy—it simply does not fit those reasons (see note 14).

Another solution, which enjoyed a long period of favor, was to see the letters as pseudepigraphic but to argue that the author used some genuine fragments of Pauline letters.[37] Although this might help to explain some of the genuine Pauline features of the letters, it, too, runs aground on the questions of occasion and purpose, not to mention that the alleged fragments are of a piece with the rest in vocabulary and style.

More recently the Pauline elements have been explained in terms of the author's use of a variety of sources, including some authentic historical data.[38] But this view also founders on the matter of the occasion and the purpose of the letters and why there were three.

The Traditional Solution

When all has been said, the traditional solution, despite the difficulties, still seems to be the best one. It affords the distinct advantage of being able to take account of more of the hard historical data, not to mention being able to offer a satisfactory accounting of all three letters, both as wholes and in all of their individual parts, as the following commentary hopes to demonstrate.

The chief difficulty with the tradition still remains: how adequately to account for the different language and style. But on this point it must be noted emphatically that, for all the differences, they are still far more like

Paul in these matters than otherwise. The best solution is that Paul used a different amanuensis for these letters than for earlier ones (or did he actually write these himself after having used amanuenses earlier?). Although this solution admittedly has its own difficulties (e.g., the actual role of the amanuensis in composition[39]), the large number of correspondences in vocabulary with Luke-Acts makes the hypothesis of Luke as this amanuensis an attractive one.[40] But on this matter, one can only conjecture. To say that Paul is the author of the PE means that the letters ultimately come from him in the historical settings contained within them. It does not say *how* they came from him; the final answer to that question is not available to us.

Notes

1. For full arguments on either side of this question, see (against Paul) W. G. Kümmel, *Introduction to the New Testament*, pp. 367–87, or A. T. Hanson, pp. 2–47; (for Paul) D. Guthrie, *New Testament Introduction*, pp. 584–624, or J. N. D. Kelly, pp. 3–36.

2. On Timothy's circumcision, see M. Hengel, *Acts and the History of Earliest Christianity* (Philadelphia: Fortress, 1979), p. 64, who notes that because Timothy had a Jewish mother, he would have been considered a Jew. Failure to have had him circumcised would have been tantamount to supporting apostasy and thus would have effectively cut off Paul's mission as being to the "Jew first." For Paul's own statements on missionary policy, see 1 Cor. 9:19–23.

3. The refusal to have the Gentile Titus circumcised is equally in keeping with 1 Cor. 9:19–23 (see note 2). In this case the gospel as freedom for Gentiles is at stake. In Paul's Christian world view, circumcision of a Jew for ministry among Jews (Timothy) and circumcision of a Gentile in order to have standing with God as a believer (Titus) would be two radically different things.

4. This date is in keeping with the view that sees Gal. 2:1–10 as a Pauline expression of the same event as that recorded in Acts 15 (as Kümmel, *Introduction*, pp. 295–304, against Guthrie, *Introduction*, pp. 450–65, who would date it about two years earlier). In either case, Titus became Paul's traveling companion earlier than Timothy.

5. It is particularly difficult to imagine why a pseudepigrapher would have chosen Titus as the recipient of one of these letters, all the more so when one considers the evidence of Acts. This is especially true for those who argue that the author knew Acts and was dependent on it for many of his data and is likewise so for those who think the author of Luke-Acts also wrote the PE (see, e.g., S. G. Wilson, *Luke and the Pastoral Epistles*).

6. For a typical expression of this difficulty see Kümmel, *Introduction*, pp. 375–78, or E. F. Scott, pp. xvii–xx. On this matter J. A. T. Robinson (*Redating the New Testament*) rightly contends: "The very difficulty of squaring them with any itinerary deducible from Acts or the other Pauline epistles is a strong argument for their authenticity" (p. 72). At least, the matter is stalemated here, and finally depends on how one evaluates the other data.

It should be noted that Robinson's own attempt to place them at three different times in the earlier life of Paul (1 Timothy between 1 and 2 Corinthians, Titus after Romans, and 2 Timothy after Colossians-Ephesians-Philemon) founders on the fact of their homogeneity with one another and their dishomogeneity with the other letters. See note 35.

7. For a presentation of the data for and against the traditional view of the provenance of these letters, see Guthrie, *Introduction*, pp. 472–78. This is still the majority view, although Kümmel argues for the Caesarean imprisonment of Acts 23:23–26:32 (*Introduction*, pp. 346–38), and some hold to an otherwise unknown Ephesian imprisonment (most recently H. Koester, *Introduction to the New Testament*, [Philadelphia: Fortress, 1982], vol. 2, pp. 130–35, for Philippians and Philemon; Koester rejects Colossians and Ephesians as having been written by Paul).

8. It is of some interest that many who argue *for* a Roman imprisonment as the place of writing for Philippians and Philemon also argue *against* a second Roman imprisonment for 2 Timothy. This seems curious in light of the clear implications in both Philippians and Philemon that Paul expected to be released. See, e.g., E. F. Scott, *The Literature of the New Testament* (New York: Columbia University, 1932), pp. 170–72; cf. C. M. Connick, *The New Testament: An Introduction to Its History, Literature, and Thought* (Encino, Calif.: Dickenson, 1972), pp. 302–4 and 322–23.

9. This very point has been argued recently by two who hold to pseudepigraphy: Hanson, pp. 14–23 (on the mission to Crete, see esp. pp. 22–23), and J. D. Quinn, "Paul's Last Captivity."

10. One of the curiosities of some who advocate pseudepigraphy is their willingness to argue that since the author probably wrote all three letters at the same time, it is "difficult to see any particular reason why one letter should be put either before or after another" (Hanson, p. 27; cf. R. J. Karris, p. 3). But such a position seems to abuse the internal evidence rather severely. It is difficult to imagine the psychology of an author who would give so many internal clues as to the order in which the letters were to be read and then not care at all that they be read in that order. This is especially true of 1 and 2 Timothy. If, for example, the pseudonymous author intended them to be read in the order 2 Timothy–1 Timothy, why were they not numbered that way? In this case the internal evidence is decisive. By the very clues put in the letters, *the author* at least intended them to be read in their present order.

11. Scott., p. 6.

12. For example, 1 and 2 Timothy simply cannot be squared with what is otherwise known about the church in Ephesus around the end of the first century A.D. If, as most believe, the Revelation comes from this period, then this church is "orthodox" whatever else (Rev. 2:1–7)—precisely 180 degrees from the picture that emerges in the PE. A similar picture of impeccable orthodoxy appears in Ignatius' letter to this church (ca. A.D. 110–115). Given these data, it can hardly have been the church in Ephesus that was capitulating in the time of our alleged author. Why, then, one wonders, these fictions about *this* church? and *for* whom specifically? But such questions are simply avoided by the proponents of pseudepigraphy.

13. See Hanson, pp. 28–31, 42–47; cf. D-C and esp. Gealy, who takes this position to its most radical stance.

14. The avoidance of this crucial question is one of the puzzles of scholarship on the PE. The closest thing to an answer is offered by R. J. Karris (pp. 3–6, 45–47), who tries to resolve this under the rubric of an author's "fictionalizing" his or her audience in order to communicate with them. That may help to explain how 1 and 2 Timothy can differ so much from one another, but it scarcely answers the real question, Why *three* letters? Furthermore, an author "fictionalizes" the audience only when he or she is writing more generally (such as in the case of this commentary); it is not the stuff of letters, which are *ad hoc* and intended to address specific, identifiable situations.

Hanson seems to offer that the reason for three letters has to do with the nature and amount of material the author had in hand and wanted to include. But this founders, as Hanson himself is forced to admit, with the existence of Titus: "one is led to suspect that Titus was written last of all and that the author was beginning to run short of material" (p. 47). This very acknowledgment demonstrates the difficulty—which is never adequately addressed.

15. For such a view from the perspective of authenticity, see Guthrie, pp. 52–53, or Kelly, pp. 59–60 and throughout. How deeply entrenched this point of view is came home forcefully to me when a student who had sat through my course began his term paper with this sentence: "The Pastoral Epistles are not private letters but rather are for the regulation of ecclesiastical discipline"!

16. Interestingly, this datum is almost totally disregarded by scholarship—on both sides of the question of authorship. It seems to have been overlooked by conservative scholars because of their view of the purpose of these letters—to establish church order—and this passage in Acts did not seem to fit that view. Others have disregarded it because they consider the speech to be unhistorical, created by the author of Acts himself (see, e.g., E. Haenchen, *The Acts of the Apostles: A Commentary* [Philadelphia: Westminster, 1971], pp. 595–98). But that scarcely resolves anything. Even if the author created the speech, its very creation "after the fact" argues strongly for the fact itself. Hence whether actual prophecy or "prophecy from hindsight," the data of this speech strongly support the position taken in this commentary.

17. By and large scholarship has subsumed the question of *who* the heretics were under that of *what* the heresy was, and it is generally assumed, if not always articulated, that the opponents were outsiders. An exception may be found in E. E. Ellis, "Paul and His Opponents," p. 114: "Unlike the earlier letters, the opponents appear to include a considerable number of former co-workers whose apostasy creates an especially bitter situation."

18. For a recent and very helpful discussion, see P. T. O'Brien, *Colossians, Philemon*, WBC 44 (Waco, Tex.: Word, 1982), pp. xxvii–xli.

19. See, e.g., G. D. Fee, "1 Corinthians 7:1 in the NIV," JETS 23 (1980), pp. 307–14; cf. W. E. Phipps, "Is Paul's Attitude towards Sexual Relations Contained in 1 Cor. 7.1?" NTS 28 (1982), pp. 125–32.

20. For an overview of this perspective, see P. T. O'Brien (note 18), pp. xxxvi–xxxviii, and the literature there cited.

21. This view of the opposition is similar to that presented by E. E. Ellis, "Paul and His Opponents," pp. 101–15, esp. 112–15. The ties of this heresy to that found earlier in Colossae were first spelled out in some detail (although I differ some in emphasis) by J. B. Lightfoot, *Biblical Essays*, pp. 411–18.

22. This is one of the features of the PE that is commonly pointed out as being non-Pauline. Note, e.g., how this becomes crucial for the argument in R. J. Karris, "The Background and Significance of the Polemic of the Pastoral Epistles."

23. One of the less convincing perspectives on the PE advocated by some suggests that "one of [their] most remarkable features . . . is their single-minded emphasis on Paul's apostolic authority" (Hanson, p. 24; cf. R. F. Collins, "The Image of Paul in the Pastorals," *LTP* 31 [1975], pp. 147–73). But one wonders how this could have been seen at all apart from a prior commitment to non-Pauline authorship. In comparison with Galatians or 2 Corinthians, for example, the emphasis on Paul's own authority in the PE is rather mild.

24. For a fuller development of this position, see Kümmel, *Introduction*, pp. 382–84, or any of the commentaries that hold to non-Pauline authorship (e.g., D-C, Easton, Hanson,

Scott).

25. One can be sure, for example, that if we did not have 1 Corinthians, one of the "assured results" of NT scholarship would be that Paul and his churches knew nothing of the Eucharist. Indeed, but for the abuses in the church in Corinth, one can only imagine what other assured results based on silence there might be.

26. J. Denney, cited by A. M. Hunter, *Introducing the New Testament*, 2d ed. (London: SCM, 1957), p. 155.

27. D-C, p. 8.

28. See, e.g., Hanson, pp. 31–38.

29. See esp. Bernard, pp. lvi–lxxv.

30. *Against Marcion* 5.21.

31. For a full display of this evidence, see Bernard, pp. xiii–xxi.

32. See esp. the useful summary in Barrett, p. 6.

33. See, e.g., the assessment by N. Turner, *Style,* vol. 4 of J. H. Moulton, *A Grammar of New Testament Greek* (Edinburgh: T. & T. Clark, 1976), p. 105: "We cannot say that the Greek style is the most elegant in the NT, but it is the least Semitic, most secular, and least exciting. It is commonplace."

34. This is especially true of P. N. Harrison's classic study, *The Problem of the Pastoral Epistles.* See the literature cited by Guthrie, *Introduction,* p. 607, notes 1 and 2.

35. P. 24.

36. As, e.g., E. F. Scott.

37. This was the position espoused by Harrison in *The Problem of the Pastoral Epistles:* It especially had a period of long favor with British scholars. For a critique, see Kelly, pp. 28–30.

39. There is evidence from Cicero that he used two different amanuenses, with two considerably different styles of dictation, when his purposes for writing differed (*Letter to Atticus* 13.25.3; see G. J. Bahr, "Paul and Letter Writing in the First Century," CBQ 28 [1966], pp. 465–77). In the case of the PE one would have to allow for more than simple dictation; the amanuensis seems also to have become partly writer. Why Paul would have changed his compositional style at this point in his life has not been adequately explained.

40. See esp. C. F. D. Moule ("The Problem of the Pastoral Epistles: A Reappraisal"), who sees them as written by Luke for Paul during Paul's lifetime. For the view that Luke is their author, but as a pseudepigrapher after Paul's death, see S. G. Wilson, *Luke and the Pastoral Epistles,* and J. D. Quinn, "The Last Volume of Luke: The Relation of Luke-Acts to the Pastoral Epistles."

Salutation

1 TIMOTHY 1:1–2

From Paul, an apostle of Christ Jesus by order of God our Savior and Christ Jesus our hope— ²To Timothy, my true son in the faith:

May God the Father and Christ Jesus our Lord give you grace, mercy, and peace.

The letter begins with the standard form of salutation found in almost all the letters from the Greco-Roman period. Where such a letter in our time would have begun, "Dear Timothy," and concluded something like, "Your affectionate father in Christ, Paul," ancient letters began with the name of the writer, followed by the address-ee and a greeting. Usually these were terse: "Paul, to Timothy, greet-ings." Such a terse greeting may be found in Paul's earliest existing letter (1 Thessalonians), but as time went on, each part of the salutation tended to become elaborated ("Christianized") in a variety of ways. These elabo-rations, especially the longer ones, often reflect the urgencies of the letter in hand. This seems to be true of our letter.

1:1 / Paul regularly calls himself **an apostle of Christ Jesus** (1 Corinthi-ans, 2 Corinthians, Galatians, Ephesians, Colossians; cf. Romans), espe-cially in those letters in which his authority was in question or what he was about to say needed the weight of apostolic authority. In more person-al letters his self-designation is "servant" (Philippians; cf. Romans) or "prisoner" (Philemon). Why, then, does Paul use the designation **apostle** when writing to his longtime missionary companion and **son in the faith**? Probably because, as was noted in the Introduction, Paul is writing to Timothy with the full expectation that the church in Ephesus will over-hear. The errors being spread in the church call for Timothy's strong action, action ultimately based on Paul's apostolic authority.

Paul's authority is further emphasized with the addition **by order of God**. Ordinarily he speaks of his apostleship as "by the will of God" (cf. 2 Tim. 1:1); but in this letter he is going to charge Timothy to "order" the church, or the errorists, to do or refrain from doing certain things. Thus he who gives orders is himself under orders.

The source of Paul's authority is **God our Savior and Christ Jesus our hope**. It is Paul's habit especially in the salutations to qualify the mention of God, but only in the PE (Pastoral Epistles) does he designate God as Savior. This title has its roots deep in OT (Old Testament) piety, where God is often referred to as (my) "Savior" (Deut. 32:15; Pss. 24:5; 25:5; 27:9; 42:5, et al.; cf. Luke 1:47 and Jude 25). Here the emphasis is on God as the source of salvation, which in turn leads Paul to refer to Christ Jesus as **our hope**, who will complete our salvation at his appearing. (Note how these ideas all come together in Christ himself in Titus 2:13.)

1:2 / The designation of Timothy as his **true son in the faith** also seems to reflect the authority motif. (Note that in the more personal 2 Timothy he is simply called "my dear son.") The word translated **true** literally refers to a legitimate child. Since Paul similarly refers to an unknown brother in Philippians 4:3 as a "true" yokefellow, one should perhaps not overstress the concept of legitimacy here. But it fits Paul's concern well, not simply reassuring Timothy himself, but also ensuring that the church does not reject him (see 4:6–16).

The meaning of **in the faith** is debated (see disc. on v. 5 for the word *faith* in the PE). There is no article in the Greek text. Since elsewhere in these letters, where Paul unambiguously means to say "*the* faith," he always uses the article, it is much more likely that **in faith** is meant here. That is, Paul is referring either to Timothy's own **faith** (*by* his having **faith** in Christ he thereby also became Paul's **son**) or to the sphere of his relationship with Paul (**in** his **faith**[fulness] to Christ he is a **true**, faithful **son**). The latter is probably what is meant. Although Paul often uses parent-child imagery to reflect his relationship to his converts (e.g., 1 Cor. 4:14–15; Philem. 10), the evidence in Acts 16:1–3 does not suggest that Timothy was in fact Paul's own convert. Paul's feelings for his younger colleague may often have been paternal, but in most references to him in the earlier letters, Timothy is spoken of as a co-worker (e.g., 1 Thess. 3:2; Phil. 2:19–20). In 1 Corinthians 4:16–17 Paul had already used language similar to what he uses here, and in that case the emphasis on his being Paul's "dear and faithful son *in the Lord*" was that by watching "son" Timothy's example, his Corinthian "children" would know how to behave like their "father." Thus the church in Ephesus is to recognize Timothy as Paul's **true son** because of his **faith**.

The greeting proper, the prayer-wish that Timothy receive **grace, mercy and peace**, is (apart from the addition of **mercy**) the standard Pauline formula. Early on, Paul had already transformed the Greek greeting *chairein* ("Greetings!") into *charis* ("Grace") and brought it alongside the Hebrew greeting *shalom* ("Peace"). In Paul's theology, and therefore in his greeting and prayer for his converts, **grace** comes from **God** through **Christ** and issues in **peace**. The combination **mercy and peace** has Jewish roots and had been used earlier by Paul in Galatians 6:16. Thus in the final letters the salutation has become complete.

Additional Notes

For a collection of scores of examples of salutations from letters in the papyrus finds, see F. X. J. Exler, *The Form of the Ancient Greek Letter of the Epistolary Papyri (3rd c. B.C.–3rd c. A.D.)*, pp. 23–68.

1:1-2 / It is Paul's habit in his *salutations* to refer to Christ as **Christ Jesus** (although in several instances some early scribes reversed the order to Jesus Christ). However, in his earlier letters he also speaks of "Jesus" (e.g., Rom. 8:11; 2 Cor. 4:10; Gal. 6:17), "Christ" (Rom. 5:6, 8, and throughout), "Jesus Christ" (e.g., Rom 1:8; 3:22; and throughout), and "our Lord Jesus Christ" (e.g., Rom. 1:4; 7:25; and throughout). By the time of the PE, the title **Christ Jesus** predominates (twenty-six times to two) and has become something very close to a full proper name.

Sōtēr (savior), along with *kyrios* (lord), was a common title for the deities of the Hellenistic mystery cults. Already the title had been taken over and applied to God in Hellenistic Judaism by Philo of Alexandria. Therefore, many scholars see this as a non-Pauline term, used by our author who has himself imbibed Philonic Hellenistic Judaism and adapted it to fit Paul. However, the title is thoroughly biblical, and it is just as likely that Paul's use of it in these letters reflects the emphases of the errorists.

Indeed, **God our Savior** could be argued to be a very Pauline idea. Only once does Paul call Christ **our Savior**, in the thoroughly eschatological context of Phil. 3:20 (the usage in Eph. 5:23 does not seem to be an appellation). But the subject of the verb *save*, or the verbal idea in the noun *salvation*, is never Christ, only God (1 Cor. 1:21; 1 Thess. 5:9). In Paul's view of things, "we shall be saved [by God] through him [Christ]" (Rom. 5:9). Thus it should not be surprising that eventually he should come to call both God and Christ *our Savior*, especially since the former has already happened in Hellenistic Judaism.

It is often argued that there are non-Pauline elements in the salutation that betray another hand than Paul's (**by order of God, God our Savior**, the addition of **mercy**, and the word order **God the Father and Christ Jesus our Lord**). One could note in response how many genuinely Pauline features there are as well. In fact one might have expected an imitator to be more slavish in copying Paul. The modifications in this salutation just as easily argue *for* Paul, since such modifications are his regular habit. Of course, an imitator could have noted that as well. So the argument is a standoff here.

2

The Charge: Stop the False Teachers

1 TIMOTHY 1:3–11

I want you to stay in Ephesus, just as I urged you when I was on my way to Macedonia. Some people there are teaching false doctrines, and you must order them to stop. ⁴Tell them to give up those legends and those long lists of ancestors, which only produce arguments; they do not serve God's plan, which is known by faith. ⁵The purpose of this order is to arouse the love that comes from a pure heart, a clear conscience, and a genuine faith. ⁶Some people have turned away from these and have lost their way in foolish discussions. ⁷They want to be teachers of God's law, but they do not understand their own words or the matters about which they speak with

so much confidence.

⁸We know that the Law is good if it is used as it should be used. ⁹It must be remembered, of course, that laws are made, not for good people, but for lawbreakers and criminals, for the godless and sinful, for those who are not religious or spiritual, for those who kill their fathers or mothers, for murderers, ¹⁰for the immoral, for sexual perverts, for kidnappers, for those who lie and give false testimony or who do anything else contrary to sound doctrine. ¹¹That teaching is found in the gospel that was entrusted to me to announce, the Good News from the glorious and blessed God.

Paul begins the letter proper in a way that is uncharacteristic of him—without the standard thanksgiving. Of his earlier letters, only Galatians (significantly enough) lacks the thanksgiving. The absence of one here supports the observation already made that 1 Timothy is really for the sake of the church as much as, or more than, for Timothy himself; what is taking place in the church gives no cause for thanksgiving.

Instead Paul launches immediately into the occasion and purpose of the letter. Indeed, all the crucial matters that make up the framework and content of 1 Timothy are set out in the opening paragraph (vv. 3–7). The church has been greatly endangered by some elders (probably), who think of themselves as **teachers of God's law** (v. 7), but who in fact **are teaching false doctrines** (v. 3). Timothy has been left in Ephesus to stem the tide. He is not the "pastor"; rather, he has been left to act on Paul's behalf while Paul is away. This letter will authorize Timothy—before the church—to oppose those deceivers and their followers. Thus the stage is set: The whole letter is a response to the presence of the false teachers.

1:3 / The opening sentence gives the occasion of the letter, plus all the significant "actors"—Paul, Timothy, the church (implied in the **in Ephesus**), and the false teachers.

Although it is not certain whether Paul had recently been in Ephesus, that seems to be implied by his **urging** Timothy **to stay** there, while he himself **was on** his **way to Macedonia**. Later we learn (3:14) that he had hoped to go to Ephesus soon; however, in case of delay (which indeed happened, given the evidence of 2 Timothy), Paul wanted his younger colleague to "have in writing" the reason for his being there.

The beginnings of the church **in Ephesus** are somewhat shrouded in mystery (Acts 18:19–21; 18:24–20:1), although it is clear from the account in Acts, corroborated by passing references in 1 Corinthians 16:8–9, 19, and 2 Corinthians 1:8–9, that it was a Pauline church (perhaps composed of many house-churches; see 1 Cor. 16:19). Ephesus itself was both the provincial capital and the religious center of the province of Asia. Because of the silting of its harbor, it was in Paul's time in commercial decline; this was still offset, however, by its past importance and the presence of its Temple of Artemis (Diana), one of the Seven Wonders of the World and a tourist attraction that obviously netted no small gain to enterprising hawkers of religious souvenirs (Acts 19:23–41). The cult of Artemis reflected religious mixture (syncretism) but basically was an Oriental fertility rite, with sensuous and orgiastic practices. The Ephesian church was very important in Paul's missionary strategy; hence his concern to root out the error in this key center.

There is no hint in either letter to Timothy that the **some people there** who were **teaching false doctrines** were outsiders, as was the case in Galatia (Gal. 2:4) and Corinth (e.g., 2 Cor. 11:4, 12–15). Moreover, Paul's farewell address to the Ephesian elders, as recorded in Acts 20:17–35, clearly predicts that the "fierce wolves" who "will not spare the flock" will be "some men from your own group" (vv. 29–30). That the false teachers were therefore probably elders is supported by several items from 1 Timothy: their presuming to be "teachers of God's law" (v. 7), a responsibility of the elders (5:17; cf. 3:2); the fact that two are named and excommunicated by Paul (1:19–20), not by the church as in 2 Thessalonians

3:14 and 1 Corinthians 5:1–5; and the repeated concern about elders in this letter, both as to their qualifications—with no mention of duties—in 3:1–7 and their discipline and apparent replacement in 5:19–25.

The word translated **teaching false doctrines**, apparently coined here and found subsequently only in Christian writings, literally means "to teach other things," or "novelties." It is reminiscent of the false teachers in Corinth, who preached "a different Jesus" and a "gospel completely different" (2 Cor. 11:4; cf. Gal. 1:6). But the "novelties" are not innocent trivialities; they are clear perversions of the pure gospel. Timothy's purpose in remaining there, then, was to **order them to stop**.

1:4 / Timothy is also to **tell** the erring teachers **to give up** their fascination for **legends and those long lists of ancestors** ("myths and endless genealogies," RSV). These two words, among the few in the letters to Timothy that give any indication of the content of the false doctrines, are also among the more puzzling. As Kelly says, "They come tantalizingly near disclosing the content of the heresy"! (p. 44). In 4:7 they are again characterized as "godless le ...us, which are not worth telling" (lit., "old wives' tales"). A sir ... phenomenon has also emerged in Crete, where they are called "*Jewish* legends" (Titus 1:14); the "genealogies" reappear in a list that includes "quarrels and fights about the Law" (Titus 3:9).

It has often been suggested that these words reflect the alleged Gnostic character of the heresy, supported further by such language as "foolish arguments . . . wrongly call[ed] 'knowledge' " (6:20) and by the ascetic practices mentioned in 4:3 (cf. 5:23). Thus the **legends** and "genealogies" are seen to refer to the speculative cosmologies of the later Gnostics with their systems of aeons (spiritual beings) that emanate from God (the Father of the All), such as one finds in Valentinus. (This position seems to be reflected in the Living Bible, which reads: "Their idea of being saved by finding favor with an endless chain of angels leading up to God.")

But the terms translated **legends** (*mythoi*) and **ancestors** (*genealogiai*) are never used in descriptions of these Gnostic systems. They do, however, regularly appear in Hellenism and Hellenistic Judaism to refer to traditions about peoples' origins. The term *mythoi* in this literature is almost always used in a pejorative sense (as throughout the PE), to contrast the legendary character of many of these stories to historical truth.

Therefore, given the lack of any real concern in 1 and 2 Timothy for characteristically Gnostic motifs, plus the fact that in verse 7 the errors are specifically related to the Law, it is more plausible that these "myths and endless genealogies" reflect Jewish influence of some kind, undoubtedly with some Hellenistic overlays. But what they were precisely is not available to us, although there have been several suggestions (such as the kinds of speculations one finds in the *Book of Jubilees* or in Philo's *Questions and Answers on Genesis* or in Pseudo-Philo's *Book of Biblical Antiquities* or even in the Jewish haggadic tradition [illustrative commentary on the OT]). It must finally be admitted that we simply do not know, because Paul does not give us enough clues.

What we do know is that he stands boldly against such things, not so much because of their content (although such **legends** are quite unrelated to the truth [4:6–7; 2 Tim. 4:4]) but because such teaching has two net effects: (1) "fruitless discussions" (1:6; cf. 6:20; 2 Tim. 2:16; 3:7), which (2) result in quarrels and strife (6:3–5; 2 Tim. 2:14, 23).

It is the utter futility of it all that grips Paul at this point. Indeed, the word translated **long list** more likely refers to the "endless, wearisome" nature of the teaching. What such "myths and endless genealogies" **produce** is "speculations" (RSV; lit., a "seeking out"), not **arguments** (GNB). Thus **legends** and **genealogies** are interminable tediums, promoting foolish speculations, "full of sound and fury," but "signifying nothing."

Furthermore, such "speculations" have nothing to do with **God's plan, which is known by faith**. The word translated **plan**, when used in its literal, nonfigurative sense, refers to the "management" of another's household (as in Luke 16:2–4). As a metaphor it means either "a stewardship entrusted by God" (cf. 1 Cor. 9:17; Eph. 3:2) or, as in the GNB, **God's plan**, meaning God's "arrangements for people's redemption." This latter is more likely the intent, since the emphasis in this context does not seem to be on the failure of the false teachers to exercise faithful stewardship but on the gospel as **God's plan** and work, based on or **known by faith**, in contrast to the futility of the "novelties."

1:5 / Having given the occasion for writing (v. 3), plus some reaction to what the erring elders are doing (v. 4), Paul now returns to his **order** that they stop (v. 3). The **purpose of this order**, he says, is **love**. This is probably not a general statement about the gospel, in contrast to the errors; rather, Paul is specifically giving the reason for Timothy's involvement, namely, **to arouse the love that comes from a pure heart**. The false teachers are involved in speculations (v. 4) and foolish discussions (v. 6) that are full of deception (4:1–2) and lead to quarrels and suspicions (6:4–5). The purpose of ordering them to stop is to bring the church back to the proper result of "God's work, based on faith," namely, their loving one another. (Note how often **faith** and **love** appear together in the PE as

7

the truly Christian virtues: 1 Tim. 1:14; 2:15; 4:12; 6:11; 2 Tim. 1:13; 2:22; 3:10; Titus 2:2).

The Christian grace of **love** springs **from a pure heart, a clear conscience, and a genuine faith**. These motivations to love stand in stark contrast to those of the false teachers, who are deceived and deceitful (4:1–2; 5:24; 2 Tim. 2:26; 3:13; cf. 1 Tim. 2:14; 5:15; 2 Tim. 3:5–7), have "branded" consciences (4:2), "and have made a ruin of their faith" (1:19).

A **pure heart** reflects Paul's biblical background (Pss. 24:4; 51:10; cf. Jesus' beatitude, Matt. 5:8). The concept of a **clear** (lit., "good") **conscience** derives from his Hellenistic environment. The **conscience** is the capacity, or seat, of moral consciousness, common to all people (Rom. 2:15; 2 Cor. 4:2). In Paul's earlier letters (Romans, 1 and 2 Corinthians only) the conscience arbitrates one's own—and others'—actions (see esp. 1 Corinthians 8–10). But it is also clear that it can be informed, either by one's pagan past or present existence in Christ. In the PE, the term **conscience** is often, as here, accompanied by a descriptive adjective (good, pure, branded), implying the seat of moral decision-making to have been "purified" by Christ or "branded" or "defiled" by Satan (see disc. on 1 Tim. 4:2 and Titus 1:15–16). It is clear from this context and from 1:19 that a **pure heart** and **clear conscience** are synonymous ideas.

The qualification of **faith** as **genuine** is comparable to his qualifying love in the same way in Romans 12:9. In a sense, neither can be so qualified. Either you have faith, or love, or you do not. But the word **faith** has a broad usage in Paul, ranging from "trust in God" (most common), to a Christian virtue coming very close to the idea of "faithfulness" (e.g., 1 Thess. 3:6; 5:8, and frequently in the PE; see disc. on 1:2), to the content of Christian belief (e.g., Gal. 1:23; also frequently in the PE). Here **genuine faith** refers to the Christian virtue, meaning trust in God that is truly there, in contrast to the deceptive nature of the errorists' "faith."

1:6–7 / That these sources of Christian love are expressed in this way so as to stand in contrast to the false teachers is now made clear. **Some people**, namely, the false teachers, **have turned away from these** (that is, "a pure heart, a clear conscience, and a genuine faith"; cf. 1:19). The concept of **turning away from** faith (or *the* faith) recurs throughout the PE, sometimes with this verb (6:21; 2 Tim. 2:18), but also with several others ("repudiate" [GNB, "have not listened to"], 1:19; "abandon," 4:1; "turn away," 1:6; 5:15; "wander away," 6:10; "turn away," 2 Tim. 4:4). This "apostasy" on the part of both the erring elders and their followers is the great urgency of 1 Timothy.

Not only have they **turned away from** true faith and integrity, but in its place they **have lost their way in foolish discussions**. This repeats the themes of tediousness and speculations from verse 4. The word for **foolish discussions** is a compound of *mataios* ("empty, vain") and *logos* ("speech"). These "discussions" are elsewhere characterized as "empty sounds" (6:20; 2 Tim. 2:16).

Paul has one final designation for the straying teachers in this opening salvo: **They want to be teachers of God's law**. It is not easy to determine precisely what is intended by **teachers of God's law** (a compound word in Greek: *nomos*, "law"; *didaskalos*, "teacher"). The word is a strictly Christian one, used by Luke of the rabbis in Luke 5:17 and of Gamaliel in Acts 5:34. Here it may be a pejorative epithet (they are merely taking the role of Jewish rabbis); but more likely it is a description of what the false teachers were really aspiring to—to be teachers of the Law (meaning probably both interpreters of the laws, 4:3, and speculative interpreters of the OT stories and genealogies about beginnings, 1:4).

In either case, as the next paragraph will elaborate, they neither **understand their own words** (because they are full of speculations and empty talk) nor **the matters about which they speak with so much confidence** (the meaning of the Scriptures). They are simply "pontificating on the unknowable." The theme of the "ignorance" or "mindlessness" of the heretics will recur in these letters (6:4, 20; 2 Tim. 2:23; Titus 1:15; 3:9; cf. 2 Tim. 3:7).

1:8 / The next paragraph (vv. 8–11) is something of a digression, which will lead in turn to a second digression (vv. 12–17; note how vv. 18–20 resume the argument of vv. 3–7). But in typical Pauline fashion it is a digression that bears significantly upon the point at hand. In response to the false teachers' improper use of the "Law," Paul sets forth its real intent, which, as expressed here, is that it is for the ungodly.

Interestingly, he fails to go on to say *how* or *why* it is for them; but in Galatians 3:23–4:7 and Romans 7:7–25, he had previously spoken to this question and suggested two reasons: to put a restraint on sin (Galatians) and to expose the sinners' desperate sinfulness, causing them to throw themselves upon God's mercy (Romans). More likely it was the former that was in mind as this paragraph begins.

The opening sentence evolves out of verse 7. The false teachers wish to be teachers of the Law but do not know what they are doing. It is clear that Paul's intent here is not to argue for a correct, Christian use of the Law. Rather, he is pointing out the folly of the false teachers, including the fact that they use the Law at all. That **the Law is good** repeats an assertion made in Romans 7:12–13 and 16 (albeit in a different context). Implied in both instances is that it is **good** because it truly does reflect God's will. Nonetheless, as Kelly points out, the Law is not gospel, but remains a species of law. Here its "goodness" is related to its being **used as it should be used**, that is, treated as law (intended for the lawless, v. 9) and not used "illegitimately" as a source for legends and endless genealogies, or for ascetic practices.

1:9–10 / Paul continues by describing what one does who treats the Law as law. Although the Mosaic Law is still in view, the Greek text lacks the definite article, hence the GNB translation **laws are made**. What is true of God's Law, thought of as law, is of course true of all laws. It was given, **not for good people** (better, "the just person"), **but for lawbreakers and criminals, for the godless and sinful**. By saying that the Law was not intended for "the just person," Paul reflects a point made earlier in Galatians, that those who have the Spirit and bear its fruit have entered a sphere of existence in which the Law no longer performs its legal functions (Gal. 5:22–23).

The mention of **lawbreakers** launches Paul into a whole list of such sinners. Vice lists like this are typical of the apostle (see e.g., Rom. 1:29–31; 1 Cor. 5:11; 6:9–10; Gal. 5:19–21; and 2 Tim. 3:2–4). What amazes one is that no single sin is specifically repeated in them all (even in the three earlier letters). They seem in each case to be *ad hoc* catalogues, although they also seem to be somewhat adapted to contexts. Of the sins in this list, only **the immoral** and **sexual perverts** (v. 10) are found in earlier lists (1 Cor. 6:9). But what is more striking is the two-part nature of the catalogue. First, there are three pairs of general classifications: **lawbreakers and criminals** (or the rebellious), the **godless** (inwardly irreverent) **and sinful** (outwardly disobedient), and **those who are not religious or spiritual** (unholy and profane). Thereafter the catalogue has a remarkable coincidence with the Ten Commandments (the fifth through the ninth), often giving more grotesque expressions of these sins.

Thus these lawless are **those who kill their fathers or mothers** (fifth commandment); **murderers** (sixth commandment); **the immoral** (lit., "fornicators") and **sexual perverts**, a word for male coital homosexuality (seventh commandment); **kidnappers**, probably slave-dealers (eighth commandment); and **those who lie and give false testimony** (ninth commandment). Such coincidences can scarcely be accidental. But what is the reason for such a list here? It is certainly not a hidden reference to the sins of the false teachers, who are guilty of their own kinds of sins, but not these. Most likely the list is a conscious reflection of the Mosaic Law as law and expresses the kinds of sins such law was given to prohibit. *This*, Paul says, is why God gave his Law, not for idle speculation and foolish discussions.

Paul rounds off this list in a manner similar to Romans 13:9 and Galatians 5:21, so as to include all other sins as well: those **who do anything else contrary to sound doctrine**. But in this case the "rounding off" words bring Paul back once again to the warnings against false teachings. The term **sound doctrine** will appear regularly in these letters (6:3; 2 Tim. 1:13; 4:3; Titus 1:9, 13; 2:2, 8). It is a medical metaphor referring to the "healthiness" of teaching "found in the gospel" (v. 11) and stands in opposition to the "sickly craving" (6:4; GNB, "unhealthy desire") of the errorists, whose "teaching is like an open sore that eats away the flesh" (2 Tim. 2:17). Such a metaphor is not found earlier in Paul. Its source, especially as a polemic device, is most likely contemporary itinerant philosophers, who would have been well known to the Ephesians. That Paul should borrow such metaphors is no more surprising than his use of the body metaphor, a well-known contemporary political metaphor, in 1 Corinthians 12, or his use of athletic metaphors in 1 Corinthians 9:24-27 and in these letters (1 Tim. 6:12; 2 Tim. 2:5; 4:7-8). In these Epistles, the metaphor of healthy teaching becomes a thorough-going polemic against the diseased false teachers. But the concern of the metaphor is not with the *content* of doctrine; rather, it is with behavior. Healthy teaching leads to proper Christian behavior, love and good works; the diseased teaching of the heretics leads to controversies, arrogance, abusiveness, and strife (6:4).

1:11 / Having mentioned behavior that is "contrary to sound doctrine," Paul concludes by describing the true source and measure for such **teaching**. It is **found in the gospel, the Good News from . . . God**. The **gospel**, as God's **Good News** over against the bad news of humanity's grotesque sinfulness, is Paul's favorite word for God's activity in Christ Jesus on behalf of sinners. "Sound doctrine" accords with the gospel message, both in content and resultant behavior; the "diseased" teaching of the straying elders does not.

In mentioning **the gospel** Paul makes two elaborations: It **was entrusted to me to announce**, and it proceeds **from the glorious and blessed God**. (GNB transposes these two phrases for clarity of expression but thereby weakens the connection between vv. 11 and 12.)

11

The gospel is first of all the **Good News from the glorious and blessed God** (lit., "the gospel of the glory of the blessed God"). This kind of genitive ("of-phrase") construction is particularly difficult to make sense of in English (and there are about fourteen possibilities for its meaning in Greek). Although the phrase "of the glory" is often used in a descriptive way in the NT (e.g., Eph. 1:17, "the glorious Father"; Col. 1:11, "his glorious power"), it is far more likely in this case that the whole phrase describes, not the *source* of the gospel, but its *content* (as in most translations and commentaries). The gospel Paul announces reveals the "glory," or majesty, of God himself, here described as **the blessed God**. This latter term, found also in 6:15, does not so much mean that we ascribe blessedness to God, but that all blessedness resides in him and proceeds from him.

This gospel, which reveals the very glory of God, Paul concludes, **was entrusted to me to announce**. This is typically Pauline. To mention the gospel, God's gracious activity for sinners, is often to mention his own role as recipient and servant, or steward (cf. 1 Cor. 9:17; Gal. 2:7; Eph. 3:2; 1 Thess. 2:4). But in this case he is probably also harking back to the authority motif (see disc. on v. 1). This theme is so important, in fact, that it will be more fully elaborated in the next paragraph.

So the paragraph concludes, apparently at some distance from where it began, as a slight digression on the purpose of the Law, which has been totally missed by the Law-teachers. However, this brief excursion to mention the gospel as the revelation of God's majesty and Paul's relationship to it is not so far afield from his main concern—to check the spread of false teaching. And having gone this far, he will now elaborate even further, again not without contextual purpose.

Additional Notes

1:3 / The opening sentence in Paul's Greek is ungrammatical, although it might be merely elliptical (some examples are given in Moulton-Milligan, p. 314). It begins, "Even as," a construction that needs a "so now" to complete it. Paul intended either something like what the GNB translates or something like, "Even as I urged you when I was on my way to Macedonia, so now I urge you in writing, stay in Ephesus."

Whether Paul had recently been in Ephesus is a moot point. Guthrie, probably because of how Paul expresses himself in 3:14, suggests that he may have "left Timothy en route for Ephesus, and charged him to *abide* there" (p. 57). More recently, J. D. Quinn, who does not think Paul wrote the letters, has offered the very attractive alternative that the author intended them to be read in the order Titus, 1 Timothy, 2 Timothy; so that Paul moved from Nicopolis (Titus 3:12), whence he dispatched Timothy while on his way to Macedonia (1 Tim. 1:3), intending to come himself shortly (3:14). But en route he was arrested at Troas (2 Tim. 4:13), whence he was taken to Rome (see "Paul's Last Captivity"). The stance taken here presupposes that Paul had been on hand personally to excommunicate Hymenaeus and Alexander (v. 20).

1:4 / For a discussion of the "myths and endless genealogies" as reflecting Gnostic or Greek ideas, see the commentaries by D-C and Hanson. For the perspective adopted here, see further in F. J. A. Hort, *Judaistic Christianity*, pp. 132–33; and F. Büchsel, *TDNT*, vol. 1, pp. 663–65. Cf. the commentaries by Kelly and Bernard.

The word translated **arguments** (*ekzētēteis*) occurs here for the first time in Greek literature. The verb form is well attested and means to "seek out." Since the companion, noncompounded word *zētēteis* (substituted here in later MSS) appears elsewhere in the PE (1 Tim. 6:4; 2 Tim. 2:23; Titus 3:9)—and *does* mean "arguments"—Paul surely intended something different here by using *ekzētēteis*.

BAGD, followed by the RSV and others, suggests "divine training" as a translation for **God's plan**; but there is no known use of the word with this meaning before the late second century A.D., and either of the other meanings, both well established by Paul's time, fits the context well.

1:5 / Many argue that the qualifications of both **conscience** and **faith** are dead giveaways of the non-Pauline character of the *ideas* of the PE. But this often assumes a static Paul, on the one hand, and seems to misread the earlier evidence, on the other. For example, D-C argue that "faith" has been transformed here into "a human attitude" (p. 18). But this is both to neglect the evidence for its being a Christian virtue, often in conjunction with love, in the earlier letters and to miss the point here, which really does have to do with trust in God.

1:8 / In the Greek this sentence has an apparent wordplay, hard to reproduce in English. "The Law (*nomos*) is good, provided it is used 'lawfully' (*nomimōs*)."

1:9-10 / The word translated **good people** is *dikaios* ("just" or "righteous"), Paul's favorite forensic term, which in its verb form is usually translated "to justify." The translation **good**, as with BAGD's "the law-abiding person," with no connotation of the religious aspect is not adequate. After all, Paul could have used *agathos* or *kalos* (both meaning "good"), as he does regularly in these Epistles. The whole passage breathes forensic ideas, though it does move in a somewhat different sphere from Paul's ordinary "justification by faith."

For an analysis of the possible source(s) and function of the vice lists in the PE, see N. J. McEleney, "The Vice Lists of the Pastoral Epistles."

The word for **kidnappers** has been suggested by BAGD (as a possibility) to mean "procurer," thus linking it with the previously mentioned sexual sins. But it almost certainly refers to slave dealing. Moreover, there is evidence for a very early understanding among the rabbis of the eighth commandment referring to slave dealing. See Str-B, vol. 1, pp. 810–12.

1:11 / There has been a long debate on the meaning of **sound doctrine** in the PE. For a critique of that debate and a full presentation of the position adopted here, see A. J. Malherbe, "Medical Imagery in the Pastoral Epistles."

3

A Testimony About the Gospel

I give thanks to Christ Jesus our Lord, who has given me strength for my work. I thank him for considering me worthy and appointing me to serve him, ¹³even though in the past I spoke evil of him and persecuted and insulted him. But God was merciful to me because I did not yet have faith and so did not know what I was doing. ¹⁴And our Lord poured out his abundant grace on me and gave me the faith and love which are ours in union with Christ Jesus. ¹⁵This is a true saying, to be completely accepted and believed: Christ Jesus came into the world to save sinners. I am the worst of them, ¹⁶but God was merciful to me in order that Christ Jesus might show his full patience in dealing with me, the worst of sinners, as an example for all those who would later believe in him and receive eternal life. ¹⁷To the eternal King, immortal and invisible, the only God—to him be honor and glory forever and ever! Amen.

This paragraph is so clearly a digression in the argument of the letter that it is easy to read it, or comment on it, apart from its immediate context. But to do so is to miss a large part of its significance. The whole paragraph flows directly out of the preceding one. First of all, it is a presentation of "the gospel" (v. 11) as a bold expression of God's grace toward sinners. Even though it takes the form of personal testimony (note the fourteen occurrences of **I** or **me**), the emphasis throughout is on God's grace set forth in Christ, which in turn prompts the doxology in verse 17. As such, the paragraph stands in contrast with verses 8–10, where, although it is not expressly said, Paul has again shown the helplessness of the Law, which was said to exist for sinners. But the Law can only "keep them in check," as it were; God's **grace** brings with it **faith** and **love** and offers **eternal life**.

This affirmation of the gospel is made, however, in the form of personal testimony, flowing directly from the words "entrusted to me." In sheer wonder at the grace lavished upon him, Paul puts himself forward as "Exhibit A" of such grace for all sinners. The testimony, too, serves as a contrast to the false teachers. Paul's *authority* finally lies in the *authentic* nature of his gospel, as he both preached and experienced it.

1:12-13 / Having mentioned "the gospel" that "was entrusted" to him,

Paul does a natural thing for him—bursts into thanksgiving (cf. Rom. 6:17; 7:25; 1 Cor. 15:57; 2 Cor. 2:14; 8:16; 9:15). Although most of these thanksgivings are short, this one, very much like 2 Corinthians 2:14, expands into a personal word, reminding his hearers of his own relationship to the gospel (cf. 1 Cor. 15:9–10; 2 Cor. 2:14–7:4; Eph. 3:1–13).

It is unusual for Paul to direct his thanks **to Christ**, rather than to God, but this has been determined here by the qualifier **who has given me strength for my work** (which precedes **Christ Jesus** in the Greek text). For Paul, this verb ordinarily refers to the work of Christ rather than to that of the Father (see Phil. 4:13; Eph. 6:10; 2 Tim. 2:1; 4:17). In saying that Christ **has given me strength**, Paul is not referring to his having received inward strength of some kind (as in Phil. 4:13). Rather, the verb refers to the "entrusting" in verse 11 and therefore might be better translated, "who enabled, or empowered, me **for my work**" (cf. NEB: "made me equal to the task"). His gratitude also embraces two further realities: Christ's **considering me worthy** and thus **appointing me to serve him.** By **considering me worthy** (better, "trustworthy"; see note), Paul does not mean that he received appointment because God thought so highly of him—such an idea would contradict the whole passage—but that it is all the more amazing to him that God would ever entrust him with the gospel at all, as verses 13 and 14 make clear. To restate his point: "To think that he would consider *me*, of all people, worthy of this trust." His appointment here, it must be noted, is referred to not as apostleship but as the work of a servant, **to serve him** (*diakonia*, "service, ministry," a Pauline favorite).

As in 1 Corinthians 15:9–10 and Galatians 1:13–16, passages very similar to this one, Paul's understanding of his conversion and ministry as expressions of grace finds its focus in the vivid memory of his past. The wonder for him—and what thus magnifies God's grace—is that Christ should ever have considered him at all (v. 12), since at the time of his call he actively **spoke evil of him** (lit., "was a blasphemer") **and persecuted and insulted him** (or "acted violently" against him). This, of course, refers to his persecution of the church (Acts 8:3; 9:1–2; 22:4–5; 26:9–11). He not only denied Christ ("blasphemed") but, by persecution and violence (cf. Gal. 1:13, "made havoc of it"), tried to force others to do the same, until finally he was himself arrested—by grace.

But God was merciful to me, he goes on, **because I did not yet have faith and so did not know what I was doing**. At first blush, this sounds contradictory, as though he received mercy because he had it coming. But the whole paragraph indicates otherwise. Paul is here reflecting on the

OT distinction between "unwitting" and "purposeful" sinning (e.g., Num. 15:22–31). His former conduct is not thereby less culpable or grotesque, but for Paul this distinction at least explains why he became an object of God's compassion rather than his wrath.

1:14 / Still caught up in the wonder of it all, Paul says it again, only this time the emphasis shifts from his ministry (vv. 11–12) to his actual conversion. Although stated with some unusual turns of phrase (e.g., **our Lord** [Christ Jesus] as the bestower of grace), the theology of this passage is thoroughly Pauline. **Abundant grace** had been **poured out on** him, a grace that brought about both his **faith** and his **love**. For Paul, God's is always the prior action. **Faith** is a response to **grace** (Rom. 3:23–25; Eph. 2:8), and **faith** acts in **love** (Gal. 5:6; cf. 1:5). Moreover, that **faith and love** are **ours in union with Christ Jesus** shows clearly that they are not human qualities but indications that grace has been operative. They are "visible expressions of a living relationship with the Savior" (Kelly).

All of this is surely in contrast to the erring elders, who have turned away from faith and love (1:6), who "blaspheme" (1:20) and are engaged in strife (6:4), and who have thus abandoned the gospel of grace here being illustrated.

1:15-16 / Having given this personal word about how the grace of Christ overflowed to a former persecutor, Paul is reminded that what happened to him is in full accord with a (probably) well-known saying, which apparently has roots in Jesus himself (Luke 19:10; cf. John 12:46; 18:37). He begins with the formula **this is a true saying** (lit., "faithful is the saying"), which will recur four more times in these letters (3:1; 4:9; 2 Tim. 2:11; Titus 3:8) and which has been the subject of considerable discussion. In this instance, the formula precedes the saying, and the extent of the saying itself is clear. Such is not always the case (e.g., 3:1 and 4:9). Furthermore, nothing quite like it occurs elsewhere in the NT. However, the similar formula, "faithful is God," is common in Paul (e.g., 1 Cor. 1:9; 10:13; 2 Cor. 1:18) and probably is the source of this present formulation.

The emphasis in Greek lies on the trustworthiness of the saying, hence the GNB's **true saying**. This is emphasized further by the addition **to be completely accepted and believed**. There is some ambiguity here about whether there is an intensive (GNB, **completely**; cf. RSV, NEB, NIV), or extensive ("accepted by all," Weymouth, Book of Common Prayer), sense to the adjective *pasēs*. A similar formula in 6:1 that can only be intensive ("worthy of all respect") lends support to the GNB translation; however, a good case can also be made from the context for an emphasis on its being worthy of universal acceptance.

In the saying itself, **Christ Jesus came into the world to save sinners**, two points are made: Incarnation and Redemption, with the emphasis on the latter. To say that he **came into the world**, of course, does not in itself necessarily imply pre-existence, but such an understanding would almost certainly have been intended. Here the reason for his coming, and Paul's reason for including it, is emphasized—**to save sinners. Sinners!** That was a term common enough in Pharisaic Judaism (Paul's own tradition). It referred to all those who did not stringently keep the Law, especially Gentiles (even Paul can so use it in Gal. 2:15). But here, and elsewhere in Paul, **sinners** is a universalizing term. All humanity, both Jew and Gentile, belong together at this one point (Rom. 3:19–20, 23). But Christ came **to save** such.

Salvation for Paul is primarily an eschatological term; that is, it has to do with human destiny, what happens to people at the end (Gk., *eschaton*). But such eschatological salvation has already begun in the present in the work of Christ, hence "saving sinners" also means **to save** them from their present sinfulness. Both the present and future aspects seem to be in view here (cf. v. 16, "believe unto eternal life").

To personalize the saying, Paul adds, **I am the worst of them**, not as a form of hyperbole, as some would have it, or because he was morbid about his sinful past, but precisely because of his own experience of God's mercy and grace. Such statements are to be understood in light of the intersection in Paul's life of the simultaneous overwhelming sense of his own sinfulness and utter helplessness before God and the fact of God's grace lavished freely on him and God's unconditionally accepting him despite his sin. It should also be noted that he says **I am**, not "I was." Even one like Hanson who believes the letter to be a forgery admits that this is a "truly Pauline touch." But it is so, not because of Paul's abiding sense of sinfulness (as Bernard and others), but because he recognized himself as always having the status of "sinner redeemed."

With the addition of that last word, **I am the worst of them**, Paul is now in position to make his final point in this testimony to God's grace. The reason for Christ's saving Paul, **the worst of** sinners, was that he could thereby set Paul forth as a primary exhibit for all other sinners **who would later believe in him** for salvation. Paul's point is simple: "If God would—and could—do it to me, given who I was and what I did, then there is hope for all" (cf. 2:3–7). And so he repeats, **God was merciful to me**, but now adds this new reason.

By saving Paul, **Christ Jesus** has demonstrated **his full patience** (or, "the full extent of his forbearance") **in dealing with** sinners. Forbearance as a characteristic of the deity in dealing with human rebellion is a thoroughly Pauline idea (Rom. 2:4; 3:25–26; 9:22–23; cf. 2 Pet. 3:9, 15). Such **patience** is seen in his dealing with **me, the worst of sinners**, precisely so that Christ might have an **example**, a prototype, **for all those who would later believe in him** and thus also **receive eternal life**. The Greek for **eternal life** means not so much life with endless longevity as it does the "life of the coming age," life that is ours now in Christ to be fully recognized at his "appearing" (see 6:12–15; 2 Tim. 4:6–8; Titus 2:11–14).

1:17 / What began as thanksgiving and then moved on to testimony of God's abundant grace now concludes with doxology. How else? Reflecting on God's grace often does that to Paul (e.g., Gal. 1:5; Eph. 3:21; Phil. 4:20). A similar doxology appears at 6:15–16. What marks off these two from earlier doxologies is their emphasis on God's "otherness" and eternity. Both have a decidedly liturgical ring to them, being deeply rooted in Hellenistic Jewish piety. They probably reflect doxologies from the Diaspora synagogue, where Paul had his own roots as well as where he began his missionary endeavors.

The **eternal King** (lit., "the King of the ages") picks up the theme of **eternal life** in verse 16. God is **eternal** in that he rules in/over all the ages. God is likewise the **immortal** (lit., "incorruptible," a term from Hellenistic Judaism), **invisible** (a recurrent OT motif; cf. Rom. 1:20; Col. 1:15), and **only** (the primary OT motif) **God**. Therefore all **honor and glory** (cf. Rev. 4:9, 11; 5:12, 13; 7:12) are due him **forever and ever**. The **amen** pronounced in the synagogues in assent to doxologies and benedictions had already passed into Christian worship (see esp. 1 Cor. 14:16) and often concludes the NT doxologies as well (e.g., Gal. 1:5; Rom. 16:27).

With this doxology, Paul brings the digression to a sudden conclusion. He has indeed come a considerable distance from the opening charge to Timothy to remain in Ephesus to oppose the false teachers (vv. 3–4). But as we have seen, none of this is without purpose. Lingering just behind every word are the erring elders and their "diseased" teaching (1:11), with its emphasis on Law and speculations, which stands over against the pure gospel of grace that produces faith and love. Now it is time for him to return to the matter at hand.

Additional Notes

1:12-13 / Some early MSS have the verb for "strengthens" in the present tense, "who strengthens me," but this is a harmonization to Phil. 4:13 and rather thoroughly misses Paul's point here.

By translating **considering me worthy**, the GNB misses what appears to be a play on words. Paul was en*trust*ed (v. 11), was considered *trust*worthy (v. 12), and even though he was among the un*trust*ing (v. 13; GNB, "did not yet have faith"), God's grace to him came with faith (*trust* in God, v. 14).

D-C argue that "only the designation 'persecutor' applies to the specific case of Paul," and that the man who wrote Phil. 3:4-6 could not have used "blasphemer" to describe his past. But that is to miss too much. From the standpoint of his former life in Judaism, it is true that Paul could not have seen himself in this way, but the standpoint here is his present life in Christ; from this perspective his former attitude toward Christ must be considered "blasphemy"—just as the attitudes of the false teachers are now considered blasphemy (v. 20).

The words **I did not yet have faith** literally say, "I acted in [a state of] unbelief." Three times in Romans he says a similar thing about the Jewish response to Christ (3:3; 11:20, 23).

1:14 / **Poured out . . . abundant grace** translates the verb *hyperepleonasen* (lit., "super-abounded"). The verb occurs nowhere else, but such *hyper* compounds are a Pauline trademark (see e.g., "more than conquerors," Rom. 8:27; "highly exalted," Phil. 2:9; "exceeding joyful," 2 Cor. 7:4; "groweth exceedingly," 2 Thess. 1:3 [all KJV], plus six others).

1:15-16 / For a full discussion, with complete bibliographies, of the five "faithful sayings" see G. W. Knight, *The Faithful Sayings in the Pastoral Letters*.

Although the precise formulation found in the saying does not occur elsewhere in Paul, it most assuredly reflects his theology. See esp. Gal. 4:4-5 and Phil. 2:5-11.

The word for **worst** is actually "first" in Greek, but "first" in the sense of "foremost," hence **worst**. The KJV, therefore, misses the point by translating, "of whom I am chief . . . that in me first." Paul's point is as the GNB translates: **I am the worst . . . in order that . . . [in] me, the worst.**

1:17 / Some later copyists added the word *wise* after **only** on the pattern of Rom. 16:27.

4

The Charge Renewed

Timothy, my child, I entrust to you this command, which is in accordance with the words of prophecy spoken in the past about you. Use those words as weapons in order to fight well, ¹⁹and keep your faith and a clear conscience. Some men have not listened to their conscience and have made a ruin of their faith. ²⁰Among them are Hymenaeus and Alexander, whom I have punished by handing them over to the power of Satan; this will teach them to stop their blasphemy.

The argument that began in verses 3–7 returns full circle in this final paragraph of chapter 1. In fact, one might note how easily verses 18–20 read hard on the heels of verse 7. The resumptive nature of the paragraph is even clearer in the Greek text, where the word here translated **command** (v. 18) is the same translated **order** in verses 3 and 5 (cf. the RSV, which consistently translates "charge").

This paragraph, however, does not simply repeat verses 3–7; rather, by way of verses 12–17, Paul now charges Timothy in a very personal way to "stick it out." He does so by reminding Timothy of his own call to ministry, and by setting that in contrast to two who failed.

1:18–19a / Reverting to the vocative of familiarity (lit., "child Timothy"), Paul renews **this command**, first given in verse 3. Here Paul **entrusts** it to him, a different Greek word from that in verse 11, which has to do with entrusting something into someone else's care (cf. 6:20; 2 Tim. 1:12, 14; 2:2).

To reinforce the entrusting of the charge, Paul reminds Timothy of his calling. It is not Paul, finally, who has left Timothy "in charge," but the Holy Spirit. This **command** is **in accordance with the words of prophecy spoken in the past about you**; and it is with **those words as weapons** that Timothy is **to fight well**.

But what are these **words of prophecy**? Paul will mention this event in Timothy's life twice more in these letters. In 4:14 he refers to Timothy's ministry (apparently) as a "spiritual gift," and there we also learn that the **words of prophecy** were accompanied by the elders' laying on of hands. In 2 Timothy 1:6, where the concern is with their own personal relationship, Paul narrows the focus to his own laying on of hands. But what precisely happened, and when, is not known. Most likely Paul is referring to an experience in Timothy's early days whereby he was recognized to have received the gift of the Spirit for ministry, a recognition that was made clear through some **words of prophecy**.

In any event, Paul reminds him of those prophecies so that he might use them **as weapons** as he engages in the current **fight** (lit., "that by means of them" or "in the strength of them" he might "wage the noble war"). **Fight** here is a military metaphor (cf. 2 Tim. 2:3–4). In contrast to his athletic metaphors of "fighting" (1 Cor. 9:24–27; 1 Tim. 6:12; 2 Tim. 4:7–8), where the general contest of the Christian life or his ministry in general is in view, Paul regularly uses the military metaphor in contexts where the struggle is against opponents of his gospel or against spiritual forces (2 Cor. 10:1–6; Philem. 1 [cf. Col. 4:17]; Eph. 6:10–17). Thus Timothy's **fight** is against the false teachers and their errors, and he is further to engage in the fight holding fast at all times to his **faith and clear conscience** (see v. 5).

1:19b–20 / As in verses 5 and 6, the mention of **your faith and a clear conscience** prompts Paul to reflect on some men who **have not listened to their conscience**. Literally, he says they have "repudiated" or "rejected," both **faith** (trust in God) and **conscience**. In so doing, with a typical change of metaphor, Paul adds, "they have made shipwreck of" (GNB, **made a ruin of**) **their faith**. The GNB does not appear to capture Paul's point here. It is not **their faith** that is shipwrecked—although that, too, has happened—but *the* faith. By rejecting **faith** (their complete trust in God's grace), they are at the same time in the process of bringing *the* faith (the gospel itself) to **ruin**.

A rather unusual thing now happens. Paul gives names. **Hymenaeus** will be mentioned again, with Philetus, in 2 Timothy 2:17, as well as in the second-century apocryphal *Acts of Paul and Thecla*. He is otherwise unknown. An **Alexander** is mentioned two other times in connection with Ephesus: In Acts 19:33–34 a Jew by that name is shouted down by the mob, and in 2 Timothy 4:14–15 Paul warns Timothy of an Alexander the metalworker, about whom it is ambiguous whether he was inside or outside the church. At least two different people seem to be involved. The **Alexander** mentioned here is sometimes identified with the metalworker in 2 Timothy; others identify the Acts and 2 Timothy references and see the present one as someone else. There is simply no way that one can be sure (but see disc. on 2 Tim. 4:14–15 for a hypothesis). In any case, the two men mentioned here are almost certainly leaders, therefore probably elders, as in 2 Timothy 2:17–18.

What Paul means next has been the subject of some debate. Literally, he says, "I turned them over to Satan." Much of the debate is related to one's understanding of the phrase "for the destruction of the flesh" that appears in a similar sentence in 1 Corinthians 5:5. Probably in light of this, the GNB understands the clause to mean that Paul has handed **them over to the power of Satan** with the expectation of physical punishment. It seems more likely, however, that the phrase "hand over to Satan" simply means "to put back out into Satan's sphere," outside the church and the fellowship of God's people; whether he also expected some physical harm to occur is a moot point, but less likely.

Paul expects that such an "excommunication" **will teach them to stop their blasphemy**. The word to **teach**, which he uses again in 2 Timothy 2:25, probably means in this instance to "correct by discipline." At least Paul expects his action to have an educative element. What they are to learn is **to stop their blasphemy**. What this means is not at all certain; but in verse 13 Paul describes his former self as a "blasphemer," and in 6:4 "blasphemies" (GNB, "insults") is listed as one of the results of the false teachers' "sickly appetite for controversy." It is probably the latter, the conscious rejection of God's grace in favor of arguments, that Paul has in mind here. When this excommunication took place is not stated, but see the note on verse 3.

With this paragraph the reason for the letter is brought to its conclusion. Timothy has been left in Ephesus to stop the false teachers. After some digressions that offer contrasts with these teachers and their errors, Paul concludes with this personal charge to Timothy himself, but once again with the false teachers clearly in view.

Additional Notes

1:18–19a / The **this** of **this command** points forward in this sentence to Timothy's "waging the good warfare" (RSV). Nonetheless, it also refers back to the charge given earlier.

There is a difference of opinion as to whether the word *proagousas* means **spoken in the past** (GNB), or "pointed to you" (RSV), or "first pointed you out to me" (NEB). But the GNB is the far most likely, both because the prefix *pro* is almost always a temporal reference and (more significantly) because the point in the context has to do with Timothy's recalling his own call to ministry, not how he was first discovered by Paul.

Many would differ with the interpretation offered here that sees 1:18; 4:14; and 2 Tim. 1:6 as all referring to the same reality. The objections arise from an apparent need to reconcile the language of each with greater precision. But the differences are no more than what often happens when one repeats the same event but does so in each case to make a different point. Nothing in the language is in fact irreconcilable. Furthermore, the very differences point to authenticity; a pseudepigrapher could have been expected to be more careful.

O. Bauernfeind (*TDNT*, vol. 7, p. 711) suggests that the military metaphor in this verse has as its starting point "human life in general, and hence also of the Christian." But this seems to miss the context rather widely.

1:19b–20 / The nature and purpose of "excommunication" in the three relevant NT texts (2 Thess. 3:14–15; 1 Cor. 5:3–5; 1 Tim. 1:20) is a subject on which not all agree. This is due partly to the nature and meaning of some of the language used. For example, does "for the destruction of the flesh" in 1 Cor. 5:5 refer to his "sinful nature" (NIV), or to literal physical punishment (GNB)? In all three cases there seems to be a clearly redemptive concern. Yet how does Satan fit into that? The stance taken here is that Paul is using language that has become semitechnical and thus does not mean literally giving them over to Satan to "go to work on them," as it were, but simply removing them from the church, the sphere of the Spirit, where God is actively at work in people's lives and putting them back out into the sphere where Satan is still at work. What exactly Paul expects to happen seems much less certain than some would suggest.

5

Proper Objects of Prayer

First of all, then, I urge that petitions, prayers, requests, and thanksgivings be offered to God for all people; ²for kings and all others who are in authority, that we may live a quiet and peaceful life with all reverence toward God and with proper conduct. ³This is good and it pleases God our Savior, ⁴who wants everyone to be saved and to come to know the truth. ⁵For there is one God, and there is one who brings God and mankind together, the man Christ Jesus, ⁶who gave himself to redeem all mankind. That was the proof at the right time that God wants everyone to be saved, ⁷and that is why I was sent as an apostle and teacher of the Gentiles, to proclaim the message of faith and truth. I am not lying; I am telling the truth!

Following the charge to Timothy in chapter 1, which points to the presence of false teachers as the occasion of the letter, Paul now moves on to give a series of specific instructions (2:1–7 on the proper objects of prayer; 2:8–15 on the proper demeanor for prayer; 3:1–13 on qualifications for church leadership). All of this leads directly to 3:14–15, where Paul repeats his purpose for writing in terms of the believers' knowing how to conduct themselves in God's household.

Because there is no *specific* reference to the false teachers in these three sections, it is often suggested that what is being given in the two chapters is an early church manual, of the kind that would have been needed for setting a congregation in order—although some have suggested that the reason for such a manual would have been to offer church order as the proper antidote to heresy. By and large, however, the "church manual" view sees very little relationship between chapters 2 and 3 and the charge to Timothy in chapter 1.

But since the new section begins with the conjunction "therefore" (GNB, **then**), implying a result or inference from what has preceded, it seems much more likely that all of this material is a direct consequence of what was said in chapter 1. That means that these instructions are best understood as responses to the presence of the wayward elders, who were disrupting the church by their errors and controversies. In fact, Paul does not suggest at any point that Timothy is to set the church in order, as for the first time. In each case the activities seem already to be present. What Paul is doing, rather, is correcting abuses of various kinds. For example, it may be assumed that men pray, and do so with raised hands (v. 8). The instruction here is that they do so with "holy" hands, not "soiled" by anger or argument.

If that be so, then what might be the place of this first paragraph in the argument? The frequent answer is that the point lies in verse 2, that prayer be made for rulers so that the church may enjoy a peaceful existence. It has even been suggested that a correct Christian attitude toward the state is what is in view. Verses 4–7, then, are seen as nearly irrelevant to that point, but go back to elaborate on a secondary point made in verse 1 (prayer be made for **all**). However, it seems much more likely that precisely the opposite is the case. The one clear concern that runs through the whole paragraph has to do with the gospel as for **all people** (vv. 1, 4–6, and 7). In this view, the **this is good** in verse 3 refers to prayer **for all people** in verse 1, thus seeing verse 2 as something of a digression—albeit as before (1:12–17), a meaningful one. The best explanation for this emphasis lies with the false teachers, who either through the esoteric, highly speculative nature of their teaching (1:4–6) or through its "Jewishness" (1:7) or ascetic character (4:3) are promoting an elitist or exclusivist mentality among their followers. The whole paragraph attacks that narrowness.

2:1 / Although this sentence clearly begins something new, the **then** (better, "therefore") also ties it to what has gone before. But what? Most likely it goes all the way back to the charge in 1:3, but now by way of verses 18–20. What Paul says, then, is: "Even as I urged you, remain in Ephesus to stop the false teachers. **I** now **urge**, therefore, **first of all, that** . . ." The **first of all** suggests not so much that prayer itself is the first thing that needs to be discussed, but that offering prayers **for all people** is the matter of first urgency.

Four different words for prayer are used; however, the distinctions often made between them are usually oversubtle. Paul's point is not to define or distinguish the various kinds of prayer that should mark Christian worship, but to urge that **prayers** of all kinds **be offered to God for all people**, with the emphasis on **all people**. That becomes clear in verses 3–7.

2:2 / "Prayers" of all kinds "for all people" also includes the governing authorities—**kings and all others who are in authority**. The word for

26

kings usually means the emperor, but the plural here seems to make it more comprehensive, which is further substantiated by a generalizing addition; **and all others who are in authority**. It might be, of course, given the nature of things in Ephesus, that the addition refers to those **in authority** in the church. But the use of **kings**, plus the whole context, implies that all those who govern (the emperor, provincial officials, local magistrates) are proper objects for Christian prayer. In this there is nothing new: Prayers and sacrifices for pagan authorities have a long history in Judaism (see note).

Paul now adds a reason for praying for the pagan authorities: **that we may live a quiet and peaceful life with all reverence toward God and with proper conduct**. For many scholars, this sounds terribly bourgeois, even selfish. But, again, it probably reflects the activities of the false teachers, who are not only disrupting ("disquieting") the church(es) but apparently are also bringing the gospel and the church into disrepute on the outside (see esp. 3:7; 5:14; 6:1; cf. Titus 2:5, 8; 3:1–3). The concern here, therefore, is not that Christians should have a life free from trouble or distress (which hardly fits the point of view of 2 Tim. 1:8 and 3:12) but that they should live in such a way that "no one will speak evil of the name of God and of our teaching" (6:1).

This understanding is supported by two other factors: First, in 1 Thessalonians 4:11–12 Paul uses identical language ("live a quiet life") for the selfsame reason (to "win the respect of those who are not believers"), where "busybodies" are disrupting things (cf. 2 Thess. 3:11 with 1 Tim. 5:13); and second, the language **all reverence toward God** (*eusebeia*) and **proper conduct** (*semnotēs*), which is peculiar to these letters in the Pauline corpus (except for Phil. 4:8, *semnēs*), has to do with behavior that can be seen. At such points one would expect "righteousness" and "holiness" in Paul if the emphasis were on one's relationship to God or internal righteousness.

The term *eusebeia* (along with its verb and adverb) is a crucial one in these letters. In popular parlance it meant roughly what *religious* means in popular English. For many it is difficult to imagine Paul's using such a word, which belongs to Hellenism and Hellenistic Judaism (see esp. Ecclesiasticus and 4 Maccabees), to describe either the Christian faith or Christian behavior. But the answer to this, as with many such terms in the PE (see the Introduction), lies with the false teachers. This is *their* word, being used by Paul to counteract them (cf. the use of *wisdom* in 1 Cor. 1–3).

It should also be noted that the attitude toward the state reflected in this passage is quite in keeping with Romans 13:1–5. Prayer for such authorities is to be made precisely so that believers, including the elders, may freely live out their faith before "the people outside the church" (3:7). But such a point is nonetheless a slight digression, brought about by the mention of pagan officials.

2:3–4 / Paul now returns to his main concern, prayers of all kinds "for all people." The reason? Because **God wants everyone** (lit., "all people") **to be saved**. That **this is good and it pleases God** might, of course, refer to the content of verse 2. But the relative clause in verse 4 indicates otherwise. **This is good**, Paul says; that is, prayers "for all people" **is good**, and **it pleases God our Savior**, precisely because the **God** who has saved us (**our Savior**) wants his salvation to reach "all people" (**everyone**).

The appellation **God our Savior** (see the note on 1:1) emphasizes that **God** is the originator of the saving event (cf. Phil. 1:28; 1 Thess. 5:9) and that Paul and the church have already experienced it. But neither **our** salvation, nor that of an elitist few, satisfies God, for God **wants** *all people* **to be saved and to come to know the truth**. The point of the text is clear: The gospel, by its very nature, as Paul will argue in verses 5–6, is universal in its scope, and any narrowing of that scope by a truncated theology or by "novelties" that appeal to the intellectual curiosities of the few is not the gospel of Christ. And to say that God **wants** (not "wills," and therefore it *must* come to pass) *all people* **to be saved**, implies neither that all (meaning everybody) will be saved (against 3:6; 4:2; or 4:10, e.g.), nor that God's will is somehow frustrated since all, indeed, are not saved. The concern is simply with the universal scope of the gospel over against some form of heretical exclusivism or narrowness.

In this sentence salvation is closely tied to coming **to know the truth**. That does not suggest that salvation is no longer a response of faith (see disc. on 1:15–16) but that, especially in the context of false teachings, salvation also has its cognitive side, **to know the truth**, that is, to hear and grasp the gospel message (cf. 3:15; 4:3; 2 Tim. 3:8; 4:4; Titus 1:1).

2:5–6a / Paul will now offer as evidence for the contention that "God wants" all people "to be saved" some commonly held theological affirmations, probably from an early creedal formulation—although some of the present language may well be his own. The statement has three parts to it: the unity of God, Christ as mediator, and Christ's death as securing redemption. It should be noted that all three parts support Paul's insistence on the universal scope of salvation.

There is one God. This statement reflects the primary Jewish affirmation about God (see Deut. 3:4; cf. 1 Cor. 8:4). Its original intent in the OT was to stress God's unity vis-à-vis the polytheism that surrounded Israel. Unfortunately, however, it often came to be used in an exclusivistic way: "He is *our* God and he looks out for his own." But basic to the original intent, and what Paul is stressing here, was that the fact of **one God** not only meant that there were no other gods but that he is therefore the **one** God over all peoples.

And there is one who brings God and mankind together (lit., "One also is the mediator between God and man"). The presupposition of this line in relation to the first is the universal sinfulness of mankind, who need outside help in order to be rightly related to the **one God** whom they have spurned. The point being made is not only that **mankind** needs mediation with God (the presupposition) but that God himself has provided it. The word "mediator" had sometimes been applied to Moses in Judaism (e.g., Philo, *Moses* 2.166), as the one who "mediated" the Law to God's people, a notion Paul seems to allude to negatively in Galatians 3:19–20. Here, or in the creed itself before Paul used it, the background lies in the idea of a "negotiator" who "establishes a relation which would not otherwise exist" (*TDNT*, vol. 4, p. 601). Jesus Christ is the "go-between God," who reconciles fallen humanity to the **one God**, that is **who brings God and mankind together**.

The phrase **the man Christ Jesus** emphasizes both his full identification with **mankind** and his being the one human being of whom it can be said, he is **the Man** (*anthrōpos*, the generic term, not *anēr*, expressing male gender). This seems to reflect Paul's use of the Adam-Christ imagery, wherein Christ becomes the representative "man" for people of the New Age, as Adam was of the Old.

Who gave himself to redeem all mankind: This clause, of course, makes explicit what was only implicit in the first two clauses, revealing Paul's reason for citing the whole. God's desire for all to be saved is evidenced in the creed itself with its statement that Christ's death was for **all mankind**. The gospel, therefore, potentially provides salvation for all people, because Christ's atoning self-sacrifice was "in behalf of" (*hyper*) **all** people. Effectually, of course, it ends up being "especially [for] those who believe" (4:10).

The clause is very close in concept, but not so in its actual language, to Mark 10:45 and probably reflects a Hellenized form of that saying. To **give himself** up for us is a typically Pauline way of referring to Christ's self-sacrifice on the cross (Gal. 1:4; 2:20; Eph. 5:2). **To redeem** translates a noun, *antilytron*, that can mean either a "ransom" (involving "payment") or "redemption" (in the Exodus sense of delivery from bondage). In both Mark 10:45 and here, the latter is to be preferred (as well as in Titus 2:14; see the GNB's "to rescue us"). Hidden in the GNB translation is the combination of two prepositions (*anti*, "instead of," and *hyper*, "in behalf of") that seems almost certainly to imply some notion of substitution—although neither of the prepositions individually necessarily implies as much.

As often happens, therefore, when describing the work of Christ (cf. Rom. 3:24–25; 1 Cor. 1:29; 6:11), a rich combination of metaphors is used, and this creedal statement is no exception. But the point throughout is its potentiality for **all mankind**.

2:6b / The sentence **that was the proof at the right time that God wants everyone to be saved** is probably the correct, but somewhat expanded, understanding of a very difficult phrase, which seems to stand without obvious grammatical connection to what has gone before. Literally, it says, "the witness in its [or "his"] own times." "The witness" apparently stands in apposition to the whole of verses 5–6a, as the GNB implies. "His own times," which will recur at 6:15 and Titus 1:3, implies that in the "history of salvation" the time for God's showing mercy to all mankind has now arrived, as witnessed in the death of Christ, which is "for all."

2:7 / With one final stroke Paul will underscore the point of the paragraph—prayer for all because God wants all to be saved. This time, through a grammatical connection to the "testimony" mentioned in verse 6, he reasserts the purpose of his own ministry. It was for the sake of the gospel of Christ's death "to redeem all mankind" that **I was sent** (better, "appointed," as in 1:12) **as an apostle and teacher of the Gentiles**. The emphasis in Paul's Greek sentence is not on his apostleship but on his being a **teacher of the Gentiles**, which picks up the theme of the universal scope of redemption. This is demonstrated by the sudden insertion of the protestation **I am not lying; I am telling the truth**! (cf. Rom. 9:1; 2 Cor. 11:31) before **teacher of the Gentiles**. Such an emphatic outburst seems quite out of place, except for the need of the church in Ephesus to hear clearly that Paul's own ministry as **teacher** (not apostle) **of the Gentiles** also demonstrates the universal nature of the gospel. This phrase in particular would seem to suggest some form of Jewish exclusivism as lying at the heart of the problem (cf. esp. Titus 1:10–16).

In the phrase **to proclaim the message of faith and truth**, the GNB has brought together (legitimately) two ideas that in fact are separate in the sentence. Paul says first that he was appointed a "herald" (translated as a verb, **to proclaim the message**), a word that occurs only here and in the companion passage in 2 Timothy 1:11 in Paul and that images the apostle as the announcer of good news. The words **faith and trust** actually modify **teacher**, but the sense is that of the GNB. Paul's message is "the true faith" (NEB, NIV), over against the exclusivism of the false teachers.

Although it is not directly Paul's point in this paragraph, these words function as one of the more significant missions/evangelism passages in the NT. The same reason that Paul was "appointed" a proclaimer of the good news for the Gentiles is why the church must always be involved in missions. It is inherent in the very character of God, **who wants** *all people* **to be saved and to come to know the truth**, and in the redemptive work of Christ, **who gave himself to redeem all mankind**. It is therefore incumbent on God's people to proclaim that good news.

Additional Notes

2:1 / The first three words for prayer in this verse may have slightly different nuances, but in fact all three simply mean "prayer." The first two, *deēsis* and *proseuchē* are interchangeable synonyms in the NT (e.g., cf. 1 Thess. 1:2, *proseuchē*, with Phil. 1:4, *deēsis*), and when they appear separately, they are simply translated "prayer." The word for **requests** appears again in 1 Tim. 4:5 and is usually translated "prayer" (although the context suggests that the prayer is a thanksgiving!). In this list, however, it may well lean toward "intercession." **Thanksgivings** (*eucharistiai*) has been suggested to refer to the Eucharist, but that is surely an anachronism. The earliest attempt to draw fine lines between these words was made by Origen, *On Prayer* 14; he has been followed, among others, by Bernard, Hendriksen, and Barclay.

2:2 / The following Jewish texts speak about Jews praying, or offering sacrifices, for the authorities: Ezra 6:9–10; 1 Macc. 7:33; *Letter of Aristeas* 44–45; *Pirke Aboth* 3.2; Jos. *Wars* 2.196. See also in first- and second-century Christian authors: 1 Clement 60:4–61:1; Tertullian, *Apology* 30.

2:3–4 / There is, of course, a long history of theological urgency in the church that has been generated by this sentence. Much of it stems from an Augustinian-Calvinist view of election that appears to be at odds with the plain sense of the text. Various suggestions have been offered, such as **all** meaning "all kinds of" (that is, people from all races and stations) or "all the elect." Much of this discussion has been carried on quite apart from Paul's context and thereby assumes the text to be intending some kind of theological pronouncement; or else an author's theology has been already in hand before approaching the text, and the discussion has been a kind of skirmish with it. All of this applies to v. 6 as well.

2:5–6a / In the second line of the creed, the structure of the Greek, which, as in our literal "translation," has the *kai* ("and," "also") following the word **one**, allows the possibility that the statement emphasizes the deity of Christ. That is, the **one God** is **also** the one who mediates, with the following appellation, **the man Christ Jesus**, then emphasizing his humanity. See I. H. Marshall, "The Development of the Concept of Redemption in the New Testament," p. 166.

For a discussion of "ransom, redemption" words in the NT, see L. L. Morris, *The Apostolic Preaching of the Cross*, pp. 9–59; D. Hill, *Greek Words and Hebrew Meanings*, pp. 49–81, whose influence is evidenced on these pages; and the Marshall essay just mentioned.

2:7 / There is an emphatic **I** in Paul's sentence here, but the verb is in the passive, indicating that his ministry was not of his own choosing but of God's.

The prepositional phrase **of faith and trust** could be adverbial and refer to the faithfulness and veracity with which Paul taught. But given the emphasis on *the* truth in v. 4, the GNB probably captures Paul's intent.

6

Proper Demeanor in Prayer

In every church service I want the men to pray, men who are dedicated to God and can lift up their hands in prayer without anger or argument. ⁹I also want the women to be modest and sensible about their clothes and to dress properly; not with fancy hair styles or with gold ornaments or pearls or expensive dresses, ¹⁰but with good deeds, as is proper for women who claim to be religious. ¹¹Women should learn in silence and all humility. ¹²I do not allow them to teach or to have authority over men; they must keep quiet. ¹³For Adam was created first, and then Eve. ¹⁴And it was not Adam who was deceived; it was the woman who was deceived and broke God's law. ¹⁵But a woman will be saved through having children, ª if she perseveresᵇ in faith and love and holiness, with modesty.

a. will be saved through having children; *or* will be kept safe through childbirth. b. if she perseveres; *or* if they persevere.

I n this paragraph Paul continues his instructions on "prayers" begun in verse 1. But now the concern is for proper demeanor on the part of the "pray-ers." But *why* these concerns, and why in this way? And why the inordinate amount of time devoted to the women in comparison with the men? Again, the solution lies with the false teachers. The word to the men is an obvious response to their controversies and strife. The word to the women, therefore, may be assumed also to respond to this conflict. But how?

The answer lies close at hand—in 5:3–16 and 2 Timothy 3:5–9. It is clear from the latter passage that the false teachers are finding their most fruitful hearing among some "weak women who are burdened by the guilt of their sins and driven by all kinds of desires, women who are always trying to learn but who can never come to know the truth." According to 1 Timothy 5, among these women are some younger widows who have "given themselves to pleasure" (v. 6), have become "foolish talkers and busybodies, *talking of things they should not*" (v. 13), and by so doing are bringing the gospel into disrepute (v. 14). Some of them, Paul says, "have already turned away to follow Satan" (v. 15; cf. 2:14 and 4:2). His advice there is similar to what is given here. They should marry (cf. 4:3), have children (cf. 2:15), and take care of their homes (5:14). Within that context, both the instructions on modest dress and on neither teaching nor having authority over men, as well as the illustration of Eve, who was equally deceived, plus the final instruction in verse 15 on bearing children, can all be shown to make sense.

Whether any of this is also related to the predominance of women in the local Artemis cult (see disc. on 1:3) is a moot point, but it is certainly possible.

2:8 / This sentence is tied to what precedes by the conjunction *oun* ("therefore"), untranslated in the GNB (probably because it was understood to be transitional). "Therefore," Paul says, "while we're on the subject, as the people gather to pray be sure it is for prayer and not in **anger** or for **argument**." That is, the instruction is neither that men *should* pray nor that *only* men pray nor that they should do so with uplifted hands, but that *when* at prayer they should do so without engaging in controversies.

This is to be so **in every church service**, or perhaps more likely, "in every place where believers gather in and around Ephesus" (the house-churches). **To lift up their hands** while **in prayer** is the assumed posture of prayer in both Judaism and early Christianity (see note). The phrase **men who are dedicated to God** is actually the adjective "holy" and modifies **hands**. The imagery is that of ritual purity, hands cleansed before praying, and here refers to their not being "soiled" by **anger or argument**, the particular sins of the false teachers.

2:9-10 / Paul turns next to **the women** (actually **women**, without the definite article, implying a broader context than merely wives). The concern has to do first of all with their dress and demeanor. It is not easy from our vantage point to understand the reason for this concern, but probably it is related to their becoming "wanton against Christ" (5:11, RSV) and their being "driven by all kinds of desires" (2 Tim. 3:6). There is a large body of evidence, both Hellenistic and Jewish, which equated "dressing up" on the part of **women** both with sexual wantonness and wifely insubordination (see note). Indeed, for a married woman so **to dress** in public was tantamount to marital unfaithfulness (see, e.g., *Sentences of Sextus* 513: "A wife who likes adornment is not faithful"). Given the close tie here between trumpery (vv. 9–10) and the need "to learn with all submissiveness" (v. 11, RSV), it is most likely that Paul is viewing the actions of some of the women from within this same general cultural framework (see esp. disc. on 2 Tim. 3:6–7).

Thus **women** are to be **modest and sensible** (that is, have "good judgment," or more likely here, "decency") **about their clothes and to dress properly**. This is then specifically defined as not wearing **fancy hair styles** (lit., "with plaited hair"; cf. 1 Pet. 3:3 and Juvenal, cited in the note) or **gold ornaments or pearls** (see Juvenal) **or expensive dresses**.

Indeed, women who are believers are to be "clothed" in better things—**with good deeds**, which will later be defined as, among other things, "bringing up her children well" (5:10). The point is that "healthy teaching" (see disc. on 1:10) has to do with conduct that **is proper for women who claim to be religious**, not that is immodest or indecent, like women intent on seduction.

2:11–12 / Paul now moves to the other side of the problem of immodesty, the tendency toward insubordination. **Women** are to **learn in silence and all humility**. By saying that **women should learn**, Paul is presupposing that women were a part of public worship and were included in the instruction. It simply goes too far to argue from this that he is herewith commanding that they be taught, thus inaugurating a new era for women. The rest of the data in the NT makes it clear that that had already happened among most Christians.

But she (the Greek text uses the singular from this verse until the middle of v. 15) is **to learn** "in a quiet demeanor"—not necessarily **in silence**, that is, without speaking (cf. the same word in 2:2 and the evidence from 1 Corinthians 11). Since this is the first thing said about women here in verse 11, and the last thing said in verse 12, it seems clear that the emphasis lies here. Most likely, in this context, it is against her being "up front," talking foolishness, or being a "busybody" (5:13). Her learning "in quietness" is further qualified as being in **all humility** (better, "being submissive in every way"). Paul does not say to whom she is to be submissive. Because of the Adam-Eve illustration that follows, it is often suggested that he is here addressing wives with regard to their husbands. But the implication of the **all** ("in every conceivable way") probably has a larger front in view, which includes the conduct of the younger widows and their "going around from house to house [house-churches], talking about things they should not" (5:13).

Verse 12, which begins with Paul's own personal instruction (**I do not allow**; better, "I am not allowing," implying specific instructions to this situation), picks up the three items from verse 11 and presents them with some further detail. **I am not** permitting **them to teach** corresponds to **women should learn**. Teaching, of course, is where much of the prob-

35

lem lay in the church in Ephesus. The straying elders are teachers (1:3; 6:3); the "worthy" elders, for whom Timothy is probably to serve as something of a model (4:11–16; cf. 2 Tim. 2:2), are those who "work hard at teaching" (5:17). Indeed, Paul calls himself a teacher in these letters (2:7). But he is here prohibiting women **to teach** in the (house-) church(es) of Ephesus, although in other churches they prophesy (1 Cor. 11:5) and probably give a teaching from time to time (1 Cor. 14:26), and' in Titus 2:3–4 the older women are expected to be good teachers of the younger ones.

Part of the problem from this distance is to know what "teaching" involved. The evidence from 1 Corinthians 12–14 indicates that "teaching" may be presented as a spiritual gift (14:6, 26); at the same time, some in the community are specifically known as teachers (cf. Rom. 12:7), while more private instruction is also given (Acts 18:26; here by a woman). Given that evidence and what can be gleaned from the present Epistles, teaching most likely had to do with instruction in Scripture, that is, Scripture as pointing to salvation in Christ (cf. 2 Tim. 3:15–17). If that is what is being forbidden (and certainty eludes us here), then it is probably because some of them have been so terribly deceived by the false teachers, who are specifically abusing the OT (cf. 1:7; Titus 3:9). At least that is the point Paul will pick up in verses 14 and 15.

Such an understanding is supported further by the woman's being forbidden **to have authority over men**, which corresponds to her "being submissive in every way" in verse 11. The word translated **authority**, which occurs only here in the NT, has the connotation "to domineer." In context it probably reflects again on the role the women were playing in advancing the errors—or speculations—of the false teachers and therefore is to be understood very closely with the prohibition against teaching. Rather, Paul concludes, **they must** be **quiet**, which exactly repeats the prepositional phrase of verse 11. Thus some kind of disruptive behavior, which perhaps included boisterous affirmation of the heresies, seems to lie behind these instructions.

2:13–14 / Paul now turns to Scripture to support what has been said in verses 9–12 (not simply vv. 11–12). However, he does not do so in his usual way, by citing Scripture itself, but by referring to two realities from the narratives in Genesis 2 and 3. First, he notes that **Adam was created first, and then Eve**. Although he does not explicitly say so, nor is it implied in the text of Genesis 2, the priority of Adam in creation is apparently seen as support of a woman's needing to dress modestly and "being submissive in every way." A similar point seems to be made by Paul earlier in 1 Corinthians 11:8–9, although there the context has no suggestion of submission, and in verses 11–12 he sharply qualifies verses 8–9 lest they be misapplied. In any case, Paul here neither explains nor elaborates; he simply states the facts of the order of creation.

Paul does, however, elaborate his second point, based on Eve's statement in Genesis 3:13 that she **was deceived** by the serpent. Since the concluding sentence in verse 15 follows directly from her deception and subsequent fall into sin, this appears to be the basic reason for his appeal to the Genesis account. As Adam has served elsewhere as the representative man, through whose sin all mankind came into sinfulness (Rom. 5:12, 19), so here Eve serves as the "representative" woman, who through her deception by Satan **broke God's law** (lit., "came to be in transgression"). Likewise it is through the deceptions of the false teachers, who themselves are involved in "the teachings of demons" (4:1), that some women have "already turned away to follow Satan" (5:15). To say that **it was not Adam who was deceived** simply means that he was not deceived by the "snake." But Eve was, and that led to her downfall.

2:15 / Paul will now bring this instruction on women to a conclusion by picking up several strands from the preceding verses. In so doing, he expresses himself in a way that has been troubling for generations of Christians, because it seems so contradictory to his own theology, on the one hand, and somewhat demeaning to women, on the other. But as a conclusion to this argument in this context, it in fact makes good sense.

Having said that **the woman was deceived** and thus fell into sin, he now says: **But** she **will be saved**. There is a subtle shift here from Eve to the women in Ephesus. The subject of the verb **will be saved** is in fact **the woman** in verse 14. Obviously Paul is not talking about Eve's salvation but "the woman" in Ephesus; hence the change back to the plural in the middle of verse 15. How she **will be saved** is what has created the problems—**through having children**! Can he mean that? Many have said no and have suggested as one alternative that the clause means "will be kept safe through childbirth" (GNB margin; cf. NIV). But besides simply not being true to reality—many Christian mothers have died in childbirth—Paul's use of the word **saved** throughout these letters disallows it (he always means redemption, from sin and for eternal life, as in 1:15–16 and 2:4). Moreover he uses an entirely different word for the idea of being "kept safe" throughout his letters (see, e.g., 2 Tim. 3:11 and 4:18). A second suggestion is that they shall be saved from the errors in verses 11–

12. But besides having against it the same things as the first alternative, it is nearly inconceivable that Paul would use the verb **saved** in an absolute way, as he does here, without some qualifier (e.g., "from these errors"), if he had intended to refer to verses 11–12. A third alternative is that "through having children" should be translated through *the* Childbirth, that is, through Mary's giving birth to Jesus, thus reversing the role of Eve by referring to the so-called *protevangelium* of Genesis 3:15. But besides this being a most obscure way of trying to say that, Paul nowhere else suggests that salvation is by the Incarnation, or by Mary's deed (since the word under no circumstances can be stretched to mean "Mary's child"). Moreover, this noun always has to do with the fact of bearing children, not to the event of a single birth (that is, the word has to do with the activity of "bearing," not with the noun "birth" or "child"). It should also be noted that nowhere in all of Jewish interpretation was Genesis 3:15 ever understood to mean anything other than the natural enmity between humans and poisonous reptiles. The earliest extant Christian interpretation of this text to refer to the death of Christ comes from Irenaeus in the second century.

More likely what Paul intends is that woman's salvation is to be found in her being a model, godly woman, known for her good works (v. 10; cf. 5:11). And her good deeds, according to 5:11 and 14, include marriage, bearing children (the verb form of this noun), and keeping a good home. The reason for his saying that she **will be saved** is that it follows directly out of his having said "the woman came to be in transgression."

But Paul could never leave the matter there, so he immediately qualifies, "Provided of course that she is already a truly Christian woman," that is, a woman who **perseveres in faith and love and holiness**. This is obviously where her salvation lies, as is always true with Paul. It is assumed such a woman already has **faith**, which is activating **love and holiness**. But the whole context of the letter, and the present argument in particular, has generated this rather unusual way of putting it. Even at the end, however, he has not lost sight of where he began, so he adds, **with modesty**.

Thus, as with the instruction on the proper objects of prayer (all people), so with the proper demeanor in prayer (men without arguments; while women's place is the worshiping community is to be a quiet one), the reason for these particular instructions in this particular way is best understood as a response to the activities and teachings of the wayward elders.

Additional Notes

2:8 / Some have suggested that the words "in every place" (GNB, **in every church service**) mean "everywhere" (NIV), that is, in all the churches universally. But when Paul intends that, he usually says it (1 Cor. 11:26; 14:33). Besides, that seems to miss Paul's point altogether. Most likely this is a reference to house-churches in and around Ephesus.

For references to prayer with uplifted hands in Judaism, see, among others, 1 Kings 8:54; Pss. 63:4; 141:2; 2 Macc. 14:32; Philo, *Flaccus* 121; Jos. *Antiquities* 4.40; for early Christianity, see esp. Tertullian, *On Prayer* 17.

2:9-10 / For but one example of this perspective, see Juvenal's *Satire* 6: "There is nothing that a woman will not permit herself to do, nothing that she deems shameful, when she encircles her neck with green emeralds and fastens huge pearls to her elongated ears. . . . So important is the business of beautification; so numerous are the tiers and storeys piled one upon another on her head! . . . Meantime she pays no attention to her husband" (Loeb, pp. 121 ff.). Cf., among others, 1 Enoch 8:1–2; Testament of Reuben 5:1–5; Ps-Phintys 84–86; Perictione 135; Seneca, *To Helvia* 16:3–4; Plutarch 26.30–32; *Sentences of Sextus* 235.

The words **fancy hair styles** and **gold ornaments or pearls** may go together and have to do with tiered hair decorated with gold and pearls. See J. B. Hurley, *Man and Woman in Biblical Perspective*, pp. 198–99.

2:11-12 / In requiring learning "in a quiet demeanor" Paul is hardly adopting a view like Plutarch's: "Her speech as well ought not to be for the public. . . . For a woman ought to do her talking to her husband or through her husband" (26.30–32, Loeb). Plutarch's view had to do with all woman in all public circumstances. Paul's statement is specifically related to the problem in Ephesus. He obviously did not take this position about women in general (see, e.g., Rom. 16:1–3; Phil. 4:2–3).

By saying, "I am not permitting," Paul focuses particularly on the situation in Ephesus. Such language as this, as well as the "I want" in v. 8, lacks any sense of universal imperative for all situations. This is not to say that he does not see his word as authoritative, but that it simply lacks the thrust of a universal imperative (cf. 1 Cor. 7:25).

There are some who see the word **authority** here to refer to juridical authority in the church or the transmission of the authoritative teaching of the church, but such a view assumes a much more advanced structure than actually emerges in these letters. It simply makes too much of a simple point, namely, that a woman's place in the worshiping community is to be a "quiet" one.

The hermeneutical question, whether these verses apply to all situations at all times, is a live one. For the view that it does, see D. J. Moo, "I Timothy 2:11–15: Meaning and Significance," and J. B. Hurley, *Man and Woman in Biblical Perspective*. For the other side, see P. B. Payne, "Libertarian Women in Ephesus: A Response to Douglas J. Moo's Article," and G. D. Fee and D. Stuart, *How to Read the Bible for All Its Worth*, pp. 57–71.

2:13-14 / The argument often made that the "order of creation" precedes the Fall and is therefore eternally binding is neither made by Paul (nor Moses) nor relevant, since that is *not* his concern here. Rather, Paul is concerned with her subsequent deception and fall into sin.

The "deception of Eve" had a long history of speculative interpretation in Judaism, seen sometimes as sexual seduction on the part of the serpent (e.g., 2 Enoch 31:6; 4 Macc. 18:6-8; *Yebamoth* 103b; *Rabbah Genesis* 18.6) and at other times as the result of her being the weaker sex (e.g., Philo, *Questions on Genesis* 1.33, 46; *Pirke Rabbi Eliezer* 15a). Even if Paul knew these traditions, he is not here alluding to them. He is only interested in the *fact* of her deception, as a vital illustration of the current problem. Note the comparable use of it in 2 Cor. 11:3.

2:15 / For a recent and helpful discussion of the various options for interpreting this verse, see D. J. Moo, "I Timothy 2:11–15," pp. 71–73.

Qualifications for Overseers

1 TIMOTHY 3:1-7

This is a true saying: If a man is eager to be a church leader, he desires an excellent work. ²A church leader must be without fault; he must have only one wife,ᶜ be sober, self-controlled, and orderly; he must welcome strangers in his home; he must be able to teach; ³he must not be a drunkard or a violent man, but gentle and peaceful; he must not love money; ⁴he must be able to manage his own family well and make his children obey him with all respect. ⁵For if a man does not know how to manage his own family, how can he take care of the church of God? ⁶He must be mature in the faith, so that he will not swell up with pride and be condemned, as the Devil was.⁷ He should be a man who is respected by the people outside the church, so that he will not be disgraced and fall into the Devil's trap.

c. have only one wife; *or* be married only once.

To this point, Paul has addressed some concerns related to the community at worship and corrected some abuses generated by the activities of the erring elders. Now he turns to the elders themselves and sets forth some qualifications for "office."

He begins, in verses 1-7, with a group called *episkopoi* ("overseers"); then moves in verses 8-13 to a group called *diakonoi* ("servants," "deacons"), with a note also about some "women" in verse 11. The GNB distinguishes between these two as **church leaders** and **church helpers**, thus avoiding the technical terminology of a later time, "bishops" and "deacons" (cf. Phil. 1:1). It is altogether likely, however, that *both* of these groups come under the larger category *presbyteroi* ("elders"). In any case, the evidence from Acts 20:17 and 28 and Titus 1:5 and 7 indicates that the terms *episkopoi*, "overseers" (Acts 20:28; Titus 1:7), and *presbyteroi*, "elders" (Acts 20:17; Titus 1:5), are partially interchangeable. So at least the **church leaders** (*episkopoi*) of this first paragraph are church elders. (For some brief comments on early church order see the Introduction, pp. xxxii–xxxiv).

It must be noted that in contrast to Titus (1:5), Timothy has not been left in Ephesus to *appoint* elders. Indeed, everything in 1 Timothy, as well as the evidence from Acts 20, indicates that there already were elders in this church. Why, then, *this* instruction? Again, the evidence points to the character and activities of the false teachers. In this regard two things must be noted: First, most of the items in the list stand in sharp contrast to what is said elsewhere in the letter about the false teachers. Second, the list itself has three notable features: It gives qualifications, not duties; most of the items reflect outward, observable behavior; and none of the items is distinctively Christian (e.g., love, faith, purity, endurance; cf. 4:12; 6:12); rather, they reflect the highest ideals of Hellenistic moral philosophy. Since the whole passage points toward and concludes with verse 7, that is, concern for the overseer's (and the church's) reputation with outsiders, this suggests that the false teachers were, by their behavior, bringing the gospel into disrepute. Therefore, Paul is concerned not only that the elders have Christian virtues (these are assumed) but that they reflect the highest ideals of the culture as well.

If our identification of the false teachers as elders is correct, then Paul's reason for this set of instructions is that Timothy must see to it that elders are living according to their appointment, that is, by these standards. At the same time, of course, the whole church will be listening in and will thus be given the grounds for discipline (cf. 5:22, 24–25).

3:1 / The section begins with our second **true saying** (see 1:15). Because the **saying** itself has seemed rather pedantic, and because the word "save" (cf. 1:15) appears in 2:15, some have argued that the preceding verse is the **true saying**. But 2:15 does not have the characteristics of a "saying," and 3:1 does—despite its noncreedal content. Perhaps too much has been made of the concept "saying," as though all these "true sayings" were in wide circulation in the church (as 1:15 probably was). More likely, this became for Paul a kind of reinforcement formula: "What I am about to say has special import" or "can be generally accepted as true."

The **saying** itself, **if a man** (better, "anyone") **is eager to be a church leader, he desires an excellent work**, appears to lend some credence to the commonly held view that people were "running for office." But there is no other evidence in the NT that people "aspired to" positions of leadership in the church. The little evidence we do have implies that men from among the earliest converts were normally appointed to such positions (Acts 14:23; cf. 1 Cor. 1:16 and 16:15–16).

The **saying** in fact focuses less on the *person* than on the *position*. Thus Paul is not commending people who have a great desire to become leaders; rather, he is saying that the position of **church leader** is such a significant matter, **an excellent work**, that it should indeed be the kind of task to which a person might aspire. Thus, despite the activities of some, he does not for that reason negate the position itself.

3:2–3 / Because being a **church leader** is such an **excellent work**, Paul is concerned that the elders in Ephesus manifest truly exemplary lives. **The church leader**, therefore, **must be without fault**. That would seem to *default* any aspiring person! The term **without fault**, however, which is repeated regarding the widows in 5:7 and of Timothy himself in 6:14 (in an eschatological context), has to do with irreproachable *observable* conduct. Here it seems to be intended as the general, covering term for the following list (mostly single words in Greek) of eleven virtues, or qualities, that should characterize a **church leader**.

The first item on the list, **must have only one wife** (lit., "the husband of one wife"), is one of the truly difficult phrases in the PE (cf. 3:12; 5:9, of the "true" widows, and Titus 1:6). There are at least four options: First, it could be requiring that the overseer be married. Support is found in the fact that the false teachers are forbidding marriage and that Paul urges marriage for the wayward widows (5:14; cf. 2:15). But against this is that it emphasizes **must** and **wife**, while the text emphasizes **one**, that Paul, and most likely Timothy, were not married, and that it stands in contradiction to 1 Corinthians 7:25–38. Besides, it was a cultural presupposition that most people would be married.

Second, it could be that it prohibits polygamy. This correctly emphasizes the **one wife** aspect; but polygamy was such a rare feature of pagan society that such a prohibition would function as a near irrelevancy. Moreover, it would not seem to fit the identical phrase used of the widows in 5:9.

Third, it could be prohibiting second marriages (GNB margin: "be married only once"). Such an interpretation is supported by many of the data: It would fit the widows especially, and all kinds of inscriptional evidence praises women (especially, although sometimes men) who were "married only once" and remained "faithful" to that marriage after their partner died. This view would then prohibit second marriages after the death of a spouse, but it would also obviously—perhaps especially—prohibit divorce and remarriage. Some scholars (e.g., Hanson) would make it refer only to the latter.

Fourth, it could be that it requires marital fidelity to his **one wife** (cf. NEB: "faithful to his one wife"). In this view the **church leader** is required to live an exemplary married life (marriage is assumed); faithful to his **one wife** in a culture in which marital infidelity was common, and at times assumed. It would, of course, also rule out polygamy and divorce and remarriage, but it would not necessarily rule out the remarriage of a widower (although that would still not be the Pauline ideal; cf. 1 Cor. 7:8–9, 39–40). Although there is much to be said for either understanding of the third option, the concern that the church's leaders live exemplary married lives seems to fit the context best—given the apparently low view of marriage and family held by the false teachers (4:3; cf. 3:4–5).

The next word, **sober**, often means temperance with regard to alcoholic beverages. However, since that is specifically said in verse 3, **sober** is probably used figuratively to mean "free from every form of excess, passion, or rashness" (cf. 2 Tim. 4:5). The leader must also be **self-controlled and orderly**, words that often occur together in pagan writings as high ideals of behavior. A Christian leader is to be more than, and therefore certainly not less than, such ideals.

The church leader **must** also **welcome strangers in his home**. This, too, was a Greek virtue, but it also was a thoroughgoing expectation of all Christians in the early church (cf. 5:10; Rom. 12:13; 1 Pet. 4:9; Aristides, *Apology* 15). Likewise **he must** also **be able to teach**. This is the one item in the list that also implies duties, a matter that will become clear in 5:17. This adjective recurs in 2 Timothy 2:24 and Titus 1:9, whose contexts suggest that **able to teach** means the ability both to teach the truth and to refute error.

In adding that the church leader **must not be a drunkard**, is Paul also setting out a contrast to the false teachers? Perhaps not, in light of their asceticism noted in 4:3. But they may have been ascetic about certain foods and overindulgent about wine. In any case, drunkenness was one of the common vices of antiquity; and few pagan authors speak out against it—only against other "sins" that might go along with it (violence, public scolding of servants, etc.). The **church leader** is not necessarily to be a total abstainer (5:23), but neither is he to **be a drunkard** (cf. 3:8; Titus 1:7); this is uniformly condemned in Scripture.

The next three qualities probably go together, and do indeed seem to reflect the false teachers' behavior. The **church leader** is not to be **a violent man, but gentle and peaceful** (lit., "not quarrelsome"). The description of the false teachers in 6:3–5, as well as in 2 Timothy 2:22–26 (cf. Titus 3:9), suggests that they are given to strife and quarrels. The true elder is to be **gentle**, even in correcting opponents (2 Tim. 2:23–25).

The list concludes with **he must not love money**. According to 6:5–10, greed turns out to be one of the "deadly sins" of the false teachers, being directly responsible for their ruin. Thus a word against avarice appears in every list of qualifications for leadership (3:8; Titus 1:7; cf. Acts 20:33). On this matter, see especially discussion on 6:5–10 and 2 Timothy 3:6–7.

3:4–5 / Paul now moves on in verses 4–7 to address three further concerns. The church leader must have an exemplary family (vv. 4–5), must not be a new convert (v. 6), and must be a person of good reputation with outsiders (v. 7). These, too, probably reflect the situation in Ephesus.

This passage also assumes the *episkopos* will be married (but does not thereby require it; cf. v. 2). Moreover, as verse 5 implies, there is the closest kind of relationship between family and church. The man who is a failure at one (family) is thereby disqualified for the other (church). Indeed, as 3:15 and 5:1–2 indicate, the word *oikos* ("household"; GNB, **family**) is for Paul a pregnant metaphor for church.

The **church leader**, then, must be able **to manage his own family well**, because he must also **take care of the church of God**. The word for **manage** is used again of the elders in 5:17 (GNB, "work as leaders") as it was earlier in 1 Thessalonians 5:12 (GNB, "guide"). It carries the sense of either "to rule, govern," or "to be concerned about, care for" (cf. "giving their time to" in Titus 3:8). The clue to its meaning here lies with understanding the companion verb about the church in verse 5, **to take care of**, which carries the full force of that idiom in English. That is, **to take care of** implies both leadership (guidance) and caring concern. In the home and church neither has validity without the other.

Such a person will be known to give the kind of leadership at home that will "have" (not **make**, as in GNB) **his children obey him** (lit., "have children in submissiveness," as 2:11). The force of the phrase **with all respect** probably means not so much that they will **obey** with **respect** but that they will be known for both their obedience and their generally good behavior. In Titus 1:6 this is further elaborated to include their being believers, along with a concern for their reputation with outsiders. There is a fine line between demanding obedience and gaining it. The church leader, who must indeed exhort people to obedience, does not thereby "rule" God's family. He **takes care of it** in such a way that its "children" will be known for their obedience and good behavior.

3:6 / The church leader, therefore, also **must be mature in the faith**, a metaphor in Greek that literally means "no newly planted person." As will be repeated in a different way in 5:22, an *episkopos* must not be a recent convert. The reason for this is the great danger of swelled-headed-ness, **so that he will not swell up with pride**. Since this is precisely what is said of the false teachers in 6:4 (cf. 2 Tim. 3:4), one wonders whether some of them were recent converts, whose "sins are seen only later" (5:24).

In any case, to **swell up with pride** means also to **be condemned, as the Devil was**. Although Paul's Greek is a bit ambiguous (lit., "fall into the judgment of the Devil"), he is probably reflecting the common theme that in Christ's ministry, especially in his death and resurrection, Satan was dealt his decisive defeat, to be realized fully at the End (cf. Rev. 12:7–17 and 20:7–10).

3:7 / Finally, he comes to the concern that the church leader be a person **who is respected by the people outside the church**. As noted in the discussion on 2:2, this is a genuinely Pauline concern in the NT. Indeed, this concern is what puts the foregoing list into perspective. That list has to do with observable behavior of a kind that will be a witness to **the people outside the church**. As in verse 6, Paul's Greek is not altogether clear, but the emphasis seems to be that a bad reputation with the pagan world will cause the *episkopos* to be **disgraced**, or slandered, and thus the church with him; and that would be to **fall into the Devil's trap**. It is a **trap** set by the **Devil** when the behavior of the church's leaders is such that outsiders will be disinclined to hear the gospel. One wonders again whether the greed and abusive conduct of the false teachers is not bringing disgrace to God's household in Ephesus, especially when one considers that Paul himself had been so accused in Thessalonica (1 Thess. 2:1–10) and that pagan moralists in particular condemned such activities among the "false" philosophers (see esp. Dio Chrysostom, *Oration* 32 and Lucian's *Philosophies for Sale*).

Additional Notes

3:1 / There are some who favor a textual variation that reads "This is a popular saying" (NEB). But that variant is found only in a few so-called Western sources that are not known for their reliability. Furthermore, the very noncreedal nature of the saying accounts for the change. See the discussion in Metzger, *TCGNT*, p. 640.

3:2-3 / The fact that *ton episkopon* ("the overseer") is singular here has led some to argue that this office represents the monepiscopacy (single person as pastor) whereas the plural *diakonoi* ("deacons") serve under him (as in most contemporary Protestant churches). However, the singular here is almost certainly generic, as "the woman" is in 2:11–12. The sure clue for such a view, besides the plural at 5:17, is Titus 1:5 and 7, where the plural "elders" appears in v. 5, then shifts to the generic singular in vv. 6 and 7. Furthermore, the "if anyone" clause in v. 1, which has led to the singular in this verse, is a nonlimiting, or generalizing, conditional sentence. It recurs in 1 Tim. 5:8 and 6:3, and in both cases—esp. 6:3—refers to a group of more than one.

Many scholars see this list of twelve qualities as "bourgeois," containing very little specifically Christian. Thus it is argued that an alleged pseudepigrapher had a "schema" of such virtues, as one finds in Onosander's *Strategikos* for the qualities desired in a general, and adapted them for his purposes (see esp. D-C, pp. 158–60). The correspondences with Onosander are indeed striking; however, they are very likely coincidental, as are the equally striking correspondences between 1 Thess. 2:1–10 and Dio Chrysostom's *Oration* 32. The *language* belongs to the milieu; the presence of the false teachers explains the specifics. The lack of "a specifically Christian element" is to be explained as something Paul *assumes* for elders. Such an element is hardly missing from 1 Timothy (see 4:12 and 6:11).

For a more thorough presentation of the view taken here on "have only one wife," see C. H. Dodd, "New Testament Translation Problems II," pp. 112–16. On the several options, see Hanson, pp. 77–78.

Kelly thinks that both hospitality and teaching reflect official duties. But since hospitality is expected of all believers, it is difficult to see anything "official" here.

It is possible that since drunkenness often leads to violence, these two go together in the list (as in the GNB), and that the mention of violence then reminds him of the false teachers and leads to the contrasts, **gentle** and "not quarrelsome."

3:4 / Some think that **with all respect** modifies **he** (the father) and should be translated "he must manage his own family well, with all seriousness," or "true dignity." But the order of words favors the interpretation given here.

3:6 / The phrase "fall into the judgment of the Devil" could refer to some form of judgment that Satan metes out and thus correspond to v. 7, where the Devil's trap is a snare he sets. But that is highly unlikely in this case. The NT is thoroughgoing that God metes out judgment, not Satan.

8

Qualifications for Deacons

1 TIMOTHY 3:8–13

Church helpers must also have a good character and be sincere; they must not drink too much wine or be greedy for money; ⁹they should hold to the revealed truth of the faith with a clear conscience. ¹⁰They should be tested first, and then, if they pass the test, they are to serve. ¹¹Their wives^d also must be of good character and must not gossip; they must be sober and honest in everything. ¹²A church helper must have only one wife,^e and be able to manage his children and family well. ¹³Those helpers who do their work well win for themselves a good standing and are able to speak boldly about their faith in Christ Jesus.

d. Their wives; or Women helpers.
e. have only one wife; or be married only once.

Paul now turns his attention to the **church helpers** (*diakonoi*; see disc. on vv. 1–7). As with the **church leaders**, the instruction basically presents qualifications with no hints as to duties. Absent in this case is the word *didaktikon* ("able to teach"); included are items one would expect to be applicable to the overseers as well—holding fast **the truth** (v. 9) and being **tested first** (v. 10). How these two groups are otherwise to be distinguished (apart from teaching) is simply not known to us. An appeal to Acts 6:1–6 is of no value, since those men are not called deacons. In fact they are clearly ministers of the Word among Greek-speaking Jews, who eventually accrue the title "the Seven" (Acts 21:8), which distinguishes them in a way similar to "the Twelve." Thus we are left with the almost certain reality that *episkopoi* and *diakonoi* are distinguishable functions in the church, but without knowing what they were.

3:8–9 / The GNB is helpful in designating these men as **church helpers**, as long as one does not infer that they were not "leaders" as well. The word *diakonos*, in fact, is a favorite of Paul's to describe his own and his fellow workers' ministries (e.g., 1 Cor. 3:5; 2 Cor. 3:6; Rom. 16:1; Col. 1:23; 4:7) and is so used of Timothy in 4:6. However, as with "prophet" and "teacher," the word seems to fluctuate between an emphasis on a *function* and a description of a *position*; by the time of Philippians it describes an "office" (Phil. 1:1), whereas in the relatively contemporary

Ephesians and Colossians *diakonos* still describes a function. Here, as in Philippians 1:1, it refers to a position of some kind.

The first word in the deacons' list is also a "cover" term, describing a kind of personal dignity that makes one worthy of respect. They **must also** (like the overseers) **have a good character** (Gk., *semnous*; cf. 2:2, "proper conduct," and 3:4, "with all respect"). This is followed by three prohibitions: "not double-tongued" (GNB, **sincere**), that is, fully trustworthy in what one says; "**not** indulging in **much wine**" (NIV), like the overseers (v. 3); and not **greedy for money**, also like the overseers (v. 3), but here with the connotation of not "pursuing dishonest gain" (NIV), that is, loving money to the point of questionable integrity.

From these characteristics Paul turns to a positive: **They should hold to the revealed truth of the faith with a clear conscience**. As we already know from 1:5–6 and 1:19–20, the false teachers in Ephesus have turned away from **a clear conscience** (1:6; 1:19) and have made shipwreck of **the faith** (1:19). **Church helpers** are to do the opposite. **Revealed truth** is one of Paul's favorite words to describe the gospel, literally meaning "mystery" (1 Cor. 2:1, 7; 4:1; Eph. 3:3–9). For Paul, the "mystery" **of the faith** was not something "secret" but rather a truth once hidden (in God) and now revealed by the Spirit, hence **revealed truth**.

3:10 / With this sentence we come to something new, but not surprising, in light of the situation in Ephesus. The deacons are to be **tested first**, before they **serve**. Although one cannot be sure, this may be assumed to be true of the overseers as well. There is an "also" at the beginning of Paul's sentence, untranslated in the GNB, which probably refers back to the overseers (cf. NEB, "no less than bishops"). It may, however, simply refer to verse 10; that is, they should *also* be tested, to see whether they **hold** fast **the faith**.

But what is the nature of this testing? by whom? testing what? Some believe, and the GNB seems to lean this way, that a formal examination of some kind is in view, including a probation period (cf. Weymouth's translation, "must undergo probation"). This would be carried out either by Timothy or the other elders, to test the candidate's understanding of the faith. But that seems to reflect the outlook of a later period. More likely what Paul intends here is the selection of "approved" men, who have been "examined" in the sense of 1 Corinthians 16:3 ("the men you have approved") or 2 Corinthians 13:5 ("Put yourselves to the test, . . . to find out whether you are in the faith").

This view seems to be supported by the words "if they are irreproachable" (not the GNB **if they pass the test**). This word is a synonym for the "without fault" (v. 2) required of the *episkopoi*. (Cf. Titus 1:6, where this word, translated "without fault" by GNB, takes the place of its synonym in 1 Tim. 3:2 at the head of the list.) Paul is saying, therefore, that when you find men "who hold to the revealed truth of the faith with a clear conscience," that is, people whose behavior is above reproach, then let such "approved" men **serve** (the verb form of *diakonos*). This obviously implies that, as with the overseer, such a person would not be a recent convert (3:6). Again contrast with the false teachers seems certain.

3:11 / This sentence is one of the genuine puzzles in 1 Timothy. Scholarship is divided as to whether Paul is turning his attention to the deacons' **wives** (GNB text) or the "women helpers" (GNB margin), since the word *gynē* can mean either "wife" or "woman."

In favor of **wives** is that the deacons are addressed on either side of this verse. It is also argued that one might have expected more detail if a third category were envisioned. In favor of "women helpers" is the structure of the sentence itself, which is the exact equivalent of verse 8, both of which in turn are dependent on the verb **must** in verse 2 (thus implying three categories). It is further argued that had the wives of deacons been in view, Paul might have been expected to say *their* **wives** (as the GNB does without any warrant whatsoever). Since there was no word in Greek for "woman helper" ("deaconess" may be too formal), it is likely that "women" here would have been understood to mean women who served the church in some capacity.

This view seems to be supported further by the list of four qualities that should characterize the "women helpers," which are roughly the equivalent of four qualities of the deacons in verses 9–10. They **must be of good character** (the feminine form of the same word that heads the deacons' list). Then there are two prohibitions: they must **not gossip** (lit., "be slanderers"; cf. Titus 2:3), the equivalent of the deacons' "not double-tongued," and **they must be sober** (cf. "not given to much wine," v. 8), although **sober** here may mean "temperate" in a broader sense, as in verse 2. Finally, they must be **honest in everything**. This probably means that they are to be absolutely trustworthy (cf. NEB).

Whichever view one holds on this verse, these qualifications stand in marked contrast to the descriptions of the women in 5:11–15 and 2 Timothy 3:6–7. Their being mentioned, therefore, probably reflects the negative influence of the false teachers on the women of the church.

3:12-13 / If Paul intended **wives** in verse 11, then verse 12 must be understood as a return to deacons because of what he has just said of their wives. It reminds him that what was true of the *episkopoi* is likewise true of the *diakonoi*. **A church helper must** also "be faithful" to his **one wife** (v. 2), and he must **manage** his own family well (v. 4).

If Paul intended "women helpers" in verse 11, as seems more likely, then this verse is something of an afterthought."Oh yes, back to the deacons for a minute . . ." On the meaning of the verse itself, see the discussion on verses 2 and 4.

With verse 13 Paul brings the qualifications of the church **helpers** to a conclusion by holding before them the "reward" they may expect for doing **their work well**. First, they **win for themselves a good standing**. The word **standing** literally means "a step." Used figuratively, as here, it probably refers to their influence and reputation in the believing community, although it could refer to their **standing** with God. The former finds more support from the next phrase. Those who by their good labor gain a good reputation are also those who will be **able to speak boldly about their faith in Christ Jesus**.

The meaning of this last phrase is not as clear as the translation suggests. The word **to speak boldly** often means just that, in the sense of having boldness or openness toward others (cf. 2 Cor. 3:12; Phil. 1:20; Philem. 8). But the word can also refer to one's "confidence" before God, as in Ephesians 3:12 (cf. Heb. 10:19, 35). Hence the NIV translates "great assurance in their faith in Christ Jesus." This is not an easy decision. On the one hand, it would add a further dimension to what it means to have good standing, namely, the confidence in speech that comes from soundness in life and work. On the other hand, it could refer to the double nature of the "reward," namely, a good reputation with other people and confidence before God. On the whole, the latter is to be preferred, because the qualifying prepositional phrase says "in **faith**" (not in *the* faith), implying, as throughout 1 Timothy, one's own **faith in Christ**.

These two commendations, of course, are precisely what the false teachers lack. Their "diseased teaching" (see disc. on 1:19), which includes improper behavior and a soiled reputation, also has caused them to abandon genuine faith in Christ (1:5).

Additional Notes

3:10 / The content of this verse might seem to support the "church manual" view (see disc. on 2:1-7), that these are instructions for "setting the church in order." The view taken here is that there is tension throughout 1 Timothy between some already in these positions who *lack* the qualifications set out and others who will be appointed in the future to replace those who are disciplined.

3:11 / It is of some interest to note that the majority of recent commentaries in English (Hanson excepted) take the view favored here, whereas many of the newer translations favor **wives** (GNB, NEB, NIV).

3:12-13 / Some have argued that the **standing** referred to has to do with "an advance in rank" in spiritual progress, such as one finds in Clement of Alexandria or the later Hermetic writings. But such an idea seems to be much later in time, as well as too esoteric for this context.

9

The Purpose of the Letter

1 TIMOTHY 3:14–16

As I write this letter to you, I hope to come and see you soon. ¹⁵But if I delay, this letter will let you know how we should conduct ourselves in God's household, which is the church of the living God, the pillar and support of the truth. ¹⁶No one can deny how great is the secret of our religion:
He appeared in human form,
was shown to be right by the Spirit,ᶠ
and was seen by angels.
He was preached among the nations,
was believed in throughout the world,
and was taken up to heaven.

f. was shown to be right by the Spirit, *or* and, in spiritual form, was shown to be right.

The letter has now come a considerable distance. It began with a clear statement of its occasion: a charge to Timothy to stay on in Ephesus to oppose some false teachers and their errors, including a digression by way of personal testimony illustrating the truth of the gospel (chap. 1). In chapters 2 and 3, Paul moves through several concerns that reflect some of the disorders in the church, which had surfaced in their gatherings for worship (chap. 2) and in the lives of some of the church leaders (chap. 3).

He now concludes this section of the letter with a further statement of its purpose. The church must give heed to what Paul has written because it alone has been entrusted with the truth (v. 15), truth that is illustrated by an early Christian hymn.

3:14-15 / The grammar of the opening sentence is a little rough, but the meaning is clear. Here we learn that Paul had been intending all along **to come and see** Timothy (and therefore the church) **soon**. In fact the probable force of the Greek participle **hope** is concessive, that is, *even though* **I hope to come soon**, in case I am delayed (v. 15, as it probably seemed likely to him), I will take the occasion to **write this letter** (lit., "these things," that is, chaps. 1–3) **to you** now. (On the question of whether Paul had recently been in Ephesus, see note on 1:3).

With verse 15 the real urgencies of the letter come into focus. The church itself is at stake. **If I delay**, it is crucial that people **know how** to behave as **God's** people, because they are the **church of the living God, the pillar and support of the truth**. The church has been entrusted with **the truth**; the conduct of the false teachers has been an abandonment of the truth (cf. 6:5; 2 Tim. 2:18; 3:8; 4:4). Thus it is extremely important that Timothy not only stop the false teachers (1:3-11) but get people back in touch with the truth.

To emphasize this point, Paul mixes some metaphors in a way similar to Ephesians 2:19-22. He begins with **conduct** (behavior) **in God's household**. This metaphor for "family," already hinted at in 3:4-5, flows naturally from the recognition of God as Father, believers as brothers and sisters, and apostles as "stewards" (household managers). Paul's point, therefore, is not, as the KJV reads and others imply, to know how "to behave . . . in the house of God" (that is, "in church"), but as the NAB happily renders it, "what kind of conduct befits a member of God's household." Such a statement of purpose hardly fits the "church manual" approach to the letter.

The metaphor then shifts slightly, from **household** to building (cf. Eph. 2:19-20). The terms **pillar and support** ("bulwark" and "foundation") and the language **of the living God** (cf. 2 Cor. 6:16) indicate that Paul's common image of the church as God's temple is in view (cf. 1 Cor. 3:16-17; 2 Cor. 6:16; Eph. 2:21). Just as **the living God** dwelt in the sanctuary of Israel, so now by the Spirit God indwells his new temple, the church, and as such they are to "uphold the truth and keep it safe" (JB).

With these two images, family and temple, Paul expresses the two urgencies of this letter: his concern over proper behavior among believers vis-à-vis the false teachers, and the church as the people entrusted to uphold and proclaim the truth of the gospel.

3:16 / The mention of **the truth** ("of the gospel" always being implied by this word) leads Paul to the exclamation: **No one can deny how great is the secret** ("revealed truth," as in 3:9) **of our religion**. The word **religion** (*eusebeia*), a favorite in 1 Timothy (see disc. on 2:2 where it is translated "reverence toward God"), has to do with "godliness" (NIV), understood as "the duty which people owe to God." But here, as often with "faith" in these letters, it is not referring to the quality of "godliness" as such but "*the* godliness," thought of in a more objective way as the content or basis of the Christian **religion**.

What follows is an expression of some of the content of the "revealed truth" of the "godliness" entrusted to God's people. The passage itself is a hymn, or hymn fragment, in six rhythmic lines. Each line has two members, a verb standing in first position, each in the aorist (past) tense, passive voice in Greek, ending with the rhythmic -*thē*, followed by a prepositional phrase (Gk., *en*, "in" or "by"). The implied subject of each verb is Christ.

On that much all modern interpreters are agreed; but on the structure itself, the meaning of a couple of the lines, and the meaning of the whole, there has been considerable debate, with nothing like a consensus. It has been viewed as a single stanza of six consecutive lines (see the JB), as two stanzas with three lines each (but in a variety of patterns [cf., e.g., the GNB with the RSV]), as three stanzas with two lines each (cf. NIV), or in other, not easily classified combinations. Moreover, three of the lines (2, 3, and 6) are not perfectly clear as to their meaning, a difficulty raised in part by some apparent parallels and/or antitheses between the lines and in part because the whole seems to have a degree of chronology, moving from the Incarnation to further aspects of Christ's life and ministry, yet breaking down in line 6. In view of so many difficulties and disagreements, one offers an interpretation with some reservation.

Let us begin with what appears to be somewhat certain. Line 1, **he appeared in human form** (lit. "he was manifested in the flesh"), has been universally recognized as an affirmation of the Incarnation, comparable to John 1:14 or Romans 1:3. Even more than in 1:15, such language implies pre-existence. In Christ, God himself has appeared "in flesh."

Line 4, **he was preached among the nations** (or "Gentiles"), is likewise generally recognized to refer to the period of early apostolic history when the gospel was proclaimed throughout **the nations** of the known world.

Line 5, **he was believed in throughout the world**, seems to accompany line 4 as a word about the response to the proclamation of the gospel.

The content of these lines, therefore, which begin with Christ's own entry into the world, and in 4 and 5 take up the apostolic witness to Christ, has caused most interpreters to view it as some form of *heilgeschichtliche* hymn, that is, a hymn that tells the story of salvation (cf. J. Wilbur Chapman's "One Day," or Fanny Crosby's "Tell Me the Story of Jesus"). If these observations are correct, then the problem that remains has to do with the meaning of the other three lines and how they all relate to one another.

Let us turn, then, to what is less certain. Line 2, **he was shown to be right by the Spirit**, presents considerable difficulties. Literally, it says "he was justified in spirit [or Spirit]." In the Greek there seems to be a parallel between "in flesh" in line 1 and "in spirit" in line 2. But does it refer to the Holy Spirit, or (more likely, given the parallel) to his spiritual nature? If the latter, then the point of this line, with some poetic license, is at least "vindication," perhaps "exaltation," referring to Christ's resurrection. Thus the first two lines hymn Christ's humiliation and exaltation (incarnation and resurrection) in a manner similar to the splendid prose of Romans 1:3 and 4 (cf. 1 Pet. 3:18).

Line 3, he (there is no **and** in the Greek text) **was seen by angels**, is likewise puzzling. This is the only line without the Greek preposition *en* ("in" or "by"). This verb (**was seen by** or "appeared to"), with the person(s) to whom he appeared in the Greek dative case (as here), is the regular formula in the NT for resurrection appearances (Luke 24:23; Acts 9:17; 1 Cor. 15:5–8). In this case, however, it more likely refers to the worship given by angels to the ascended, glorified Christ. If so, then the first three lines sing Christ's incarnation, resurrection, and glorification and form a stanza about Christ himself, as he is seen "from glory to glory."

In such a scheme, the next two lines (4 and 5) offer a similar parallel to lines 1 and 2, but now sing the ongoing ministry of Christ through his church. But the problem arises at line 6, he **was taken up to heaven** (lit. "was taken up in glory"). The word **was taken up** elsewhere in the NT refers to the Ascension (Luke 9:51; Acts 1:2, 11, 22; cf. Mark 16:19). How, then, does the Ascension follow the apostolic ministry? The answer seems to lie with the phrase "in glory," which would not refer to his being taken up *into* heaven, but to his exaltation that is "glorious," or "accompanied with glory." Like line 3, then, this line also emphasizes his triumph and glorification more than the actual event of the Ascension itself, chronologically understood. Indeed, in this view, line 6 is the glorious climax of the whole that begins in line 1 with the humiliation of Incarnation.

On this understanding, then, the hymn has two stanzas of three lines each. The first stanza sings Christ's earthly ministry, concluding with a word of triumph and glorification. Similarly, the second stanza sings the ongoing ministry of Christ through his church, concluding again with the theme of glorification. In a certain sense both stanzas reflect the theme of humiliation and exaltation.

Thus the great "mystery of the godliness" we believe in, Paul sings, has to do with Christ's own humiliation and exaltation and the church's ongoing witness to him, who is now the exalted, glorified one. This double focus, especially the emphasis on the ongoing ministry to the nations, returns to a theme sounded earlier in the creedal words of 1:15 and 2:4–6.

But the question still remains: Why *this* hymn with *these* emphases at this point in the letter? The answer to that is not easy, but two possibilities commend themselves (perhaps it is a combination of both): First, the double emphasis on humiliation/exaltation, focusing on the present, triumphant glory of Christ, probably stands in some kind of contrast to the Christology of the false teachers. This is especially so, if, as we have argued in the Introduction (pp. xxii–xxiii), there are some affinities between what is going on in Ephesus and what had earlier been afoot in Colossae and Laodicea. Second, Paul is about to return to a censure of the false teachers, with an exhortation to Timothy to stand in sharp contrast to them. This hymn prepares for that censure by boldly expressing what the truth is all about, as a contrast to their demonic errors.

Additional Notes

3:14–15 / In Paul's Greek sentence the subject of the infinitive "to conduct one-self" is not expressed. The KJV supplies "thou . . . thyself," a most unlikely option; the GNB has **we . . . ourselves**, but "people . . . themselves" (NIV; cf. NEB) is much to be preferred. The Living Bible's "you will know what kind of men you should choose as officers for the church" is altogether unwarranted.

3:16 / The original text of line 1 begins with the Greek relative pronoun *hos* ("he who"). Because this word would have been written OC, somewhere around the fourth century this was mistakenly read as $\overline{\Theta C}$, the abbreviation for God. This reading eventually came to predominate in the Greek church (never in the West, since the translation into Latin happened before the variant arose). Hence the KJV translated "God was manifest in flesh." See the discussion in Metzger, *TCGNT*, p. 641; and G. D. Fee, "The Majority Text and the Original Text of the New Testament," esp. 117–18.

The most common alternative to the view of the hymn presented here is to see it as having three sets of two lines, each alternately expressing humiliation and exaltation (or the realm of earth and heaven). The lines then form two sets of chiasmus (*a b   b a   a b*—a form of rhetoric in which the words or ideas in the second or subsequent units in otherwise parallel structures are in reverse order); the sets sing respectively his incarnation and resurrection, his ascension and proclamation on earth, his reception on earth and in heaven. As common—and in some ways attractive—as this interpretation is (RSV, Kelly, Bernard, D-C, et al.), some of the alleged parallels seem forced and probably would never have been seen as such if it were not for the flesh-spirit pair in lines 1 and 2. Moreover, the words "in glory" are highly unusual if line 6 was intended to parallel line 5. In that case the expected phrase would be "in heaven," which is the only antithesis to "earth" used in the NT.

The bibliography for this passage is extensive. The most complete discussion is in German: W. Stenger, *Der Christushymnus 1 Tim. 3, 16. Eine strukturana-lytische Untersuchung.* The most useful recent discussion in English is R. H. Gundry, "The Form, Meaning, and Background of the Hymn Quoted in I Timothy 3:16."

10

The False Teachings Censured

1 TIMOTHY 4:1–5

The Spirit says clearly that some people will abandon the faith in later times; they will obey lying spirits and follow the teachings of demons. ²Such teachings are spread by deceitful liars, whose consciences are dead, as if burnt with a hot iron. ³Such people teach that it is wrong to marry and to eat certain foods. But God created those foods to be eaten, after a prayer of thanks, by those who are believers and have come to know the truth. ⁴Everything that God has created is good; nothing is to be rejected, but everything is to be received with a prayer of thanks, ⁵because the word of God and the prayer make it acceptable to God.

Because of the content of 3:14–16—the statement of purpose climaxed by the hymn—it is easy to think of chapter 3 as bringing us to some kind of conclusion, or major break, in the middle of the letter. But to view 3:14–16 that way is to miss the very close tie between chapter 4 and what has preceded.

Paul is about to elaborate in some detail upon the two matters expressed in the charge in chapter 1: the nature of the errors of the false teachers (4:1–5; cf. 1:3–11, 19–20) and Timothy's role in Ephesus (4:6–16; cf. 1:18–19). The intervening instructions of chapters 2–3, on "what kind of conduct befits a member of God's household," are themselves to be understood against the backdrop of the teachings and activities of the straying elders. Now, in 4:1–5, Paul returns to these teachers. First, he says that their emergence should have come as no surprise—the Spirit clearly forewarned about them; second, he indicates that the true source of their teaching is demonic; and third, he gives some specifics of their errors and the reasons why they are errors.

4:1-2 / This paragraph is joined to 3:14–16 by the conjunction *de* (untranslated in GNB), which could mean "now" (as KJV, meaning "to move on to the next matter"), or "however." The latter seems preferable. In 3:15–16 Paul declared that the church has been entrusted with **the truth**—the truth we sing about Christ. "However," he goes on, **the Spirit**

says clearly that some people will abandon the faith [i.e., the truth] **in later times**.

But who are these **some people**? In this case—and surely this is the great urgency of the letter—they are the members of "God's household" (3:15), who are being led astray by the **deceitful liars** (the false teachers) of verse 2. Note how this same concern is expressed in 2 Timothy 2:16–18; 3:13; and 4:3–4.

We are not told how **the Spirit says clearly**. Such a formula is never used by Paul when referring to the OT. But whether this refers to the prophetic Spirit's having spoken in the church (as Barrett) or to the Spirit speaking to Paul as he writes (or earlier, as in Acts 20) cannot be known. In any case, Paul sees the present "apostasy" (he has here used the verb form of *apostasia*, "rebellion, falling away") as something **the Spirit** has plainly announced beforehand.

In later times refers to their present situation. The early church had long before seen the advent of the Spirit as the beginning of the End. Paul himself believed, and belonged to a tradition that believed, that the End would be accompanied by a time of intense evil (cf. 2 Thess. 2:3–12), including a "falling away" of some of the people of God (see 2 Tim. 3:1; cf. Matt. 24:12; Jude 17–18; 2 Pet. 3:3–7). Thus the present scene was clear evidence for Paul of their living in the **later times** (the time of the End).

What had only been hinted at before (2:14; 3:6–7) is now boldly stated. The ultimate source of the false teachings is Satan himself. The **lying** ("deceiving") **spirits** and **teachings of demons**, which **some people obey** and **follow**, probably refer to the same reality—the demonic nature of teaching that opposes the gospel (cf. 2 Cor. 4:4; 11:3, 13–14).

That **such teachings are spread by deceitful liars** is a particularly strong indictment against the false teachers. Not only are their teachings demonic in nature, but they themselves are **liars** (lit., "speakers of falsehood"). The translation **liar** could be somewhat misleading, since it implies a deliberate attempt to state as fact what one knows not to be true. The Greek word implies simply that they are saying things about the gospel that are not true; that is, they are speaking falsehood rather than truth. These "lies" are furthered **by deceitful** means (lit., "by hypocrisy"), implying that they are outwardly false and therefore that their abstinence in verse 3 is mere pretense or outward show.

Finally, they are characterized as men **whose consciences are dead, as if burnt with a hot iron**. Paul's Greek is not all that clear. The implication of the GNB (also RSV, NIV, NAB) is that they have had the seat of their moral judgments totally seared (we get the word *cauterized* from this verb); thus they are unable to discern truth from falsehood. But it is equally possible that he intends to suggest that their consciences carry Satan's brand (as NEB, Bernard, Kelly). This seems more in keeping with the context. By teaching in the guise of truth what is actually false, they have been branded by Satan as belonging to him and doing his will.

4:3a / As illustrations of the "teachings of demons spread by" the "deceitful liars," Paul mentions two items: **It is wrong to marry and to eat certain foods**. These catch us a bit by surprise, although they are perhaps related to these men "wanting to be teachers of the Law" (1:7). It is not altogether easy to see how these items relate to the "myths and wearisome genealogies" of 1:4 or the teaching that "our resurrection has already taken place" (2 Tim. 2:18). Some kind of asceticism, perhaps similar to that in Colossae (Col. 2:16–23), is probably involved. This may have also been mixed with a kind of over-realized eschatology (that the End had not just begun, but had arrived in fullness; cf. 2 Thess. 2:1–2; 1 Cor. 15:12). In Corinth this kind of view about the End was apparently linked to Hellenistic dualism, which believed matter to be corrupt, or evil, and only spirit to be good. Just as some Corinthians denied a future bodily resurrection (1 Cor. 15:12, 35), and some at least took a dim view of sex (7:1–7) and marriage (7:25–38), it is altogether likely that something very much like that is being given out as "Law" in Ephesus. Hence the road to purity was marked off for them through abstaining from marriage (to be like the angels after the resurrection [Matt. 22:30]?) and from **certain foods**. (See the Introduction, pp. xxi–xxii, for further discussion.)

We have already noted (2:8–15) how this teaching **that it is wrong to marry** had probably affected some of the women in Ephesus (cf. 5:6, 11–15). For the rest of this paragraph, Paul will respond only to the prohibition against **certain foods**.

4:3b–5 / Paul has had to contend with the matter of eating or not eating **certain foods** several times before—in 1 Corinthians 10:23–33; Romans 14:1–23; Colossians 2:16, 21. Each of these situations was different, thus accounting for what appears to have been some ambivalence on his part. However, some consistent guidelines emerge: Food is a matter of indifference; therefore, one may or may not partake as one wishes. However, one who abstains may not judge the one who partakes (Rom. 14:3, 10; 1 Cor. 10:29–30), and when one goes beyond mere "judging" to **demanding** abstinence for religious or theological reasons, as in Colossians 2, Paul comes out fighting. One may do as one wishes before God, but one may not impose those "wishes" as regulations for others to follow. The response here combines some things said in 1 Corinthians 10:25–26 and 29–30 within a context of anti-abstinence polemic similar to Colossians 2:16 and 21–23.

The reasons given for Paul's anti-abstinence stance are basically two-fold—repeated and elaborated several times: **God created those foods to be eaten**; and they are **eaten** (lit., "shared in," "partaken of") **by believers after a prayer of thanks**.

The first point speaks directly against any form of dualism that would impute impurity, ritual or ethical (although the context is ritual here), to any created thing (see also Titus 1:14–16). **God created those foods**— those rejected by the false teachers, but by implication, all foods—to be partaken of **by those who are believers and have come to know the truth** (for this combination, cf. Titus 1:1). Those who believe the gospel are freed from the food laws (cf. Mark 7:19; Acts 10:9–16). One reason for this is an appeal to a repeated motif in Genesis 1—what **God has created is good**. That is, the very fact that God created something has inherent in it the fact of its goodness. Therefore, **nothing is to be rejected**, implying rejection for reasons of ritual uncleanness (cf. Rom. 14:14: "Nothing is unclean of itself").

The second reason appeals to the common fact that a benediction, or **prayer of thanks**, always accompanied meals in Judaism and the early church. This is evidenced both in the Gospels (Mark 6:41; 8:6; 14:22–23 and synoptic parallels; Luke 24:30) and in Paul (1 Cor. 10:30; Rom. 14:6). Indeed by the second century in Judaism, "it is forbidden a man to enjoy anything of this world without a benediction" (Babylonian Talmud, *Berakoth* 35a). Paul's point is the same as in 1 Corinthians 10:30: How can one condemn another for eating that for which the thanksgiving has been offered? Implied in this is not that **the prayer** in itself **makes it acceptable to God**, but that the prayer of thanksgiving has inherent in it the recognition of God's prior creative action. It is thus the believer's response to God as Creator, and **the word of God and the prayer** together **make it acceptable** (lit., "sanctify it," keeping the ritual imagery).

There has been considerable debate as to what **the word of God** means in verse 5. Many see it as referring to the words of the OT often used in the thanksgiving prayer (e.g., Ps. 24:1, used by Paul in his argument in 1 Cor. 10:25–26). However, Paul does not use the term **word of God** to refer to the OT as an objective, inscripturated reality. In the PE, **the word of God** invariably refers to the gospel message (2 Tim. 2:19; Titus 1:3;

2:5; cf. 1 Tim. 5:17; 2 Tim. 2:15; 4:2). If that is the case here, then it reflects the idea of believers' having **come to know the truth** (v. 3) that in Christ there are no food laws. On the other hand, it may (perhaps more likely in the context) refer to the word God spoke in Genesis 1 that declared everything created by God to be good, not referring to an OT text per se but to the fact of God's having declared all food good.

Abstinence, therefore, has nothing to do with the gospel; mandatory abstinence from marriage or foods is ultimately the teaching of demons, and the church in Ephesus is not to be deceived thereby.

Additional Notes

4:1-2 / The fact that early Christians understood themselves to be living **in later times**, at the time of the End, often perplexes twentieth-century Christians. But one must be careful not to overstress the idea of "imminence"—although it may well often have been there. Rather, living **in later times** has to do with a new understanding of existence. The End has already begun; believers are to be the people of the Future in the present age, even though the consummation of what has begun still lies in the Future. Thus Christian existence always belongs to the **later times**, already begun with the advent of the Spirit. For an overview of this framework of understanding in Paul, see, e.g., G. E. Ladd, *A Theology of the New Testament*, pp. 360-75.

4:3a / For the possibility that the heresy involved a form of "over-realized eschatology," see W. L. Lane, "I Tim. iv 1-3. An Early Instance of Over-realized Eschatology?"

4:3b-5 / There are at least three other interpretations of **the word of God** in this sentence, including the possibility that the prayer itself functioned as God's word, that it meant a word of blessing from God in response to the prayer (Hendriksen), or that it referred, in a most circuitous way, to the bread and wine of the Eucharist (Hanson).

11

Timothy's Personal Responsibilities

1 TIMOTHY 4:6-16

If you give these instructions to the brothers, you will be a good servant of Christ Jesus, as you feed yourself spiritually on the words of faith and of the true teaching which you have followed. ⁷But keep away from those godless legends, which are not worth telling. Keep yourself in training for a godly life. ⁸Physical exercise has some value, but spiritual exercise is valuable in every way, because it promises life both for the present and for the future. ⁹This is a true saying, to be completely accepted and believed. ¹⁰We struggle ᵍ and work hard, because we have placed our hope in the living God, who is the Savior of all and especially of those who believe.

¹¹Give them these instructions and these teachings. ¹²Do not let anyone look down on you because you are young, but be an example for the believers in your speech, your conduct, your love, faith, and purity. ¹³Until I come, give your time and effort to the public reading of the Scriptures and to preaching and teaching. ¹⁴Do not neglect the spiritual gift that is in you, which was given to you when the prophets spoke and the elders laid their hands on you. ¹⁵Practice these things and devote yourself to them, in order that your progress may be seen by all. ¹⁶Watch yourself and watch your teaching. Keep on doing these things, because if you do, you will save both yourself and those who hear you.

g. struggle; *some manuscripts have* are reviled.

P aul turns at last to say some things to Timothy personally, things we might have expected much earlier in the letter, given the address (1:2) and the charge with which it began (1:3, 18–19a). But even here, these matters are subordinated to the main concern of the letter.

The instructions in the first paragraph are clearly given vis-à-vis the false teachers. In contrast to these false teachers, who have been deceived by Satan and in turn are deceiving others, Timothy must guard his own life and the teaching of the truth with great care. The appeal is for Timothy personally, that he not get caught up in their **godless legends**, but rather keep himself **in training** for true godliness (v. 7). This latter is an athletic metaphor that Paul then typically exploits to further advantage.

But the second paragraph (vv. 11–16), though filled with personal matters, makes it plain that Paul thereby wants Timothy to function as a model (vv. 12, 15), both for godly living (v. 12) and for ministry (vv. 13–14)—all for the sake of his hearers (vv. 15–16).

4:6. / The first paragraph begins by gathering up what has been said from 2:1 to 4:5 and urging Timothy to **give these instructions to the brothers**. **The brothers**, of course, means not the church leaders, but as always in Paul, the church community as a family of brothers and sisters (cf., e.g., Phil. 4:1, which moves on in v. 2 to address some of the sisters). By giving **these instructions** to the church Timothy will fulfill his own ministry as **a good servant** (*diakonos*, see disc. on 3:8) **of Christ Jesus**. The first concern, then, as throughout, is for the church in Ephesus.

But Paul then elaborates for Timothy's sake—without losing sight of the church—what it means for him to **be a good servant**. He will be so **as** he continues to **feed** himself **spiritually**, a metaphor from child rearing, having to do with nurturing (training or nourishing). The source of such spiritual nourishment is **the words of faith** (better, *the* **faith**) **and of the true** (lit., "good," "excellent") **teaching**. By **words of** the **faith** Paul clearly means the content of the gospel; but it is not quite so clear whether **the true teaching** also refers to the gospel, or to the correct use of Scripture (as in 2 Tim. 3:14–16). In either case, this appeal includes a reminder of Timothy's long association with Paul: **which** teachings **you have** always **followed** (cf. 2 Tim. 1:13; 2:2; 3:10). (The gist of this sentence will be repeated with more detail in 2 Tim. 3:14–16.)

4:7–8 / Almost as a reflex action, Paul's mentioning **the true teaching** calls forth a contrast with the false kind. Indeed, the word order, with the imperative coming last, serves to highlight the contrast. **But** the **godless legends, which are not worth telling, keep away from**. For **legends**, see discussion on 1:4. Here they are characterized as **godless**, meaning profane in the sense of being radically opposite to what is sacred, and **not worth telling** (lit., "old wives' ") **legends**, a sarcastic expression often used in philosophical polemic comparing an opponent's position to the tales perpetuated by the older women of those cultures as they would sit around weaving and the like.

In contrast to **godless** and "old wives' " **legends**, which promote speculations and have nothing to do with genuine godliness (*eusebeia*), Paul urges Timothy to give himself vigorously to the latter. In doing so he changes metaphors—from child rearing (v. 6) to athletics: **Keep yourself in training** (*gymnaze*) for *eusebeia* ("a **godly life**"). Paul's point is that, like the athlete, Timothy should **keep** himself **in** vigorous **training** for the practice of genuine godliness, understood here as both the content of the truth and its visible expression in correct behavior (see disc. on 2:2 and 3:16).

Having used the metaphor of physical **training**, Paul, in typical fashion, pauses to reflect on the metaphor itself for a moment. There is another kind of **training**, he says, **physical exercise** itself (*gymnasia*), which **has some value**. This statement has been the cause of some puzzlement. Is Paul herewith trying to encourage Timothy to take a little **physical exercise**? Almost certainly not. Such a concern is irrelevant to the context and quite beside the point. What, then? Most likely the reason for it lies with the metaphor itself. Having just urged *gymnaze* (**keep in training**) for *eusebeia* ("godliness"), Paul now picks up both ends of that sentence, and with perfectly balanced sentences presses home the reason for Timothy's training himself in godliness. Paul will allow that **physical exercise** (*gymnasia*) **has some value**, a value, however, that is limited strictly to this age. But he says that only to set up his real concern. *Eusebeia*, translated **spiritual exercise** in keeping with the metaphor, is where the real value is. It **is valuable in every way**, because it holds **promise** for **life, both for the present and for the future**. (The idea of godliness as holding promise of life is reiterated in Titus 1:2.) Here is a clear reference to Paul's understanding of Christian existence as basically eschatological. **Life**, which means "eternal life" (see 1:16), has already begun. The **life** of the future is therefore both a **present** reality and a **future** hope. (See further the note on 4:1.)

Paul's argument has strayed a bit, but not without purpose. The word *eusebeia* ("true godliness") is used throughout 1 Timothy to express genuine Christian faith—the truth and its visible expression. It is this quality that the false teachers lack. Thus "godliness," though contrasted with **physical exercise**, really stands in contrast to the **godless legends**, precisely because it has to do with **life**, both **present** and **future**.

4:9 / This is the third time (cf. 1:15; 3:1) we meet the **true saying** formula, in this instance exactly as it is in 1:15, with the addition of **to be completely accepted and believed**. But what is the saying? Four options have been suggested: (1) What immediately follows in verse 10 (NEB): "With this before us we labour and struggle, because we have set our hope on the living God, who is the Saviour of all men." (2) The second half of verse 10 (NIV): "We have put our hope in the living God, who is the Savior of all men, and especially of those who believe." (3) All of verse 8, with the balanced pairs of **physical exercise** and "godliness" (Barrett, Knight). (4) The second part of verse 8: "Godliness is profitable in every way, because it promises life both for the present and the future" (NAB, Kelly).

For several reasons the fourth seems by far the best option. First, as we shall see, verse 10 is not an independent saying but a further reflection on verse 8b, and totally dependent on it. Second, even though verse 8 starts with balanced pairs, the point is only in the second part. The first part, as we have seen, comes about because of what has been said in verse 7 and exists strictly to set up a contrast for what follows in 8b. Third, verse 8b has the epigrammatic nature of a saying, and that alone is what verse 10 will go on to elaborate.

4:10 / Unfortunately, the two connectives that tie this verse to the saying of 8b have been left untranslated in the GNB. It begins with a "for," referring to why this "true saying" is "to be completely accepted and believed" (v. 9); then Paul says "for this reason," that is, the promise of life found in true godliness (v. 8b), **we struggle and work hard**. These two verbs occur frequently in Paul and refer to his and others' ministries (cf. Col. 1:29, where they also occur together). The first verb, **we struggle**, has to do with engaging in athletic contests (see disc. on 6:12; cf. 2 Tim. 4:7; 1 Cor. 9:25) and thus continues the athletic metaphor begun in verse 7. The verb **work hard** is more frequent; it occurs again in 5:17 regarding the teaching ministry of the elders.

The **because** clause that concludes the paragraph simply gives further elaboration of the true saying and in so doing picks up several earlier themes in the letter. For this, the present and future life that true godliness promises, **we** "contest" **and work hard, because we have placed our hope in the living God**, who alone can give life now and to come. Our hope rests in him, because **he is the Savior of all**, that is, he would save (give life to) all people (see disc. on 2:4–6), but his salvation is in fact effective only for **those who believe**. This latter addition makes it clear that the universal scope of salvation argued for so strongly in 2:4–6 is not at the same time an expression of universalism.

This paragraph, therefore, that began as a word to Timothy vis-à-vis false teachers moves by way of these contrasts to an exhortation to discipline himself in true godliness and concludes by telling him why: The result is **life**, now and forever, not only for those of us who **have placed our hope in the living God**, but for **all who** will **believe** (cf. 1:16).

The next paragraph (vv. 11–16) returns to Paul's personal concern for Timothy, both his life and ministry, but does so in the context of his relationship to the church. The paragraph is a string of ten imperatives (commands), whose content is summarized in verse 16: **Watch yourself** (v. 12) and **watch your teaching** (vv. 13–14), for by so doing, **you will save both yourself and those who hear you** (vv. 11–12, 15).

4:11 / Paul begins by reminding Timothy that the pursuit of true godliness with its promise of life is not just for him but for the church as well. **Give them these instructions** (the same verb as the "charge" in 1:3, 5,18) and **these teachings**. Note how this charge is repeated throughout (5:7; 6:2b; 2 Tim. 2:2, 14; Titus 2:15).

4:12 / We now discover what is probably a hidden agenda that made it necessary for Paul to write this letter—Timothy's youthfulness. To say, **do not let anyone look down on you because you are young**, is very likely two-edged. It is first of all a word of encouragement to Timothy, because he was in fact a younger man (thirty to thirty-five)—and perhaps timid (cf. 1 Cor. 16:10–11; 2 Tim. 1:6 ff.). In a culture where "elders" were highly regarded, and in a church where the elders would have been older than he, this is not an insignificant encouragement. But for the same reasons, it is likewise a word to the community, to let them know that, despite his youth, he has Paul's own authority to "command and teach these things" (v. 11, RSV).

On the contrary, not only are they **not** to **look down on** him **because** he is **young**, but they are to "look up" to him. He is to **be** (lit., "become") **an example for the believers**. That the people of God are to learn Christian ethics by modeling after the apostolic example is a thoroughgoing, and crucial, Pauline concept (see 1 Thess. 1:6; 2 Thess. 3:7, 9; 1 Cor. 4:6; 11:1; Phil. 3:17; cf. 2 Tim 1:13).

The virtues Timothy is to model for them are those that some scholars have felt to be missing in the list of qualifications for church leadership (see note on 3:2). But even here they stand in contrast to the conduct of the false teachers: **in your speech** (not involved in arguments; cf. this virtue in Col. 3:8; 4:5–6); **in your conduct** (the broad term for behavior and a favorite of 1 Peter); **your love, faith** (which the false teachers have abandoned; 1:5–6); **and purity** (the real thing, in contrast to their false asceticism; cf. 5:22–23).

4:13–14 / From instructions regarding personal conduct, Paul turns to Timothy's ministry while in Ephesus. **Until** Paul himself arrives back on the scene (cf. 3:14), Timothy is to **give** his **time and effort to the public reading of the Scriptures and to preaching and teaching**. Many are tempted to see here a kind of pattern of public worship, modeled after the synagogue. Although this certainly refers to what Timothy is to do in public worship, it is too narrow a view to see this as intending to provide a model. We know from other sources that public worship included prayers (2:1–7; 1 Cor. 11:2–16), singing (Col. 3:16; 1 Cor. 14:26; cf. 1 Tim. 3:16), charismatic utterances (1 Thess. 5:19–22; 1 Cor. 11:2–16; 12–14), and the Lord's Supper (1 Cor. 11:17–34).

Rather than providing an example of the pastor's specific duties in worship, these three items basically refer to the same thing—the reading, exhortation, and exposition of Scripture—and as such are to be Timothy's positive way of counteracting the erroneous teachings (cf. 2 Tim. 3:14–17). The last two words, **preaching and teaching**, are repeated as imperatives in 6:2b about what Timothy is to do with the contents of this letter.

The next imperative, **do not neglect the Spiritual gift that is in you**, follows naturally out of verse 13. That is, **the spiritual gift** [*charisma*] **that is in** him almost certainly has to do with his calling and gift for ministry as a preacher/teacher of the Word. It is precisely through his role as preacher/teacher that he is to overcome the influence of error, a point made even more clearly in 2 Timothy (1:13–14; 2:15; 2:24–26; 3:14–4:5). But Timothy must ultimately rely on the Holy Spirit, who, as 2 Timothy 1:6–7 and 14 make plain, is the source of the **spiritual gift** he is **not** to **neglect** (*amelei*, "disregard," or "not take care of").

The **spiritual gift** of ministry, as in 1:18, is said to have been given **when the prophets spoke** (better, "through prophecies"; cf. 1:18). In this instance, however, because of the broader concern for Timothy's relationship to the community, Paul adds that the giving of the gift through prophetic utterances was "accompanied by" (the Greek *meta* means "with," not "through" as the NEB) the laying on of the **hands** of the **elders** (lit., "the presbytery"). The precise relationship of the three elements (Timothy's spiritual gift, the prophecies, and the laying on of hands) is not altogether clear and is ambiguous in the NT itself. The background for such laying on of hands is found in the OT (Deut. 34:9; cf. Num. 27:18–23) and appears in contemporary Judaism. The most probable analogy, however, is to be found in Acts 13:1–3, where the Spirit speaks (v. 2), apparently through the prophets (v. 1), in response to which the prophets and teachers lay on hands in some form of consecration. In any case, the evidence there and elsewhere (2 Tim. 1:6–7) indicates that the Spirit is the crucial matter; the laying on of hands, though not insignificant, is the human side (response) to the Spirit's prior activity. It is probably something of an anachronism to refer to this event as an "ordination," although the language surely reflects a concern to note the believing community's recognition of Timothy's ministry from the very beginning.

4:15-16 / Paul now sums up the concerns of the previous verses: **Practice these things and devote yourself to them**. The first verb may mean "give your mind to" (cf. KJV, "meditate upon"), but it also frequently is used for "cultivating" or "practicing," the latter thus picking up the athletic metaphor from verses 7-10.

The purpose for such practice and devotion to **these things** is **that your progress may be seen by all**. The evidence from 2 Timothy 2:16 and 3:9 suggests that **progress** was one of the slogans of the false teachers, perhaps as a kind of elitist appeal to those who wanted to "advance" into "deeper truths" by engaging in their speculative nonsense (see disc. on 1:3-4, 6-7; 6:20-21). If so, then this is a bold counterstatement to their kind of **progress**, which in 2 Timothy 2:16 is ironically labeled "progress in ungodliness [*asebeia*]." By Timothy's being a faithful minister of the word of the gospel, the people will be able to see the real thing.

The final verse in the paragraph partly repeats the injunctions of verse 15, but it does so in such a way as to summarize the whole. The first two admonitions clarify the meaning of **these things** in verse 15. **Watch yourself**, Paul says, referring to his being an example *for* the believers (v. 12); **and watch your teaching**, referring to his ministry *to* them (vv. 13-14). So one more time Paul enjoins, **keep on doing these things**, because by so doing Timothy **will save both** himself, **and** especially **those who hear** him. As in 2:15 above and 1 Corinthians 7:16, the language may not be theologically precise, but the meaning is clear. Salvation involves perseverance; and Timothy's task in Ephesus is to model and teach the gospel in such a fashion that it will lead the church to perseverance in faith and love, and hence to final, eschatological salvation. Thus both paragraphs in this section conclude with the great concern of the gospel—people's salvation (cf. 1:15; 2:4-6; 4:10).

Additional Notes

4:6 / Some see **these instructions** as limited to 4:1-5. But since the last personal charge to Timothy was in 1:18-20 and everything since then has been instruction for the church, the *tauta* ("these things") logically includes the whole of 2:1-4:5.

The verb translated **give** means "to set before" or "enjoin." Some interpreters, enamored of its derivation from two words that mean "to lay under," see a metaphorical reference to laying a foundation for the church. But such etymological understandings are seldom relevant at a later stage in a word's use and are certainly irrelevant here.

The present participle translated **as you feed yourself spiritually** in the GNB was translated as though it were an aorist (past tense) or perfect in the NIV ("brought up in") and NEB ("bred"). Not only does this do injustice to the Greek, but it seems to miss the point, making it refer to Timothy's earlier training rather than his current need.

4:7-8 / For a similar use of "old-wives' fables" in a polemical context, see Lucian, *Lover of Lies* 9: "Your stories still remain old wives' fables."

There has been a significant tradition of interpretation that sees **physical exercise** to be a metaphor in these sentences to refer to a degree of allowable asceticism (e.g., Bernard, Calvin, Easton): "the discipline of the body . . . to be practiced in moderation . . . is profitable for a little" (Bernard). But as Kelly says, "It . . . seems incredible that, after denouncing the sectaries' asceticism as devilish, Paul should end up by conceding that physical mortification has a limited value" (p. 100). Indeed, the very use of such a metaphor more likely speaks directly against their extreme asceticism. See V. C. Pfitzner, *Paul and the Agon Motif*, pp. 171–77, although he, too, allows that "the verdict that it has little value does not amount to a complete negation of the necessity for self-denial and control over the body" (p. 174).

4:9 / For a more detailed discussion of the problems with this **saying**, see G. W. Knight, *The Faithful Sayings in the Pastoral Letters*, although he argues for the third option.

4:10 / The older versions (Latin and Syriac) and the majority of later Greek manuscripts have "we suffer reproach" for **we struggle**. This variant probably arose from the ideas expressed in 2 Tim. 1:8, 12; 2:9–10. See Metzger, *TCGNT*, pp. 641-42.

Some interpreters (e.g., Calvin, Guthrie, Barrett) perceive theological difficulties with the final clause of this verse and suggest that **Savior** means "Preserver." All are thus "preserved" by God, but only the believers obtain eschatological salvation. But this seems to miss the obvious tie to 2:4–6 and argues for a usage of **Savior** found nowhere else in the NT. **God is the Savior of all** in the same sense that Christ gave himself a ransom for all (2:6). Neither sentence suggests that all people will indeed be saved.

4:12 / For a substantial collection of evidence that men in their thirties were often referred to as young, see the footnote in Bernard. That Timothy must have been thirty to thirty-five is based on the date of his joining Paul (ca. 49–50) and the date of this letter (ca. 62–64).

4:13-14 / Because the singular "presbytery," reflecting **the elders** as a body, seems awkward to some, it has been suggested that the genitive, "of the presbytery," should be seen as a Greek rendering of a Hebrew term, thus producing "your ordination as an elder" (NEB margin). But this suggestion produces a most unnatural meaning of the Greek phrase, including a disregard of the definite article *the*. It also seems to miss the point in context, which is not that Timothy was ordained an elder but that he received a **spiritual gift** through prophecy.

It is often argued that "ordination" is in view, on the basis of rabbinic ordination, which Paul, or the pseudonymous author, borrowed from Judaism. But the date of such ordinations, as well as their nature, is not very clear from the texts; and in any case, the crucial element here, the Spirit, is missing from the Jewish texts. For a discussion of "ordination" in early Judaism, see M. Warkentin, *Ordination: A Biblical-Historical View*, pp. 16—28.

12

Responsibilities
Toward Believers

1 TIMOTHY 5:1–2

Do not rebuke an older man, but appeal to him as if he were your father. Treat the younger men as your	brothers, ²the older women as mothers, and the younger women as sisters, with all purity.

This paragraph serves as something of a transition in the argument. On the one hand, it flows naturally out of 4:11–16, with a set of two more imperatives to Timothy (in the second person singular), and the content continues to reflect concern over Timothy's relationship to the church community, now in very specific ways related to his own youthfulness.

This content, on the other hand, also serves as a kind of introduction to what follows: a long section on widows, old and young (vv. 3–16), a section on elders (vv. 17–25), and a concluding brief word to believing slaves (6:1–2). Thus, in form and concern the paragraph belongs with 4:11–16; in content it anticipates, with some general guidelines, the specific instructions of 5:3–25.

5:1-2 / In 4:12 Paul reminded Timothy, "Do not let anyone look down on you because you are young." On the other side of that coin he now says, "See to it that you **do not rebuke an older man**." But **not** to **rebuke** (a Greek word that suggests harshness) does not mean he should not "exhort," or "urge," **an older man** toward right conduct. Therefore, Timothy should **appeal** (the same word translated "urge" in 1:3 and 2:1, and "preach" in 4:13 and 6:2) **to him as if he were your father**. In God's household (note the "family" theme in each case) there is an appropriate way for the leader to treat people—exactly as one does in one's own family (assuming a cultural ideal of great deference and respect in the home).

Similarly with other age groups, Timothy is to **treat** (the next three are all objects of the verb **appeal to**) **the younger men as your brothers,**

the older women as mothers (cf. Paul's attitude in Rom. 16:13), **and the younger women as sisters**. To the latter Paul adds **with all purity**, not only because of the special nature of this relationship, but perhaps also because this may have been an area of special concern with some in the community (see disc. on 2 Tim. 3:6–7; cf. 5:11).

Additional Note

5:1 / The word for **older men** (*presbyteros*, sing.) is the same as that translated "elders" in 5:17. Some, including the NEB, have therefore translated it thus here, implying the church leaders mentioned in 4:14 and 5:17–25 are in mind. But the context demands the more general term, which would include the "elders" but would not be limited to them.

13

Instructions for Widows

Show respect for widows who really are all alone. ⁴But if a widow has children or grandchildren, they should learn first to carry out their religious duties toward their own family and in this way repay their parents and grandparents, because that is what pleases God. ⁵A widow who is all alone, with no one to take care of her, has placed her hope in God and continues to pray and ask him for his help night and day. ⁶But a widow who gives herself to pleasure has already died, even though she lives. ⁷Give them these instructions, so that no one will find fault with them. ⁸But if anyone does not take care of his relatives, especially the members of his own family, he has denied the faith and is worse than an unbeliever.

⁹Do not add any widow to the list of widows unless she is over sixty years of age. In addition, she must have been married only once[h] ¹⁰and have a reputation for good deeds: a woman who brought up her children well, received strangers in her home, performed humble duties for fellow Christians, helped people in trouble, and devoted herself to doing good.

¹¹But do not include younger widows in the list; because when their desires make them want to marry, they turn away from Christ, ¹²and so become guilty of breaking their earlier promise to him. ¹³They also learn to waste their time in going around from house to house; but even worse, they learn to be gossips and busybodies, talking of things they should not. ¹⁴So I would prefer that the younger widows get married, have children, and take care of their homes, so as to give our enemies no chance of speaking evil of us. ¹⁵For some widows have already turned away to follow Satan. ¹⁶But if any Christian woman has widows in her family, she must take care of them and not put the burden on the church, so that it may take care of the widows who are all alone.

h. married only once *or* faithful to her husband.

The next two large sections, on widows and elders, now bring into specific focus instructions on how Timothy is to deal with the two problem elements in the church—the younger widows and the erring elders (probably the false teachers). Therefore, although the material is new, the letter has been moving toward these instructions right along. It will conclude, following these guidelines on the handling of specific cases, with a final, ringing exposure and condemnation of the false teachers (6:3–10) and a final exhortation to Timothy (6:11–16, 20–21).

This section on widows has long been one of the puzzling items in the letter. The problems are intrinsic. It begins and ends with concern about the care of widows. Yet in verse 9 widows are to "be enrolled" (RSV), and the description that follows in verse 10 has caused many to believe that an order of widows existed, who had prescribed duties and who in return were cared for by the church.

The greater urgency of the section, however, does not seem to be with the enrollment and duties of the older widows at all, but with the reprehensible activities of some younger ones. Indeed, the whole section basically presents two concerns: how to identify "real widows" (RSV) so that the church may care for them and why the younger widows are not to be "enrolled" as real widows but should marry a second time.

A careful analysis of the whole indicates that the second matter is the more urgent. It is true that there is genuine concern that the "real widow" be cared for. The first paragraph begins and ends on that note (vv. 3–4 and 8), and it is brought up again at the end (v. 16). But the *descriptions* of these "real widows" in verses 5–7 and 9–10 stand in sharp contrast to the activities of the younger ones (vv. 11–15). Thus the real widow seems to be set up as an ideal to contrast to the young widows in much the same way that Timothy is in contrast to the false teachers (4:6–16; 6:11–16).

We have already suggested (see disc. on 2:8–15) that the probable reason for this concern about the younger widows lies with their relationship to the false teachers. If we are correct in identifying them with the "weak women burdened by the guilt of their sins and driven by all kinds of desires" of 2 Timothy 3:6–7, then the unusual emphases of this section make good sense, not to mention its inordinate length compared with anything else in the letter.

5:3 / The section begins with the concern that the church **show respect for widows who really are all alone** (lit., "honor widows who truly are widows"). The imperative **show respect for** is not easy to translate, because in verse 17 the same noun implies some sort of remuneration, whereas in 6:1 it means simply **respect**. But the context of the whole section, finally clarified in verse 16, suggests that "honor" in the sense of "caring for" is what is in view. Whether they are also to be honored because they serve the church in some way is not so clear, but the commendation for good deeds in verse 10 would certainly allow it.

It must be noted that, even though this section has ultimately been shaped by the activities of the younger widows, the care of genuine widows is indeed a real concern. Such concern has deep roots in the OT (e.g., Exod. 22:22; Deut. 24:17, 19–21; Job 29:13; Ps. 68:5; Isa. 1:17) and very early found a place in the church as well (Acts 6:1–6; 9:36, 39, 41; James

1:27). The urgency here, however, is not to exhort the church to care for widows but to give guidelines to determine who qualifies for such care.

It is likewise too restricting to translate "who truly are widows" (repeated in vv. 5 and 16) as **who really are all alone**. The addition of the qualifier "left alone" in verse 5 and the argument of verses 4–8 make it clear that her being a true widow means at least that she is **all alone**, that is, that she has no family to support her. But it is equally clear that the "real widow" is one who is godly, given to prayer.

In the final analysis there are two classes of widows who do not qualify: those who have family and friends to care for them (vv. 4–5, 8, 16) and the younger widows of verses 11–15.

5:4 / This sentence gives the first qualification for identifying who are not "real widows," namely, those who have **children or grandchildren**. This verse, as well as verse 8, is directed toward widows' families, to remind them that caring for parents is their **first** order of business. Such care for **parents and grandparents** is *eusebein* (see disc. on 2:2; 3:16; 4:7–8): It is **to carry out their religious duties**. As with the overseers and deacons (3:4–5, 12), so with the community as a whole; genuine Christian behavior begins at home with **their own family** (*oikos*, "household," as in 3:4–5, 12, 15).

The next clause, **and in this way repay their parents and grandparents**, refers of course to a widowed mother or grandmother. This clause itself stands as a kind of appositive to the preceding one, so that it spells out *how* the children are "to put their religion into practice" (NIV)—by "repaying" the earlier care they themselves have received. Such "repayment" of a parent or grandparent **is what pleases God**, which is almost certainly a reflection on the fifth commandment.

5:5-6 / The next two verses give the second qualification for the "real widow"—she must herself be a godly woman. Although the sentences are descriptive, they are also clearly directed toward the widows themselves. Verse 5 begins, "Now the real widow" (GNB, **a widow who is all alone**), "being one who has been left all alone" (GNB, **with no one to take care of her**). It thus ties what is about to be said to verses 3 and 4. The "Now [Gk. *de*] the real widow" picks up the words of the opening imperative (v. 3); the phrase "being one who has been left all alone," meaning to be left without family at the death of her husband, reflects the widow whose case does not fit verse 4.

But such a widow must also be a woman who **has placed her hope in**

God. This language is obviously appropriate to widowhood, but more, it reflects the language of the psalms, where the poor (which includes widows) place their trust and **hope in God**. In this case her **hope in God** is found in her continuing **to pray and asking him for his help night and day**. The words **to pray and ask for** appear in 2:1 as the first two in that list. The words **night and day**, which reflect the Jewish understanding of the day (cf. Gen. 1; 1 Thess. 2:9), reinforce the concept of praying continually. The remarkable way this passage coincides with the description of Anna in Luke 2:36-38 leaves one with the distinct impression that what is given here is a kind of ideal for widowhood, similar to the ideal for Christian womanhood in 2:9-15.

Such an impression is strengthened by the contrast in verse 6. The true widow is a trusting, prayerful woman, who, contrariwise, does not **give herself to pleasure**. This verb, found also in James 5:5, regularly implies self-indulgence of all kinds and seems to fit the further description of the younger widows in verses 11-13. A woman such as these, Paul says, **has already died** (i.e., she is spiritually dead) **even though she lives** (the precise opposite of John 11:25).

5:7 / The urgency of the situation brought on by the behavior of the younger widows causes Paul at this point, immediately following verse 6, to exhort Timothy to **give them these instructions**. The following purpose clause, **so that no one will find fault with them**, seems to limit **these instructions** to what has been said to the widows in verses 5-6, not to the families in verse 4. This is further supported by the fact that it occurs here, not after verse 8, and that the word "blameless" (GNB, **find fault with**; the same word that began the list of overseers' qualifications, 3:2) refers to the kind of behavior spoken to in verses 5-6. An even stronger word of judgment to the families will follow in verse 8.

Thus, even though the thrust of the whole paragraph (vv. 4-8) is to define "genuine widows," who are to be "honored" by the church, this sudden imperative to Timothy to "charge" (same word as in 1:3, 5, 18) the widows with **these instructions so that** they might be "blameless" suggests very strongly that the problem lies here. Compare the similar urgency and the solemn interruption in 5:21.

5:8 / Before continuing these instructions for the widows themselves, however, Paul returns once more to the children and grandchildren of verse 4—this time to pronounce judgment on **anyone** who fails to **take**

care of his own. In so doing, he has created a chiastic (*ab ba*; see note on 3:16) structure in this first paragraph:

a words to the relatives (v. 4)
    b words to the widows (v. 5)
    b judgment on disobedient widows (vv. 6–7)
a judgment on disobedient relatives (v. 8)

Thus the **but** that begins this verse goes back to verse 4.

The combination **his relatives, especially the members of his own family** (lit., "his own household") is particularly emphatic about **family members** living under one's own roof. It perhaps suggests that someone in the believing community (cf. v. 16) was neglecting or turning over to the church the care of a widowed mother or grandmother. Such dereliction is tantamount to having **denied the faith**. One is hardly prepared for such a strong word of judgment for this kind of behavioral lapse. However, the next words, **and is worse than an unbeliever**, gives us the clue. It fits with the concern expressed throughout the letter (see 2:2; 3:1–7; 5:14; 6:1) that Christian behavior be circumspect before the outsider and therefore at least be ethically equal to theirs—although obviously more is expected as well. Paul is not condemning unbelievers; on the contrary, he is saying that they do in fact take care of their own widows. To *do* less is therefore to *be* less **than an unbeliever**; it equals a denial of **the faith**, since it is to act worse than a person who makes no profession of faith.

The second paragraph (vv. 9–16) of this section adds a new dimension to what has been said, and at the same time also helps to clarify some of the items in verses 4–8. Here we learn that a "genuine widow" is to be put on **the list of widows**, provided she has met further qualifications of godly living (vv. 9–10). Then the widow given to self-indulgent living (v. 6) is exposed in detail (vv. 11–13), with instructions for her to remarry (v. 14). Verse 15 makes it clear that all of this was very existential for the church and therefore is not a "church manual" on "what to do with widows in the ongoing church." A final word is added (v. 16) to bring the other urgent matter—genuine concern for widows—into focus also.

5:9–10 / The language of this sentence is what has generated much of the debate over this material. First, Paul speaks of **adding** a **widow to the list of widows**. The verb **add to the list** may be a general term ("count among") or a more technical term for "enrolling" or "enlisting" in some kind of official list. Second, Paul gives three qualifications: **she** must be

over sixty, **have been married only once**, and **have a reputation for good deeds**, five (or four) of which are then appended.

Some see this as indicating that there was by this time in the church an official "order of widows," who were expected to perform the "duties" of verse 10 and would in return be cared for by the church. But that seems to ask too much of what is actually said in the text, as well as to read far too much into the second-century evidence called in for support (see note). Furthermore, it seems to miss the greater concern of the paragraph, namely, verses 11–15.

More likely what is happening here reflects Paul's twofold concern: to establish further who shall be "counted among" the "genuine widows" to be cared for by the church; and to set these women in contrast to the younger widows who follow. In so doing, he is not so much setting up duties in verse 10—indeed, the Greek text hardly allows such an interpretation—as he is arguing that she must *already* (probably before as well as after her husband's death) have gained **a reputation for good deeds**.

That **she must be over sixty years of age** probably reflects the cultural norm both for "old age" as well as for the age beyond which remarriage would have been out of the question. The cultural ideal of a widow who has **been married only once** is amply illustrated from literature and epitaphs (cf. Luke 2:36–37). As with 3:2 this may mean "faithful to her one husband," but for a widow such faithfulness would extend to exclude a second marriage. The fact that younger widows are counseled against this ideal hardly speaks against this interpretation (as Hanson), since they are already, for several reasons, being excluded from among the genuine widows.

Her reputation (lit., "having had witness born of her") **for good deeds** includes four specific items, plus a generalizing conclusion (**devoted herself to doing good**; NAB, "In a word, has she been eager to do every possible good work?"). This last item suggests that the list is merely representative of her godliness, not definitive of her duties.

Included are (1) **A woman who brought up children well**. That this should be included as a good deed reflects both a cultural and a biblical ideal for womanhood (see disc. on 2:15). (2) A woman who **received strangers in her home**. As with the overseer (3:2) and all other Christians (Rom. 12:13), she must also have a reputation for "practicing hospitality." (3) A woman who has **performed humble duties for fellow Christians** (lit., "washed the feet of God's people," as in the first ed. of GNB; cf. 1 Sam. 25:41). As in John 13:17, it is not clear whether footwashing is intended literally or figuratively (for **humble** service). Part of the difficulty is a general lack of knowledge of local customs. At any event it certainly would be the kind of thing that if done literally, as seems very likely, would also be an example of her **humble** servanthood. (4) A woman who **helped people in trouble**. There is no way to know what specifically this might refer to. But it should be noted that these last three all reflect a woman of a generous and serving spirit. Such widows, alone in the world and full of good deeds, should be cared for by the church.

5:11-12 / But it is otherwise with **younger widows**; **do not include** them **in the list**, basically for two reasons: They become wanton and do not wish to remain as widows (vv. 11–12) and, as widows, they do not live according to the model of godly widows (v. 13).

Although some of the details of this sentence (vv. 11–12) are difficult, the point seems clear enough. The **younger widows** are **not** to be "counted among" the "real widows," first of all, because they will not remain as widows—**their desires make them want to marry**. And despite verse 14, it seems equally clear that this desire to remarry is seen as a judgment against them. This is quite in keeping with the perspective of 1 Corinthians 7:8–9, 39–40, where remaining a widow is called for but remarriage is conceded, although without the rather harsh verdict of this passage. The greater problem here is to reconcile the apparent harshness of this sentence about remarriage with the unequivocal desire of verse 14 that they do remarry.

The clue seems to lie in two places: First, Paul really does see widowhood as a high honor. He would, with Luke, certainly applaud Anna, as he does the widows of verses 9–10. But secondly, he says that **when they turn away from Christ** (NAB, "when their passions estrange them from Christ"), they **want to marry** (not the other way about, as the GNB). One often, as GNB, tends to read verse 11 in light of a certain understanding of verse 12 that implies that their very wish to remarry is tantamount to abandoning the faith in some way. But what is actually said is that their desire to remarry tends to outweigh their devotion to Christ, to the point that they will allow sensual desire to supersede that devotion.

Although Paul does not say so here, one wonders whether the problem is not related to what he says in 1 Corinthians 7:39, where he concedes remarriage to Christian widows. She is free to remarry, he says, only it must be "in the Lord" (GNB, "but only if he is a Christian"). What seems to be envisioned in the present passage is a remarriage that includes abandoning her faith in Christ; that is, her sensual desire is more important than her faith in Christ to the point that she would marry a nonbeliever in order to fulfill that desire.

By thus abandoning Christ in their wish to marry, they become **guilty of breaking their earlier promise to him** (lit., "incurring judgment because they have set aside the first faith"). Three options have been suggested for the meaning of this difficult clause: that the word *pistis* ("faith") means "pledge" and has to do with her pledge to widowhood (like a vow of "celibacy" in joining the "order"; cf. Hanson), which she nullifies by wanting to remarry; that the word *pistis* means "pledge" but has to do with her "faithfulness" to her first husband and thus reflects her abandoning the ideal of being married only once (v. 9); or that the word *pistis*, as it does elsewhere in these letters, means "faith in Christ" or "the faith," and her judgment comes in a kind of remarriage that has inherent in it an abandoning of Christ himself.

The first two options see the judgment in remarriage itself. Of these, the second is more easily reconciled with verse 14. Their desire to remarry is only one among other things (v. 13) that shows the younger widows to be going after Satan (v. 15). But Paul will in fact concede remarriage (v. 14) as the way of finally redeeming them, by thus allowing them to become women who will be well known for their good works, as the true widows have been. But all told, the third is probably the best option. Not only does it fit with the interpretation of verse 11, but it recognizes that the whole paragraph is concerned with redeeming these women for the "faith"—because some have already abandoned faith—rather than with simply getting them to see the fault in desiring to remarry.

5:13 / The second reason (*hama de kai*: "along with that they also") for not counting the younger widows among true widows is that in their present singleness they are not doing what they should be doing (prayer, v. 5, and the good works of vv. 9–10) and, they are doing things they should not.

First, **they learn to waste their time** (lit., "they are learning to be idlers") **in going around from house to house**. This stands in direct contradiction to the good works of the real widows, whose activities are primarily centered in their own homes. Given the existence of house-churches and the nature of the problems in Ephesus, one wonders whether the problem here is simply that of wasting their own time, and that of others as well, or whether perhaps it involves a disrupting of the various worshiping communities.

Such a possibility seems to be supported by what is said next. **But even worse** (lit., "not only are they idlers") implies that not only are they doing nothing *con*structive but their activities are actually *de*structive.

They have become **gossips and busybodies, talking of things they should not**. The translation **gossips** (*phlyaroi*) is quite misleading, suggesting on the basis of "going from house to house" that they are involved in "idle talk about the affairs of others." The Greek word, however, means to talk nonsense, or foolishness, and is used most often in contexts of speaking something foolish or absurd in comparison to truth. Thus, the young widows are described in terms very much like the false teachers, whose talk is foolish (1:6) and empty (6:20), and who are also **talking** about **things they should not** (cf. 1:6–7; 4:7; 6:3–4). It is probably as the "idle" purveyors of the false teachings that they are **busybodies**, and thus this becomes one of the reasons they are to be in all submissiveness and not to teach (2:11–12).

5:14 / The activities of the younger widows in promoting the false teaching is also the best explanation for what now appears as contradictory to verses 11–12. Precisely because the behavior described in verse 13 stands in contradiction to the godly behavior described in verses 9–10 (**so**, "therefore," in view of v. 13, perhaps also 11 and 12), the younger widows are now encouraged to emulate the good works of the older ones. But to do so they must **get married**, so that they may **have children and take care of their homes** (cf. v. 10). The verb **have children** is the same word as in 2:15, by which the problem in 2:9–15 is finally resolved. Paul's point is that by their giving attention to their true task, the satanically induced problems of the Ephesian church would tend to be brought to an end.

But does this in fact contradict verses 11–12? Not really. In verses 11–13, Paul was giving reasons why they should *not* be counted among the real widows—basically because they fail to meet the qualifications given in verses 9–10. Now he advises what young widows *should* do, since they are rejected as being "true widows."

Nor does this contradict 1 Corinthians 7:39–40. There Paul said she is *free* to remarry (a believer), but it is *better* to remain single. Here he still holds that it is *better* to be single (5:9, 12), but the situation in Ephesus has now caused him to *advise* remarriage (again, as vv. 11–12 imply, to a believer).

As so often in this letter (see disc. on 2:2; 3:6; 5:8), the behavior encouraged by Paul in contrast to the false teachings is **so as to give our enemies no chance of speaking evil of us. Our enemies** in Greek is "*the* enemy, or adversary." Most likely this refers to Satan, although of course the **speaking evil of us** is carried out through human instrumentality.

5:15 / The emphatic word order **for already** of this sentence indicates that we have now come to the urgency that called most of this section forth. This sentence also makes it clear that verses 11–13 are not simply hypothetical, as though Paul were saying, "This is what will most likely happen to young widows; therefore do not add them to the list."

The problem is existential—and urgent. **Some widows have already turned away to follow Satan**. As noted earlier (see disc. on 1:6), the language **turned away** recurs in 1 and 2 Timothy to reflect the situation there, both of the teachers and of those whom they have deceived. To describe such turning away as **to follow Satan** reflects what was said in 4:1–2 and what was implied of the women in 2:14.

5:16 / Having now dealt with the urgent problem of the defection of some of the younger widows, Paul returns a final time to the concern with which the section started—the care of the genuine widows. This sentence clarifies what was only hinted at before, that **the church** is to **take care of the widows who are all alone** ("the true widows"). In so doing he also repeats the substance of verses 4 and 8, that relatives should **take care of widows in** their own **family** so as **not** to **put the burden on the church**.

The surprising element in the sentence is the subject, **if any Christian** ["believing"] **woman**, rather than, "if anyone" (as in v. 8). So surprising is this term that some early copyists altered the text (thinking they were correcting it) to read "any believing man or believing woman."

It is this kind of surprise that reminds one of how immediate the historical situation and the substance of the letter would have been for its original recipient(s) and how far we are removed from it, which leads to so many of our uncertainties (as is true in so many places in the NT Epistles). Possibly this feminine subject tells us that the problem behind verses 4 and 8 was a specific case of a younger widow of means rejecting the care of a widowed mother and/or grandmother. She would then be the "anyone" in verse 8. If so, then even the concern for the care of "genuine widows" was prompted by the activities of one of the younger ones.

The alternative would be that a wealthy **Christian woman** such as Lydia (Acts 16:14–15) or Chloe (1 Cor. 1:11) had already taken in widows as a part of her household (the words **in her family** are not in the Greek text). Paul would then be encouraging this to continue, so that the widows who need care by the church (as defined in vv. 4–10) would not need to include such widows already receiving care.

Additional Notes

5:6 / A nearly identical expression about being dead while living occurs in Philo (*On Flight and Finding* 55) and is used by some as evidence of Philonic influence on the alleged pseudepigrapher. But such an idea is certainly not substantively Philonic. Indeed, it is found also in Rev. 3:1.

5:7 / The placing of this charge at such a point in the argument creates difficulties for those who deny Pauline authorship. Thus they must see it either as "a rather feeble connecting sentence" (Hanson) or simply fail to comment on it altogether (D-C). But like 5:21, the charge is such an urgent interruption, one wonders how a pseudepigrapher could have created it.

5:9-10 / It has sometimes been argued (e.g., Bernard) that vv. 3–8 and 9–10 refer to two groups: widows who are the recipients of charity and others who have official duties. The argument is that "the Church would not limit her charity to the needy by strict conditions like those of *vv.* 9, 10" (p. 81). But this argument misses the point of the whole section as well as puts too much weight on what is not certain—that an "order of widows" ministered in the church.

Kelly (p. 112) argues from statements in Ignatius (*Smyrnaeans* 13.1; *Polycarp* 4.1), Polycarp (*Philippians* 4.3), and Tertullian (*On the Veiling of Virgins* 9) that a ministering order of widows was fully developed in the second century. But none of these statements remotely suggests such a ministering order. To the contrary, the passages allude to their existence as a recognizable entity and reflect concern for their care, as does a similar passage in Justin (*First Apology* 1.67). Cf. the more cautious approach of Barrett (p. 74) and Lock (p. 56).

For a literary reference praising women who were married only once, see Seneca, *On Marriage* 72–77 (translated in J. P. V. D. Balsdon, *Roman Women* [Westport, Conn.: Greenwood Press, 1962], p. 208); for epitaphs, see M. Lightman and W. Ziesel, "Univira: An Example of Continuity and Change in Roman Society."

Some (e.g., Kelly; cf. Hanson) want the term **brought up her children well** to be a broader idea reflecting her duties, thus suggesting that it be translated "looking after children" and refer to caring for orphans. Likewise **received strangers in her home** is argued to refer to a duty, "alongside the overseers (cf. iii, 2), in the reception and entertainment of itinerant evangelists, preachers,"etc. (Kelly, p. 117). But that is to let the idea of "duties" determine the meaning of the text, and it fails to take seriously enough that this list reflects a **reputation** already gained through these kinds of **good deeds**.

The question of whether "foot-washing" had become a rite cannot be concluded one way or the other on the basis of the evidence available. The first clear reference to such a rite is found in Augustine, *Letters* 55.33.

5:13 / Both Kelly and Hanson point out that the word for **busybodies** is used in the neuter plural in Acts 19:19 as a euphemism for "spells" or "magic arts."

They make the interesting, but improbable, suggestion that this word is "discreetly veiled language" (Kelly, p. 118) for such incantations, and thus to talk **of things they should not** reflects the use of such formulas. Barrett's and D-C's suggestion, seeing this as reflecting the ideas of 2 Thess. 3:11, seems much closer to the mark.

5:14 / To suggest "the enemy" means **our enemies** is to bring forward an idea found nowhere else in 1 and 2 Timothy, namely, that there was some outside opposition in Ephesus. To refer to Satan as ultimately responsible for the activities of opponents (or unknown circumstances) is probably how one is also to understand 1 Thess. 2:18.

5:16 / Despite the fact that the reading "the believing woman" is clearly the more difficult and better attested, the NEB, Moffatt, and Easton prefer the reading "Christian man or woman" (NEB). Such a choice assumes the words *pistos ē* ("Christian man or") dropped out because a scribe's eye jumped over these words to the similar *pistē* ("believing woman"). But the evidence for *pistē* is so early and so diverse that one would almost have to argue for such a phenomenon to have occurred more than once, which seems highly unlikely.

14

Instructions About Elders

1 TIMOTHY 5:17-25

The elders who do good work as leaders should be considered worthy of receiving double pay, especially those who work hard at preaching and teaching. [18]For the scripture says, "Do not muzzle an ox when you are using it to thresh grain" and "A worker should be given his pay." [19]Do not listen to an accusation against an elder unless it is brought by two or more witnesses. [20]Rebuke publicly all those who commit sins, so that the rest may be afraid.

[21]In the presence of God and of Christ Jesus and of the holy angels I solemnly call upon you to obey these instructions without showing any prejudice or favor to anyone in anything you do. [22]Be in no hurry to lay hands on someone to dedicate him to the Lord's service. Take no part in the sins of others; keep yourself pure.

[23]Do not drink water only, but take a little wine to help your digestion, since you are sick so often.

[24]The sins of some people are plain to see, and their sins go ahead of them to judgment; but the sins of others are seen only later. [25]In the same way good deeds are plainly seen, and even those that are not so plain cannot be hidden.

As with the preceding section on widows, this section on elders has long been a puzzling one. Besides the difficulties in the meaning of "elders," there are the problems of context (What is it doing *here?*) and of structure (How do vv. 21-25 relate to 17-20, and what is the point of the personal admonitions to Timothy in vv. 21 and 23?). If our view of things thus far has been correct, then the answer to these puzzles lies with the historical situation in the church in Ephesus, namely, the activities of the false teachers.

The structure of the argument has some interesting similarities to the foregoing section on widows. Just as the concern there was twofold (genuine care for widows, in the context of some who have rejected faith), so here Paul begins with a genuine concern for the care of the elders (vv. 17-19) but then moves on to the greater urgency—the impartial reproof of those who are sinning (vv. 20-21). Replacements for the sinning elders are to be selected with great care (v. 22), because some people's sins, unfortunately, are not always immediately evident (v. 24). But never one to leave a matter on such a negative note, Paul adds that the same is often true of good deeds as well. Verse 23, the great puzzler, is a slight digression, prompted by what is said in verse 22 but expressed in light of both the asceticism of the false teachers (4:3) and Timothy's personal health.

But why is all of this said here, and not after chapter 3, for example, or 4:1-5? The answer to that probably lies in the overall argument of the letter. After the charge in chapter 1, Paul began with conduct in the community vis-à-vis the false teachers (chaps. 2-3) then moved to an exposure of the false teaching itself—and its source (4:1-5). After a renewed charge to Timothy and his own responsibilities in the situation (4:6-5:2), Paul gives instructions about how to deal with the two specific groups who are the problem element—some young widows (5:3-16) and their "captors," the straying elders (this section). Thus its location in the argument is related in part to the relationship of the false teachers to the younger widows and in part to the need finally to deal with the elders specifically (good and bad, but prompted by the bad).

5:17-18 / Verses 17 and 18 form a clear unit, connected by **for** (v. 18), telling Timothy and the church that **the elders** responsible for **teaching and preaching** are to receive **pay**, because Scripture supports it.

Although "elders" ("older men") were mentioned in 5:1, this is the first use of this term in 1 Timothy for those in positions of leadership (see the disc. on 3:1-7). That **the elders** include at least the overseers of 3:1-7 is supported by the evidence of Titus 1:5-7 and Acts 20:17, 28. Probably the term covers all the **leaders** and thus includes the deacons as well. The choice of the term itself (see also Acts 14:23; 15:4) undoubtedly reflects the church's Jewish heritage; elders were already a permanent feature of the synagogue (see BAGD, 2a).

Three things are said about them here: First, they **work as leaders** in the church. The term **work as leaders** is the one used in 3:4 and 12 for "managing" one's own family. Although not frequent in Paul, it is in fact the earliest term he uses for church leaders (1 Thess. 5:12; cf. Rom. 12:8); it is found in the singular as a noun in Justin Martyr (ca. A.D. 150; *First Apology* 1.67) for the one who by then had emerged as the single leader of a congregation. The concern here is that such **elders** do their work *well* (**do good work**).

Second, among **the elders** are **those who** do the **work** of **preaching and teaching**. Not all who **work as leaders** are also teachers, but the teachers are counted among the leaders. The verb **work hard at** was used earlier of his own and Timothy's ministries (4:10) and is one of Paul's favorites for labor in the gospel (e.g., 1 Thess. 5:12; 1 Cor. 15:10; 16:16;

Romans 16 throughout). What they **work hard at** is **preaching** (lit., "in word," or "in speaking") **and teaching**.

Third, such **elders** who **work hard** in word **and teaching** are to **be considered worthy of receiving double** "honor." It is clear from verse 18 that "honor" here includes at least **pay**. But it is highly unlikely that "double honor" means **double pay**, implying either twice as much as others who do not teach or twice as much as the widows. Rather it means "twofold honor," the honor and respect due those in such positions as well as remuneration. Paul thus reiterates a point made elsewhere that those who give leadership to the community in the ministry of the word should be maintained by the community (see esp. 1 Cor. 9:7–14; cf. 1 Thess. 2:7; 2 Cor. 11:8–9).

The **for** that begins verse 18 implies that what follows will explain or give support for the contention of verse 17, and what follows are two citations that argue for teachers' receiving a stipend (but with no hint of double pay). The formula that introduces the citations, **for the scripture says**, is typically Pauline (cf. Rom. 9:17; 10:11; 11:2; Gal. 4:30). The citations themselves reflect the same two kinds of supporting evidence as in 1 Corinthians 9:9 and 9:14. The first citation is from Deuteronomy 25:4: "**Do not muzzle an ox when you are using it to thresh grain.**" In Corinthians Paul had argued, in good rabbinic style, that Moses said that for the sake of Christian ministers, who should be supported by the people they are "laboring" for. The same obvious point is made here without the elaboration.

In the argument of 1 Corinthians 9:13–14, as something of an afterthought, Paul reminded the Corinthians that priests get their share of the food sacrifices and that Jesus, too, had commanded "that those who preach the gospel should get their living by it." There he appeals to the content of what he here cites: "**A worker should be given his pay.**" This is a saying of Jesus, exactly as it appears in Luke 10:7 (cf. the slightly different version in Matt. 10:10). It should be noted that in the only other instance where Paul actually cites the words of Jesus (1 Cor. 11:24–25), he also cites a version he shares with Luke, in contrast to Mark and Matthew. This should surprise us none, given Paul's apparent closeness to Luke.

The point of all this, of course, is *not* to give a definition of who elders are and what makes up their duties; Paul's concern is with the elders in Ephesus who are responsible for teaching. These men are **worthy** of twofold honor, including remuneration, when they do their **work** *well*.

Unfortunately, not all are doing so in Ephesus, so he must now address that problem.

5:19-20 / These verses take up a second item with regard to elders—the matter of discipline. Basically Paul gives two guidelines: (1) No unsupported charges are to be brought against an elder (v. 19), but (2) there must be *public* rebuke of those who are found guilty (v. 20). These obviously follow one another, and the second assumes that valid charges have been brought.

In charging that no **accusation against an elder** be listened to **unless it is brought by two or more witnesses**, Paul is not arguing for something that would be different for anyone else (see 2 Cor. 13:1; cf. Deut. 19:15; John 8:17; Heb. 10:28). But he says this in the hearing of the whole church for the sake of the elders, because of their visibility and position, on the one hand, and because some are in fact sinning (v. 20), on the other. This guideline protects an elder from capriciousness or maliciousness.

The second charge is probably the reason for the whole section, since verses 21–25 follow naturally out of this. **Those who commit sins** (lit., "those who *are* sinning," not "those who have sinned") are to experience public **rebuke**. This word could also mean "expose publicly," and is so translated by Kelly and Moffatt. In either case the emphasis is on the public nature (NASB, "in the presence of all") of the action. This may seem a bit harsh and unloving, but as the next clause indicates, it is for the sake of the whole community: **so that the rest may be afraid**. The word **afraid** in English has connotations that might mislead one. The point is that **the rest** will experience "the fear of God" by such a public rebuke, which seems to be supported by the solemn charge that follows (v. 21). But who are **the rest** who are to fear? The Greek word ordinarily means "the others in the same category." It at least means that here, that is, that the other elders will fear God. But given the public nature of the action, there is no reason to exclude **the rest** of the church as well—although the word was probably not used primarily about them.

As before, all of this makes sense if it is addressing the *ad hoc* situation in Ephesus. If so, then the emphasis is on verse 20, not verse 19. Timothy is to expose, or **rebuke**, those who are persisting in their waywardness. But Timothy is not to be on a vendetta, so Paul begins with the caution— no private or unsupported charges.

5:21 / That verse 20 is the real urgency is supported by this solemn charge to Timothy **to obey these instructions without showing any prejudice**

or favor to anyone. Although the GNB and others (e.g., D-C) see this verse as the beginning of a new paragraph, that is highly unlikely, given the less-than-urgent nature of the instructions that follow. **These instructions** have to do with seeing that *judgment* is carried out **without showing any prejudice**, on the one hand (as, e.g., in v. 19), and totally without favoritism, on the other. Such judgments must be carried out without prejudgment and partiality because Timothy and the church also stand before the heavenly tribunal (**in the presence of God and of Christ Jesus and of the holy angels**), both as their representatives in these actions and as those who themselves will someday be judged. For this kind of solemn charge, see also 2 Timothy 4:1 (cf. 1 Tim. 6:13).

The inclusion of **the holy** (lit., "elect") **angels** is unusual and serves to intensify the solemnity of the charge. "Elect" may either refer to the angels as the chosen ministers of God who carry out his will (Bernard) or serve as a contrast to the fallen angels (Kelly), probably the latter, given the context of judgment.

The urgency of this appeal is what makes one think that these are not simply general instructions in dealing with elders but reflect the specific, historical situation. But rather than "concrete . . . cases of scandal arising out of the preferential treatment which erring elders have received," as suggested by Kelly (p. 127), the concern is more likely with erring elders who, as false teachers, are having considerable influence in the community.

5:22 / The first imperative of this sentence, **be in no hurry to lay hands on someone**, follows naturally out of what has been said. Verse 20 indicates that some elders *are* sinning; verse 21 implies that their public exposure, or rebuke, must be carried out. Now some guidelines will be given for their replacement. The words **to dedicate him to the Lord's service**, although not in the Greek text, are therefore the correct understanding of "the laying on of hands" in this passage (cf. 4:14).

The point of this imperative is as in 3:6, that Timothy must exercise proper caution before laying hands on people to be recognized as elders. The reason for caution has to do with sin, that is, the fact that some are now sinning (v. 20) and that not all people's sins are readily apparent (v. 24).

This concern over the "sins" of some of the elders leads to the next imperative: **Take no part in the sins of others**. This could mean either "Do not be yourself involved in those kinds of sins that have caused some elders to need to be judged" or "By being hasty in the laying on of hands and thus ordaining people who turn out to be sinners, you thereby become a partner in their sins." This latter would seem to be supported by verses 24–25, where the reason for patience is spelled out in more detail. However, the additional imperative, **keep yourself pure**, seems to favor the first option, especially in light of the similar concern in 4:12. As in 4:6–16, therefore, the concern about the sins of others leads Paul to a short aside to Timothy personally about the ordering of his own life.

5:23 / Paul, however, is quick to qualify that brief personal word to Timothy. If he does not want Timothy sharing in their sins, neither does he want him to get caught up in the false teachers' view of purity, namely abstaining from certain foods (4:3), which apparently included wine.

Thus he says, **do not drink water only**. Every other known use of this verb in antiquity means to **drink water only** in the sense of abstaining from wine. Therefore, Paul is saying, by **keep**ing **yourself pure**, I do not mean to live as an "abstainer." Indeed abstinence is a part of the hypocrisy of the false teachers, one of their "sins." On the contrary, Timothy is to **take a little wine**, for the sake of his own good health. The use of wine will **help your digestion** (lit., "for the sake of your stomach"), **since you are sick so often**. In making this recommendation Paul is merely reflecting the widespread use of wine for medicinal purposes among both Jews and Greeks.

The mention of Timothy's being **sick so often** helps to contribute to the picture of timidity that emerges in the various texts (see disc. on 4:12).

5:24–25 / Having made a short digression by way of a personal note to Timothy, Paul now returns to the matter of the "sins" of the elders and gives his basic reason for no haste in laying on of hands. First, he says, **the sins of some people are plain to see, and their sins go ahead of them to judgment**. That is, when judgment finally comes on some people, it will be no surprise because of their evident sins. But Paul has been badly disappointed by some of the elders in this church, so he warns Timothy, **the sins of others are seen only later**.

What is not said throughout this section, of course, is what **sins** are involved. But the close proximity of the final indictment of the false teachers in 6:3–10 makes one wonder whether the hidden sins might not have been their pride, unhealthy desire to argue, jealousy (6:4), and especially, their avarice (6:5–10).

In typically Pauline style, however, the word of caution in verse 24 needs its positive counterbalance. The same thing that is true about some people's sins is also true of others' **good deeds**. Most **good deeds are plainly seen**, but in any case, **even those that are not so plain cannot be hidden** forever. This final clause is not so clear in the Greek. It could mean **even those** deeds **that are not** *good*, but in the light of what has already been said in verse 24, the GNB probably has given the right sense. It is also not clear when Paul thinks they might be no longer hidden. Kelly thinks at the judgment, but more likely it balances the word of verse 24 and thus also goes back to verse 22. Just as caution is required because some people's sins are not always immediately evident, so the same caution will work in Timothy's favor with regard to the **good deeds** of others. In time they, too, will manifest themselves, so that truly worthy people will eventually come to the fore.

Additional Notes

5:17-18 / This passage is the one where some would draw distinctions between "ruling" elders and "teaching" elders, although the "teaching" elders are also "ruling" elders. The problems with such distinctions have to do with how little we can say on the basis of all the evidence. What this passage does allow is that not all who were responsible for leading the church were in fact teachers. But beyond that the evidence is more ambiguous.

Bernard (p. lxxii) argues that the terms *episkopos* and *presbyteros* are not interchangeable, at least in the sense of an *episkopos* also being a *presbyteros*; but his argument is based on some very questionable exegesis. See disc. on Titus 1:5, 7. For a presentation similar to the one argued for in this commentary, see J. P. Meier, "*Presbyteros* in the Pastoral Epistles," pp. 325–37.

The formula **the scripture says** technically introduces only the citation of Deut. 25:4. If Paul wrote (or dictated) these words, then Luke's Gospel had almost certainly not yet assumed written form. Many would argue that by using the formula **scripture** for a saying in the Gospels, a later pseudepigrapher thereby betrayed himself. But in this case that will hardly work, since the term *scripture* meant *only* the OT for Christians until the end of the second century. Even a writer at the end of the first century is not likely to have referred to a word of Jesus as "scripture," even though, of course, his words were fully authoritative for them (see *graphē* in Lampe's *Patristic Lexicon* for the evidence; cf. 1 Clement, Ignatius, Polycarp, Justin, etc.). Very much as Mark says, "it is written in the prophet Isaiah" (1:2), and then cites Malachi and Isaiah, Paul writes, **the scripture says** and cites "scripture" itself, but then adds another authoritative word without necessarily meaning the term *scripture* to apply to it. It is altogether possible, as A. E. Harvey has argued, that the second citation was something of a proverb. However, Paul almost certainly intends to be citing what for him was already known to be a saying of Jesus.

It should also be noted that the citation of Deut. 25:4 differs from that in

1 Cor. 9:9, using the verb *phimōseis*, with the LXX, rather than *kēmōseis*. Some see this evidence for non-Pauline authorship. But if a pseudepigrapher *were* using 1 Cor. 9 for this passage, why not cite what is found there? In any case, 1 Cor. 9:9 follows the word order of the LXX, which is abandoned here, so neither citation fully reflects the LXX—which is typically Pauline. Note the two different citations of Isa. 40:13 in 1 Cor. 2:16 and Rom. 11:34.

5:19-20 / Kelly suggests that no emphasis should be placed on the present tense of the participle, "those who are sinning." But if Paul had intended to refer to some who had been "caught" in some kind of sin, one would have expected the Greek aorist, "those who have sinned." This verb form does in fact imply that "sinning" is going on.

Bernard (and others) would limit the phrase "in the presence of all" to "in the presence of all his *co-presbyters*" (p. 87), thus rejecting the translation **publicly**. But nothing in the context would suggest such a delineation. If that were Paul's intent, this would be the appropriate place for *loipoi*, **the rest**, making it clear that fellow elders were to be the "court."

5:22 / It has been argued by some (e.g., Lock, D-C), that the concern over elders is limited to vv. 17–19, since the word *elder* occurs only in those verses. Verses 20–25, then, deal with those in the community as a whole who sin, and v. 22 in particular deals with the laying on of hands for the reclamation of the penitent: "Don't be too quick to bring them back in," for the reasons given in vv. 24–25.

But against this stand these data: that one can make such good sense of the whole section as dealing with elders, that such a practice is unknown before the third century, and that laying on of hands elsewhere in the PE refers to recognizing special gifts for ministry.

5:23 / The place of this verse in its context has long been one of the puzzles of 1 Timothy, so much so that Moffatt omitted it altogether from his translation. For those who deny Pauline authorship, both its placement and the details of its content present problems. As Kelly correctly notes: "The very banality of the verse strikes a note of authenticity" (p. 128).

The medicinal use of wine, especially for stomach problems, is reflected in such varied sources as the Talmud (*Berakoth* 51a; *Baba Bathra* 58b), Hippocrates (*Ancient Medicine* 13), Plutarch (*Advice About Keeping Well*), and Pliny (*Natural History* 2.19). Kelly includes Prov. 31:6–7, but on what appears to be very doubtful exegesis.

15

Instructions for Slaves

1 TIMOTHY 6:1–2a

Those who are slaves must consider their masters worthy of all respect, so that no one will speak evil of the name of God and of our teaching. ²Slaves belonging to Christian masters must not despise them, for they are their brothers. Instead, they are to serve them even better, because those who benefit from their work are believers whom they love.

These two verses, which give instructions about the attitudes of slaves toward their masters, present difficulties for the contextual questions: What's the point of all this, and what is it doing here? The section is related to the preceding two sections on widows and elders in its concern for *timēs* ("honor," or **respect**; cf. 5:3, 17). However, it also differs considerably from them in that both of the previous sections were concerned that the church both honor genuine widows and worthy elders as well as discipline the erring ones. Here the words are strictly for the slaves, with no corresponding word either to the church or to the masters.

But why these words at all? First, it needs to be noted that slavery in the first-century Greco-Roman world was considerably different from that of recent American history; it was rarely racially motivated. Most people became slaves through war or economic necessity, although by the time of this letter, the majority of slaves were so by birth (born of slaves). Manumission, the freeing of slaves, was a common occurrence, although in many cases slavery was preferred to freedom because it offered security—and, in some cases, good positions in a household.

Nonetheless, slavery was the bottom extreme of the human social condition and was scarcely a desirable status. Slaves, along with most freedmen, constituted a large element of "the poor" to whom the gospel came with good news of acceptance with and freedom before God. From the evidence of the NT and beyond, it is clear that slaves made up a considerable portion of early Christian communities in the Hellenistic world. Hence this passage fits in with several others in the NT that speak to the behavior of slaves (Col. 3:22–25; Eph. 6:5–8; 1 Pet. 2:18–25; Titus

2:9–10) or their situation (1 Cor. 7:21–24; Philem. 10–17). It is perhaps worthy of note that the other two Pauline passages (Colossians and Ephesians) were written to churches in this same geographical area, and that in each case the word to slaves is much longer than the corresponding words to masters or parents and children. One wonders, therefore, whether the false teachings being propagated in this part of the world were putting considerable tension on the master/slave relationship in the church.

One cannot be sure that such was the case here, but it is altogether likely in view of the position of this section in the argument. Furthermore, as with the two preceding sections, the concern seems to be with the second item taken up, namely, the attitudes among believers. If so, then perhaps problems have arisen among some Christian slaves and their attitudes toward Christian masters similar to those among the younger widows. Has an over-realized eschatology or an elitist spirituality caused them to disdain the old relationships that belong to the age that is passing away? One cannot have certain answers to such questions, of course, but such a reconstruction does make sense of Paul's instructions. In any case, it is clear that Paul's concern, as before (2:2; 3:7; 5:14), is not only with relationships within the church but also with how the problem was affecting the church's witness.

6:1 / Because Paul mentions believing masters in verse 2, it is common to interpret verse 1 as referring to attitudes toward pagan masters. That is altogether possible. However, it seems very likely that verse 1 is introductory—and general—and therefore has to do with attitudes toward all masters, but that even here it is anticipating verse 2.

Those who are slaves, Paul says, **must consider their masters worthy of all respect**. GNB has omitted a redundant "under yoke" following **slaves**. That redundancy, "slaves under yoke," may point to the chafing of some under their pagan masters; or it may be a Pauline reminder to the believing slaves that even though their status in Christ is that of freedmen, they are otherwise still in the old social order.

The instruction that they should **consider their masters worthy of all respect** tends to strike a discordant note to twentieth-century ears, especially if such masters were pagans and unworthy of "all honor." What if their orders violated conscience? Why not speak out *against* slavery? But Paul's instruction is quite in keeping with the entire NT understanding of Christian behavior as essentially reflecting servanthood (cf. Mark 10:43–45; 1 Cor. 9:19; Gal. 5:13; Eph. 5:21; 1 Pet. 2:16–17) and of Christian existence as basically eschatological—the form of this world is passing away; as an eschatological people, our present status is irrelevant (1 Cor. 7:17–24, 29–31). Therefore, precisely because it is essentially irrelevant, one may live one's present status in loving obedience.

The purpose clause, **so that no one will speak evil of the name of God and of our teaching**, picks up the recurring concern about how the church is viewed by those on the outside (see disc. on 2:2; 3:7; 5:14). Such a concern would be immediate if Christian slaves for some reason were being disobedient to pagan masters. But it could equally reflect a concern for how pagans might view the church if they were seeing Christian slaves throwing off "the yoke" of their Christian masters.

The language **speak evil of** (lit., "blaspheme") **the name of God** comes from Isaiah 52:5, a text similarly quoted by Paul in Romans 2:24 to mean that God's name was being dishonored among the Gentiles because of the "ungodly" behavior of God's people, who bore his name. In this passage such dishonor to God's **name** means that the outsiders **will speak evil of our teaching**—the gospel itself. For Paul, to blaspheme the gospel is to blaspheme the source of the gospel, and Christian slaves should do nothing as slaves to cause that to happen.

6:2a / As suggested above, this verse probably gives us the *ad hoc* reason for this short section. There is an untranslated *de* at the beginning of the sentence. If verse 1 were dealing with Christian slaves/pagan masters then this *de* is adversative: "*But* those slaves . . ." If verse 1 is more general, or prefaces verse 2, then the *de* means, "Indeed, those slaves . . ."

The latter would seem to make more sense of the whole of verse 2. The problem in the church probably lay right here: **Some slaves belonging to Christian masters** were disdaining them as masters. The word **must not despise** is the same as that translated "look down on" in 4:12 and almost certainly means something like that here (cf. RSV, "be disrespectful," or NAB [and Kelly], "take liberties with"). Being on equal footing in Christ does not mean that one is thereby free to abuse the slave/master relationship; it does mean that the old relationship is worked out in an entirely new sphere. Thus, the reason given for slaves not treating Christian masters with disdain is precisely *because* [for] they are their brothers. Being **brothers** together in God's household sets the whole relationship on a new footing.

In light of that new relationship, believing **slaves** must **serve them even better**, not meaning better than they would pagans, but "all the more so" because they are fellow **believers**. The words, **who benefit from their work**, could refer to the masters, and be translated "who devote themselves to good works" (BAGD; D-C), or "who reciprocate in good service" (Hendriksen). But these seem to miss the emphasis on the service of slaves for masters, **whom**, Paul says, these slaves **love**—although this translation might reflect a more ideal condition than the word *agapētoi* warrants. What Paul intends is that these masters are **believers** and therefore part of the brotherhood who are "beloved" (or "dear to us").

Thus Paul's word to Christian slaves is, Be Christians toward fellow Christians whom you serve as slaves, (1) so that unbelievers will not blaspheme God's name or our teaching and (2) because such masters are *fellow* believers.

Additional Notes

6:1 / Barrett has made the intriguing suggestion that this material belongs to what has immediately preceded, and that the correlative *hosoi* ("as many as") that begins the sentence should be translated, "As many elders who are slaves should . . . " If so, that would in fact intensify the problem as suggested in the interpretation presented here.

6:2 / It is not exactly clear in the Greek how the clause **for they are their brothers** is to be understood. The NIV, and others, take it to go with the verb: "not to show less respect for them [just] because they are brothers." That would fit well with our understanding of v. 1. Nonetheless, that seems to miss the point of the *hoti* (**for**, "because"), which, as in GNB, more likely serves to qualify the whole clause and explains *why* they **must not despise them**.

D-C argue that *agapētoi* should be translated "beloved by God," on the grounds that "slaves who must be admonished to serve cannot, in the same injunction, be expected to act out of love for the masters." But besides taking quite a low view of the power of grace, that argues for a meaning of the word not found elsewhere in Paul.

16

Final Indictment of the False Teachers

1 TIMOTHY 6:2b–10

You must teach and preach these things. ³Whoever teaches a different doctrine and does not agree with the true words of our Lord Jesus Christ and with the teaching of our religion ⁴is swollen with pride and knows nothing. He has an unhealthy desire to argue and quarrel about words, and this brings on jealousy, disputes, insults, evil suspicions, ⁵and constant arguments from people whose minds do not function and who no longer have the truth. They think that religion is a way to become rich. ⁶Well, religion does make a person very rich, if he is satisfied with what he has. ⁷What did we bring into the world? Nothing! What can we take out of the world? Nothing! ⁸So then, if we have food and clothes, that should be enough for us. ⁹But those who want to get rich fall into temptation and are caught in the trap of many foolish and harmful desires, which pull them down to ruin and destruction. ¹⁰For the love of money is a source of all kinds of evil. Some have been so eager to have it that they have wandered away from the faith and have broken their hearts with many sorrows.

Paul is about to bring the letter to its close. One more time he exhorts Timothy to **teach and preach these things**. But before he concludes, the exhortation to teach and urge **these things** leads Paul to go back over the two dominant concerns one more time: the false teachers and Timothy's role.

In this section he presents the final exposure and indictment of the false teachers. Much that is said in the first paragraph (vv. 3–5) is reminiscent of the language of chapter 1. But much is new as well. Here the picture is filled out in greater detail. These teachers, who are the reason for everything—Timothy's presence in Ephesus, this letter, the "falling away" by some in the church—turn out to be **swollen with pride**, having a sickly craving for arguments. And all of this, it turns out, because the bottom line is greed. They think "godliness" is a means of financial gain—just like the religious hucksters of the Artemis cult (Acts 19:23–41).

The second paragraph (vv. 6–10), therefore, is Paul's response to their greed and pronounces their sentence of ruin.

6:2b / For the final time in this letter, Paul charges Timothy **to teach and preach** ("urge," or "exhort") **these things**. As before (3:14; 4:6, 11; 5:7, 21), **these things** refer to what has already been said, in this case at least to 5:3–6:2, although given the concluding nature of what follows it may go all the way back to 2:1.

6:3-5 / In contrast to **these things** that Timothy is to teach, there are those who **teach a different doctrine** (the same word translated "teaching false doctrines" in 1:3). Verses 3–5 are a single conditional sentence in Greek, of a type known as a simple present particular, meaning that both parts of the sentence express the way things actually are. Such conditional sentences are used when an author is quite certain of his premise. In this case the protasis (the "if" part, v. 3) describes what the false teachers are *not* doing that they should be doing. The apodosis (the "then" part, vv. 4–5) describes the results.

Most of what is said in verse 3 has been said before. That they **teach a different doctrine** was said in 1:3; **the true words** are a repetition of the medical metaphor of "sound doctrine" first met in 1:10 (a metaphor that is slighted in the GNB; unfortunately so, since the whole sentence is a play on this metaphor); the combination of **true words** and **teaching** to describe the truth of the gospel occurred in 4:6; and that the teaching must be that which "accords with godliness [*eusebeia*]" (RSV, which captures the sense better than **the teaching of our religion**) reflects the "mystery of godliness" in 3:16 and the true godliness that stands in opposition to godless myths in 4:7–10.

What is new in the sentence is the expression **the true** ("healthy," "sound") **words of our Lord Jesus Christ**. Some think this refers to what is found in a written Gospel, and thus means the words spoken by Christ. But that misses Paul's emphasis, namely, that the false teachers have abandoned the truth of the gospel, which comes from our Lord Jesus Christ himself, who is the ultimate origin of the faith, or "godliness," Paul proclaimed. Their abandonment of Christ (i.e., his gospel) is their grave error.

Verses 4–5 describe the results of the false teachers' having turned away from wholesome teaching. Paul begins by characterizing the false teacher himself in two ways: First, he **is swollen with pride and knows nothing** (cf. the NEB's "pompous ignoramus"). This indictment reflects a common motif in Paul, namely, that those who abandon the truth of the gospel think of themselves as wise, or "in the know," and are thus bloated with self-importance, when actually they **know nothing**. (See disc. on 1:7; cf. Titus 1:15–16 and the argument in 1 Cor. 1:18–4:21; 8:1–3; 2 Cor. 10–12; Col. 2.)

Second, **he has an unhealthy desire to argue and quarrel about words**. With a nice play on words, Paul describes the opposite of "healthy teaching" as a sickness, a "morbid craving" (BAGD) for controversy. We have already noted that their teachings lead to "foolish discussions" (see disc. on 1:4, 6); we were forewarned by what was said in 2:8 that such "discussions" engendered strife. Now all of this is spelled out clearly (cf. 2 Tim. 2:23–25; Titus 3:9). What are at first merely "idle speculations" (1:4) eventually lead to **quarrels about words** (a compound word in Gk. from *logoi*, "words," and *machē*, "a fight," meaning "word battles").

This **pride** and sickly craving **to argue** and carry on word battles in turn have two devastating effects. First, they lead to a disrupted and unhealthy *community*. When teachers abandon the gospel and argue and quarrel, this brings on **jealousy** or envy—people take sides—which is one of the deadly sins (see Gal. 5:21; Rom. 1:29). **Jealousy** usually breaks out in **disputes** (or "strife, quarreling"). This, too, is on the lists in Galatians 5:20 and Romans 1:29. The two words appear together characterizing Paul's opponents in Philippians 1:15 (cf. 1 Cor. 3:3). **Disputes** (cf. Titus 3:9) in turn bring on **insults** (cf. Titus 3:2) and **evil suspicions**. How self-centered is the teaching of error—and how destructive! And how often it is done in the name of "knowledge" and wisdom (cf. 1:7; 6:20–21)! Finally, these result in **constant arguments**. This word occurs only here in the NT and means either "constant friction" (Moffatt) or "mutual irritation" (Goodspeed) between people.·

The second result of their "sickness" is what it has done to the false teachers themselves. Their **minds do not function** (lit., "corrupted in mind"); this carries the sickness metaphor to its final conclusion: decay and corruption of the mind. That such corrupted minds **no longer have** (lit., "have been robbed," or "defrauded of") **the truth** repeats a common theme. Believers have come to know **the truth** (2:4; 4:3; 2 Tim. 2:25); these men have been robbed of it (cf. 2 Tim. 2:18; 3:7, 8; 4:4).

Their corrupted **minds, no longer** having **the truth**, are finally evidenced in their thinking that **religion** (*eusebeia*, "godliness"; cf. 3:16; 4:7–8) **is a way to become rich**. This final indictment, hinted at in 3:3, 8, seems to unmask what they have been up to all along. The Greek word *porismos* means simply "financial gain" or "profit"; to translate **to be-**

come rich probably carries the quantity factor too far. These men were teaching because for them it was a means of "turning a dollar." Although we are not told precisely what this meant for them, teaching philosophy as a "cloak for greed" (1 Thess. 2:5, RSV) was a common accusation in antiquity (see, e.g., Dio Chrysostom, *Oration* 32) and one that Paul had to defend himself against on at least one occasion (1 Thess. 2:4–9; cf. Gal. 1:10). Probably these false teachers have picked up some clues from the culture and are teaching to curry people's favor—and eventually their money. It should be noted finally how many things said in these verses have their counterpoints in the qualifications for church leaders in 3:2–12.

This matter of the false teachers' greed is such a crucial one that Paul now turns to give it some special attention (vv. 6–10). He responds to their thinking of *eusebeia* as a way of turning a profit in two ways: in verses 6–8, by showing the relationship between true godliness and money—the latter is irrelevant to the former—and in verses 9–10, by showing the true end of those who desire money.

6:6 / This verse stands in immediate contrast to the last words in verse 5, with a striking play on terms. *They* think godliness "is a way to become rich." **Well** (Gk., *de*, "indeed"), they are right. There *is* great profit (now used metaphorically) in godliness **(religion does make a person very rich)**, provided it is accompanied by a "contented spirit" (Moffatt, Kelly), that is, **if** one **is satisfied with what** one **has** and does not seek material gain.

The word *autarkeia* ("contented spirit") expresses the favorite virtue of Stoic and Cynic philosophers, for whom it meant "self-sufficiency," or the ability to rely on one's own inner resources. There are some (D-C, Hanson, Brox, et al.) who see that philosophical tradition as lying behind all of verses 6–8, and they translate "if it is coupled with self-sufficiency" (D-C; cf. NEB, "whose resources are within him"). But Paul has already used this word in an analogous context in Philippians 4:11; there he "turned the tables" on the Stoics by declaring that genuine *autarkeia* is not *self*-sufficiency but *Christ*-sufficiency. For Paul, therefore, the word means "contentment," the empowering *Christ* gives to live above both want and plenty (Phil. 4:13). Moreover, there is no hint in 1 Timothy that its author considered anything like self-sufficiency to be a virtue. Life for him is all of grace and dependent on God's mercies (1:12–17), and his ministry comes from Christ who appointed and empowered him for it (1:12).

Paul's point, of course, is to combat the greed of the false teachers and, incidentally, of any others who might be tempted to lean in that direction.

6:7-8 / Paul now gives two reasons why a "contented spirit" should accompany "godliness" and why, when it does, one has "great profit." The first reason (v. 7) is primarily eschatological: We can take nothing with us at death (or the Parousia), so material gain is irrelevant—and greed is irrational. The Greek text is indicative—and particularly awkward (see note)—in form, but the questions of the GNB capture the sense. **We** brought **nothing** material **into the world** at birth; nor **can we take** anything **out of** it at death. This sentiment can also be found among the Stoics, but it is precisely the point of view of Job 1:21: "Naked I came from my mother's womb, and naked shall I return" (RSV; cf. Eccles. 5:15; Philo, *On the Special Laws* 1.294–95, where he expresses himself in terms very close to Paul's and then supports it by alluding to Job 1:21). Paul's emphasis is on the second clause, **we can take nothing out of the world**; in light of this eschatological reality, greed makes no sense at all.

So then, Paul adds as a second reason, **if we have food and clothes, that should be enough for us** (lit., "we shall be content," the verb of the same noun as in v. 6). Again, it is argued that this "reflects the spirit of Stoicism" (D-C, p. 85), which indeed it does. But it also reflects more precisely the teaching of Jesus (Luke 12:22–32; Matt. 6:25–34), which in both Gospels is independently placed in a context condemning greed (Luke 12:16–21; Matt. 6:24). Thus, the contacts with Stoicism are incidental; what seems to have happened in verses 7–8, on the contrary, is very similar to what Paul did in 5:18: He gives an allusion to an OT text (v. 7) followed by an allusion to the teaching of Jesus (v. 8).

The point is clear enough. Godliness is not something to make material gain in or from (v. 5); rather, it is itself the greatest gain (v. 6). True godliness, however, is accompanied by contentment (v. 6). Since we can take nothing with us at death (v. 7), if we have life's essentials, we can be content with these (v. 8); and such an attitude obviously excludes greed.

6:9-10 / Now, by way of contrast with verses 6–8 **(but)**, Paul returns to the false teachers and their avarice. What is said in verse 9, of course, reaches out more broadly and is true of all **those who want to get rich**. The letter after all is written so that God's household will behave in accordance with the truth and true godliness. Thus he generalizes at first by describing the results of greed that would apply to all. But verse 10 makes it clear that some have already capitulated, which ties the whole paragraph to verse 5.

Thus verses 9–10 are Paul's final sad commentary—and judgment—on the false teachers. They **want to get rich**.

The results of greed are a downward spiral. First, the greedy **fall into temptation**. Avarice has a way of causing people to look in directions they may never have looked in otherwise. And as the hunter well knows, the enticement **(temptation)** leads to the prey's getting **caught in the trap**. The two go together. The **trap** in this case is **many foolish and harmful desires**. The word **desires** often has sexual connotations, but there is no reason to think so here. The **many foolish desires** are probably for wealth itself, which are **foolish** because wealth has nothing to do with true godliness and **harmful** because they ultimately **pull** the greedy **down** (lit., "plunge them") **to ruin and destruction**.

Paul's point is that the very desire for wealth has inherent spiritual dangers, partly because (vv. 6–8) wealth itself is unrelated to godliness in any way and partly because (v. 9) the **desire** is like a **trap** set by Satan himself to plunge one into spiritual **ruin**. To put that in a different way: Why would anyone **want to get rich**? Wealth has nothing to do with one's eschatological existence in Christ; on the contrary, the desire leads to other desires that end up in ruin, of which truth the false teachers themselves are Exhibit A (v. 10).

In verse 10, a much-abused text, Paul concludes his indictment of the false teachers in two ways. First, he cites, or alludes to, a well-known proverb that supports his contention in verse 9 about the evil effects of the desire for wealth. Second, he brings all of this into focus on the false teachers, who vividly illustrate the truth of what was said in verse 9.

For, Paul says, now as supporting evidence, in this case the common proverb is quite right: **The love of money is a** [better, "the"] **source of all kinds of evil**. This text neither says, as it is often misquoted, that **money** is the root of all evil nor intends to say that every known evil has avarice as its **source**. A proverb very much like this ("The love of money is the mother-city of all evil") is widely attested in Greek antiquity. It is the nature of proverbs to be brief, particular expressions of a truth, often imprecise, and for effect, often overstated. Thus, Paul's point is not theological precision on the relationship of greed to all other sins. Both Jews and Greeks had long before come to realize the disastrous effects that avarice had on people's lives, and they expressed it in proverbs. Paul is simply citing a proverb as support for his contention that greed is a trap full of many hurtful desires that lead to all kinds of sin.

The living proof of all this is found in the wayward elders in the church of Ephesus. **Some have been so eager to have** money **that they**

have wandered away from the faith. They have "sold out" the gospel for different doctrines and in so doing **have broken their hearts** (lit., "impaled themselves") **with many sorrows**.

Thus their final indictment is a tragic one, and for Paul a painful one. Here were good men, who had emerged as leaders in the church of Ephesus. But they had allowed themselves to be ensnared by Satan. Who knows how or why they became enamored of new ideas, fell in love with speculative interpretations, or made themselves look good by appealing to an ascetic ideal, an elitist Christianity. But underneath they had come to love money, and it did them in. They went astray **from the faith** and pierced themselves through, as with a sword, **with many sorrows**.

Additional Notes

6:3–5 / A textual addition that seems to have developed in the Latin church, but eventually came to predominate, concludes v. 5 with a personal note to Timothy: "Keep away from such people." But not only does this imperative interrupt the argument, the Greek is not the language of the PE (*paraitou*, not *aphistaso*, is used elsewhere to express this idea: 4:7; 2 Tim. 2:23; Titus 3:10). See also Metzger, *TCGNT*, p. 643.

6:6 / Some see the *de* in this sentence as an adversative (e.g., NIV, "but godliness with contentment is great gain"). But that misses the *irony* of the sentence.

D-C make the remarkable statement about this paragraph that there is an "absence of a strict connection between the sayings, which are simply placed in a series" (p. 84). On the contrary, the whole paragraph is a clear argument and is specifically relevant to the situation in Ephesus (cf. Kelly, p. 138).

For *autarkeia* as a Stoic-Cynic virtue, D-C cite Stobaeus, *Ecl*. 3, "Self-sufficiency is nature's wealth," and Epictetus, "The art of living well is contingent upon self-control and self-sufficiency, orderliness, propriety, and thrift."

6:7–8 / The awkwardness of v. 7 is due to a *hoti* ("because" or "that") that introduces the second clause. Various attempts have been made to make sense of it including: a textual variation that would read, "it is certain that" (RSV margin); an attempt to make the second clause causal in some way (thus Barrett: "There is no sense in bringing anything into the world with us, *because* we shall not be able to take anything out); and ignoring it altogether, or seeing it as resumptive and thus not translating it (e.g., Bernard, GNB). For the textual variation, see Metzger, *TCGNT*, p. 643.

For the sentiment of this verse found elsewhere, see in Judaism, Eccles. 5:15; Wisd. of Sol. 7:6; and Philo; and in Greco-Roman thought, Seneca, *Epistle* 102.25.

The two words translated **food** and **clothes** are not found elsewhere in the NT, but neither are they the words used by the Greek philosophers in such contexts (cf. Diogenes Laertius 6.106; 10.131). The second word literally means "covering" and could refer to shelter, but "clothing" seems much more likely in this context.

It is perhaps noteworthy that D-C should be so enamored of the affinities of this verse with Greek philosophy that they should fail altogether to mention the much closer affinities with Jesus himself.

6:9-10 / Although it is possible to translate the Greek *rhiza* ("root") as *a* **source**, both the emphatic word order and the so-called Colwell's rule (that a definite predicate noun that precedes its verb is usually without the article, as in John 1:1) suggest the intent is *the* source, as in all the other expressions of the proverb.

For the proverb itself, see Stobaeus, *Ecl.* 3; Diogenes Laertius 6:50; Ps.-Phocylides 42; Polycarp, *Philippians* 4:1; cf. Test. Jud. 19:1; Diodorus Saeculus 21.1; Philo, *On the Special Laws* 4.65; Apollodorus Comicus, *Philadelph. fragmenta* 4.

For the use and meaning of biblical proverbs, see Douglas Stuart, in G. D. Fee and D. Stuart, *How to Read the Bible for All Its Worth*, pp. 195–98.

17

Final Exhortation to Timothy

1 TIMOTHY 6:11–16

But you, man of God, avoid all these things. Strive for righteousness, godliness, faith, love, endurance, and gentleness. [12]Run your best in the race of faith, and win eternal life for yourself; for it was to this life that God called you when you firmly professed your faith before many witnesses. [13]Before God, who gives life to all things, and before Christ Jesus, who firmly professed his faith before Pontius Pilate, I command you [14]to obey your orders and keep them faithfully until the Day when our Lord Jesus Christ will appear. [15]His appearing will be brought about at the right time by God, the blessed and only Ruler, the King of kings and the Lord of lords. [16]He alone is immortal; he lives in the light that no one can approach. No one has ever seen him; no one can ever see him. To him be honor and eternal power! Amen.

The preceding paragraph, with its final indictment of the false teachers, was the third such exposure of these teachers in 1 Timothy (cf. 1:3–7, 18–20 and 4:1–5). In the two preceding instances, the direct word against the false teachers was accompanied by a corresponding personal word to Timothy to resist them and to be their antithesis in the church in Ephesus (cf. 1:3, 18–19; 4:6–16). In each case that charge included an appeal to Timothy's spiritual beginnings (1:18; 4:14). That pattern is what we meet again in this paragraph. Even though Paul has yet a further word on riches, to the already wealthy (vv. 17–19), the final exposure and indictment of the false teachers calls forth an immediate final exhortation to Timothy.

Even though it is not altogether clear as to what events either in Timothy's past (vv. 12 and 14) or in Christ's life (v. 13) form the basis of the appeal, the argument of the paragraph itself is easy enough to discern. Paul begins with a series of four imperatives (vv. 11–12), exhorting Timothy both to avoid the sins of the errorists and to carry on the present struggle of the faith until the final triumph, and to do so by keeping his own calling and confession before him. This leads to a solemn charge (vv. 13–14), which in turn leads to a final doxology (vv. 15–16) full of rare descriptions (for the NT) of God's eternal majesty. The whole of the appeal is placed against the backdrop of Christian eschatological certainties.

But what is Paul calling him to? Is the concern for his ministry per se, or is it for his personal commitment to Christ that would also include his ministry? The answer to this question is most likely to be found in 2 Timothy 4:6–8, where in similar language Paul reflects on his own spiritual history and is there almost certainly referring to his ministry—although for Paul that also includes his whole life in Christ.

6:11–12 / The exhortation of these verses stands in emphatic contrast to the "sickness" and greed of the false teachers: **But you, man of God, avoid all these things**. The **all** supplied by GNB is not in the Greek text; it is an attempt (correctly) to help the reader to see that **these things** Timothy is to **avoid** (lit., "flee") include more than just the greed of verses 6–10. They also include the "different doctrines" (v. 3, and therefore also 1:4 and 4:3, 7), as well as the divisiveness and destructiveness of their controversies (vv. 4–5).

The vocative, **man of God**, although somewhat unusual (cf. 1:18; 6:20; 2 Tim. 2:1), is used again as an appellation for Timothy as minister of the Word of God in 2 Timothy 3:17. The background for the term is the OT, where in each case it refers to one of God's servants or agents: Moses (Deut. 33:1; Josh. 14:6), David (Neh. 12:24), or one of the prophets (1 Sam. 9:6; 1 Kings 17:18; 2 Kings 4:7). It is probably called forth here as a sharp contrast to the false teachers, who, by having abandoned Christ, have also ceased to be servants of the Word of God.

Rather (there is a *de*, "but," untranslated in GNB), Timothy is to **strive for** virtues and behavior that are the opposite of the false teacher and that reflect the gospel. **Righteousness**, in the sense of "uprightness" in conduct (cf. Phil. 1:11), and **godliness** (*eusebeia*; cf. 3:16; 4:7–8; 6:5–6), having to do with one's relationship toward God, reflect the horizontal and vertical dimensions of the faith, with emphasis on observable conduct. **Faith** and **love** are the supreme Christian virtues and together appear on every such list in the PE (1 Tim. 1:5; 2:15; 4:11; 2 Tim. 2:22; Titus 2:2). The final two, **endurance and gentleness**, are especially Pauline understandings of Christian attitudes (see, e.g., Gal. 5:23; Col. 3:12; Eph. 4:2)—and are clearly appropriate to the appeal of this paragraph, that Timothy continue in the noble contest until the end.

From the contrasts of fleeing the pursuits of the false teachers and pursuing those graces that reflect the gospel, Paul flows naturally into a second set of imperatives, calling for perseverance. The first, **run your best in the race of faith**, is, as GNB translates, an athletic metaphor from the Games. The metaphor could imply running (suggested by the collocation with "finishing the course" in 2 Tim. 4:7) or boxing/wrestling (cf. the usage in 1 Cor. 9:25–27) or simply, more generally, any of the contests (thus Montgomery, "keep contending in the noble contest of the faith"). The word **faith** has the article, *the* **faith**, but it is not clear whether Paul means for him to contend for the gospel itself (thus referring back to vv. 3–10) or whether it includes that but now, also, in light of verse 11, refers in a broader way to the whole of his Christian life as a great contest requiring discipline and purpose. Probably Paul's concern is to address Timothy both regarding his own personal life and his faithfulness in ministry, but that depends in part on how one interprets the rest of the paragraph. In any case, the present tense of the verb implies a persevering in the struggle.

The second imperative, **win eternal life for yourself**, extends the metaphor to focus on the prize (lit., "*the* **eternal life** unto which you were called"). Both the language (**eternal life**, cf. disc. on 1:16) and the nature of the metaphor, as well as the parallel in 2 Timothy 4:7–8, imply that the main thrust of the imperative is eschatological; that is, Timothy is to continue in the contest until it consummates in triumphant conclusion. But as usual in such texts, there is an inherent tension between the "already" and the "not-yet" of the believer's eschatological existence. The imperative, **win for yourself** (or "take hold of," RSV, NIV), implies a present action as well. **Eternal life** is that **life** to which **God called** him, and which is therefore already in his grasp (cf. 4:8).

The idea that **God called** Timothy to life is a thoroughly Pauline idea (cf. 1 Cor. 1:9; 7:17–24; 2 Thess. 2:14). God's is the prior action, but there must also be response. In this case Paul reminds him of **when you firmly professed your faith** (lit., "confessed the noble confession") **before many witnesses**. Some argue that this refers, as with 1:18 and 4:14, to Timothy's call to ministry and his own "ordination vows." But the call here is not to vocation per se, but to Christian life as vocation. It is far more likely, therefore, that the event Paul refers to is that of Timothy's becoming a believer, very possibly to his baptism, by which event, or in conjunction with it, he confessed his **faith before many witnesses**.

Thus the imperatives exhort Timothy to persevere both in his life in Christ *and* his ministry (the present) and thereby to secure the awaited prize (the future), by being reminded of his beginnings—God's call and his own response (the past).

6:13–14 / The imperatives in verses 11–12, which are very personal words to Timothy but given in the context of the false teachers, are now summed up in the form of a solemn charge (cf. 5:21). As one who stands **before God** and **Christ Jesus**, Timothy is charged (GNB, **I command you**; cf. 1:3, 5, 18) to "keep the commandment."

The **God** before whom Timothy is given this charge is described as the one **who gives life to all things**. Actually this verb (*zōogoneō*), which may mean "to endue with life," means in both the LXX and NT (Luke 17:33; Acts 7:19) "to preserve, or maintain, life." Given the context as a call for steadfastness, this nuance seems the more likely here. Similarly, the appeal to **Christ Jesus** as the one **who firmly professed his faith before Pontius Pilate** is almost certainly to be understood as an encouragement to steadfastness on Timothy's part. But it is not at all certain what Paul specifically intended. GNB has correctly recognized the parallels with Timothy's confession in verse 12. But the verb and preposition are different here. Literally, it reads, "who *bore witness* to the noble confession **before** [or, "in the days of"] **Pontius Pilate**." If it means **before Pilate**, then it could refer to either a confession he actually made or his having borne a good witness during trial. If it means "in the days of" Pilate, then it could refer to either the witness of his entire life and ministry or, more specifically, to his death. Good reasons can be given for all of these, although the appeal to Christ's death—which was *for* Timothy—as His own witness and noble confession is particularly appealing.

As Timothy is called upon to stand before the life-preserving God and the Christ who made the greatest "confession" of all, Paul now charges him "to keep the commandment [GNB, **I command you to obey your orders**] without spot and above reproach." Most of the difficulties in understanding the paragraph stem from this charge, which is at once quite ambiguous, yet the point of everything.

The "commandment" he is charged to keep has been variously understood as the exhortations in verses 11–12, collectively understood; an alleged baptismal charge to which allusion is made in verse 12; an ordination charge (the GNB's **obey your orders and keep them faithfully** seems to fit here); the whole Christian faith thought of as a kind of new law; and a commandment to Timothy to persevere in his own faith and ministry, as in 4:16, so as to save himself and others. This last seems to move in the right direction in light of the context itself and the similar expressions in 6:20 (to guard what has been entrusted to him) and 2 Timothy 4:7 ("I have kept the faith"). Thus it really summarizes the basic thrust of the letter, that Timothy will best stem the tide of the false teachers as he himself is steadfast in his faith and calling.

That the emphasis is still on his perseverance is made plain by the eschatological addition, **until the Day when our Lord Jesus Christ will appear**. The word **appear** (*epiphaneia*), which is used of Christ's incarnation in 2 Timothy 1:10 (cf. Titus 2:11), is the word used consistently in these letters to refer to the Second Advent (2 Tim. 4:1, 8; Titus 2:13). Paul's more common term is *parousia*; however, both words occur together as early as 2 Thessalonians 2:8. Although it is not certain, this usage may be another reflection of the Hellenistic religious terminology that occurs frequently in these letters.

It is often suggested that this last phrase implies that Paul (or a later author) is writing at a time when the imminence of the Parousia is no longer alive. But that is to read far too much into one phrase (read, of course, in light of 2 Tim. 2:6–8). It also misses the eschatological urgency of these letters (1 Tim. 4:1; 2 Tim. 3:1), as well as the ambiguity elsewhere in Paul. As early as 1 Corinthians, the very letter that has so much of the urgency in it (7:29–31), Paul speaks of "awaiting the revelation" (1:7; cf. 11:26), and in Philippians one finds the same tension between his readiness to die (1:21–23) and "awaiting the Lord Jesus from heaven" (3:20–21). If the present text implies anything, it is that Timothy will experience the Parousia, and that scarcely reflects the perspective of a church settling in for a long life in the world.

6:15-16 / What is of greater moment about this mention of the Second Advent is Paul's insistence in verse 15 about both its certainty ("which God will bring about," NIV) and its resting in God's sovereign control (**at the right time**, lit., "in his own time"). This last phrase occurred in 2:6, and will recur in Titus 1:3, to express the coming of Christ and the gospel as in God's own time. What was true of his first **appearing** will likewise be true of the second.

This emphasis on the Second Advent as belonging to God's sovereignty then triggers a series of epithets about God that are at once striking and majestic. Each of the terms has OT and Hellenistic Jewish counterparts; taken together they sound a note for the transcendent majesty of the Eternal God matched in the NT only by the splendid imagery of Revelation 4. Kelly is probably right in calling this "a gem from the devotional treasury of the Hellenistic synagogue which converts had naturalized in the Christian Church" (p. 146).

The God who will bring about Christ's **appearing** in his own time is:
The blessed and only Ruler: The word **Ruler** (*dynastēs*), used of God only here in the NT, is common in Hellenistic Judaism (e.g., Ecclus. 46:5; 2 Macc. 12:15) and emphasizes God's sovereignty. Paul has used the

language **blessed** of God in 1:11 and **only** in 1:17 (cf. 2:5). The latter, of course, is primary in Judaism (Deut. 6:4), whereas **blessed** had become the currency of the period (cf. Philo, *On Abraham* 202; *On the Special Laws* 1.209; 2.53; Jos. *Against Apion* 2.190; *Antiquities* 10.278).

The King of kings and Lord of lords: These terms have separate histories in the OT. **King of kings** was first used of the Babylonian and Persian emperors (Ezek. 26:7; Dan. 2:37; Ezra 7:12) but by the time of 2 Maccabees 13:4 is applied to God. **Lord of lords** was used in conjunction with "God of gods" to express God's absolute sovereignty over all other "deities" (Deut. 10:17; Ps. 136:2–3). The two terms had already been joined in Judaism in 1 Enoch 9:4; they are joined again as designations of Christ in Revelation 17:14 and 19:16. Here they emphasize God's total sovereignty over all powers, human and divine.

He alone is immortal. See the discussion on 1:17, where a different word is used. (This word occurs with **blessed** in Philo, *On the Unchangeableness of God* 26, evidencing its use in Hellenistic Judaism.)

He lives in light that no one can approach. The description reflects Psalm 104:2. It arose in Judaism in conjunction with the concept of his blinding glory, which no human eye can see (cf. Exod. 24:15–17; 34:29–35; 1 Kings 8:11). The motif of God as pure light is played on from several angles in the Johannine literature (John 1:7–9; 3:19–21; 1 John 1:5–7).

No one has ever seen him; **no one can ever see him** (cf. "invisible" in 1:17). These clauses reinforce his dwelling **in light that no one can approach** and reflect a common OT theme (Exod. 33:20; cf. 19:21). The emphasis in these last two items is not the Greek one, that God is unknowable, but the Jewish one, that God is so infinitely holy that sinful humanity **can** never **see him** and live (cf. Isa. 6:1–5).

To him be honor and eternal power! (On the **Amen**, see disc. on 1:17.) This final ascription turns the whole thing into a doxology. But instead of "honor and glory" as in 1:17 (and elsewhere), Paul says **honor and eternal power**, thus picking up the theme of God's absolute sovereignty begun in verse 15. For this combination, see Revelation 5:13 (cf. "glory" and **eternal power** in 1 Pet. 4:11; Rev. 1:6).

But why, one wonders, this doxology with these glorious ascriptions right here? It begins in a context emphasizing the certainty of the Second Advent to be brought about by the Mighty God. Is this to reinforce courage in Timothy to persevere in the difficult situation in Ephesus? Perhaps. But it is probably for the sake of the church as well. Ephesus was not only the haven of Artemis, but an early center of emperor worship as well. This doxology, therefore, is Paul's parting shot that the God with whom the church has to do in the gospel of Christ is none other than the supreme Ruler of the universe, the Lord over all other lords.

Additional Notes

6:11-12 / D-C use a rather circuitous route to argue that the vocative **man of God** "refers to any Christian . . . who has been endowed with the spirit of God, and who henceforth 'serves' God." It would in this sense also be applicable to Timothy, "the prototype of a 'man of God' since he is the leader of the congregation" (p. 88). But again this seems to miss the genuinely *ad hoc* character of this Epistle.

It is common to argue (e.g., Gealy, Hanson) that Paul could never say, "strive for righteousness or faith," since in Paul those are "God's gifts, not man's achievements" (Gealy, p. 452). But such an argument confines Paul's own usage of these terms too narrowly. **Righteousness** as "right-standing" and **faith** as "trusting response" are indeed God-given; but both terms also become Christian virtues, which, like **love**, are both gifts (Gal. 5:22) and something pursued (1 Cor. 14:1).

For a presentation of the argument that the athletic metaphor in v. 12 applied to both Timothy's life and his ministry, see V. C. Pfitzner, *Paul and the Agon Motif* (see note on 4:7-8), pp. 177-81. The view that vv. 12-14 reflect a baptismal confession and charge may be found in the commentaries by Kelly and Spicq, among others. For a defense of "ordination vows," see the commentaries by D-C, Barrett, Hanson, and esp. the article by E. Käsemann, "Das Formular einer neutestamentlichen Ordinationsparänese," in W. Eltester, ed., *Neutestamentliche Studien für Rudolf Bultmann* (Berlin, 1957), pp. 261-68. The argument for a confession before a tribunal was presented by J. Thurén, "Die Struktur der Schlussparänese 1. Tim. 6, 3-21," *ThZ* 26 (1970), pp. 241-53.

6:13-14 / The word *epiphaneia* ("appearing") had a considerable history in Hellenism as a technical term for "a visible manifestation of a hidden divinity, either in the form of a personal appearance, or by some deed or power by which its presence is made known" (BAGD). It thus became a common term in Hellenistic Judaism for "manifestations" of the power of God (see, e.g., 2 Macc. 2:21; 3:24; 3 Macc. 5:8; *Letter of Aristeas* 264; Jos., *Antiquities* 2.339; 3.310). For an argument for a more strictly Jewish background for this term, see M. McNamara, *The New Testament and the Palestinian Targum to the Pentateuch*, AB 27 (Rome: Pontifical Biblical Institute, 1966), pp. 246-52.

6:15-16 / Hanson (pp. 112-13) minimizes Spicq's attempt to argue for this doxology as a Pauline composition. But there are no good historical reasons for denying the possibility that Paul has borrowed heavily from the Hellenistic synagogue, where he himself spent so much time.

18

A Word for Those Already Rich

1 TIMOTHY 6:17–19

Command those who are rich in the things of this life not to be proud, but to place their hope, not in such an uncertain thing as riches, but in God, who generously gives us everything for our enjoyment. [18]Command them to do good, to be rich in good works, to be generous and ready to share with others. [19]In this way they will store up for themselves a treasure which will be a solid foundation for the future. And then they will be able to win the life which is true life.

After the exalted language of the preceding doxology (vv. 15–16), these words come as such a surprise that some scholars doubt whether they really belong here and suggest they are an interpolation. But if the "logic" of all this is not perfect, there is no difficulty in seeing what has happened.

Paul was bringing the letter to its close with a final word against the false teachers, a word that turned out to be such a strong judgment against their greed that it included a warning to "*all* those who want to get rich" (v. 9). But there would have been some in the church who were *already* **rich in the things of this life** (v. 17), especially those in whose homes the church met (cf. also 5:16). However, since Paul's first concern was with the false teachers and Timothy's own role in combating them, he followed his words about them with an immediate final exhortation to Timothy— to keep contending in the noble contest until the End. Now, having given that noble charge to Timothy, he returns to say a few words for the already rich, lest they feel condemned by verses 6–10.

What he says to them is again predicated on his thoroughly eschatological view of Christian existence, but without the asceticism of the false teachers. Such people may be rich in the things that pertain to the present life; but these things, even though they may be for our enjoyment, belong only to this present age and are therefore uncertain. The rich should therefore hold their possessions loosely, not placing their hope in them but being generous with them, using them for good works. Their hope must be placed in God and their riches used to store up treasures for the future, for the life which is true life. One might note that there are some close affinities in this passage (including 6:7) with Ecclesiastes 5:8–20.

6:17 / Timothy is called upon to give one more **command** (the same word as in 1:3, 5; 4:11; 5:7), this time to **those who are rich in the things of this life**. Paul nowhere else speaks to the wealthy as a class, but that merely indicates the *ad hoc* nature of his letters. His theology of the cross clearly recognizes the OT stance that God champions the cause of "the poor" (1 Cor. 1:26–31). And in Corinth, where the majority are in this class, he gives the wealthy a considerable dressing down for their treatment of the "have-nots" (11:20–22). But he must often have been the beneficiary of the well-to-do (cf. Philem. 1–2, 5–7, 22), so he is hardly against the wealthy as such. He simply expects those who "have" to be generous to those who "have not" (Rom. 12:8, 13; 2 Cor. 9:6–15).

Paul's **command** strikes at the twin perils of the wealthy: **not to be proud**, or **to place their hope . . . in such an uncertain thing as riches**. The word for **proud** is a compound of two words that mean "to think, or cherish, exalted thoughts" (KJV, "high-minded"; cf. Rom. 11:20; 12:16). Pride is the deadly sin of all people, but it seems to be the special curse of the rich. Not only that, but they tend to put altogether too much confidence **in such an uncertain thing**. The *uncertainty* of wealth is underscored in the Proverbs (23:4–5); here this theme is tied to its being only for **this life** (lit., "the present age," in contrast to "the coming one," v. 19). Putting hope in wealth was denounced by the prophets (e.g., Jer. 9:23) and seems to be the one thing above others that closed the door of the Kingdom to some in the ministry of Jesus (cf. Mark 10:17–27; Luke 12:15, 16–21).

As with all others (4:10), especially the poor widows (5:5), the wealthy are **to place their hope in God**. As in the two earlier texts, salvation expressed as **hope in God** carries a decidedly eschatological connotation, as well as that of trust and endurance.

But Paul is no ascetic. That the wealthy should not place confidence in their wealth does not carry with it an attitude of total rejection. Thus, even here he takes a swipe at the false teachers (see disc. on 4:1–5 and 5:23). **God**, he says, **generously gives us everything for our enjoyment** (cf. 4:3–4; see also Eccles. 5:19–20). **Enjoyment**, however, does not mean self-indulgent living (5:6). The reason **everything** may be enjoyed lies in the recognition that everything, including one's wealth, is a *gift*, the expression of God's gracious generosity.

6:18 / The "enjoyment" of "everything" as God's generous gift leads away from "high-mindedness" and false security to the freedom of giving generously. Indeed, the whole of this verse repeats in four ways that the wealthy are to use their wealth for the benefit of others. It begins, **command them** (repeated from v. 17 for clarity) **to do good**, which is then repeated with a play on "riches" (cf. 2 Cor. 8:9): **to be rich in good works**. And in case that is not clear, **good works** is further defined as being **generous and ready to share with others**. This last item, an adjective form of *koinōnia* ("fellowship"), implies the liberal sharing **with others** what is one's own. Hence true "riches" is found in the giving, not in the having.

6:19 / Having used "riches" metaphorically in verse 18, Paul now extends the metaphor eschatologically. In so doing, he makes what appear to be some very un-Pauline comments (as in 2:15). But the awkwardness is the result of the metaphor(s), not of a theological shift. Salvation is to put one's hope in God; it is not achieved by "buying shares in heaven"!

Nonetheless, very much as Jesus said (Luke 12:33; 18:22; cf. Matt. 6:19–21), Paul reminds them that **in this way** (by generous giving to the needy) **they will store up for themselves a treasure . . . for the future**. This is not to "buy off" God or to earn salvation. It is simply to emphasize again what was begun in verse 17. True "riches" have not to do with earthly possessions, which are uncertain and belong to this age only. True "riches" are obtained by the generous and liberal sharing of the "riches of this life." Thus for the rich to give riches away is not to suffer loss but rather **to store up for themselves a treasure** of a different kind. It is, in a typically Pauline shift of metaphors, "to store up" **a solid foundation for the future**. In this regard one should note the sayings of Jesus that Luke has placed together in 12:32–33. The Kingdom as gift leads to selling possessions and giving to the needy and thereby providing for oneself "a treasure in heaven."

Finally, lest any of this be misunderstood, Paul sets forth the nature of the treasure, the same eschatological goal that all believers share (cf. 1:16; 4:8, 10; 6:12): **And then they will be able to win the life which is true life**. This clause is very similar to what was said to Timothy in 6:12, except that what was an imperative there is here a purpose clause, expressing the final goal of their hope in God and their resultant good works. By so doing they **win** ("secure for themselves," or "take hold of") **the life which is true life**, meaning, of course, eternal life, eschatologically understood.

Additional Note

This paragraph is actually a single sentence in Greek that makes a considerable play on the word "riches" and related ideas. The word itself occurs four times in four different forms (a substantival adjective, "the rich"; an abstract noun, **riches**; an adverb, "richly" [GNB, "generously"]; and a verb, **to be rich**). Thus "the rich" are not to trust in **riches**, but in God who "richly" gives all things, and therefore are **to be rich** in good deeds, which then, to extend the metaphor, is their way to **store up . . . a treasure** for the future.

6:17 / That the riches of this age should be for one's **enjoyment** creates considerable difficulty for those who see 6:6–8 as the author's borrowing from Cynic-Stoic ideals (cf. Gealy, "it is another tone than 6:7–10," p. 457). But it fits in well with Paul's own view set forth in Phil. 4:10–13, where the believer, strengthened by Christ, can live above *both* want (6:6–10) *and* plenty (6:17–19).

The Final Charge

1 TIMOTHY 6:20–21

Timothy, keep safe what has been entrusted to your care. Avoid the profane talk and foolish arguments of what some people wrongly call "Knowledge." [21]For some have claimed to possess it, and as a result they have lost the way of faith. God's grace be with you all.

That the preceding paragraph was an afterthought to verses 6–10 is now made clear as Paul brings the letter to its conclusion. The letter could well have ended with a final greeting after the solemn charge and doxology of verses 13–16 (see Phil. 4:20–23 and 2 Tim. 4:18–22, where the final greetings immediately follow a doxology). But the need to reassure the already rich prevented that, so now he repeats the charge to Timothy and does so, as always, vis-à-vis the false teachers. Thus the two great urgencies of the letter, and especially from 6:2b and on, are expressed one final time.

What is most remarkable about this conclusion is the lack of any final greetings. All the Pauline letters, including this one, sign off with a final grace, or benediction. But only 1 Timothy and Galatians have no greetings from Paul and friends to the recipient and friends (cf. 2 Tim. 4:19–21; Titus 3:15). To the very end this letter is characteristically "all business," and except for some new language, this final charge merely summarizes that business.

6:20 / With a final vocative, O **Timothy** (the emotional interjection "O," untranslated in GNB, occurs often in Paul [6:11; Rom. 2:1, 3; 9:20; Gal. 3:1]), Paul appeals to his younger colleague: **Keep safe what has been entrusted to your care**. This is the third such charge in the letter (cf. 1:18–19; 6:13–16; the fourth if one sees 4:6–10 as a charge). The imperative (lit., "keep the deposit") is a metaphor, drawn from common life, reflecting the highest kind of sacred obligation in ancient society, namely, being entrusted with some treasured possession for safe-keeping while another is away. A person so entrusted was under the most binding sacred duty to keep "the deposit" safe (see, e.g., Lev. 6:2, 4, where this word, *parathēkē*, is used in the LXX; cf. Tob. 10:13; and esp. 2 Macc. 3:15). So Paul concludes the letter by placing Timothy under such a trust (cf. 1:18; 2 Tim. 1:14).

But what is the "deposit" that **has been entrusted** to Timothy's **care**? Many think the "sound teaching" of the gospel, which he then is to entrust to others (2 Tim. 2:2). But that is probably to read too much back into 1 Timothy from the considerably altered circumstances of 2 Timothy. The best answer is to be found in the context of the entire letter: Timothy has been entrusted with the task of resisting the false teachers, which in this letter includes keeping his own life pure (4:11–12; 5:22–23; 6:11–12), and of faithful proclamation and teaching of the truth (4:13–14; 6:2b; etc.).

Such an interpretation is supported by the rest of verses 20–21. One final time Paul charges Timothy to resist the teachings of the wayward elders: **Avoid the profane talk** (cf. 4:7) **and foolish arguments** (cf. 1:6; and esp. 2 Tim. 2:22, where this imperative is repeated nearly verbatim) **of what some people wrongly call "Knowledge."**

Many are ready to see these last words as the giveaway that the author is really battling some form of Gnosticism (from the Gk. word *gnōsis*, "knowledge") and are thus ready to date the letter much later than Paul's time (see also disc. on 1:4). But that is to make far too much of this language. The essential matters for a Gnostic heresy (speculations about spiritual hierarchies and the soul finding its salvation by "knowledge" of its escape from the world of matter) are simply not found in 1 Timothy. Paul has previously had trouble with those who opposed his gospel in the name of wisdom and *gnōsis* (1 Cor. 1:10–4:21; 8:1–13), which had become a semitechnical term for philosophy. Furthermore, deviations from the gospel in the name of philosophy had already plagued the churches in this area just a few years earlier (see esp. Col. 2:1–10). This relationship to Colossians more than adequately explains this use of words.

6:21 / For Paul, even though such false teaching must be resisted, there is always a tragic element to what has happened in Ephesus: **For some** (the false teachers and their followers?) **have claimed to possess it, and as a result they have lost the way of faith**. It is this losing **the way of faith** ("miss the mark with regard to the faith," BAGD; cf. 1:6) by **some** within the church that has exercised Paul throughout and is ultimately the reason for the letter (see 1:3–7, 19–20; 4:1–2; 5:15, 20; 6:10; cf. 2:14; 3:6–7; 5:5–6, 24–25).

Finally, with an abruptness that has within it its own pathos, Paul signs off with his typical benediction: **God's grace be with you all**. This final plural **you** (**all** is added to make that clear) is certain evidence that Paul intended the letter to be read aloud in the church(es). Some see the lack of greetings as evidence against Pauline authorship but then must argue that the author outdid himself in imitating Paul in 2 Timothy and Titus. One can only guess at the reasons for this lack. A similar thing happens in Galatians, where in the "signature" (6:11-18) he takes one last swipe at the opponents (vv. 11-15), but prays for peace on those who follow the gospel (v. 16), before the final grace. It is perhaps worthy of note that these two letters lack the opening thanksgiving as well (see disc. on 1:3). Apparently, the distress of the situation in both these churches makes the letters to them all business.

The **grace** itself is a typically Pauline feature. The standard "good-bye" in ancient letters was *errōsthe* (lit., "be strong"), found in the letter of James (Acts 15:29) and the letters of Ignatius (cf. 2 Macc. 11:21, 33; Jos. *Life* 227, 365). But as with the salutation (see disc. on 1:1-2), Paul "Christianizes" all the formal elements of the ancient letter. Thus he prays for **God's grace** to **be with** them **all**. Only here and in Colossians is it so terse. Since **God's** is not in the text, and in the other letters it is the "grace of our Lord Jesus Christ," that is probably his intent here as well.

The final "amen" in the KJV is not in the earlier manuscripts; it was added at a later time when the letter was regularly read in church as a part of Scripture.

Thus 1 Timothy comes to a conclusion. Paul is away and hopes to return (1:3; 3:14-15; 4:13); meanwhile the situation in Ephesus is so desperate that he had to leave (or send) his younger colleague to "straighten out the mess." Above all else, Timothy himself is to guard this trust, by not being attracted to so-called knowledge and by doing his best to stop its pervasive influence in the church. As we have seen throughout, everything in the letter in some way touches this concern.

Additional Notes

Because of the words *antitheseis* (**arguments**) and *gnōsis* (**knowledge**), it was argued in an earlier time (Baur, Harnack) that this final charge was an anti-Marcionite interpolation (since Marcion [ca. 150] was called a Gnostic and his work was entitled *Antitheseis*). But no one currently subscribes to such a view.

6:20 / For a helpful discussion of *parathēkē* in 1 and 2 Timothy, see esp. W. Barclay, "Paul's Certainties, VII. Our Security in God—2 Timothy i.12." For a powerful illustration of the meaning of the term, see the story of the Apostle John and the young man he entrusted to a bishop's care as a *parathēkē* as told by Clement of Alexandria, *The Rich Man's Salvation* 42 (Loeb, pp. 357-65).

1

Salutation

From Paul, a servant of God and an apostle of Jesus Christ.

I was chosen and sent to help the faith of God's chosen people and to lead them to the truth taught by our religion, ²which is based on the hope for eternal life. God, who does not lie, promised us this life before the beginning of time, ³and at the right time he revealed it in his message. This was entrusted to me, and I proclaim it by order of God our Savior.

⁴I write to Titus, my true son in the faith that we have in common.

May God the Father and Christ Jesus our Savior give you grace and peace.

What is striking about the salutation to Titus is its considerable differences from those in 1 and 2 Timothy, especially its lengthy elaboration of Paul's apostleship (vv. 1–3), a phenomenon found elsewhere only in Romans. These verses, which form a single, extremely complex sentence in Greek, conclude with a note about his apostleship as a trust. The main thrust, however, emphasizes the *purpose* of that apostleship: to bring God's people to faith and truth, and thus to life. That life, he explains, was promised by God before time began but has only now been revealed—through Paul's preaching.

What is less clear is the reason for such an elaboration in *this* letter. Only in part does it seem to exist to authenticate Paul himself. The central concern is with the truth of the gospel that the Cretans have embraced as the result of Paul's preaching, a concern that seems to fit the prophylactic nature of the letter. Paul wants to encourage the people in their new faith, which is based on the gospel (**the truth**) and contains the hope of eternal life. At the same time the content of the salutation serves as a safeguard or warning against any false teaching or teachers.

1:1a / Paul's first self-designation in this letter, **a servant of God** (lit., "God's slave"), suggests at the outset that the life-setting of this letter is not as urgent as in 1 and 2 Timothy. Although this exact form does not appear earlier, Paul begins both Romans and Philippians with the designation "Christ Jesus' slave." Given his own personal attitude toward his ministry and relationship to his Lord (see, e.g., 1 Cor. 4:1–2, 9; 2 Cor. 2:14–17), this would probably be his favorite, or ordinary, self-designation. But most of his letters, including this one, are written out of urgencies that require his apostolic authority; hence he adds, **an apostle of Jesus Christ**.

1:1b–3 / Ordinarily Paul qualifies his apostleship by some note as to its source (e.g., "by the will of God"); here, as in 2 Timothy, he feels constrained to say something about its purpose. **I was chosen and sent to help the faith of God's chosen people** paraphrases (correctly) "according to the faith of God's elect" (KJV). The word "according to" does not mean that his apostleship was regulated by their faith in some way or that it was in keeping with orthodoxy. Rather it connotes *goal* or *purpose* (BAGD, II, 4) and could be translated "with a view to." His apostleship existed "for **the faith of God's** elect" (NIV), which probably refers to their coming to trust Christ, not to their advancing in or better understanding *the* faith. The designation **God's chosen people** (or "elect"; cf. Rom. 8:33; Col. 3:12; 2 Tim. 2:10) is another typical instance of Paul's referring to believers as the people of God by using OT language (e.g., Ps. 105:43; Isa. 65:9, 15; cf. his use of "saints").

His apostleship is also "with a view to their coming to know the truth" (GNB, **to lead them to the truth**). In the PE **the truth** regularly recurs as a designation of the gospel (see disc. on 1 Tim. 2:4); here it refers to the cognitive side of faith (cf. esp. 1 Tim. 4:3, "those who are believers and have come to know the truth"). **The truth** is that **taught by our religion** (on this word, *eusebeia*, see disc. on 1 Tim. 2:2 and 3:16). This word is in another "according to" phrase and probably in this instance is intended to define **the truth** as that which accords with true godliness, the gospel of Christ, as it is visibly manifested in godly behavior.

The next phrase, translated in the GNB as a clause, **which is based on the hope for eternal life**, is very difficult, both as to its meaning and what it modifies. Many (e.g., Kelly, D-C) see it as further defining Paul's apostleship, which was to promote faith, knowledge of the truth, and hope. GNB sees it as modifying **our religion**. More likely, it modifies the whole of the two preceding ideas and is sequential to them. That is, the *goal* of God's people is **eternal life**. Faith and knowing the truth therefore lead to **eternal life**. As elsewhere in the PE (1 Tim. 1:16; 6:12, 19; 2 Tim. 1:10; Titus 2:13; 3:7), and everywhere in Paul, salvation has a decidedly eschatological flavor.

This life, Paul now adds, was **promised us** by **God**. With this clause he turns our attention momentarily away from his apostleship and its purpose to the source of all things—both the gospel and his apostleship—God himself. The point in his saying this is probably similar to 1 Timothy 6:14–16, to reinforce the certainty of the future. **The hope** of **eternal life** is predicated on the twin facts that the **God** who promised it **does not lie**, an idea not pressed elsewhere in Paul but found in Numbers 23:19 (cf. Heb. 6:18) and that he promised us this life (cf. 1 Tim. 4:8; 2 Tim. 1:1) **before the beginning of time, and at the right time** (meaning *now*) has **revealed it**. The phrase **before the beginning of time** (lit., "before eternal times") is sometimes interpreted as referring to the OT promises (cf. RSV, "ages ago"). But as in 1 Corinthians 2:7–10 (cf. 2 Tim. 1:9; Eph. 1:4), Paul's point is that what believers are now experiencing belongs to the eternal counsels of God and has been hidden in God until revealed by the Spirit in the New Age through the work of Christ (cf. Rom. 16:25–26; Col. 1:25–26).

The clause **and at the right time** (cf. 1 Tim. 2:6) **he revealed it in his message** (lit., "his word") expresses the present fulfillment of the promise mentioned in verse 2. However, Paul's Greek is slightly different from the GNB. Although it may be implied that **it** (eternal life) is what has been **revealed**, the sentence actually reads, "but **at the right time he revealed** his word" (i.e., the **message** of the gospel, as elsewhere in PE; 2 Tim. 2:9; 2:15; 4:2; Titus 1:9; 2:5). Thus, God promised life, and now, **at the right time, he revealed** his word "in the preaching that **was entrusted to me**" (to be more literal). If that does not make a nicely balanced set of ideas, the thought is clear enough. Paul simply brings his sentence back to its point of origin, his apostleship. The revelation of the promised life has actually taken place in Paul's proclamation of God's **message**, as attested by the Cretans' faith (v. 1). As always for Paul, such preaching, hence his apostleship itself, is not of his own choosing but is a sacred trust (see 1 Tim. 1:11; cf. 2 Tim. 1:11; 1 Cor. 9:17; Gal. 2:7). And all of this, finally, is **by order of God our Savior** (see disc. on 1 Tim. 1:1). Paul's preaching, like his apostleship, is in keeping with God's **order**, his divine injunction on Paul's life.

1:4 / After that long elaboration on the purpose and authentication of his apostleship, Paul now moves to the address and greeting proper. As with Timothy (1 Tim. 1:1), **Titus** (see the Introduction) is to be recognized by the Cretans as Paul's **true son**; that is, he is a legitimate child of Paul in carrying on Paul's ministry. His legitimacy comes at the one crucial point, **in the faith that we** (i.e., Paul the Jew and Titus the Gentile) **have in common**.

Thus he greets Titus with his own Christianized salutation: **May God the Father and Christ Jesus our Savior give you grace and peace** (see disc. on 1 Tim. 1:1). In keeping with all the other Pauline letters (except 1 and 2 Timothy) the greeting is **grace and peace**. Although in these letters Paul more often calls God **our Savior** (as in v. 3), because salvation originates in God the Father, it is effected by **Christ Jesus our Savior**. The interchanging of this title between God and Christ Jesus (cf. 3:4, 6) reflects the high Christology found in Paul from the beginning.

Additional Notes

1:1a / The doublet **servant of God** and **apostle of Jesus Christ** is typical of these letters—and occurs earlier in Paul as well. Cf. "God our Savior/Christ Jesus our hope" (1 Tim. 1:1) esp. and 1 Tim. 6:13: "God, who gives life to all things, and . . . Christ Jesus, who firmly professed his faith before Pontius Pilate." This probably explains why Paul says "God's slave," rather than "Christ Jesus' slave," as we might have expected (Rom. 1:1; Phil. 1:1). To suggest the usage is un-Pauline and would mean "authorized revealer of God" rather than "God's own property" (as Hanson, following Hasler) is to move far beyond the evidence.

The word order "Jesus Christ" occurs only here and at 2 Tim. 2:8, except for four occasions where it occurs in conjunction with another title (1 Tim. 6:3, 14; Titus 2:13[?]; 3:6). Probably no important distinction is to be made from this word order here, although in 2 Tim. 2:8 that may not be the case (which see).

1:1b-3 / It seems prejudicial that such a thoroughly Pauline idea as **the hope** of **eternal life** having been **promised . . . before the beginning of time** should be seen by some as reflecting a Platonic idea: "Salvation belongs to the timeless eternal world; only revelation belongs to time" (Hanson, p. 170).

2

The Appointment of Elders

I left you in Crete, so that you could put in order the things that still needed doing and appoint church elders in every town. Remember my instructions: [6]an elder must be without fault; he must have only one wife,[a] and his children must be believers and not have the reputation of being wild or disobedient. [7]For since a church leader is in charge of God's work, he should be without fault. He must not be arrogant or quick-tempered, or a drunkard or violent or greedy for money. [8]He must be hospitable and love what is good. He must be self-controlled, upright, holy, and disciplined. [9]He must hold firmly to the message which can be trusted and which agrees with the doctrine. In this way he will be able to encourage others with the true teaching and also to show the error of those who are opposed to it.

a. have only one wife; *or* be married only once.

As with 1 Timothy, Paul begins without the typical thanksgiving, which is perhaps not surprising given the letter's almost total lack of personal notes (see Introduction, p. xxiv). This letter, like 1 Timothy, is all "business," not a personal communication to Titus (cf. the very different 2 Timothy).

But unlike 1 Timothy, the "business" is not primarily that of stopping false teachers(-ings). Such teaching is indeed a threat, and still comes from within; but its source is different. Instead of established elders leading people astray, the threat is coming from "the circumcision party" (1:10, RSV). Moreover, the problem does not seem to have the same urgency as in Ephesus, probably because the churches are relatively new. The antidote to the problem in Crete, therefore, is not for Titus himself to ferret out the error but to see that the churches are set in order with duly appointed elders/overseers, who are themselves to resist the errorists. Hence, the letter begins with this matter of setting the churches in order (vv. 5–9) and then takes up the false teachers (vv. 10–16).

This paragraph, especially verses 6–8, has very close resemblances to 1 Timothy 3:1–7. As with 1 Timothy 3, there are fifteen qualifications given; five are identical, and five or six others have points of correspondence. What *differs* is what is significant: (1) Titus is to **appoint** these elders (what is said here is to serve as qualifications for that appointment). (2) At least one item of *duty* is clearly spelled out (v. 9): They are to be the teachers of the truth and must also refute those in error. (3) The whole list has a more orderly arrangement, so that the household matters are brought to the fore, followed by five vices to be avoided and six virtues to be sought. Thus the whole, though reflecting 1 Timothy, seems to be a more studied presentation.

1:5-6 / Paul begins the letter by reminding Titus why he has been left **in Crete** (cf. 1 Tim. 1:3), which in turn also indicates the purpose of the letter. Both the verb **I left you** (cf. 2 Tim. 4:13) and the context imply that Paul himself had been on **Crete** and had **left** Titus behind. Since this cannot have been the incident mentioned in Acts 27:8, a recent mission, following Paul's first imprisonment, must be assumed, although nothing more is known of this mission or of the church's early days on this island. (Some Cretans were present on the Day of Pentecost [Acts 2:11] and may have brought back the tidings of that event to the synagogues, but that is largely speculative.)

In any case the mission seems to have been recent enough so that the assemblies in the various towns on the island had not yet been fully set **in order**. Hence Paul had **left** Titus **in Crete, so that** he **could put in order the things that still needed doing**. This verb, **put in order**, usually means "to correct" or "set right," but the phrase **the things that still needed doing** (lit., "what is lacking") makes it clear that the "correcting" is not so much *re*formation as it is formation, namely, the completion of a task left unfinished.

That this is the correct understanding is verified by the next clause, which defines what has been left undone **that still needed doing**. Titus is to **appoint church elders in every town**. The rest of the paragraph details what that means. We are still left with a lot of unanswered questions. Did Titus **appoint** them by himself? How many **in every town**? Did they have duties besides teaching? In any case, the absence of a caution that they must not be recent converts (see 1 Tim. 3:6 and 5:22) adds to the overall sense that this is a new thing.

The clause translated **remember my instructions** in GNB and made to point forward hides a more complex sentence in Paul's Greek. The clause literally says, "as I instructed you," and goes with what has preceded as well. Thus Paul's point goes something like this: "I left you in Crete to complete the unfinished task, just as I instructed you, of appointing elders in all the churches. But those instructions, you will recall (and now for the sake of the churches, they are being put in writing), had the following kinds of guidelines."

The first guidelines, given in verse 6, take the form of indirect questions, and instead of imperatives (as the GNB, and most translations), they might better be put in the form of questions (see NEB; cf. NAB on 1 Tim. 5:10). Is a man **without fault**? This is not the same word as in 1 Timothy 3:2, but the synonym used of the deacons in 3:10. Nonetheless, it functions in exactly the same way—to head the list as a covering term for a variety of behavioral concerns. One should note the shift to the singular, **an elder must be**, occasioned by the form of the indirect question ("if anyone . . ."; see the note on 1 Tim. 3:2).

The first two items wherein the elder must be **without fault** have to do with the quality of his home life (which appear first and thirteenth in 1 Tim. 3:2, 4, but are brought together as an afterthought for the deacons, 3:12). Does he **have only one wife** (see disc. on 1 Tim. 3:2: "Has he been faithful to his one wife?")? Are **his children . . . believers**, who do **not have the reputation of being wild or disobedient**? Although this reflects 1 Timothy 3:4, it is said in a slightly different and more positive way. These represent two sides of the same coin. Children are to **be believers** themselves; that is, the potential elder is to be such a person that his children have followed him in adopting his faith. Or it could mean they are "faithfully" to reflect the behavior of "the faithful." In either case, the flip side of the coin is that they are **not** to **have the reputation of** (or "be open to the charge of") **being wild** (or "dissipation," "debauchery"; cf. Eph. 5:18) **or disobedient** (a word used in the LXX of Eli's sons, 1 Sam. 10:27). The word **disobedient** is repeated later (v. 10) of the false teachers ("who rebel"). Here we have the first hint of what will become the dominant theme of the letter—good works and a concern for what outsiders think.

It is probably significant for newer churches that, before Paul gives a further list of vices and virtues, these two items should head the list of qualifications. A good look at the man's home life will tell much about his character and his ability to give leadership to the church.

1:7–8 / It is easy, because of the inherent difficulty of translation, to miss the very close connection of verse 7 to verse 6. An explanatory **for** ties the two sentences together. The one (v. 7a) now gives reasons *why* the **church leader** (*episkopos*) must be **without fault** in the sense of verse 6 (i.e., as a faithful husband and father), namely, because he will also serve as "God's household manager" (a metaphor one might miss by translating **in charge of God's work**). Hence the same point is being made as in 1 Timothy 3:5: If a person is not exemplary in his own household, how can he care for God's? It should also be noted that **God's** is a possessive. The *episkopos* is **God's** "household manager," not the church's; nor is the "household" his own.

The easy movement from *presbyteroi* (pl., "elders," v. 5) to *tis* (sing., "anyone," v. 6) to *ton episkopon* (sing., "the overseer," or **church leader**) indicates some of the difficulty we have in determining precisely who and how many these **church leaders** were. This much seems certain: The *episkopos* is clearly an **elder** (both in 1 Tim. 3:2 and Titus 1:9 the *episkopos* is a teacher, and 1 Tim. 5:17 makes it clear that the teachers are also elders). It also seems likely that not all elders are *episkopoi*, and therefore the words are interchangeable only in a limited sense. Whether or not a given assembly had several elders and one of them was the *episkopos* is a moot point, but it is not highly probable at this stage, given the plural in Philippians 1:1. Therefore, a **church leader** is probably a generic term, as in verse 6.

Having repeated that a **church leader** must be **without fault**, Paul now reverts to a list of eleven adjectives, much like 1 Timothy 3:2–3, only in a more ordered fashion. There are five vices to be avoided (which are certainly not exhaustive, but representative). The first two form a pair, not found in 1 Timothy 3: **He must not be arrogant** ("self-willed"; cf. 2 Pet. 2:10) or **quick-tempered** (cf. "gentle and peaceful" in 1 Tim. 3:3). It is in keeping with all the NT for **not arrogant** to head the list. God's household manager must be a servant, not stubbornly self-willed, since it is God's household, not his own (cf. Mark 10:41–45; 1 Cor. 3:5–9; 4:1–2).

On the next two, not **a drunkard or violent**, which also form a pair, see discussion on 1 Timothy 3:3. The fifth vice, **greedy for money**, is the same word used in the deacon's list (1 Tim. 3:8) and recurs in verse 11 about the false teachers. Barrett is probably correct in noting, "It is the sordidness of making profit out of Christian service, rather than dishonest gain, that is here condemned" (p. 129).

A look at the close ties between the false teachers and the reputed character of the Cretans in verses 10–13 will make the significance of this list readily apparent—although they are obviously appropriate for church leaders in any age!

In contrast to these vices Paul lists six representative virtues. **He must be hospitable** (see disc. on 1 Tim. 3:2) **and love what is good** (a word found frequently on inscriptions in praise of worthy people). Here again the "good works" motif of the letter emerges (see disc. on v. 6). **He must also be self-controlled** (see disc. on 1 Tim. 3:2 and Titus 2:2, 5), a favorite word in the PE, which probably means something close to "having his wits about him." The next two, **upright** and **holy**, occur regularly together both in and out of Scripture reflecting duty toward other people and duty toward God (cf. Luke 1:75; Eph. 4:24; 1 Thess. 2:10). And he must be **disciplined** (or "self-controlled"); the noun form of this word is the last of the fruit of the Spirit in Galatians 5:23.

Though it is true that this list has some affinities to similar lists in the Hellenistic world, it is also true that four of the six are clearly Pauline words and that all of them are obviously appropriate for church leaders. (On this question, see the note on 1 Tim. 3:2).

1:9 / Finally, and significantly, the list of qualifications concludes in the form of a duty. **He must hold firmly to the message which can be trusted and which agrees with the doctrine**, a somewhat awkward way of repeating his need to be absolutely devoted to the gospel (cf. 1 Tim. 3:9 about the deacons). But he must be so not just for himself but because **in this way** he will be able to fulfill his twofold task of exhorting/encouraging the faithful and confuting the opponents of the gospel.

It should be noted that these are exactly the tasks enjoined on Timothy in 1 Timothy (cf. 2 Tim. 4:2). Here, even though Titus is to lead the way (see disc. on 1:13), these tasks are to be entrusted to the elders/overseers. The "church leader" must **be able to encourage** (better, "exhort"; cf. 1 Tim. 4:13; 5:1; 6:2) **others** by means of **the true teaching** (i.e., "sound doctrine"; see disc. on 1 Tim. 1:10). He must **also** be able **to show the error of** (or "refute," "convict"; cf. 1 Tim. 5:20; 2 Tim. 3:16; 4:2) **those who are opposed to it**. This final qualification will lead directly to the next section of the letter.

Additional Notes

D-C make a considerable point of the similarities between vv. 6–9 and 1 Tim. 3:1–7, 8–12, and 2 Tim. 2:22–25. They seem to find a few more correspondences than actually exist. Their point is that the author is simply borrowing from a common "schema," and therefore that the actual items listed would hardly reflect what Paul would require of a Christian church leader. But D-C make far more of the possibility of a common schema than the evidence suggests. Their very attempt to make the two lists look more alike than they are, without recognizing the more ordered nature of this list or the fact that both lists fit their particular life-settings so well, probably betrays some prior interests on their part.

1:5-6 / Some argue that the verb *apelipon* (**I left**) does not necessarily imply **I left behind**, as does the variant reading *katelipon*, found in the majority of witnesses. But that is to make too much of the variant, which merely substitutes a stronger synonym to express the same idea. The two uses of this verb in 2 Timothy (4:13 and 20) clearly mean "to leave behind" (see also BAGD), and the context as a whole implies that Paul, too, had been on Crete.

Hanson (p. 172), following LSJ, argues that **put in order the things that still needed doing** should be translated "complete unfinished reforms." "It therefore implies that the church in Crete, far from being recently founded, had existed long enough to grow corrupt and was in process of being reformed." Hanson's reason for this position is that it thereby "suggests a state of affairs more likely to prevail at the end of the century than in Paul's day." But that is to put far too much weight on a dubious rendering of *ta leiponta* ("what is lacking"). As the exegesis shows, the weight of evidence points to a new situation, especially when compared with 1 and 2 Timothy (e.g., the repeated concern in 1 Timothy that new appointees not be new converts, which fits the established church of Ephesus but would make little or no sense here and is therefore missing).

1:9 / The thirteenth-century MS 460 has the following interesting addition after v. 9: "Do not appoint those who have been married twice, nor make them deacons; nor may they have wives from a second marriage; neither let them approach the altar for divine service. As a servant of God, rebuke the rulers who are unjust, swindlers, liars, and merciless."

3

Warnings Against
False Teachings

TITUS 1:10–16

For there are many, especially the converts from Judaism, who rebel and deceive others with their nonsense. ¹¹It is necessary to stop their talk, because they are upsetting whole families by teaching what they should not, and all for the shameful purpose of making money. ¹²⁻¹³It was a Cretan himself, one of their own prophets, who spoke the truth when he said, "Cretans are always liars, wicked beasts, and lazy gluttons." For this reason you must rebuke them sharply, so that they may have a healthy faith ¹⁴and no longer hold on to Jewish legends and to human commandments which come from people who have rejected the truth. ¹⁵Everything is pure to those who are themselves pure; but nothing is pure to those who are defiled and unbelieving, for their minds and consciences have been defiled. ¹⁶They claim that they know God, but their actions deny it. They are hateful and disobedient, not fit to do anything good.

This paragraph is closely tied to verses 5–9 (by the **for**) and elaborates especially on "the opponents" of verse 9. This is the major reason why Titus must appoint worthy elders, because there are some people **who rebel** (v. 10) and "are opposed to" wholesome teaching (v. 9).

Along with 3:10–11, this is the only indication in the letter of the presence of false teachers. Yet their lack of genuine good works (v. 16) plus the emphasis throughout on observable good works by those who know the truth (2:5, 7, 8, 10, 14; 3:1, 8, 14) suggest that their presence is a major reason for the letter—even if it lacks the urgency of 1 Timothy.

The picture of the opponents that emerges has many correspondences to the situation in Ephesus (1 and 2 Timothy) and also to the slightly earlier situation in Colossae-Laodicea (cf. esp. Col. 2:16–23). It looks as if this subtle, and apparently attractive, deviation was "catching on" all over this part of the world. In this instance, its particularly Jewish nature comes to the fore. It is in fact being promoted by some Jewish Christians (v. 10), and the whole of verses 14–16 reveals an emphasis on ritual regulations, comparable to the asceticism in 1 Timothy 4:3 but of a decidedly Jewish character.

The paragraph as a whole expresses a twofold concern over the character and conduct of these rebels (seen to be in keeping with the well-known reputation of Crete) and their teaching itself.

1:10 / With a causal **for**, Paul now gives the reasons why the elders/overseers must be of blameless character (vv. 6–8) and able to teach truth and refute error. **There are many . . . who rebel**, the same word translated "disobedient" in verse 6, which here has the nuance of "insubordinate" (Moffatt). Their rebellion, or insubordination, is in the first instance a matter of rejecting the truth of the gospel (v. 14, and by implication the lordship of Christ and the authority of Paul). It expresses itself in their deceiving **others with their nonsense**. The word for **nonsense** is the same as in 1 Timothy 1:6 (which see). As with the false teachers in Ephesus, Paul sees the teaching being put out in Crete as "foolish discussions" that mislead or **deceive others** (cf. 1 Tim. 4:2; 2 Tim. 3:13).

But unlike those in Ephesus, where some of the false teachers are named (1 Tim. 1:20; 2 Tim. 2:17) or otherwise referred to with the indefinite "some people" (1 Tim. 1:3, 6, etc.), these rebels are **the converts from Judaism** (lit., "those of the circumcision"; cf. Acts 10:45; 11:2; Gal. 2:7–9, 12). The word **especially** (cf. 2 Tim. 4:13) in this instance probably means something like "in other words" and implies, not that many others as well are insubordinate, but that the problem is from Jewish **converts** in particular (see note). Thus Paul would have meant something like this: "Make sure your appointees are qualified people, because there are already many insubordinates at work with their deceptions; I am referring in particular, as you know, to the converts from Judaism."

Does this mean that all Jewish converts are going this way? Not necessarily, but it does imply that the threat from Judaism is no longer, as formerly, about circumcision (e.g., Galatians), but involves some subtleties in other areas that are described in verses 14–16.

1:11 / This verse comes the closest in the Epistle to expressing urgency over the situation in Crete. **It is necessary to stop their talk**. This verb (lit., "to stop the mouth") could mean either "to silence" or simply "to hinder." In this context it must mean that they are to be silenced in some way. Why? **Because they are upsetting** (better, "overturning," or "ruining") **whole families** (better, "households"; cf. 1 Tim. 3:5, 15; 2 Tim. 3:6–9) **by teaching what they should not**.

The picture that emerges is one of a somewhat less than cohesive church structure in which a lot of the teaching activity takes place in various households. In some cases, **whole** households are being overturned by the false teachers, rather than, as some have suggested, some families being upset by the defection of one or two within them.

The language **teaching what they should not** reflects 1 Timothy 5:13 (cf. 1 Tim. 1:6–7; 6:3–4). Again as in Ephesus (1 Tim. 6:5–10), the bottom line for the false teachers is greed, not truth or godliness or God's "honor." They have become religious mercenaries, who are trying to win converts **all for the shameful purpose of making money**. On the meaning of this term in Titus, see discussion on verse 7.

1:12-13 / Before pursuing these opponents further about their teaching, Paul gives the argument an unexpected turn. He is reminded that the conduct of these false teachers is very much in accord with the known reputation of Crete, expressed in an epigram of Epimenides (ca. 600 B.C.): **"Cretans are always liars, wicked beasts, and lazy gluttons."** What he intends by this seems clear enough. It is not a blanket indictment of all Cretans; rather, he is reminding them that in the case of the false teachers, Epimenides, **a Cretan himself**, certainly **spoke the truth**. These teachers are **liars** (cf. "deceive others with their nonsense," v. 10). Perhaps they also fit the rest of the description (**wild beasts,** "who rebel" [v. 10]; **lazy gluttons**, "shameful purpose of making money'). In any case, he is trying to shame them—both the teachers and any who would follow them—by saying, "It's all very Cretan of them," in the sense of the island's unsavory reputation on the outside.

The quote itself has an interesting history. According to a well-established tradition found in Callimachus' *Hymn to Zeus* 8 (305–240 B.C.) and Lucian's *Lover of Lies* 3 (cf. *Timon* 6; ca. A.D. 120–180), the reason that **Cretans are always liars** was that they claimed to possess a *tomb* of Zeus, who, of course, as a god, cannot have died!

But what did Paul mean by calling Epimenides **one of their own prophets**? Possibly he intended something similar to John 11:49–51, where Caiaphas spoke prophetically without necessarily intending to do so. More likely Paul is reflecting the common reputation of Epimenides, whom Plato called a "divine man" and of whom Aristotle said, "He used to divine, not the future, but only things that were past but obscure" (*The*

Art of Rhetoric 3.17, Loeb). The **truth** of what he had said about Cretans now evidenced in the false teachers makes the title a permissible one.

For this reason, he continues, **you** (Titus) **must rebuke them sharply**. This is the only time in the letter that Titus himself is called upon to address the false teachers (cf. 1 Timothy everywhere). The word **rebuke** (*elengchein*) occurred in verse 9 as the task of the elders (**show** or "refute"; cf. 1 Tim. 5:20; 2 Tim. 3:16; Titus 2:15). Used with the adverb *apotomōs* (**sharply**) the imperative more likely means "correct them rigorously" (Goodspeed), since the intent is **so that they may have a healthy faith** (again, see disc. on 1 Tim. 1:10).

This last clause opens the question about to whom **them** and **they** refer. To the false teachers? or to the Cretan believers as well? The context demands that the antecedent is primarily the false teachers. But the corrective aim of the **rebuke**, as well as the content of verse 14, may point beyond them to all the believers (however, see disc. on 2 Tim. 2:25-26, where Paul possibly still holds out hope for the opponents themselves).

1:14 / In typical fashion, **healthy faith**, which is seldom defined, is set in contrast to the unhealthy teaching of the errorists, which is. "They" are **no longer** to **hold on to Jewish legends** (cf. 1 Tim. 1:4; 4:7). Although "genealogies" are not mentioned here (but see disc. on 3:9), these **legends**, specifically described as **Jewish**, very likely reflect the similar phenomenon condemned in 1 Timothy 1:4 (which see).

More significantly, in the sense that Paul will comment on it further in verses 15-16, they are also not to **hold on . . . to human commandments**. Literally, this says, "the **commandments** of men," and reflects Isaiah 29:13 (LXX: "In vain they worship me, teaching commandments and doctrines of men"), a passage cited by Jesus about Pharisaic regulations (Mark 7:7/Matt. 15:9) and alluded to by Paul about ascetic practices in Colossae very similar to these (Col. 2:22). As elsewhere (e.g., 1 Tim. 6:5; 2 Tim. 4:4), the perpetrators of such **human commandments** are described as **people who have rejected the truth**.

1:15 / The final two verses in the paragraph spell out Paul's indictment of the false teachers with their "commandments of men." It is clear from these verses that the problem again has to do with prohibitions of some kind, probably food laws, given the emphasis on purity and defilement (see 1 Tim. 4:3; cf. Col. 2:16-23, esp. 20-23). In any case the language throughout reflects decidedly Jewish concerns.

Paul begins with the positive: **Everything is pure to those who are**

pure. Although the concern here is different, this restates Paul's position given in Romans 14:20. It reflects a clear understanding of Jesus as found in Mark 7, that what people eat cannot defile them. Paul's point is clear: **Everything**, including those things thought to be unclean by some, **is** [ritually] **pure**—that is, nothing is unclean of itself (cf. 1 Tim. 4:4, "nothing is to be rejected")—**to those who are themselves** [morally] **pure**, since they have been "cleansed" by faith in Christ.

The opposite of this is that, contrary to the stance of the false teachers, **nothing is** [ritually] **pure to those who are** [morally] **defiled**, who are further described as **unbelieving**. At this point Paul is picking up the common Jewish motif that whatever a defiled person touches is by that fact likewise defiled (cf. Hag. 2:10–14; Philo, *On the Special Laws* 3.208–9). But his devastating punch is that, instead of becoming or keeping themselves pure by eating only pure things, the very fact that they consider anything impure and therefore need regulations for their own purity is the demonstration that the false teachers **are** themselves **defiled**. They are so precisely because they are also **unbelieving**, that is, not putting their trust in Christ. Thus in the New Age, everything is new. The one who seeks purity by obedience to regulations, that is, human commandments, turns out not to be one of God's people at all, but among the **unbelieving**.

To make sure his point is not missed, he adds, **for their minds and consciences have been defiled**. The **their** brings the point of the two statements on purity to rest on the false teachers. They are not the **pure** for whom **everything is pure** but are those who believe **nothing is pure**. The problem is not external, one of defilement through food, but internal—**defiled minds** (cf. 1 Tim. 6:5) **and consciences** (see disc. on 1 Tim. 1:5, clean ["pure"] conscience). In this case **their minds and consciences have been defiled** because they think that they will be defiled by eating certain foods, but even more so because they would lay such human commandments on God's people.

1:16 / Now comes the most stinging indictment of all. **They claim** (lit., "confess") **that they know God, but their actions deny it**. Although Barrett, and others, see this as "the Gnostic tendency of the heretics" (p. 133; cf. Kelly, p. 237), surely that is secondary. It was, after all, the special boast of the Jews, who are specifically singled out as the rebellious ones in verse 10, **that they** knew **God**—over against the pagans who did not. Paul himself reflects this understanding in such passages as 1 Thessalonians 4:5; 2 Thessalonians 1:8; Galatians 4:8; and Romans 2:17–18. This point is similar to 1 John 2:4 or James 2:14–16, where the false teachers profess to **know God** and thus are appealing to others to let them lead them to God.

But **their actions** (lit., "works") **deny** the claim. Not only do they not know the truth about God as revealed in the gospel, but their behavior in particular demonstrates their lack of knowledge. It is not clear what **actions** are being referred to. Some think their ascetic practices; more likely it is their greed, strife, and so forth, since this is the concern throughout the letter and is noted at the end of the verse, **not fit to do anything good**.

Finally, these people are described as **hateful and disobedient**. It is questionable, however, whether the word *bdelyktos* should be thought of as active (GNB, **hateful**) or passive (KJV, "abominable"; RSV, NIV, "detestable"). In this context the latter is preferable, since the word is an OT one reflecting what is detestable or abominable in God's sight, especially in connection with idolatry. This then is the ultimate irony. As D-C have well said: "These persons who find 'abomination' everywhere are themselves 'abominable' " (p. 138). They obey **human commandments**, but they are **disobedient** to God himself. Therefore, they are **not fit to do anything good** (lit., "unqualified for any good work"). So Paul concludes with the sharpest kind of distinction between their works, predicated on human commandments, and what God wants by way of good works, which will now be spelled out in 2:1–3:11.

Additional Notes

1:10 / On the meaning of the word *malista* (**especially**) proposed here, see the article by T. C. Skeat, " 'Especially the Parchments': A Note on 2 Timothy IV.13." He has mustered a convincing array of evidence that in *ad hoc* documents the word frequently means something like "in other words" or "I mean," by defining or particularizing a general term.

There is substantial evidence for a large number of Jews on Crete: Philo, *On the Embassy to Gaius* 282; Jos. *Antiquities* 17.327; *Life* 247. Cf. Acts 2:11; 1 Macc. 15.23.

1:11 / The greed of the Cretans was an established reputation. For example, Polybius says: "So much in fact do sordid love of gain [same word as in Titus 1:7 and 11] and lust for wealth prevail among them, that the Cretans are the only people in the world in whose eyes no gain is disgraceful" (6.46, Loeb). But since this problem existed also in Ephesus, perhaps one should not make as much of its particularly Cretan character as some do.

At the end of this verse MS 460 (see note on v. 9) adds this remarkable sentence: "The children who abuse or strike their parents you must check and reprove and admonish as a father his children" (Metzger's translation, *TCGNT*). This reflects a considerably different stance on the "upsetting" of households!

1:14 / Although the word for **commandments** differs from that of the LXX, which is used in Mark 7:7/Matt. 15:9 and Col. 2:22, the allusion is certainly to Isa. 29:13. The interchange of the Greek synonyms involved also occurs in Mark 7:7, 8.

1:15 / Barrett implies that the author of Titus takes a different view from Paul in Romans 14–15, even to the point of suggesting that "in Titus, it is the weak . . . who are not protected, but attacked" (p. 132–33). But such language reflects an unfortunate confusion of two considerably different life-settings. Except for the language used, there is scarcely any other point of contact with Romans 14.

It is common to view the language used and the problem addressed in vv. 15–16 as reflecting a Gnostic view of things. That such ascetic regulations may indeed have been influenced by Hellenism is scarcely deniable. Nonetheless, there is not a single word or idea of any kind in this paragraph, or in 3:8–11, that primarily suggests Greek influence. But every word fits the Jewish milieu specifically singled out in vv. 10 and 14.

4

Instructions for Groups of Believers

But you must teach what agrees with sound doctrine. ²Instruct the older men to be sober, sensible, and self-controlled; to be sound in their faith, love, and endurance. ³In the same way instruct the older women to behave as women should who live a holy life. They must not be slanderers or slaves to wine. They must teach what is good, ⁴in order to train the younger women to love their husbands and children, ⁵to be self-controlled and pure, and to be good housewives who submit themselves to their husbands, so that no one will speak evil of the message that comes from God.

⁶In the same way urge the young men to be self-controlled. ⁷In all things you yourself must be an example of good behavior. Be sincere and serious in your teaching. ⁸Use sound words that cannot be criticized, so that your enemies may be put to shame by not having anything bad to say about us.

⁹Slaves are to submit themselves to their masters and please them in all things. They must not talk back to them ¹⁰or steal from them. Instead, they must show that they are always good and faithful, so as to bring credit to the teaching about God our Savior in all they do.

Although this section has affinities to several passages in both the PE and the rest of the NT, the material nonetheless appears here in a unique way. It picks up the *framework* of 1 Timothy 5:1–2, where people are grouped by age and sex, and in verses 2–8 fleshes out some details, not in terms of Titus' relationship to them but of their own attitudes and conduct. The *language* of the details echoes that used for the overseers, deacons, and women in 1 Timothy 3:1–13 and 2:9–15. The passage then concludes in verses 9–10 with a word to slaves, reminiscent of 1 Timothy 6:1–2. Imbedded in the instructions for the younger men is a word to Titus himself (vv. 7–8), reminiscent of 1 Timothy 4:12–13.

Some have seen a similarity between this material and the so-called house codes in Colossians 3:18–4:1, Ephesians 5:21–6:9, and 1 Peter 2:18–3:7. However, the similarities are merely surface at best, since in those passages the entire concern was about relationships within the household. Here the concern is chiefly about character and conduct in general; only the instructions for the younger women and slaves is relational, and in both of these, submission is advised for the sake of the gospel's reputation with outsiders.

Thus the concern throughout the passage is on observable behavior, obviously in contrast to that of the "opponents" described in 1:10–16, who are finally judged as unqualified for any good work. The language used is quite general and very much that which was current in pagan philosophical and religious circles, here adapted to Christian life. One gets the feeling, therefore, that the passage does not so much address *ad hoc* problems in Crete as it does in a more general way call for good works and a lifestyle on the part of Christians that "will make the teaching about God our Savior attractive" (v. 10, NIV).

All of this adds to the overall sense of the letter as being less urgent than 1 Timothy and somewhat prophylactic. Christians of both sexes and all ages are urged to consider their conduct, not so much toward one another, but before the world.

2:1 / The **but you** that begins the section stands in clear contrast to 1:10–16. The same formula occurred in 1 Timothy 6:11, immediately following the final indictment of the false teachers (cf. 2 Tim. 3:10, 14). However, in contrast to its occurrences in 1 and 2 Timothy, where Timothy himself was urged to stand in opposition to the false teachers, here Titus is urged to **teach what agrees with sound doctrine**, so that the *people themselves* will live differently from the false teachers. The verb to **teach** literally means "to speak," a milder term than the imperatives of 1 Timothy ("exhort," "charge," "teach"). Titus is to "rebuke sharply" the opponents (1:13); he is to "speak" to the people. On **sound doctrine**, see discussion on 1 Timothy 1:10 (cf. Titus 1:9, 13). Here it stands in contrast to the "human commandments" of 1:14–16. Again, it will be observed that **what agrees with sound doctrine** has not so much to do with the cognitive side of the gospel as the behavioral.

2:2 / Paul begins with instructions for **the older men** (cf. 1 Tim. 5:1; on this word, Philo, *On the Creation* 105, cites Hippocrates as referring to the sixth of seven periods of a man's life, ages fifty to fifty-six; Philo himself uses it to refer to a man over sixty in *On the Special Laws* 2.33). It is chiefly from among these men that the elders/overseers of 1:5–9 will be selected. Hence it is not surprising that the qualities urged on them correspond to what is said of the overseers and deacons in 1 Timothy 3:2, 8.

They are to be **sober** (cf. 1 Tim. 3:2), **sensible** ("worthy of respect"; cf. 1 Tim. 3:8, "have a good character"), and **self-controlled** (cf. 1:8; 1 Tim. 3:2). This last word, *sōphronas*, which is a favorite in the PE, is repeated below of the younger women (v. 5) and younger men (v. 6). It has especially to do with being "sensible" or "sound-minded" (see disc. on 2 Tim. 1:7).

They are also **to be sound** (cf. v. 1 and 1:13) in the three cardinal virtues of **faith, love, and endurance** (hope?). These three words occur together in the exhortation to Timothy in 1 Timothy 6:11 (cf. 2 Tim. 3:10) and are found together in Paul as early as 1 Thessalonians 1:3 (though not quite in this way). The triad **faith, love**, and *hope* appears to be a very early piece of Christian ethical instruction (see note). That "hope" has been replaced by **endurance** probably reflects an emphasis on perseverance that the word *hope* itself does not always connote. Thus "what accords with sound doctrine" for **the older men** is that they should be respectable in every way (esp. in light of 1:12!); above all they should be exemplary of the cardinal Christian virtues: **faith** toward God, **love** toward all, **endurance** to the End. Although nothing like the latter is explicitly said of the following groups, it may be assumed that such is expected of all.

2:3 / **In the same way** (a word that similarly connects 1 Tim. 2:9 to 8, and 3:8 and 11 to 3:2) Titus is to **instruct the older women** (a related but different word from 1 Tim. 5:2; used by Philo, *On the Special Laws* 2.33, of women past sixty). Interestingly, especially in light of what is said next of the younger women, these instructions do not reflect 1 Timothy 5:9–10, but only 3:11.

First, they are **to behave as women should who live a holy life**. The word translated **live a holy life**, *hieroprepeis*, often means simply "holy" (e.g., 4 Macc. 9:25; 11:20), but it could also carry the more specialized sense of "acting like a priestess," resulting from its use to describe the conduct of a priest. Since it is an unusual word (occurring only here in the Gk. Bible), it may well be that Paul intends this broader connotation. In demeanor they are to be what would be fitting for temple service.

Then he adds two injunctions: **They must not be slanderers** (as 1 Tim. 3:11) **or slaves to wine** (cf. 1 Tim. 3:8, 11). It is a negative reflection on first-century culture itself, which often admired heavy drinkers, that both the **older men** and **older women** in the church are urged to set a different example.

Finally, **they must teach what is good**. This represents a single compound word in Greek, *kalodidaskalous*, which occurs only here in all Greek literature. The word itself does not necessarily mean formal instruction. Indeed, it probably implies nothing more than informal teaching by word and example, since the content of the instruction in verses 4–5 has to do with being a model, godly wife.

2:4–5 / Paul next directs his instruction to **the younger women** but does so by way of the "older women" in verse 3. The latter are to be teachers of good, so that they may **train the younger women**. The verb translated **train**, *sōphronizōsin* (see disc. on v. 2, *sōphronas*, "self-controlled), is highly unusual, literally meaning to "bring someone to his or her senses," although there is some evidence for it to mean something like "advise," or "urge." Since what follows is reminiscent of the instructions to the women in 1 Timothy 2:9–15 and 5:11–14, one wonders whether Paul, in mentioning **the younger women**, is not still smarting from the problem in Ephesus. If so, then the verb probably means something like "wise them up" as to their wifely duties.

Therefore, the instructions that follow differ from verses 2–3—as well as verse 6—in that *(a)* they are very specific, all having to do with her being a good wife; and *(b)* in this case such demeanor is specifically enjoined so that outsiders will not disparage the gospel.

The younger women ("wives" is implied; the whole passage assumes a culture in which most **younger women** will be married) are advised to demonstrate six qualities—probably to be paired as the GNB suggests of the first four. They are **to love their husbands and children** (two words in Gk., found frequently in pagan antiquity in praise of "good wives"). One should note that although these two words do not appear in 1 Timothy, they are the implications behind 2:9–12, 15 and 5:9–10, 14.

The next word, **self-controlled**, is identical to what was said of the older men in verse 2. However, this is one of the most frequent words used by contemporary writers to describe a good wife, and most often it intends to describe her as a virtuous woman (see disc. on 1 Tim. 2:10). Therefore, in this context **self-controlled and pure** probably mean "virtuous and chaste." The last two words in the list, translated as a noun and adjective (**good housewives**) in the GNB, probably also form a pair. The first word means "keepers of the home" (cf. 1 Tim. 5:14); the second means "good women." However, the latter could also have the nuance of "being kind," and some have suggested it might mean "goodness" or "kindness" to members of the household (including slaves). If so, then the whole list reflects her relationships at home.

Finally, he urges that they also **submit themselves to their husbands** (cf. 1 Tim. 2:11; Col. 3:18; Eph. 5:21–23; 1 Pet. 3:1). As with the list of virtues, this, too, assumes the cultural norm of what a good wife was expected to be like (see note). Thus, very much in keeping with 1 Timothy 2:9–15 and 5:9–15, Paul sets a standard, conditioned in part by the cultural norm of what was expected of a good wife, that **the younger women's** place in Christ was to be found in the home.

The reason for their living out their faith in terms of this domestic code is for the sake of the gospel and how it would be viewed by outsiders: **so that no one will speak evil of the message that comes from God**. For this clause, see discussion on 1 Timothy 6:1. Here we have the first of several clear articulations of the need for good works for the sake of nonbelievers (see disc. on 1:6; cf. 2:10; 2:11, 14; 3:2; 3:8; 3:14).

2:6 / Paul finally turns his attention to **the young men** (note the repeated **in the same way**; cf. v. 3). However, in this case instead of giving a list of virtues, he gives a single exhortation: **Urge** them **to be self-controlled in all things**. Paul now uses the verb form *sōphroneō* (cf. vv. 2, 4, 5), and emphasizes once again the need for clearheaded, sensible Christian living in the face of much that is false (both in terms of the truth itself and resulting behavior).

The prepositional phrase, **in all things**, (perhaps better, "in all respects"), may indeed go with verse 7 as in the GNB (cf. NIV, RSV); more likely it belongs with the exhortation for **the younger men** to "keep their heads" (as in NEB, NAB, Kelly, D-C). This usage fits the style of the PE and does not negate the otherwise emphatic use of *seauton*, **yourself**, in verse 7.

2:7–8 / In the context of exhorting **the younger men** to sensible Christian behavior, Paul emphatically urges Titus to fulfill the apostolic role of "modeling" genuine Christian **behavior** (lit., "putting yourself forward as an example of good works"). This is a common theme in Paul (see disc. on 1 Tim. 4:12; cf. 1 Thess. 1:7; 2 Thess. 3:9; Phil. 3:17) and stands in contrast to those in 1:16 who are "unqualified for any good work."

This passage (vv. 7–8) is reminiscent of 1 Timothy 4:12, 13. However, instead of giving a list of **good behavior** ("works") for him to **be an example of** (as in 1 Tim. 4:12), he turns immediately to Titus' own larger responsibilities in the community (as in 1 Tim. 4:13). There, the reason was for Timothy to save himself and his hearers (4:16); here, it is **so that** "the one in opposition" **may be put to shame by not having anything bad to say about us** (v. 8).

Thus he exhorts Titus to **be sincere** (lit., "without corruption"; therefore, full of "integrity," RSV) **and serious** (*semnotēta*, see disc. on 1 Tim. 3:4; "your manner [be] such as to inspire respect," Lock) **in your teaching**. Here **teaching**, as in 1 Timothy 4:13, 16; 2 Timothy 3:16, has to do with the *activity* of **teaching**, not its content, which will be emphasized in verse 8. The concern is first of all that **in** his **teaching** Titus **set an example** of pure motive and respectful demeanor (**sincere and serious**), in obvious contrast to the "rebels" of 1:10–16.

Also in contrast to them, Titus is to **use sound words** (that word again! see disc. on 1:9, 13; 2:1, 2; cf. 1 Tim. 1:10) **that cannot be criticized**. This word occurs only here in the NT and means "uncondemned," thus "beyond reproach." It is not that Titus *will not* **be criticized**, but that in terms of the gospel itself, his teaching/preaching must be above contradiction.

If Titus' **teaching** is pure in motive, demeanor, and content, he may thereby **put to shame** his **enemies**. **Enemies** is actually singular and means "the one who is in opposition." The primary reference is almost certainly to the opponents within, although in the full context of verses 1–10 it may also include the pagan critic.

But what does it mean for them to be **put to shame**? Does Paul intend a kind of judgment; that is, they will be disgraced because they can find nothing in Titus' conduct to reproach? Or, perhaps more likely (cf. 2 Thess. 3:14), does he intend something of an offer of hope, that is, shamed into repentance, since he does **not** have **anything bad to say about us**? In either case, the word **bad** ("evil") is used invariably of evil *deeds*. So Paul's point is not that the opponent should not be able to point out evil in Titus' doctrine—although that would follow—but in his conduct, which in turn would also implicate Paul (**about us**).

Thus a passage that began as an exhortation to **the younger men** turns out instead to be a word to Titus about his life and ministry. It does not thereby exclude **the younger men**, but includes them only indirectly.

2:9-10 / This concluding exhortation to **slaves** comes as something of a surprise, since everything that has preceded is based on age and sex. It is nonetheless joined grammatically to verses 6–8 as a second indirect command with the verb "urge" in verse 6. The passage is reminiscent of 1 Timothy 6:1–2 and also has some interesting parallels with what is said to the younger women in verses 4–5. They are the two longest sections in the paragraph; in both submission is called for; and both conclude with a purpose clause on the possible effect of their behavior on how the gospel is viewed by outsiders. Although nothing specific is said in these two verses about whether the masters are pagan or Christian—and no decision has to be made—the close ties with verses 4–5 and 1 Timothy 6:1–2 probably presuppose activity within a Christian household.

Slaves are to submit themselves (reflecting correctly the Gk. middle voice, and therefore better than the passive of the NIV, et al., "be subject") **to their masters** (*despotais*, as elsewhere in PE and 1 Peter; in earlier letters Paul uses *kyrioi*). Probably, as in verses 6–7, the **in all things** is intended to go with this verb, which in turn would strengthen the suggestions that the **masters** are believers. The rest of the passage (one sentence in the Gk.) spells out some details of Christian submission.

First, **slaves** are to **please** ("give satisfaction to," Bernard) **their masters**. No one promised that Christian discipleship would be easy! This is the positive attitude that would cover all others (cf. esp. Col. 3:22–25; Eph. 6:5–8), but it is further elaborated by two injunctions: **They must not talk back to them or steal from them**. These must have been the two most common temptations of **slaves**, especially the latter (a word that implies "pilfering" [RSV] or "misappropriating funds"), since slaves were often entrusted with buying goods and also often had a degree of private ownership.

On the contrary (**instead**, a strong adversative to the two negatives), **they must show that they are always good and faithful** (lit., "demonstrate all good faith," or "fidelity"). This use of "faith" (*pistin*) to mean faithfulness is a Pauline usage in the NT (see esp. Gal. 5:22).

These attitudes—and behavior—are again for the sake of the outsider. But what was said in a somewhat negative way in verse 5 ("lest they speak evil of the message") is now given its flip side: **so as to bring credit to** (*kosmōsin*, lit., "adorn") **the teaching about God our Savior** (see disc. on 1 Tim. 1:1) **in all they do** (the same as **in all things** in v. 9). The verb *kosmōsin* implies either "win respect" (as the GNB) or, perhaps more likely, "make attractive."

Consequently, the final point about the conduct of Christian **slaves** also serves as the final point of the whole section regarding people who are to be "sound in their faith, love, and endurance" (v. 2). Paul wants the Christians in Crete not only to stand in contrast to the Cretan reputation exemplified by the insubordinates (1:10–16) but also to live in such a way that outsiders will not only not "blaspheme" the gospel (v. 5) but actually be attracted to it by the believers' behavior (v. 10). This is precisely the point of the creedal basis for such concern and behavior that now follows (vv. 11–14).

Additional Notes

It is common among commentators (see, e.g., D-C) to see this section as reflecting the house codes sections in Colossians, Ephesians, and 1 Peter. But the dissimilarities are much greater than any similarities. In fact, if it were not for the section on slaves (vv. 9–10), and to a lesser extent the young wives (vv. 4–5), one wonders what would ever have given scholars the suggestion. This is not a domestic code, but a call to exemplary behavior, with the outsider in view.

2:2 / For a discussion of the triad **faith**, hope, and **love** as a common pre-Pauline formula for ethical instruction, see A. M. Hunter, *Paul and His Predecessors*, rev. ed. (London: SCM, 1961), pp. 33–35.

2:3 / That the older women are expected to be "teachers of good" to the younger is almost totally irrelevant to the hermeneutical concerns that are often raised in conjunction with 1 Tim. 2:11–12. Formal teaching is hardly in view; rather, it is that "everyday" kind of instruction that takes place in the home by word and example.

2:4-5 / Most of the virtues mentioned for the young women occur regularly in non-Christian texts as the highest ideals of a good wife. For example, the first two appear together in Plutarch's *Dialogue on Love* 23. *Sōphronas*, as the high ideal of being virtuous, occurs frequently in that essay and others (esp. *Advice to Bride and Groom*). In this latter essay (*conj. praec.* 33) Plutarch also notes: "So it is with women also; if they subordinate themselves to their husbands, they are commended, but if they want to have control, they cut a sorrier figure than the subjects of their control" (Loeb). On these matters Plutarch speaks for all antiquity.

2:8 / There has been general disagreement about to whom Paul is referring in speaking of "the one who is in opposition" (GNB, **your enemies**). Chrysostom, alone and certainly incorrectly, suggested Satan. Bernard argued for the opponents within the church (1:10–16); Spicq, for the pagan critic (generally in view in 2:1–3:2). Scott, Kelly, and Hanson take the middle ground of allowing either, although seeing the emphasis to lie differently (within the church [Kelly]; outside [Hanson]).

5

The Theological Basis
for Christian Living

TITUS 2:11–15

For God has revealed his grace for the salvation of all mankind. [12]That grace instructs us to give up ungodly living and worldly passions, and to live self-controlled, upright and godly lives in this world, [13]as we wait for the blessed Day we hope for, when the glory of our great God and Savior Jesus Christ[b] will appear. [14]He gave himself for us, to rescue us from all wickedness and to make us a pure people who belong to him alone and are eager to do good.

[15]Teach these things and use your full authority as you encourage and rebuke your hearers. Let none of them look down on you.

b. our great God and Savior Jesus Christ; or the great God and our Savior Jesus Christ.

This marvelous passage (vv. 11–14), like its companion in 3:4–7 (cf. 2 Tim. 1:8–10), displays so much theological grist that it is easy to analyze it solely on its own merits and thereby overlook its place in the context of the letter. Furthermore, the language employed, while reflecting Pauline usage, also evidences a rather large number of affinities with Hellenism (probably by way of Hellenistic Judaism), so that for some scholars the investigation of these matters has become the major interest.

The paragraph, in fact, serves a major function in the letter—providing the theological basis (the "indicative") for the instructions of 1:10–2:10 (the "imperative"). It begins (v. 11) by picking up the concern for the "outsider" from 2:10, reiterating a major concern from 1 Timothy—the universal scope of salvation (see disc. on 1 Tim. 2:3–7; 4:10). Then Paul appeals that the same grace that makes salvation available to all should instruct God's people in proper behavior (v. 12). Salvation, however, is not merely a present reality; it also includes a sure future for God's people (v. 13), because the same Lord Jesus Christ who has already come as the manifestation of God's grace (v. 14) will come again as the manifestation of God's glory (v. 13). The aim of that grace was to create a people for God who would be characterized by their "zeal for good works" (v. 14b).

Although the whole passage reflects Paul's theology of salvation as a past-present-future reality, the structure reveals that Paul's chief concern is to advise God's people about what salvation means for their present behavior (vv. 12 and 14b). This is apparently motivated by his further concern for the universality of salvation, including the "outsiders" on Crete.

This concern to remind the people that the gospel is the basis for Christian life (repeated in a more thorough way in 3:4–7) again suggests the more prophylactic nature of this letter, whose hearers would be more recent converts than those in Ephesus (1 Timothy).

2:11 / An explanatory **for** opens the paragraph and thus closely ties verses 11–14 to 2–10. It proceeds to explain why God's people should live as exhorted in 2–10 (so that the message from God will not be spoken evil of [v. 5] but instead will be attractive [v. 10]): because **God has revealed his grace for the salvation of mankind**.

In the Greek text all of verses 11–14 form a single sentence, of which "the **grace** of **God**" stands as the grammatical subject. This **grace**, Paul says, was **revealed** (the same word translated "will appear" in v. 13; for its meaning, see disc. on 1 Tim. 6:14; *epiphaneia*), not "to all men" (as NIV, KJV), but **for the salvation of all mankind** (see disc. on 1 Tim. 2:3–6).

Paul does not indicate here the reference point for this revelation of God's **grace**. Most likely he is thinking of the historical revelation effected in the saving event of Christ (v. 14; cf. 2 Tim. 1:9–10), but it could also refer existentially to the time in Crete when Paul and Titus preached the gospel and the Cretans understood and accepted its message (cf. 1:3 and 3:3–4). That at least is when the educative dimension of **grace**, emphasized in verse 12, took place.

2:12 / If the concern in this paragraph were to present a creedal or liturgical formula, as some believe, then theological logic would demand that the content of verse 14 appear next, since that verse expresses the *historical revelation* of God's **grace**. Instead, however, the issue is first of all Christian behavior. Hence Paul appeals to the Cretans through Titus to recall their own reception of **that grace**, which occurred at their conversion, when they first heard the gospel.

As he will spell out in more theological detail in verse 14, God's **grace instructs us** ethically in two directions. First, negatively, God's people must **give up ungodly living** (*asebeia*, cf. Rom. 1:18, the opposite of *eusebeia*, for which see disc. on 1 Tim. 2:2) **and worldly passions** (for this idea Paul usually says "fleshly" **passions**; cf. Gal. 5:16, 24). They are to give up such living, he says in verse 14, because Christ "gave himself for us, to rescue us from all wickedness."

Second, positively, they must live **self-controlled** (*sōphronōs*; see vv. 2, 5, 6 above), **upright** (*dikaiōs*; cf. 1 Thess. 2:10; see disc. on 1 Tim. 6:11), **and godly** (*eusebōs*; in contrast to *asebeia*) **lives in this world** (lit., "in the present age," in contrast to "the age of come"; see disc. on 1 Tim. 1:16). This likewise corresponds to the second statement about Christ's work in verse 14 ("to make us a pure people . . . eager to do good"). Together these two sides to Christian behavioral response reflect the "two ways" tradition, found in Judaism as early as Qumran and elaborated in detail in Christian documents at the beginning of the second century (Barnabas 18–21; *Didache* 1–6). Paul often presents Christian ethical instruction in this form (cf. "putting to death/bringing to life," Rom. 6:5–14; "works of the flesh/fruit of the Spirit," Gal. 5:16–26; "putting off/putting on" like a garment, Col. 3:8–14). Regularly, as here, what one must **give up** (better, "renounce," NEB) are **worldly passions** (Rom. 6:12; Gal. 5:24; Eph. 4:22), that is, desires that reflect the values of the present age with its antigodly mind-set.

The positive side in this passage picks up language regularly used in these letters, which is also that of Hellenistic moralism. Many in fact see the three words **self-controlled, upright, and godly** as expressing three of the four cardinal virtues of Platonism-Stoicism. One can scarcely doubt the correspondence, but in this passage, conditioned as it is by verses 13–14 and the three cardinal Christian virtues in verse 2, Paul is borrowing and adapting such language for Christian purposes, just as in Philippians 4:8–9.

2:13 / As in other places in the PE, Paul sets the Christian imperative in the context of "already/not yet" eschatology (see disc. on 1 Tim. 6:11–16; 2 Tim. 1:8–12). We are "to live godly lives in" the present age, **as we** also **wait for** its glorious future consummation, **when . . . Jesus Christ will appear**. However, the way Paul expresses this **hope** in this passage has been the subject of lengthy discussion. Literally, the text reads: "awaiting the blessed hope and appearing of the glory of the great God and our Savior Jesus Christ." Some of the ambiguities in the clause can be easily resolved. "The blessed hope" probably means "the hope that brings blessing, or blessedness" (hence, GNB: **the blessed Day we hope for**). The first "and" is almost certainly equal to "even" or "namely" (thus, "the hope that brings blessing, namely, the appearing . . . ").

But after that there is wide disagreement at three points: First, how are we to understand "of the glory"? Is it descriptive ("the glorious appearing," as KJV)? Or is it objective, the "what" of the manifestation (as GNB, RSV, et al.). In this case the GNB has the better of it. The Second Coming is the final manifestation of God's full **glory**, as the first advent was the manifestation of God's "grace" (v. 11) or, as in 1 Timothy 1:11, was the beginning of the manifestation of God's glory through the gospel.

Second, did Paul mean to say **our great God and Savior** (GNB) or "the **great God and** our **Savior**" (GNB margin, KJV)? Again the GNB (NIV, RSV) has the better of it, since (*a*) the single definite article before **great God** is best understood as controlling both nouns together, (*b*) the term **God and Savior** is stereotyped terminology both in the LXX and Hellenistic religions, and (*c*) nowhere else is God the Father understood to be joining the Son in the Second Coming.

Third, to what, then, does **Jesus Christ** stand in apposition? All who side with the KJV on the second question see it as in apposition to **our Savior**, as a kind of balance to the adjective **great**. Thus: "Our great God [the Father] and our Savior Jesus Christ." Most of those who take the position of the GNB on the second question see it as in apposition to **our great God and Savior**. It thus becomes one of the few unambiguous *statements* in the Pauline corpus that Jesus is God (cf. NIV, RSV *contra* GNB on Rom. 9:5). If so, then Paul may well be using it in opposition to Hellenistic cults, including the imperial cult, as an affirmation that Jesus Christ alone is **the great God and Savior** (see Harris, Hanson). The third option, which resolves the difficulties and carries none of its own, is to see it in apposition to "the glory of God." What will finally be manifested is God's **glory**, namely, **Jesus Christ**. (On the use of **glory**, see disc. on 1 Tim. 1:11; cf. 2 Cor. 4:4, 6; for a similar grammatical construction see Col. 2:2, lit., "the knowledge of the mystery of God, namely, Christ himself.")

In order to make his present point Paul would not have had to use the name at all. What he has said about the *parousia* is sufficient: **We wait** for the manifestation of **the glory of our great God and Savior**. He then adds the personal name, **Jesus Christ**, because he has some more things he wants to say about him (as in Col. 2:2), which leads to verse 14.

2:14 / What more he has to say concerns salvation as a past event, effected in the crucifixion of Christ, in which **he gave himself for us**. This is thoroughly Pauline language (e.g., Gal. 1:4), echoing the words of Jesus in Mark 10:45. In this instance Paul offers two reasons for Christ's giving

himself for us, corresponding to the "two-way" ethical response in verse 12. First, he died **to rescue us** ("redeem us," NIV, RSV; "free us," Goodspeed) **from all wickedness** (a direct verbal parallel to the LXX, Ps. 129:8 [130:8 in English]). This corresponds to the believers' renouncing "ungodly living and worldly passions" in verse 12. Second, he died **to make us a pure people** (lit., "to purify a people for himself") **who belong to him alone**. Much of this language is verbally dependent on the LXX of Ezekiel 37:23. The adjective translated **who belong to him alone**, meaning "a people set apart for himself," is from Exodus 19:5 (cf. Deut. 7:6; 14:2; 26:18). Again, Paul has appropriated the language used of God's people in the OT for the new people of God (cf. 1:1).

The purpose of this two-sided redemptive act was to create "a people for himself" who are characterized as **eager to do good** (lit., "full of zeal for good works"; cf. Deut. 26:18). This of course corresponds to living "self-controlled, upright, and godly lives in this world" (v. 12). With this, the paragraph has come full circle. The concern throughout has been with these "good works," but they are to be seen as the proper *response* to God's grace revealed and made effective in the saving death of Jesus Christ.

2:15 / Having set before them the theological basis for "good works" (God's saving grace manifested in Christ's redemptive act), Paul now turns to urge Titus to **teach these things**. Such *tauta* (**these things**) imperatives are frequent in 1 Timothy (see 4:6, 11, 15; 5:7, 21; 6:2, 11); this is the only occurrence in Titus (again, suggesting it is less urgent). **These things** refers at least to 2:2–14, perhaps to 1:10–16 as well. In any case the charge picks up three verbs that appear earlier. **Teach** ("speak") **these things** (cf. 2:1), he is told, which is a two-sided command. **Encourage** ("urge"; 2:6) the church; **rebuke** (1:13) the wayward. And do this with **your full authority**, which, of course, is his by his relationship to Paul.

This little interlude is then concluded with a rare personal word to Titus: **Let none of them look down on you**. This is reminiscent of 1 Timothy 4:12, but it lacks any mention of Titus' youth. This may suggest that Titus is older than Timothy; at least, it reflects a slightly different concern toward what Timothy was encountering in Ephesus than what Titus might be expected to in Crete.

Following this brief aside, reminding the people, as it were, of why Titus is there and of his authority, Paul will return in 3:1–11 to his concern that God's people exhibit good works, not only as the proper response to his love, but also for the sake of the "lost" who observe their behavior.

Additional Notes

For further reading on the nature of the language of this paragraph, see esp. D-C, pp. 142–46, who see the paragraph as a wholesale adoption of Hellenistic moral-religious language, including terms from the cult of the emperor. S. C. Mott ("Greek Ethics and Christian Conversion: The Philonic Background of Titus II 10–14 and III 3–7") sees an adoption of Philonic ideas. However, in both cases what seems to be missed is the thoroughly "Paulinized" way the language is now used (as with "wisdom" in 1 Cor. 1–3; "knowledge," etc., in Colossians; and "the heavenlies" in Ephesians). Paul has regularly shown himself a master at using the language of opponents or the situation to which he is writing and "breaking" and "molding" it to his own ends (cf. on *autarkēs*, "self-sufficiency," in Phil. 4:10–13; see disc. on 1 Tim. 6:6–8).

For a very readable discussion of Paul's theology reflecting the scheme of salvation as a past-present-future reality based on the work of Christ, see A. M. Hunter, *The Gospel According to St. Paul* (Philadelphia: Westminster, 1966).

2:11 / Because of the combination of **grace** being "manifested" (*epephanē*) and "instructing" (*paideuousa*, see note on v. 12), D-C comment: " 'Grace' in this context does not recall the grace of God of which Paul writes, but rather the 'graces' of the epiphanous gods in their manifestations (as they are praised, e.g., in the cult of the ruler)" (p. 144). One can hardly imagine a comment that is at once more influenced by presuppositions and more thoroughly off the mark than this one.

2:12 / The word for **instructs** (*paideuousa*), which Paul uses in its more common LXX sense of "discipline" in 1 Tim. 1:20 (cf. 1 Cor. 11:32), is seen as the "give-away" for the non-Pauline character of this paragraph, since it is a key word in Hellenistic moral philosophy. See, e.g., the classic on the Hellenistic mind by W. Jaeger, entitled *Paideia: The Ideals of Greek Culture* (Oxford, 1939). Thus Barrett contends: "In Paul grace is not educative, but liberating." But two things must be noted: First, the use of *paideuō* reflected here has already been taken over into Hellenistic Judaism (Wis. 6:11, 25 [cf. 11:19, showing the author knew both meanings of the word]; Sir. 6:32). Thus this usage fits with what is found throughout the letters—the language of Hellenistic Judaism. Second, ethical instruction regularly occurred as a part of Paul's gospel. Otherwise, passages like 1 Thess. 1:5b–10 (cf. 4:1 ff.) and 1 Cor. 4:17 (cf. 10:33–11:1) make little sense at all.

On the matter of the possible relationship of Paul's language to the four cardinal virtues, see especially S. C. Mott ("Greek Ethics and Christian Conversion").

2:13 / There is a considerable literature on this verse. The most recent and up-to-date discussion, which will also put one in touch with this literature, is by M. J. Harris, "Titus 2:13 and the Deity of Christ." The position espoused here in this commentary was first suggested by F. J. A. Hort, *The Epistle of St. James* (London: Macmillan, 1909), pp. 47, 103–4.

2:14 / It should be noted that this concern for "good works" is not non-Pauline, as some suppose. Paul avoids this language in the earlier controversial letters because his opponents were trying to establish a righteousness based on "works of Law." But from the beginning Paul expected the encounter with grace to issue in proper behavior, which only later he calls "good works" (cf. Eph. 2:8–10).

6

Instructions for Living in State and Society

TITUS 3:1-8a

Remind your people to submit to rulers and authorities, to obey them, and to be ready to do good in every way. ²Tell them not to speak evil of anyone, but to be peaceful and friendly, and always to show a gentle attitude toward everyone. ³For we ourselves were once foolish, disobedient, and wrong. We were slaves to passions and pleasures of all kinds. We spent our lives in malice and envy; others hated us and we hated them. ⁴But when the kindness and love of God our Savior was revealed, ⁵he saved us. It was not because of any good deeds that we ourselves had done, but because of his own mercy that he saved us, through the Holy Spirit, who gives us new birth and new life by washing us. ⁶God poured out the Holy Spirit abundantly on us through Jesus Christ our Savior, ⁷so that by his grace we might be put right with God and come into possession of the eternal life we hope for. ⁸This is a true saying.

After a brief exhortation to Titus (2:15) to "teach these things" (at least 2:1-14), Paul returns in this section to the major concern of the letter—"good works" (i.e., genuinely Christian behavior) for the sake of the outsider (3:1-8), and in contrast to the false teachers (3:9-11).

This section, however, makes a decided turn in the argument. In 2:1-14 the concern for "good works" had to do largely with relationships between believers, which when seen by outsiders would keep them from "speaking evil of the message" (2:5) and perhaps would even attract them to it (2:10). Now the interest centers in the effect of Christian behavior upon outsiders (3:1-2, 8). Again, as in 2:11-14, Paul offers a theological basis for such behavior (3:3-7), this time in the form of a semicreedal statement about salvation, with emphasis on God's mercy and the Spirit's regenerating work. God's people were at one time like all others (v. 3), but in mercy God saved them (vv. 4-5a). He has recreated them by the rebirth and renewal effected by the Holy Spirit (vv. 5b-6), so that they are now heirs of eternal life (v. 7). The point, made clear by the direct way it is driven home in verse 8, advises that what God has done in mercy for the Cretan believers he wants to do for others, and their own behavior as Christians will help serve that end.

The argument of the letter will then conclude (vv. 8b–11) with an appeal for Titus to give special emphasis to the teaching of verses 4–7, so that the people will be motivated to do good works for the sake of outsiders (v. 8), all of which is once again set in contrast to the false teachers (vv. 9–11).

3:1-2 / With the imperative, **remind your people** (lit., "them"), which flows naturally out of 2:15, Paul resumes the argument of 2:1. The verb **remind** (cf. 2 Tim. 2:14) implies that they should already know these things, or at least recognize them as genuine implications of the gospel. What follows, as often in these letters, is another list, which in this case combines some duties with attitudes and virtues.

Since the concern here is specifically with behavior toward outsiders, it begins at the logical place: behavior toward governing **authorities.** Titus' **people** are to submit themselves (cf. 2:5, 9) **to rulers and authorities**, and are **to obey them**. These imperatives raise all kinds of questions for today's Christians: What about rulers who would force one to do things against conscience (cf. Acts 4:19)? What about authorities who are suppressing Christianity? What about civil disobedience in a participatory democracy when laws are blatantly unjust? But these instructions in fact are consonant with Romans 13:1–8 and reflect a time (Paul's day) when the state was still a benefactor of Christians. For this positive attitude toward **rulers and authorities**, see also 1 Timothy 2:2. When the state turns against the church (as in the Revelation), believers still **submit**—unto death(!), and they do so precisely because they must not **obey** when it contravenes conscience (see Rev. 6:9–11; 12:11; 13:14).

Having begun with civil obedience as a Christian obligation, Paul next says that they should **be ready to do good in every way** (cf. 1:16; lit., "be prepared for every good work"). Some see this as a further elaboration of civic duty (e.g., Scott: "Christians should be among the foremost in showing public spirit," p. 172; cf. Kelly, Guthrie, Hendriksen). More likely this is a generalizing imperative that prepares the way for the rest of the list. It could include civic duty, but need not be so limiting.

Actually, this and the remaining items stand in sharp contrast to the false teachers. The latter are "unqualified for any good work" (1:16); believers are **to be ready to do** "any good work." The false teachers are involved in "arguments" and "quarrels" (3:9); God's people **are not to**

speak evil of anyone (*blasphēmein*; cf. 1 Tim. 6:5, *blasphēmiai*, "insults"); nor are they to be quarrelsome (better than GNB's **to be peaceful**; see disc. on 1 Tim. 3:3). Moreover, they are to be **friendly** (the translation "conciliatory" of Moffatt and Kelly is to be preferred).

Finally, still in obvious contrast to the arguments and strife of the false teachers, God's people, who are **to be ready to do good in every way**, must **always . . . show a gentle attitude** (cf. 1 Tim. 6:11; 2 Tim. 2:25) **toward everyone** (the "all people" of 1 Tim. 2:1, 4, 6; 4:10; Titus 2:11). This showing **a gentle attitude toward everyone** is the clear concern of the paragraph. Furthermore, it seems to have evangelistic overtones, not simply an interest in Christian reputation in the world.

3:3 / Just as verses 1–2 *function* as an appeal for good works directed specifically toward outsiders but in *form* take on the character of another "virtue" list, so also this verse functions as the evangelistic *reason* for the appeal of verses 1–2, but in form takes on the character of another "vice" list. In this case, however, as one might well expect given the content of verse 2, the sins listed are much less those of the false teachers and much more those of human fallenness in general (cf. Rom. 1:29–31; Gal. 5:19–21; and esp. 1 Cor. 6:9–11; this latter passage has several interesting parallels to vv. 3–7 in both form and content).

The evangelistic intent emerges in the **for we ourselves were once like them**. One should note that whenever Paul is moved to speak about the gospel he takes up the personal self-identification of **we ourselves** (cf. 2:11–14; 2 Tim. 1:9–10; Gal. 1:4; etc.). What **we ourselves were**—and *they* by implication still *are*—includes **foolish** (perhaps "without understanding," Williams), **disobedient** ("to God" is implied; cf. 1:16), **and wrong** (better, "deceived" [NIV] or "misguided" [Kelly]; it is Pauline theology that people living in sin are "duped" by Satan: cf. 1 Tim. 4:1–2; 2 Cor. 4:4). Because they are being led astray, they become **slaves to passions** (cf. Gal. 4:8, 9; Rom. 6:6) **and pleasures of all kinds** (interestingly, the only occurrence of this common Greek word in Paul). Furthermore, human fallenness involves us in malevolent behavior of all kinds: Like others, **we spent our lives in malice** (cf. Rom. 1:29; Col. 3:8) **and envy** (cf. 1 Tim. 6:4; Rom. 1:29; Gal. 5:21). The self-centeredness of our sinfulness ultimately caused **others** to **hate us** (this could mean "full of hate," but probably is a passive idea, as in GNB) **and** in turn **we hated them**. It is not a pretty picture, but as always, such lists unerringly diagnose the human condition.

3:4 / In verses 4–7, a single sentence in the Greek text, Paul offers the divine response to the human condition. As with 2:11–14, this theological statement about salvation has a twofold function in the argument: to set before the Cretan believers the gospel in capsule form, both as a reminder of the content of "sound teaching" and as a reinforcement of the evangelistic reasons for the appeals in verses 1–2 and 8—God is in the business of saving such people as described in verse 3—and at the same time to emphasize that salvation is not based on the "good works" to which he keeps appealing but depends totally upon God's mercy.

Because the sentence is so loaded with theological content, it is often described as hymnic (e.g., Guthrie) or liturgical (e.g., Hanson; cf. Kelly, p. 254). However, despite the exalted nature of its prose, it altogether lacks the poetic elements of a hymn. More likely this is an early creedal formulation, which presents Pauline soteriology (the doctrine of salvation) in a highly condensed form. Its language, as elsewhere in these letters, is a combination of Pauline elements and Hellenism (via Hellenistic Judaism), and as before, Paul is bringing such language into the service of the gospel in new forms.

The sentence begins (v. 4) with a *when*-clause. **But** even though "we ourselves were once" like others (v. 3), there came a time **when** God mercifully intervened in our behalf. Although **the kindness and love of God our Savior was revealed** historically in the person and work of Christ (cf. 2:11), the emphasis here, as verses 5–7 make clear, is on the believers' own experience of that **kindness and love** at the time of their rebirth and renewal. This clause in particular picks up Hellenistic themes. On **was revealed** see discussion on 1 Timothy 6:14 and Titus 2:11; on **God our Savior** see discussion on 1 Timothy 1:1. Although **kindness** (better, "goodness") occurs in Paul (Rom. 2:4; 11:22; Eph. 2:7), the combination **kindness and love** (for mankind; *philanthrōpia*) occurs frequently in Hellenism and Hellenistic Judaism as the highest virtues of both deities and human rulers. Paul simply presses their language into the service of the gospel.

3:5 / *What* God did, "when" his "kindness and love" for mankind appeared, was to **save us**. This is the main subject and verb of the whole sentence. The rest of the sentence gives the *basis* (**his own mercy**), the *what* (**new birth; new life**, "put right with God"), the *means* (**through the Holy Spirit**, "by his [Christ's] grace), and the *goal* (**the eternal life we hope for**) of salvation.

The basis of salvation is expressed in thoroughly Pauline terms. It was not because of any good deeds **that we ourselves had done** (cf. Eph.

156

2:8–9; Phil. 3:9; 2 Tim. 1:9), emphasized in this way here (and not in terms of "works of Law"—found only in Romans and Galatians) because of his frequent appeal for **good deeds** in this letter (1:16; 2:7, 14; 3:1, 8, 14). On the contrary, " 'tis **mercy** all, immense and free." As throughout the OT, salvation is God's prior action, based entirely on **his own mercy** (cf. 1 Tim. 1:12–16). Paul more often uses "grace" for this idea (but see Rom. 11:30–32); here, **God** in **mercy . . . saved us** (v. 5) "by [Christ's] grace" (v. 7).

The what of salvation is expressed in three metaphors: **new birth** and **new life** in this verse and justification ("put right with God") in verse 7. Between them they condense the twofold aspect of Christian conversion: (1) a new (renewed, restored) relationship with God—the *positional* aspect—expressed by "justification" and (2) a radical change in one's inner being—the *regenerational* aspect—expressed in new birth (*palingenesia*, "regeneration") **and new life** (*anakainōsis*, "renewal"). In this sentence the aspect of re-creation is mentioned first, with emphasis on the work of **the Holy Spirit**, who accomplished it **by** his **washing us**. This latter expression is seen by the GNB, probably correctly so, as a metaphor for spiritual "cleansing," although probably also alluding to baptism.

This translation, however, takes a decided stance on a very difficult phrase, which literally reads: "through the washing of regeneration and renewal of the Holy Spirit." For this collection of genitives ("of"-phrases) there have basically been three positions (with various modifications within each):

The first position is that **washing** refers to baptism and "renewal" to the coming of the Spirit, with both words dependent on **through** and referring to two distinct realities. These two realities are variously seen as conversion and confirmation (the traditional view) or conversion and baptism in the Spirit (a "holiness"-Pentecostal view). But there are some distinct disadvantages to this interpretation, including the fact that the words **new birth** and **new life** are nearly synonymous metaphors and that such an intent seems to need a repeated **through** in order to make it clear.

The second position is that **washing** refers solely to baptism and as such controls both genitives, "regeneration and renewal," which are effected at baptism by **the Holy Spirit**. This is the more common interpretation, which in turn elicits considerable discussion over the meaning of baptism in Paul and in this passage. The two words "regeneration and renewal" can be seen either as synonyms ("the washing of regeneration and renewal, effected by the Holy Spirit") or as one phrase explaining the other ("the washing of regeneration, that is, the renewal of the Holy

Spirit"). Although this view is certainly to be preferred in terms of its understanding of the middle terms, "regeneration and renewal," it tends to put more emphasis on baptism than the full context warrants.

The third position is that **washing** probably alludes to baptism but is in fact a metaphor for spiritual cleansing and not a synonym for baptism itself, the emphasis in the entire phrase being on the cleansing, regenerative work of **the Holy Spirit**. This is the view of the GNB and the one taken here in this commentary. It is fully in keeping with Pauline theology that the Holy Spirit is the absolute prerequisite of Christian existence (e.g., 1 Cor. 2:6-16; Rom. 6-8), and it seems confirmed by the emphases in the sentence itself (see disc. on v. 6).

Of the middle terms, **new birth** is found frequently in Hellenism and Hellenistic Judaism for a whole variety of "rebirths"—of deities in the mystery cults (e.g., Plutarch, *Isis and Osiris* 35), of the Jewish homeland (Jos., *Antiquities* 11.66), of the reincarnation of souls (e.g., Plutarch, *On the Eating of Flesh* 1, 2), and of initiates into the mystery cults (see note). One might compare the eschatological "regeneration of all things" mentioned by Jesus in Matthew 19:28. The idea here, of course, reflects Paul's "death, burial, new life" metaphor found in Romans 6:4-14. The term **new life** occurs only in Paul (cf. Rom. 12:2), and later Christian literature dependent on Paul, in all of Greek literature. The idea is reflected elsewhere in Paul in 2 Corinthians 5:14-17. Thus the two words are metaphors for the same spiritual reality—the re-creating work of **the Holy Spirit** in the believer's life.

3:6 / This verse, a relative clause in Greek, seems to confirm the interpretation of verse 5 just given. The key to Christian conversion, and subsequent life, is **the Holy Spirit**, whom **God poured out ... abundantly** (lit., "richly"; cf. 1 Tim. 6:17, "generously"—no scrimping with God) **on us**. Thus, for Paul, Christian life is life in the Spirit (Romans 8; Galatians 5), and its basic imperative is, "Walk in the Spirit" (Gal. 5:16). The language of God's **pouring out the Spirit** comes from Joel 2:28-30 (LXX, 3:1-2; cf. Acts 2:17-18). That God **poured out** his **Spirit ... through Jesus Christ our Savior** is not expressly said elsewhere in Paul, but it is in keeping with the expressions in 1 Corinthians 6:11 and with the rest of the NT (cf. Acts 2:33, John 14:26; 16:7). One should also note the inherent Trinitarianism of this clause (cf. 1 Cor. 12:4-6; Eph. 1:3-14), which sees the Father, Son, and Spirit working conjointly for our salvation.

3:7 / Having mentioned "Jesus Christ our Savior" (cf. 1:4), Paul reflects again on the *what* and the *means* of salvation, with his more well known metaphor of "justification by grace," before bringing the sentence to an end by noting the eschatological *goal* of salvation.

By an act of sheer **grace**, Christ **put** us **right with God** ("justified" us). This, as always in Paul, is also a metaphor, expressing the forensic (legal), positional aspect of salvation. Some have argued that the usage here, because it lacks "by faith," is not quite Pauline. But such a view both misses Paul's emphasis elsewhere (he uses "by faith" to contrast "by works of Law," but he *always* means "by grace through faith" as in Eph. 2:8–9) and overlooks 1 Corinthians 6:11 (with its order, "washed, sanctified, justified," and its coordinate "in [by] the name of our Lord Jesus Christ and in [by] the Spirit of our God," without any mention of "faith").

Finally, as always in Paul (cf. 2:11–14; 1 Tim. 1:16; 4:8–10; 6:12–14), salvation is to be fully realized eschatologically. Believers will ultimately **come into possession** (lit., "become heirs"; cf. Gal. 4:7; Rom. 8:17) **of the eternal life** (see disc. on 1 Tim. 1:16; 6:12; Titus 1:2) **we hope for** (cf. Titus 1:2; 1 Tim. 4:10).

3:8a / As it turns out, the preceding piece of exalted prose is another of the "faithful sayings" (GNB, **a true saying**) of the PE (cf. 1 Tim. 1:15; 3:1; 4:9; 2 Tim. 2:11). This is the second instance (cf. 1 Tim. 4:9) where the formula follows the **saying** (although Scott curiously suggests that it is to be found in v. 8).

Because the other "faithful sayings" are more pithy and formulaic, there has been considerable debate over the extent of the actual saying (vv. 3–7, D-C; 5b–6, Kelly; 5–7; Spicq, Guthrie; 4–7, the majority). Surely here the majority view is correct, since verses 4–7 are the complete sentence. Some are simply overconvinced that the author has used a prior source and that *logos* must mean **saying** (see disc. on 1 Tim. 3:1). Both its position and meaning become clear when one takes the formula as the beginning of a new compound sentence, joined by an untranslated "and" (GNB and others) in the Greek text: **This is a true saying**, *and* "I want you to give special emphasis to these matters" (i.e., the content of vv. 1–7, but esp. of 4–7), which will bring the whole argument back to the concern that they do good works for the sake of outsiders.

Additional Notes

3:1 / There has been considerable debate over the terms used here for **rulers** ["powers"] **and authorities** (*archai, exousiai*). The latter is used alone of governing authorities in Rom. 13:1–7. When used together elsewhere in Paul (e.g., Col.

1:16; 2:15; Eph. 6:12), they refer to spiritual powers. Luke, however, uses them together to refer to earthly authorities (12:11). The debate has focused on whether spiritual powers are seen to be controlling the government authorities (as in O. Cullmann, *The State in the New Testament* [London: SCM, 1957], et al.) and whether the "powers" are demonic or angelic. For the latest full discussion, with bibliography, see W. Carr, *Angels and Principalities* SNTSMS 42 (Cambridge: Cambridge University Press, 1981).

3:4 / On the question as to whether or not vv. 4–7 comprise a hymnic or liturgical fragment, it should be noted that NT scholarship is all too prone to use such language even when the barest poetic requirements (structure and meter) are missing. No poetic elements appear in this sentence (despite the way it is set out in the Nestle-Aland Greek NT); it forms a compressed theological compendium, which looks as if it could be creedal, although it lacks any "we believe" formulation. On this matter see A. Lesky, *A History of Greek Literature* (New York: Crowell, 1963), pp. 759–63; and W. Goodwin, *A Greek Grammar* (Boston: Ginn, 1892), pp. 348–49.

For the Hellenistic background to the terms **kindness and love**, see D-C, pp. 143–46. S. C. Mott (see "Greek Ethics and Christian Conversion") sees these terms as personifications; however, both the language and Philonic parallels are pressed a bit too hard in order to draw such a conclusion.

3:5 / It is of more than passing interest to watch NT scholarship, already convinced of the non-Pauline authorship of these letters, argue that many features in this sentence (vv. 5–7), including the **not . . . but** clause in this verse, are not fully Pauline. In this case the failure to say "works of Law" or "by faith" is seen to be the giveaway (cf. Barrett, p. 141). But if one were to presuppose that Paul did not write 1 Corinthians, the same arguments could be used to demonstrate the non-Pauline character of 6:11 or 8:5–6! This passage, as Barrett et al. acknowledge, "conveys accurately enough Pauline doctrine." The matter of *language* in such a passage reflects the difference in historical setting, not authorship.

For a thorough discussion of the first two alternatives for understanding the middle terms of this verse, see G. R. Beasley-Murray, *Baptism in the New Testament*, pp. 209–16. For a presentation similar to the one adopted here (alternative 3), see J. D. G. Dunn, *Baptism in the Holy Spirit*, pp. 165–70.

For a discussion of rebirth in Hellenism, see D-C, pp. 148–50, although their enamorment with parallels in the mysteries seems to preclude their hearing the passage in terms of Pauline theology.

3:7 / Beasley-Murray (*Baptism in the NT*) argues that the verb "to justify" has more a dynamic than a forensic sense in this passage, as in 1 Cor. 6:11. He may be correct, but it may also be that he has not taken seriously enough the metaphorical sense of this word group in Paul.

3:8a / For a discussion of the extent and meaning of this **true saying**, see G. W. Knight, *The Faithful Sayings in the Pastoral Letters*, pp. 80–111.

7

Final Exhortations: To Good Works and Against Errors

TITUS 3:8b–11

I want you to give special emphasis to these matters, so that those who believe in God may be concerned with giving their time to doing good deeds, which are good and useful for everyone. ⁹But avoid stupid arguments, long lists of ancestors, quarrels, and fights about the Law. They are useless and worthless. ¹⁰Give at least two warnings to the person who causes divisions, and then have nothing more to do with him. ¹¹You know that such a person is corrupt, and his sins prove that he is wrong.

With these final exhortations Paul brings the "argument" of the letter, which began in 1:5, to its fitting conclusion. Actually these verses do not so much form a new paragraph as bring the paragraph begun in 3:1 to a conclusion. This is especially true of verse 8, which begins (as noted in discussion on 3:8a): "This is a faithful saying; and concerning these things, I want you to give special emphasis." At the same time, however, the contrasts picked up in verse 9, which tie to verse 8 through the motif of **useful** and **useless** deeds, also reach back to 1:10–16, thus bringing the whole letter to conclusion.

The net result is that the argument from 1:10 (which hinges on 1:9) to 3:11 forms a kind of chiasmus:

a 1:10–16—warnings against the false teachers, with their "false works"

  b 2:1–14—specific "good works" for specific believers, with the outsider in view, plus their theological basis

  b′ 3:1-8—once again, "good works" for outsiders, this time directed toward them, and again with their theological basis

a′ 3:9–11—final warning against the false teachers and their "false works"

3:8b / As noted in the discussion on 3:8a, the presence of an "and," connecting **this is a true saying** with the opening clause of this verse, indicates the closest kind of tie between verse 8 and verses 1–7. Paul **wants** (not as strong a verb as "urge"; used also at 1 Tim. 2:8 and 5:14) Titus **to give special emphasis** (a verb used of the confident assertions of the false teachers in 1 Tim. 1:7) **to these matters**. The word *tauta* (**these matters**) refers at least to verses 4–7, but perhaps Paul intends to include all of verses 1–7. As in 2:11–14, and elsewhere in Paul (cf., e.g., Rom. 12:1–2; Gal. 5–6), the appeal for truly Christian behavior is predicated on a proper hearing of the gospel.

The reason that Titus should give **special emphasis to** the **matters** of verses 1–7 is **so that those who believe in God may be concerned with giving their time to** (on this verb, see disc. on 1 Tim. 3:4) **doing good deeds** (cf. the purpose of redemption as expressed in 2:14). By **those who believe in God** (lit., "who have believed in God"), Paul obviously means Christian believers, those who have trusted God's mercy for salvation as expressed in verses 4–7 (here is the "by faith" some see as missing in that passage; see note on v. 5). By **good deeds**, as elsewhere, Paul intends all kinds of Christian behavior, including attitudes.

The expressed goal of such Christian behavior is that it be **good and useful for everyone**. In the Greek text this forms a new sentence, which literally says: "These things [*tauta*] are good and useful for people." Kelly thinks "these things" refers to the previous *tauta* (**these matters**) in the verse, and therefore translates: "These are admirable truths and useful for people." However, since the corresponding "useless" in verse 9 refers to the "evil works" of the false teachers, it is much more likely that "these things" here refers to the believers' **good deeds** (as GNB). The goal, therefore, is at least partly "evangelistic." **Good deeds** "benefit" (are **useful** for) people, not only by affecting them positively, but also by attracting them to the truth of the gospel.

3:9 / With the adversative conjunction **but**, Titus is now told to **avoid** some "evil works" that stand in obvious contrast to the **good deeds** of verse 8, as they were delineated in verses 1–2. Although the imperative is to Titus personally, the context makes it clear that the imperative is intended for the whole church as well. It is also evident, both from the language itself and from verses 10–11 that follow, that the false teachers are once more in purview.

Four of their **useless and worthless** deeds are mentioned. Titus—and the Cretans—are to **avoid**: **stupid** ("foolish"; cf. 2 Tim. 2:23) **arguments** (cf. 1 Tim. 6:4; 2 Tim. 2:23), **long lists of ancestors** ("genealogies"; see disc. on 1 Tim. 1:4), **quarrels** (or "strife"; see disc. on 1 Tim. 6:4, a word that frequently makes Paul's "vice" lists: e.g., Rom. 1:29; 13:13; 1 Cor. 3:3; 2 Cor. 12:20; Gal. 5:20), **and fights** (cf. 2 Tim. 2:23 and the compound "word battles" in 1 Tim. 6:4; 2 Tim. 2:14, plus the negated form, "not quarrelsome," in v. 2 and 1 Tim. 3:3) **about the Law.** The addition of this final adjective (translated **about the Law**) helps to put some other items in these letters into focus (see esp. disc. on 1:14–16; cf. 1 Tim. 1:6–7; 4:1–5). Thus it is not only the theological aberrations (1:10–16) of the false teachers, but their **useless** (the opposite of "useful" in v. 8) **and worthless** behavior as well, that distresses Paul.

3:10 / Having mentioned these evil deeds (obviously of the false teachers) that Titus and the people are to **avoid,** Paul turns his attention once more to the teachers themselves. Here they are described as **the person who causes divisions.** Because the adjective *hairetikon* (lit., "divisive") in later times came to be used of those who held to false doctrines (as these teachers obviously do), the KJV (cf. NEB, NAB, et al.) translated it *heretic.* But that is to read later ideas back into the text. The context (v. 9) makes it clear that the problem is with these people's behavior, not their theology per se. Hence it is their divisiveness (cf. RSV, "factious") that is in view (cf. the use of the noun in 1 Cor. 11:19; Gal. 5:20). Unfortunately, all too often in the church the "orthodox," in ferreting out "heretics" (i.e., people who hold different views from mine), have become the "divisive" ones!

Titus is to **give at least two warnings** (or "admonitions," a Pauline word on the NT) **to** this **person.** Thus he still holds out the hope of redeeming such people, as elsewhere in the PE (2 Tim. 2:25–26; see also disc. on 1 Tim. 1:20) and in Paul (2 Thess. 3:14–15; 2 Cor. 2:5–11).

But when **the person who causes divisions** pays no heed to the "admonitions," he is to be rejected: **Have nothing to do with him** (the same verb as in 1 Tim. 5:11). Does this mean then that Paul has now become untrue to himself and to what he has just said about divisive people? Hardly, as verse 11 will make clear.

3:11 / The reason the divisive person is to be rejected is precisely that, in his divisiveness, **such a person** demonstrates that he **is corrupt, and his sins prove that he is wrong.** Although this translation captures the essence of Paul's clause, it misses a fine point or two. In persisting in divisive behavior, the false teacher "has become perverted" or "turned aside" (Gk. perfect tense) "and is continuing in his sinning" (Gk. present tense), thus "being self-condemned." That is, by his very persistence in his sinful behavior he has condemned himself, thus putting himself on the outside, hence to be rejected by Titus and the church.

It is of more than passing interest that a warning against those who cause divisions, similar to these verses, appears at the same place at the end of Romans (16:17–20).

Additional Note

3:8 / The expression **giving their time to good works** is translated by Moffatt "make a point of practicing honorable occupations" (cf. RSV), thus tying it back to a narrower view of "every good work" in v. 1. However, both the immediate context of vv. 9–11 and the full context of the letter make it clear that the concern is not with "occupations" but with Christian behavior of all kinds.

Personal Instructions and Greetings

TITUS 3:12–15

When I send Artemas or Tychicus to you, do your best to come to me in Nicopolis, because I have decided to spend the winter there. ¹³Do your best to help Zenas the lawyer and Apollos to get started on their travels, and see to it that they have everything they need. ¹⁴Our people must learn to spend their time doing good, in order to provide for real needs; they should not live useless lives.

¹⁵All who are with me send you greetings. Give our greetings to our friends in the faith.

God's grace be with you all.

In a typically Pauline fashion the letter closes with some final personal instructions (vv. 12–13; cf. Rom. 16:1–2; 1 Cor. 16:5–12; Col. 4:7–9), plus a "parting shot," repeating the concern of the letter (v. 14; cf. Rom. 16:1–20a; 2 Cor. 13:11; Gal. 6:17), final greetings, including greetings *from* Paul and his companions *to* all believers in Crete (v. 15a; cf. most of the Pauline letters), and the final benediction (v. 15b; cf. all the letters).

One should compare these instructions and greetings with the two letters to Timothy. The First Letter to Timothy has none of this, except the benediction, indicating that although both letters (1 Timothy and Titus) tend to be "all business," 1 Timothy is more so, despite its more frequent personal exhortations to Timothy. The Second Letter to Timothy is more personal in every way, including an opening thanksgiving (1:3–5) and a much longer conclusion, with personal instructions (4:9–18) and final greetings (4:19–22).

The information gleaned from verses 12–13 gives us some help in piecing together the history of this period in Paul's life. As with 1 Timothy, but in sharp contrast to 2 Timothy, Paul is still ministering in the East, probably in Macedonia, directing the affairs of his churches. The casual way he invites Titus to rejoin him after Artemas or Tychicus comes to relieve him in Crete further indicates what has been observed throughout the letter—it simply lacks the ugency of the situation in Ephesus (1 Timothy). A pseudepigrapher who created these various settings, and consistently carried them through, pulled off a remarkable achievement indeed, and all the more so if trying to speak to a singular situation in the author's own day.

3:12 / Paul begins to bring the letter to a close with these personal words. Despite the directions to Titus in this letter, Paul apparently intends that soon after it is received, presumably brought by Zenas and Apollos (v. 13), Titus is to be replaced on Crete and is to return to Paul. This again reinforces our observation made throughout of the less urgent, more prophylactic, nature of this letter, which is more for the church than for Titus.

At the time of writing Paul has not yet decided on Titus' replacement, **Artemas** (of whom nothing more is known) or **Tychicus** (cf. Acts 20:4; Col. 4:7; Eph. 6:21). On the basis of Paul's eventually having sent **Tychicus** to Ephesus (2 Tim. 4:12) and of Titus' departure for Dalmatia (2 Tim. 4:10), up the coast from **Nicopolis**, we may safely conjecture that the plan eventually materialized with the sending of **Artemas**.

As for Titus himself, Paul wants him to **do** his **best** (cf. 2 Tim. 4:9, 21) **to come to** Paul in **Nicopolis**, where he has **decided to spend the winter**. The **there** verifies that Paul was not currently **in Nicopolis**, but it is quite impossible to know his location from the available information.

Nicopolis itself is considerably off the "beaten track," by both land and sea. A newer city, founded by Augustus on the site of his camp after his victory (hence *niko*, "victory," *polis*, "city") over Mark Antony at Actium in 31 B.C., it is situated about two hundred miles northwest of Athens on the north side of the Ambracian Gulf near the Adriatic Sea.

It might be noted that several details in this verse put considerable strain on the hypothesis of pseudepigraphy: Paul's "indecision" as to whom to send; the use of an otherwise unknown person (**Artemas**); the desire for Titus, to whose care the church has been "entrusted," to leave Crete; the choice of **Nicopolis** as the place of rendezvous. It is hard to believe that a later author, who allegedly used Acts as his point of departure, would have done all of this, since none of it corresponds to any data in Acts.

3:13 / Titus is also to **do** his **best to help Zenas the lawyer and Apollos to get started on their travels** (NIV, "to help on their way"), **and see to it they have everything they need**. These men presumably had been with Paul, and when he discovered that their travel plans would take them to Crete, he sent this letter along with them. Now in turn he reminds Titus of his Christian responsibility to assist them **on their** further **travels**. Such assistance for travelers was apparently a recognized Christian practice (see Acts 15:3; 21:5; Rom. 15:24; 1 Cor. 16:6, 11; 2 Cor. 1:16; 3 John 6, where the same verb, "to help on the way," occurs in each instance).

Nothing further is known of **Zenas the lawyer**, whose designation probably means that he was a jurist (expert in Roman law) by profession. It is a Pauline touch to identify a professional by his title (cf. "Luke the physician," Col. 4:14; "Erastus, the city treasurer," Rom. 16:23). **Apollos** is assumed to be the well-known, eloquent Alexandrian of that name (Acts 18:24–19:1; 1 Cor. 1:12; 3:4–22; 16:12).

3:14 / The probability that **Zenas and Apollos** were the bearers of this letter is further supported by this unexpected intrusion into these final, personal greetings. Having mentioned their names and Titus' need to assist them, Paul is also reminded of their destination and is thus prompted to give the Cretan believers themselves a final parting word: **Our people** too (there is an untranslated *kai*, "also, too," in the text) **must learn to spend their time doing good** (cf. v. 8). The infinitive phrase, **to spend their time doing good**, is an exact repetition from verse 8 of "giving their time to doing good deeds." This is the recurring theme of the entire letter (1:16; 2:7, 14; 3:1, 8). In this instance the "good works" are qualified as for the purpose of providing **for real needs** (lit., "necessary needs"). Consequently, this final word lifts the concern above those attitudinal and behavioral "deeds" that stand basically in contrast to the arguments and quarrels of the false teachers.

It remains uncertain whether **to provide for** "necessary" **needs** reflects their need to work so as to supply their own everyday needs (so NEB, JB, NAB) or to help with the "urgent needs" (Kelly) of others (RSV, NIV, et al.). The context, of both verse 8 and verse 13, suggests the latter as the better alternative. The final purpose of such good deeds is "that they might not be unfruitful" (cf. Kelly, "otherwise they will be good for nothing"), a concern that is slightly obscured by the imperative of the GNB's **they should not live useless lives**. Fruitful Christians are so as they minister to the needs of others.

3:15 / The letter closes with the final **greetings**, first to Titus from **all who are with me** (cf. 1 Cor. 16:20; 2 Cor. 13:12; Phil. 4:22; cf. also Rom.

16:21–23 and Col. 4:10–14, where those with Paul are mentioned by name). Then he tells Titus to **give our greetings to our friends in the faith**. **Our friends** is perhaps a bit weak as a translation for "all those who love us" (NIV, RSV). This way of putting it is probably an indirect reference to the fact that some in Crete have proven themselves disloyal to Paul and his gospel.

For the final benediction, **God's grace be with you all**, see discussion on 1 Timothy 6:21. Thus this letter to a longtime companion in ministry, born out of concern for the nascent churches in Crete but with considerably less urgency than that to Timothy in Ephesus, concludes with a benediction, praying for **God's grace** to **be** on them **all**.

Additional Note

For examples of the formal closings of ancient letters, see F. X. J. Exler (*The Form of the Ancient Greek Letter of the Epistolary Papyri*), pp. 69–77 and 111–13.

1

Salutation

From Paul, an apostle of Christ Jesus by God's will, sent to proclaim the promised life which we have in union with Christ Jesus—

²To Timothy, my dear son:
May God the Father and Christ Jesus our Lord give you grace, mercy, and peace.

After the long elaboration in the salutation to Titus (see disc. on Titus 1:1-4), Paul reverts to a more standard, brief form in this final letter to Timothy. Indeed, except for some slight modifications, these two verses are nearly identical to 1 Timothy 1:1-2. However, as in all his letters, these "slight" modifications reflect nuances of his changed circumstances and of his concerns in this letter.

1:1 / It may seem somewhat surprising to us that Paul in such a personal letter should style himself **an apostle of Christ Jesus**. His reason for doing so probably differs slightly from 1 Timothy 1:1 (which see). There, it was to lend authority both to the letter and to Timothy. Here it may simply be habit; more likely, however, it reflects the urgent appeal found throughout the letter for loyalty to Paul and his gospel. Because the concern is not now to establish Timothy's own authority, Paul also reverts to his more common **by God's will** (cf. 1 and 2 Corinthians, Colossians, Ephesians), in lieu of "by order of God" in 1 Timothy. Apostleship, even for one who must suffer for it, is only and always **by God's will**.

The next modifier, **sent to proclaim** (lit., "is in accordance with") **the promised life which we have in union with Christ Jesus**, is the one major difference from the salutation in 1 Timothy. In part this reflects the language of the "faithful saying" in 1 Timothy 4:8. It is not at all surprising, given the nature of this letter with its more intensified eschatological outlook, that Paul should reflect on his apostleship in such eschatological terms at the outset. The **promised life** is that which is "for the future" in 1 Timothy 4:8; but it is also ours in the present as we are **in union with Christ Jesus**. As with the resurrection and the Holy Spirit, present **union**

169

with Christ is the "first fruit" (1 Cor. 15:20) or "down payment" (Eph. 1:14) of the promised fullness of life that is yet to be.

1:2 / This verse exactly parallels 1 Timothy 1:2, except that **dear son** replaces "my true son in the faith." Again, this reflects the altered circumstances. This letter is not for the church in Ephesus; hence no need exists to legitimatize Timothy before them. Timothy is now **my dear** (or "beloved") **son**, as he has always been for Paul (see 1 Cor. 4:17). The appeal to these close ties will become a large part of this letter.

For the other matters in this verse, see the discussion on 1 Timothy 1:2.

Additional Note

1:1 / The force of the words "which is in Christ Jesus," translated **which we have in union with Christ Jesus** by the GNB, has been blunted by the NEB to say, "whose promise of life is fulfilled in Christ Jesus," and by Easton, et al., to say, "given by Christ Jesus." See Barrett for a proper critique of the NEB and Kelly for a critique of Easton.

Thanksgiving

I give thanks to God, whom I serve with a clear conscience, as my ancestors did. I thank him as I remember you always in my prayers night and day. ⁴I remember your tears, and I want to see you very much, so that I may be filled with joy. ⁵I remember the sincere faith you have, the kind of faith that your grandmother Lois and your mother Eunice also had. I am sure that you have it also.

The common practice in the Hellenistic world was to begin letters with a formalized prayer-wish for the recipient's general welfare, including good health (cf. 3 John 2). As with the salutation (see disc. on 1 Tim. 1:1–2), however, such forms in Paul's hands become thoroughly Christianized. Although a formal prayer still can be found (e.g., Col. 1:9–14; Phil. 1:9–11), more often Paul has turned it into a thanksgiving or benediction (in nine of his previous letters, excepting Galatians, 1 Timothy, and Titus; see disc. on 1 Tim. 1:3–11, Titus 1:5–9).

This present thanksgiving is quite in keeping with the more personal nature of 2 Timothy; it also resembles the earlier thanksgivings, whose contents anticipate so much of their respective letters (see esp. 1 Cor. 1:4–9; Phil. 1:3–11). Paul is about to urge Timothy to loyalty (to himself) and perseverance (in the gospel), especially in the face of hardship. In so doing he will appeal to his (Paul's) own example (e.g., 1:11–12; 2:9–10; 3:10–11), to their long association (e.g., 3:10–11), and to Timothy's own spiritual history (e.g., 1:6–7, 13–14; 3:10–15). These are precisely the items that dominate the thanksgiving.

Thus, by way of thanksgiving, he reminds Timothy of his past loyalty (v. 4) and faith (v. 5) and of their common "roots" in the faith (vv. 3 and 5). From these reminders he will launch his initial appeal for steadfastness (vv. 6–14).

1:3 / As a former Law-keeping Pharisee (Phil. 3:5), Paul would long ago have made it his habit to pray regularly. Such a practice was easily carried over to his Christian life so that he prayed **night and day** (cf. the requirement for widows in 1 Tim. 5:5). These **prayers** normally consisted of giving **thanks to God** *for* his recipients (**as I remember you always in my prayers**), *because* of something God had done in their lives (v. 5; cf. Rom. 1:8; 1 Cor. 1:4–7; Phil. 1:3–6; Col. 1:3–7; 1 Thess. 1:2–3; 2 Thess. 2:13; Philem. 4–5). The word **always**, which occurs in most of the thanksgivings, does not refer to unceasing prayer and thanksgiving (as implied in the KJV) but indicates that he **always** remembered Timothy in his regular times of prayer (as GNB).

In mentioning **God** in this case, Paul adds a remarkable qualifier: **whom I serve with a clear conscience** (for this phrase, see disc. on 1 Tim. 1:5), **as my ancestors did**. The clause itself is not so unusual (cf. Rom. 1:9, "whom I serve with my whole heart in preaching the gospel of his Son," NIV); but the final phrase is (lit., "from my forefathers," which can mean, **as my ancestors did** [GNB], or "[the God] of my forefathers" [NAB]). Because of Paul's word order, the GNB is probably correct. But what could he possibly be trying to say? Most likely this prepares the way for the reminder to Timothy in verse 5, by suggesting that Paul's service unto God stands in the true succession of the religion of the OT, that genuine continuity exists between the OT (cf. esp. 3:14–17) and his preaching of the gospel (cf. Acts 24:14; 26:6; Rom. 2:28–29; 4:9–17; 9:1–9; Gal. 3:6–9). The reason for such an emphasis here is perhaps related to the false teachers, who are also using the OT, but "falsely" so (cf. 1 Tim. 1:7; Titus 3:9). In any case, this theme will be repeated throughout the Epistle (1:9–10; 2:8, 19; 3:8, 14–17).

1:4 / Verses 3–5 form a single sentence in the Greek, whose structural relationships are somewhat blurred by the GNB. The basic sentence reads: "I give thanks to God, . . . *as* I remember you always in my prayers" (v. 3), . . . *because* (or *when*) "I remember your sincere faith" (v. 5). Verse 4, therefore, reads as something of an aside. The mention of remembering Timothy "in his prayers" (v. 3) prompts in Paul a memory of another kind—their last parting (probably that referred to in 1 Tim. 1:3). One can hardly escape the sense of pathos. "When I remember you in my prayers," Paul says, "I am filled with longing **to see you**, because I also am continually reminded of **your tears** when we last parted."

Although this deviates slightly from the main thrust of the sentence, it nonetheless strikes a note that belongs to the ultimate reason for the letter—Paul's loneliness in his final vigil and his desire for Timothy to join him, despite the unfinished work in Ephesus (hence 2:2; see 4:6–8, 9, 16, 21). Thus he **wants to see** him **very much, so that** he **may be filled with joy**.

1:5 / With this clause Paul returns to the thanksgiving proper, now expressing the basis for it—God's work in Timothy's life. This work is expressed in terms of Timothy's **sincere** (or perhaps better in these letters, "genuine"; see disc. on 1 Tim. 1:5) **faith**, which in this case means at least his genuine trust in God but also perhaps moves toward the idea of "faithfulness," that is, his continuing steadfast in his **faith**. Paul regularly considers this quality in God's people to be thankworthy (cf. 1 Thess. 1:3; 3:6–7; 2 Thess. 1:3; Rom. 1:8; Col. 1:4; Philem. 5).

Because this letter will basically be an *appeal* to Timothy to maintain his loyalty and steadfastness (to Christ, Paul, and the ministry of the gospel) in the face of suffering, he is therefore prompted to remind Timothy that the same **faith** he has—and is to be loyal to—was that **kind of faith that your grandmother Lois and your mother Eunice also had**. That is, "Don't lose heart, because just as my ministry has continuity with my forebears (v. 3), so does yours. Don't forget your roots; they go way back, and your own **faith** is like that of **your mother** and **grandmother**."

The mention of his maternal parentage is in keeping with the evidence of Acts 16:1, where we learn that **Eunice** was a Jewish Christian, whose husband was a Gentile. Paul's appeal to her **faith**, therefore, although almost certainly referring to her faith as a believer in Christ, also reflects his view that such faith is the genuine expression of the Jewish heritage, that is, that faith in Christ is the true continuity with the religion of the OT (cf. v. 3). It should also be noted in passing that, the more personal the letter, the more often Paul mentions personal names (twenty-two in this letter; cf. Philemon, nine).

Finally, to register his concern one more time, he adds, **I am sure you have it also**. This confidence in Timothy's genuine **faith** becomes the springboard for the appeal that follows (1:6–2:13). Thus, as in other letters (esp. 1 Thessalonians, Romans, and Colossians), the thanksgiving not only sets out some of the themes of the letter but actually moves directly into the letter itself.

Additional Notes

For a collection of examples of the prayer-wish in the Hellenistic letters, see F. X. J. Exler (*The Form of the Ancient Greek Letter of the Epistolary Papyri*), pp. 102–111. For a collection of the letters themselves, see A. S. Hunt and C. C. Edgar, *Select Papyri I*, Loeb (Cambridge, Mass.: Harvard University Press, 1932), pp. 268–395.

The best recent discussion of the Pauline thanksgivings is by P. T. O'Brien,

Introductory Thanksgivings in the Letters of Paul, NovT Suppl. 49 (Leiden: Brill, 1977), who, unfortunately, chooses not to include this one (p. 2). Although there are some linguistic features about the thanksgiving that are not Paul's ordinary usage (these are conveniently set out by Kelly, p. 155), the whole is so Pauline that one should wonder how a pseudepigrapher could have so thoroughly grasped the spirit of the man, yet fail to use his precise language. Changes in Paul's own linguistic patterns could be more easily accounted for.

3

Appeal to Loyalty Despite Hardship

For this reason I remind you to keep alive the gift that God gave you when I laid my hands on you. [7]For the Spirit that God has given us does not make us timid; instead, his Spirit fills us with power, love, and self-control.

[8]Do not be ashamed, then, of witnessing for our Lord; neither be ashamed of me, a prisoner for Christ's sake. Instead, take your part in suffering for the Good News, as God gives you the strength for it. [9]He saved us and called us to be his own people, not because of what we have done, but because of his own grace by means of Christ Jesus before the beginning of time, [10]but now it has been revealed to us through the coming of our Savior, Christ Jesus. He has ended the power of death and through the gospel has revealed immortal life.

[11]God has appointed me as an apostle and teacher to proclaim the Good News, [12]and it is for this reason that I suffer these things. But I am still full of confidence, because I know whom I have trusted, and I am sure that he is able to keep safe until that Day what he has entrusted to me.[a] [13]Hold firmly to the true words that I taught you, as the example for you to follow, and remain in the faith and love that are ours in union with Christ Jesus. [14]Through the power of the Holy Spirit, who lives in us, keep the good things that have been entrusted to you.

a. what he has entrusted to me; *or* what I have entrusted to him.

This section forms the first part of an appeal—extending through 2:13—that urges Timothy to be steadfast and loyal, in the face of increasing gains by the false teachers, on the one hand (2:16–18; 3:13; 4:3–4), and increasing defections of various kinds (1:15; 4:10, 16) due to Paul's (apparently political) imprisonment (1:8, 12; 2:9; 4:16–17), on the other. In light of these circumstances, he appeals for Timothy's continued loyalty to his own Spirit-given ministry (vv. 6–7, 13–14; cf. 1 Tim. 1:18; 4:14), which means in turn to be loyal to Christ and his gospel (vv. 8a, 9–10) and to Paul in his imprisonment (vv. 8b, 11–12).

The argument begins and ends with an emphasis on the **empowering of the Holy Spirit** for Timothy's ministry (vv. 6–7 and 13–14). Verse 8 sets the stage for the rest by its two-sided appeal: **not to be ashamed of**

Christ or of Paul his **prisoner** but, on the contrary, to be ready to **take** his own **part in** the present **suffering**. The basis for such an appeal is grounded in the gospel of Christ, who has given us hope by his abolition of death and revelation of life and immortality (vv. 9–10). Thus, **do not be ashamed of** Christ (v. 8a). Then he reminds Timothy of his (Paul's) own ministry, as one who is not ashamed to suffer for Christ, because God can be fully trusted to keep safe what has been entrusted to him. Thus, **do not be ashamed of me**.

Examples of those who have deserted Paul (v. 15) and of one who was not ashamed of him (vv. 16–18) follow this first appeal. The second part of the appeal (2:1–13) takes up especially the theme of Timothy's need for steadfastness as he takes his own **part in** the **suffering**.

1:6 / As noted in the discussion on v. 5, Paul moves directly from the thanksgiving to the main concern of the letter. The **for this reason** refers to the genuine faith that Paul is persuaded really does reside in Timothy. Believing that he has such faith, Paul now **reminds** him (a verb chosen almost certainly because of the threefold "remember" in vv. 3–5) **to keep alive the gift**. The verb translated **to keep alive** is a metaphor for rekindling a waning fire. It does not necessarily imply an actual wavering or dying faith on Timothy's part, but it does urge with very strong language that he "fan into flame" (NIV) **the gift that God** gave him long ago at the time of his call, **when** Paul **laid** his **hands on** him.

The picture of Timothy that emerges from these two verses (6 and 7), and throughout the Epistle, coincides with what surfaces elsewhere (cf. 1 Tim. 4:12; 5:23; 1 Cor. 16:10–11)—that Timothy is both a younger and less forceful colleague. As in 1 Timothy (1:18 and 4:14), a part of Paul's appeal, therefore, is to remind him of the spiritual **gift** (for ministry; Gk. *charisma*; see disc. on 1 Tim. 4:14) **that God gave** him at the time of his call ("through words of prophecy"; 1 Tim. 1:18; 4:14), and that was recognized by the laying on of **hands**. In 1 Timothy 4:14 (which see), where a part of the concern was to authenticate Timothy before the church, Paul mentions the laying on of hands by the elders. Here, where the interest is almost totally personal, the focus is on Paul's own part in that call, thus appealing to their close personal ties. Note a similar appeal to Timothy's beginnings in 1 Timothy 6:12–14.

1:7 / That verse 6 was dealing primarily with Timothy's "gift" for ministry, having to do with a work of the Spirit in his life, is made clear by the explanatory **for** that begins verse 7. **For**, Paul will now explain, **the**

Spirit that God has given us (probably meaning here not the gift of **the Spirit** that all receive at conversion [cf. Titus 3:5] but that special giftedness of **the Spirit** for various ministries [cf. Rom. 12:6; 1 Cor. 12:4]) **does not make us timid**. The translation **timid** is probably too weak. The word, often appearing in battle contexts, suggests "cowardice," or the terror that overtakes the fearful in extreme difficulties (cf.Lev. 26:36; 2 Macc. 3:24). It is a particularly appropriate choice of words for this letter, given Timothy's apparent natural proclivities, and now in the face of suffering and hardship.

The GNB's translation, **the Spirit that God has given us**, has almost certainly captured Paul's intent. The translation of the NIV ("God did not give us a spirit of timidity"), following the traditional English versions (KJV, RSV), is possible (since the article is absent in the Greek) but most highly improbable, as can be seen both from the following qualifiers (**power, love, and self-control**) and the parallels in Romans 8:15 and 1 Corinthians 2:12. In each case the difficulty arises from Paul's first mentioning the negative (which does not in fact fit **the Spirit** well). But it is equally clear in each case that when Paul gets to the "but" clause, he intends **the *Holy* Spirit**.

Here that is made certain by the contrasts "but of **power, love, and self-control**" (literally), which the GNB rightly translates: **his Spirit fills us with power** (a thoroughgoing NT and Pauline understanding; cf., e.g., Acts 1:8; Rom. 15:23), **love** (cf. Gal. 5:22; Rom. 5:5), **and self-control** (*sōphronismos*; a different word for "self-control" from that in Gal. 5:23). *Sōphronismos* is a cognate, and here probably a synonym, for the "soundmindedness" of Titus 2:2, 5, and so forth. In all likelihood Paul intended to call for a "wise head" in the face of the deceptive and unhealthy teaching of the errorists.

Thus Paul begins his appeal by reminding Timothy of his own "gift" of "the Spirit" for ministry, who in turn has given him the necessary **power, love, and** sound-mindedness to carry out that ministry.

1:8 / With the two imperatives of this verse (**do not be ashamed**, and **take your part in suffering**) we come to the heart of this first appeal. These imperatives are closely tied to what has preceded by the **then** (better, "therefore"). That is, for the very reason that "the Spirit God has given us" leads not to cowardice but "fills us with power" (not to mention also because of the close personal ties between them), Paul exhorts Timothy to further loyalty, both to the gospel and to Paul himself.

This appeal has its clear life-setting in Paul's present imprisonment for the sake of the gospel (cf. 2:9). As will be clearly articulated in 3:12, such suffering for the gospel has for Paul always been a part of the on-going proclamation of the gospel (cf., e.g., 1 Thess. 1:6; 2:14; 3:4; 2 Cor. 4:7–15; Rom. 8:17; Col. 1:24; Phil. 1:12, 29). In Paul's understanding this suffering is closely tied to Christ's own suffering, both the physical pain of torture and the humiliation of the shamefulness of crucifixion. Only in this context can one accurately hear the two imperatives, which are actually the two sides of a single reality.

Determining a precise meaning for the expression **do not be ashamed** poses some difficulties. The word frequently refers to "deserved" humili-ation or disgrace, but more often it is "undeserved" humiliation and, especially for the biblical writers, humiliation from which one hopes for divine vindication (e.g., Ps. 25:1–3). At other times it relates to the stigma, or embarrassment, of association with that which has shame. In this pas-sage these latter two meanings seem to coalesce. There is a stigma to being associated with a crucified Messiah (thus a state criminal) and his (politi-cal) prisoner. Yet it is "undeserved humiliation" from which there will be vindication "on that Day" (see v. 12). Thus, Paul does not want Timothy to avoid the humiliation generated by his association with Christ (**of witnessing for our Lord**, or perhaps to be understood more objectively, "of the witness [gospel] about our Lord") or by his association with **me, a prisoner for Christ's sake** (lit., "me, his prisoner"; when imprisoned *for* Christ, Paul was not in his own thinking a prisoner of the empire, but of Christ himself).

On the contrary (**instead**), Paul exhorts Timothy, paradoxically, to join in the "humiliation": **Take your part in suffering**, but not just any suffering. It is **suffering for** the gospel (**the Good News**), that is, suffer-ing that will be his both by his association with the gospel and by his own activities in its behalf (hence, v. 6: "fan into flame your gift of the Spirit for ministry"). Thus the two imperatives of this verse entreat Timothy to the three basic loyalties: to Christ (and his gospel), to Paul, and to his own ministry.

But again, aware of Timothy's character and of the difficulties ahead, Paul adds the dimension of divine help: **as God gives you the strength for it** (lit., "by God's **power**," the same word as in v. 7). This mention of **God** launches Paul into a creedlike expression of the gospel itself (vv. 9–10; the first loyalty), which is followed in turn by Paul's own example (vv. 11–12; the second loyalty), and a final exhortation to "guard the deposit" (vv. 13–14; cf. 1 Tim. 6:20; the third loyalty).

1:9–10 / In a fashion typical of these letters, Paul supports his point with a semicreedal formulation, which gives a brief, and not necessarily complete, expression of the gospel, which is at the same time particularly adapted to the concerns of the present argument (see disc. on Titus 2:11–14 and 3:4–7). In this case the emphases are particularly fitting for one whose gift needs "fanning into flame" and who is being urged "not to be ashamed of the gospel but to take his part in the suffering." (All of vv. 8–11 in fact are a single sentence in Gk.)

Having noted that Timothy's taking his part in suffering can only be accomplished "by the power of God," Paul emphasizes that this is the same God who **saved and called us**, and that this saving act resided in God's **own** gracious **purpose . . . before the beginning of time**, but was **revealed** historically as an expression of **grace . . . through the coming of . . . Christ**, whose work in this instance is defined as ending the **power of death** and revealing **immortal life**. Thus he braces Timothy's resolve by emphasizing God's sovereign grace and purpose to render death inoperative, and by insisting that this revelation resides in the very gospel for which Timothy is to "take" his "part in suffering"!

The formulation begins with a common theme in the PE: It is "God" who has **saved us** (see disc. on 1 Tim. 1:1; 2:3–4; 4:10; Titus 1:3; 2:10; 3:4–5). In a typically Pauline fashion, such salvation also constitutes our calling (see disc. on 1 Tim. 6:12; cf., e.g., 2 Thess. 2:13–14; 1 Cor. 1:9, 24, 26; Rom. 8:28–30). God both initiated and effected salvation. In this case the call is qualified as (literally) "a holy calling." This is a Semitic construction whose meaning is not altogether certain. It could be a dative of means, "*with* a holy calling" (RSV, NASB), because it comes from a holy God. More likely it is a dative of interest, "*to* a holy life" (NIV; cf. esp. 1 Thess. 4:7) or "*to be* a holy people" (cf. NEB; cf. "called to be saints" or "God's holy people," 1 Cor. 1:2, etc.). Hence, the GNB translates **called us to be his own people**, which is not altogether satisfactory, although it moves in the right direction.

As in Titus 3:5, and elsewhere in Paul (e.g., Eph. 2:8–9), God's saving act is based **not** on **what we have done**, but on **his purpose and grace**. This is a thoroughly Pauline way of saying it (cf. Rom. 8:28–30), as are the descriptions of that **purpose and grace** that follow—although the stating of them is a bit convoluted. God's saving us, Paul says to Timothy, is predicated on his **purpose and grace**, *both* of which, not just his **grace**, find expression (**he gave us**) in **Christ Jesus**. Because he is a God of **grace**, he **purposed** our salvation in **Christ Jesus before the beginning of time** (cf. Titus 1:2), **but** only **now, through the coming** (*epiphaneia*, "appearing"; see disc. on Titus 2:11, 13; 3:4; cf. 1 Tim. 6:14) **of our**

Savior, Christ Jesus (cf. Titus 1:4; 3:6) **has** it **been revealed to us**. For this very Pauline view of things, see the discussion on Titus 1:2–3 (cf. 1 Cor. 2:7–10; Eph. 1:4).

Finally, and especially significantly for this context of bolstering Timothy's resolve to take his share of the suffering, Paul describes the effect of this "manifestation": **He has ended the power of death** ("rendered death ineffectual," Berkeley) **and has revealed immortal life** (lit., "life and incorruptibility," cf. Rom. 2:7). As usual in Paul, salvation has an eschatological outlook. But the immortality that is yet to be is in a sense already ours, because in his **coming** (incarnation), and especially through the cross and resurrection, our last enemy, **death**, has already received its mortal wound. So his word to Timothy is plain: "Be steadfast; rekindle your gift; take your part in the suffering; for we are already among those who have overcome death through Christ."

All of this has been **revealed** (lit., "brought to light"), Paul notes, **through the gospel**; and just as the mention of "the power of God" at the end of verse 8 launched Paul into this creedlike statement of God's saving activity, so now this mention of the gospel will, as often before, prompt him to restate his own role in proclaiming that gospel.

1:11–12 / With this clause the sentence that began in verse 8 is brought to a close. Paul began with a twofold appeal for Timothy not to be ashamed either of the gospel of Christ or of Paul, Christ's prisoner. Verses 9–10 then function both as a reminder of the content of that gospel—why he should not be ashamed of it—and as a bolster in the face of hardship. Having concluded by noting that God's saving event, his Good News, was brought to light "through the gospel," he now affirms his own role in **the Good News**, and he does so in order to make his next point (v. 12), that it is for the sake of the gospel, and his own role in proclaiming it, that he is now in prison—which is why Timothy should not be ashamed of him as well (v. 8).

Verse 11 almost repeats 1 Timothy 2:7 but lacks the insertion "I am not lying; I am telling the truth" and the phrase "of the Gentiles" (although this latter is added to the majority of later MSS). Thus his concern here is not with the solemn affirmation of his ministry to the Gentiles but simply with his appointment as "a herald" (see disc. on 1 Tim. 2:7), **an apostle**, and a **teacher** of (lit., "for the sake of") the gospel (**the Good News**). The ordering of the three words makes it clear that the emphasis is not on his *authority* as an apostle, but on the gospel itself and his own relationship to it.

With verse 12 Paul ties his present circumstances (**that I suffer these things**, i.e., his imprisonment; cf. v. 9; 2:9) to his role as a messenger of the gospel (**for this reason**; i.e., what is said in v. 11). It is probably not his appointment or his apostleship that he has in mind as the **reason**; rather, it is the fulfilling of his commission as herald-apostle-teacher *of the gospel* that has resulted in his present trouble.

Since he is writing to Timothy so that, not only will he not retreat ("be ashamed") under these circumstances, but he will also be prepared to take his own share of suffering (v. 8), Paul encourages him by noting his own response. **I** myself **am** "not ashamed" (cf. Rom. 1:16; the GNB's positive **I am still full of confidence** unfortunately misses the tie to v. 8, and also to v. 16). But what does it mean for Paul to be "not ashamed"? It could mean "not ashamed of the gospel," despite what has happened. More likely it means, "my imprisonment causes me no personal shame," precisely because it is for Christ and his gospel. Furthermore, similar to the psalmists who hope for vindication from God in the time of their humiliation (e.g., Pss. 31:1–5; 69:9), Paul knows no shame in his imprisonment, **because** he **knows** the One (probably "God," perhaps "Christ") **whom** he has **trusted** ("believed," but in the context of this sentence **trusted** is to be preferred).

Considerable disagreement exists over the meaning of the rest of the sentence, which expresses Paul's confidence in his ultimate vindication. Literally, the text reads: "And I am convinced that he is able to guard my deposit unto that day." The problems are, first, whether "my deposit" is something God **has entrusted to** Paul (GNB text) or something Paul has entrusted to God (GNB margin; KJV) and, second, to what the metaphor "deposit" refers.

Most contemporary scholars, convinced that the metaphor itself must have the same meaning here as in verse 14, understand it to refer to the "sound teaching" of verse 13—the gospel itself—that God has entrusted to Paul (v. 12), that Paul in turn has entrusted to Timothy (v. 14; cf. 1 Tim. 6:20), and that Timothy is likewise to entrust to others (2:2). As attractive as that alternative is, it is unfortunately based on a prior commitment to the meaning of the metaphor and does not take seriously enough the plain sense of the idiom **keep safe what has** been **entrusted** ("guard the deposit"). Since it is God who is here envisioned as guarding the deposit, the idiom demands that it is therefore something entrusted *to* God (as *to* Timothy in v. 14), not something God has entrusted to another that he yet continues to guard. The clearly eschatological force of **until that Day** also supports this understanding.

What precisely the metaphor itself means is not certain. Very likely it refers either to Paul's life or to his commitment to Christ and his gospel. But in either case the emphasis parallels that of verses 9–10. Just as the gospel announces a salvation that God in grace initiated and effected, and through which he rendered death ineffective, so also the same God can be **trusted** to **keep safe until** the End the life that **has** been **entrusted** to his care.

1:13-14 / In these final two verses Paul returns to the direct appeal to Timothy, but now with some slightly different nuances. The entreaty from verses 6–12 has been very personal and directly related to Paul's present circumstances and his and Timothy's personal relationship. But Paul has not forgotten the ongoing threat of the false teachers and the havoc they have been generating. The language of the two parallel imperatives of these verses indicates that they must be understood in this light (as v. 15 also seems to suggest).

The first imperative repeats the concern throughout the PE that Timothy **hold firmly to the true words** (i.e., the "sound teaching"; see disc. on 1 Tim. 1:10). As always, the "sound teaching" is that which **I taught you** (lit., "which you heard from me"; cf. 2:2, where the same wording appears; cf. also 3:10; 1 Tim. 4:6). Such a concern elsewhere always is expressed against the backdrop of the false teachers.

Although Paul's intent in this sentence is clear enough, the actual wording is not (lit., "hold an example of sound words"). Probably this means that what Paul taught is to serve as a model for Timothy's teaching (as most interpreters; but see the NEB and Moffatt for alternatives).

The final prepositional phrase (lit., "in faith and love which are in Christ Jesus"), which the GNB reads as an additional imperative (**remain in the faith . . .**), is likewise not altogether clear. It seems certain that Timothy's **faith** (not *the* **faith**) **and love** are products of his being **in union with Christ Jesus** (see disc. on 1 Tim. 1:14; cf. Gal. 5:22). But how this phrase relates to the verb presents a more difficult problem. The sense seems to go something like this: "Let what you have learned from me serve as your model for sound teaching, but let it do so as you yourself also model faith [or faithfulness] and love."

The final imperative, **keep the good things that have been entrusted to you** (lit., "guard the good deposit"), parallels verse 13, but now in the language of 1 Timothy 6:20 (which see). "Timothy," Paul urges, "keep safe what I have deposited with you; it is a sacred trust." Since what has **been entrusted** is described as **good**, it almost certainly refers to the "sound teaching" of the gospel. He must not allow it to be purloined, or eroded, by the false teachings. But for such a charge, Timothy is not to think of himself as on his own. He is to fulfill his responsibilities **through the power of the Holy Spirit** (see v. 7), **who lives in us**.

Thus the appeal has come full circle. It began by urging that Timothy fan into flame his gift of ministry, which was his through the power of the Spirit (vv. 6–7). Then Paul urged loyalty to the gospel, and to himself, even though now a prisoner. After detailing the gospel and Paul's own loyalty to it, with emphasis on God's sovereignty, he returns to urge once more loyalty to his (Timothy's) own ministry and to the gospel; and again he is to do so **through the power of the Spirit**. From here Paul will turn to some examples of disloyalty, and of one who was especially loyal (to Paul in his imprisonment).

Additional Notes

1:6–7 / Because of the close relationship between this appeal and the thanksgiving, modern editors have not all agreed on the best scheme of paragraphing. The paragraphing followed by this commentary, which differs from the GNB (vv. 3–7, 8–10, 11–14), adheres closely to Paul's own sentencing. It is also followed by Kelly and NA[26].

Although Paul clearly says "through the laying on of my hands" in v. 6, the evidence from 1 Tim. 1:18 and 4:14 suggests that it was by **the Spirit** ("through prophetic utterances") that Timothy received his **gift**, and that it was *accompanied* by the laying on of hands. Therefore, the *dia* ("through") is either attendant circumstance (so Barrett) or simply a "telescoped" expression (like "by faith" for "by grace through faith").

Given the fully Pauline character of v. 7, it seems biased on Hanson's part to say, "but the word the author uses here, *sōphronismos*, has a slight element of prudential ethic in it that is foreign to Paul's way of thinking" (pp. 121–22). A similar thing could be said of his use of *enkrateia* ("self-control") in Gal. 5:23, if one believed Paul did not write that letter.

1:8 / For the concept of "ashamed/shame" in Paul (and the rest of the NT) see esp. H. C. Kee, "The Linguistic Background of 'Shame' in the New Testament," in *On Language, Culture, and Religion: In Honor of Eugene A. Nida*, ed. M. Black and W. A. Smalley (The Hague: Mouton, 1974), pp. 133–47.

1:9–10 / On the matter of these creedlike formulations in the PE, see disc. on Titus 2:11–14 and esp. 3:4–7. As with the Titus passages, there is nothing of the nature of a hymn here (despite Easton). The use of the word "liturgical" for these formulations (as Hanson) is likewise arguing for more than the data themselves suggest.

1:11-12 / Given the context, the order of the three titles, and the fact that when Paul wants to assert his authority he emphasizes his apostleship, it seems to miss the point of vv. 11–12 rather widely to argue (as Hanson, p. 124): "The three titles given to Paul here are intended to enhance his sole authority in the churches which he founded."

For arguments on both sides of the question of who has been entrusted with the deposit in v. 12, see Kelly or Bernard for the GNB text, and W. Barclay "Paul's Certainties VII. Our Security in God—2 Timothy i.12" for the GNB margin.

1:13-14 / See Bernard (p. 112) for a full presentation and good discussion of the alternative possibilities for understanding this sentence.

4

Examples of Disloyalty and Loyalty

2 TIMOTHY 1:15–18

You know that everyone in the province of Asia, including Phygelus and Hermogenes, has deserted me. ¹⁶May the Lord show mercy to the family of Onesiphorus, because he cheered me up many times. He was not ashamed that I am in prison, ¹⁷but as soon as he arrived in Rome, he started looking for me until he found me. ¹⁸May the Lord grant him his mercy on that Day! And you know very well how much he did for me in Ephesus.

At first sight this section may seem irrelevant to the appeal that surrounds it. It lacks any words of exhortation to Timothy (none of the second person singular imperatives that otherwise predominate in the letter); its content seems to have little in common with its context. Nonetheless, as with other such "digressions" in these letters (cf., e.g., 1 Tim. 1:12–17), this section is not without purpose. In this case the key to its significance lies in **Onesiphorus' not** being **ashamed** of Paul's imprisonment (cf. vv. 8 and 12). Apparently the mentioning of his imprisonment in verse 12, plus his appeal to Timothy to "keep" safe what has "been entrusted to" him (v. 14), reminded Paul, first, of many who had not kept that trust (v. 15), and, second, of one who in particular had not only not deserted but had gone out of his way to the share the "shame" of Paul's imprisonment.

In this paragraph we sense the pain of Paul's present situation and his loneliness, brought about both by what has happened in Ephesus (v. 15; cf. 2:14–3:9) and by his unfavorable circumstances in Rome (vv. 16–18; cf. 4:6–18). The paragraph, however, is not without its difficulties, especially in trying to reconstruct some of the historical matters to which it alludes.

1:15 / Paul begins by reminding Timothy of something of which he was all too painfully aware. **You know** all about what's going on **in the province of Asia** (lit., "**in Asia**," which may in fact refer to the whole

province, but includes at least Ephesus). But precisely because Timothy *did* know, we are left a bit in the dark as to *what* has happened—and *when* and *where*.

Paul says that **everyone in . . . Asia has deserted** him. Almost all are agreed that these deserters are **in Asia** at the time of writing. But **everyone**? Either this means that some Asians, including Onesiphorus, had come to Rome, and all but Onesiphorus had deserted him and returned home (so Bernard), or else (more likely) it means that the defections in Asia have been so staggering (Kelly, "the exaggeration [of] depression") that even friends (presumably) from whom he would have expected more—**including** [perhaps led by] **Phygelus and Hermogenes**—have **deserted** him.

If this is how we are to understand "who" and "where," then "when" probably has to do with events since the writing of 1 Timothy, perhaps a general "abandoning ship" at the news of Paul's arrest (cf. Kelly). Paul himself would have been informed of it by Onesiphorus.

But what does it mean, **have deserted me**? If our reconstruction thus far is correct, then at least it means that they have abandoned their loyalty to Paul. If so, then for him that would mean they have also abandoned his gospel, since that is about the only way one could desert the apostle; and that is precisely how the same verb is used elsewhere in the PE (4:4; Titus 1:14; a different verb is used of the personal "desertions" in 4:10).

1:16–17 / The mention of those from Asia who had **deserted** him prompts Paul to pray for **mercy** for **the family of** one who did not. This sudden bursting out in a wish-prayer (hardly intercession, as Kelly, but an expression of Paul's desires for them; cf. 2 Thess. 3:16; Rom. 15:5) for the *family* **of Onesiphorus** (cf. 4:19) means that he is not now with them (otherwise Paul would have said "to Onesiphorus and his family"). The fact that Paul should begin his reminder about **Onesiphorus** in this way, by asking for *present* **mercy** for his **family**, and that at the end (v. 18a) he should ask for *future* **mercy** (on that Day) for Onesiphorus himself, suggests very strongly that Onesiphorus had died in the meantime. If so, it could only have increased Paul's present pain and loneliness.

But the memory of **Onesiphorus** lingers on. His actions **in Rome** are a model of loyalty (for Timothy's sake surely). **He cheered me up** (lit., "refreshed me") **many times**. In a culture in which imprisonment often involved self-sustenance, such "refreshment" probably included food as well as "cheering up." Moreover, and the more significant reason for mentioning him at all, **he was not ashamed that I am in prison**. The "shame" in this case was hardly that of embarrassment. Here was a man who was willing to take the risk of regularly visiting one who was a state criminal and who would soon be condemned to die. Under such circumstances, desertions had been plentiful (see disc. on 4:16–17), but not so with Onesiphorus. Indeed, **as soon as he arrived in Rome, he started looking** [Gk., "he looked diligently"] **for me until he found me**. The implication is that Paul was not in a "public" prison, and that finding him required a considerable effort on the part of Onesiphorus.

Paul's point to Timothy is clear enough. "Don't you be ashamed of the gospel or of me, Christ's prisoner (v. 8). Some have (v. 15), but not Onesiphorus (vv. 16–17); so be like him."

1:18 / Having already entreated mercy for his family (v. 16a), presumably because of their loss, Paul now desires (again in the form of a wish-prayer) for Onesiphorus himself that **the Lord** may **grant him his mercy on that Day! On that Day**, as in verse 12, can only refer to the Second Advent. Thus it is hard to escape the implication that Onesiphorus is now dead. Why else, one wonders, especially in light of verse 16, should Paul only wish him "to find" (this word appears in the Gk.; it is a wordplay on Onesiphorus' having "found" him; v. 17) **mercy** at the End?

Does this, then, countenance prayers for the departed? Many think so. However, before one builds Christian doctrine on such a text, one needs to be cautioned that such an idea is quite singular to this one, not totally certain, text and that it merely expresses Paul's sentiment toward, or desire for, Onesiphorus. It is not, in fact, intercessory prayer (cf. the difference with Eph. 1:17, e.g.); rather, it is an acknowledgment that even one like Onesiphorus has only God's mercy as his appeal.

Almost as an afterthought, Paul remembers that Timothy will easily recognize that Onesiphorus' actions in Rome should come as no surprise. As Timothy would know very well, it was quite in keeping with the man. Timothy will recall **how much he did for** Paul **in Ephesus**. One cannot be sure whether such "service" (Gk. word for "serving," or "ministering") was rendered much earlier when Paul and Timothy were together in Ephesus (cf. 1 Cor. 4:17 with 16:8), or whether it was during Timothy's recent tenure (per 1 Timothy). In either case, it happened when Timothy was on hand to observe, and now Onesiphorus' devoted service is being recalled—as a gentle prod to Timothy.

Additional Notes

Personal notes of the kind found in this paragraph create, as Kelly notes, " a particularly vivid impression of authenticity, and also special difficulties for any theory of pseudonymity" (p. 168). So much is this so that most scholars allow that the material here is probably authentic, even if they believe the letter is not (e.g., Barrett).

1:15 / Spicq suggests that the phrase "all who are **in Asia**" may be a Semitism for "all who are from Asia," thus implying that all other Asians in Rome abandoned Paul except Onesiphorus. However, that is a forced reading of the text, and one can make sense of it as it stands.

There are still other hypotheses about the historical circumstances behind this sentence. Barrett, e.g., tentatively suggests that it might reflect a time alluded to in 2 Cor. 1:8; Hendriksen submits that these people had been summoned to testify but did not come. Most of these suggestions see the desertion only as related to Paul's imprisonment and, therefore, strictly in contrast to Onesiphorus. In fact, D-C make the surprising comment that the verb "cannot be understood to imply apostasy from the gospel, because of the comparatively mild terminology" (p. 106). But that seems to neglect too much evidence to the contrary. The overall context of 1:6–2:13, followed closely by 2:14–3:9, would seem to favor the reconstruction offered here.

1:16 / For a formal consideration of the "wish-prayer" in Paul, see G. P. Wiles, *Paul's Intercessory Prayers*, SNTSMS 24 (Cambridge: Cambridge University Press, 1974), pp. 45–155.

Hendriksen (and others) properly cautions that one cannot be certain that Onesiphorus is dead, but his argument that Paul would have explicitly said so if "this hero" had died, is special pleading. He simply does not take seriously enough the abrupt nature of introducing Onesiphorus by wishing **mercy** *for his family* or that the prayer-wish of v. 18a interrupts the text (note how smoothly it reads without it) and can only be explained as a sudden wordplay on "find," which then is expressed eschatologically precisely because he is now dead.

1:18 / The prayer-wish literally reads: "May *the Lord* grant him to find mercy from *the Lord* on that day." Several explanations for this awkward construction have been offered (see Kelly or Hanson). The most likely (adopted by Spicq, Kelly, Hanson, et al.) is that the first **Lord** refers to Christ (as in vv. 2 and 8 above, and ordinarily in Paul and the PE), and that the second refers to God and reflects the LXX.

5

The Appeal Renewed

2 TIMOTHY 2:1–7

As for you, my son, be strong through the grace that is ours in union with Christ Jesus. ²Take the teachings that you heard me proclaim in the presence of many witnesses, and entrust them to reliable people, who will be able to teach others also.

³Take your part in suffering, as a loyal soldier of Christ Jesus. ⁴A soldier on active duty wants to please his commanding officer and so does not get mixed up in the affairs of civilian life. ⁵An athlete who runs in a race cannot win the prize unless he obeys the rules. ⁶The farmer who has done the hard work should have the first share of the harvest. ⁷Think about what I am saying, because the Lord will enable you to understand it all.

After a brief "digression" in 1:15–18 that reminded Timothy of the disloyalty of "everyone in Asia," with the noteworthy exception of Onesiphorus, Paul resumes the appeal to Timothy. With an emphatic, **as for you**, in contrast to those in verse 15, Paul repeats the urgencies of 1:6–14: that he fulfill his trust and ministry (reflecting 1:6–7 and 13–14), in this instance by entrusting it to others (v. 2), and that he be ready to **take** his **part in suffering** (v. 3, reflecting the main concern of 1:8–12).

A series of three analogies (military, athletics, farming) reinforce the appeal to suffering and emphasize the need for wholehearted devotion to service (vv. 4–5) and the expectation of reward beyond the hardship (vv. 5–6). These emphases will be repeated in a different way in 2:8–13.

2:1 / This opening imperative, which in a general way gathers up the concerns of 1:6–14 and anticipates those that follow (2:2–13), is tied to what has preceded with an emphatic *su oun* ("you then," or "therefore"—not translated in the GNB). **As for you** stands in contrast to the general defection of the Asians (1:15) but in keeping with the likes of an Onesiphorus. The *oun* is at least resumptive ("then"), perhaps consequential ("therefore"), and goes back to the imperatives of 1:13–14.

You, *therefore* (having already been urged to suffer and keep the trust, and now in the light of the Asians and Onesiphorus), **be strong through the grace that is ours in union with Christ Jesus.** The imperative **be strong** (cf. 4:17; 1 Tim. 1:12; Rom. 4:20; Eph. 6:10; Phil. 4:13) is present tense (i.e., "keep on being"), passive voice, whose proper force is that one is being strengthened *by God*. The phrase **through the grace** can be either instrumental ("by means of the grace," so GNB) or locative ("in the grace"). Though it is true that **grace** is the means by which we are saved and by which we are enabled to walk in God's will, it is also true that that same **grace** is the sphere in which all of Christian life is lived (cf. Rom. 5:2). In light of the usage of this phrase in Ephesians 6:10 and elsewhere in the PE, Paul probably intends the latter. He wants Timothy to be strengthened by God himself as he stands *in* **the grace** that he has received. The source of such grace is to be found in his continual **union with Christ Jesus** (cf. 1:13).

Thus Paul places the *specific* imperatives of this appeal ("Don't be ashamed," 1:18; "Take your share of suffering," 1:8, 2:3; "Guard the deposit," 1:14) within the context of this more general imperative of allowing God to strengthen him for his task of ministry. One should note the similarities with 1:6–7, 8c, and 14.

2:2 / The first task he is to be strengthened for is tied closely to the imperatives of 1:13–14. Just as Timothy must "keep safe what has been entrusted to him," so also he is now **to entrust** (the verb form of the noun "deposit" in 1:14 and 1 Tim. 6:20) **them to reliable people, who** in turn **will be able to teach others also**.

What strikes one about this sentence is both its uniqueness in the PE and its apparent interruption in the flow of the argument (or appeal). It seems strange, therefore, that so many should see this singular text as the main point of all three letters. Paul, however, is not so much concerned about "apostolic succession" (a true anachronism), as he is with the gospel itself, in light of the reality that Timothy is being urged by this letter to leave Ephesus and join Paul in Rome (in his suffering; cf. 4:9, 21). Because Timothy must leave, he is to **take the teachings** entrusted to him **and entrust them** to others. Those to whom he entrusts **the teachings** are to be **reliable**, or trustworthy, people (cf. 1 Tim. 1:12). The same adjective in the PE often means "believing" (cf. 1 Tim. 4:3, 10, 12; 6:2; Titus 1:6), but here, as with its usage in the phrase "here is a trustworthy saying" (2:11, etc.), the emphasis is on their **reliable** character, not their status—although the genuine elders of 1 Timothy 3:1–7 and 5:17–18 are probably in view.

What Timothy is to **entrust** to them also reflects 1:13–14: **the teachings that you heard me proclaim** (lit., "what you heard from me," precisely as in 1:13, so therefore probably implying "the sound teaching" mentioned there). This tie of the gospel to Paul's own preaching is thoroughgoing in Paul, beginning as it does in his earliest letter (1 Thess. 2:13).

What is not clear in this sentence is the phrase **in the presence of** [*dia*, ordinarily "through"] **many witnesses**. If *dia* here means **in the presence of** (so Chrysostom [d. A.D. 407] and many others), it must refer to the time of Timothy's coming to faith (cf. 1 Tim 6:11–13). But it is difficult to understand the reason for such an emphasis, especially in light of 3:10–11, which makes a point of Timothy's longstanding companionship with Paul. If *dia* means "through," as seems more likely, it probably means not that Timothy himself heard Paul's **teachings** as they were *mediated* through **many witnesses**, but that, as Timothy should well know, what Paul taught is also attested to by **many** others—a needed emphasis in light of the many defections in Ephesus. (Cf. the plural "from whom" in 3:14, which also would support this interpretation.)

2:3 / With this imperative Paul returns to the second—and main—reason that Timothy needs "to be strengthened in the grace that is his in Christ," namely, that he may, as Onesiphorus, **take** his **part in** the **suffering**. Since this verb is an exact repetition from 1:8, this is by far the preferable translation to the "endure hardship" of the NIV (which has "join with me in suffering" in 1:8; cf. KJV, NEB). The verb (*syn* ["with"]-*kako* ["evil"]-*paschō* ["suffer"]) has to do with sharing **suffering**, not simply enduring difficulties, and is repeated by Paul (without the *syn*) in verse 9 (see NIV) of his own sufferings for the gospel.

On this occasion Paul qualifies the verb with an analogy from the military—**as a loyal** (lit., "good") **soldier of Christ Jesus** (which probably explains the translation in the NIV, KJV, NEB). Military imagery is common in Paul (cf. 2 Cor. 10:3–5; Eph. 6:10–17; Philem. 2) and usually occurs in a context of struggling against opponents of his gospel (cf. 1 Tim. 1:18). While the imagery here may indeed reflect that concern (cf. 2:14–19), it more likely is a general metaphor for Timothy as a minister of the gospel, whose ministry has some analogies to the life of the **soldier**. By the very nature of his occupation, the **soldier** will often be called on to **take** his **part in suffering**.

2:4 / The imagery of soldiering in verse 3 calls forth at this point a reflection on the metaphor itself, which in turn will lead to two further metaphors. In 1 Corinthians 9:7 Paul has previously used two of these metaphors; but there all three images make a singular point (ministers of the gospel have a right to expect support from those to whom they minister). Here the military metaphor makes a considerably different point (the need for perseverance), and the subsequent metaphors add yet a further nuance (the promise of eschatological reward); all of which looks forward to verses 11–13.

The metaphor itself propounds: **A soldier on active duty** [a nice touch for "serving as a soldier"] **wants to please his commanding officer and so does not get mixed up in the affairs of civilian life**. One must be careful not to press images into meanings that differ from the author's intent. Here the concern follows directly from verse 3, that Timothy is to "take his share in suffering." Thus it is not a proscription against marriage or a call for separation from worldliness, as it has often been treated by Roman Catholics or Protestant Fundamentalists. Paul's concern is singular: Timothy must give himself, even to the point of great suffering, to wholehearted devotion to his divine **commanding officer**. Indeed, it should be his desire **to please** him. Such a desire will mean obedience to the call to **active duty**, including **suffering**. The analogy does not negate "civilian life"; rather, it disallows "looking back" (cf. Luke 9:61–62) or hankering for an easier path (in this case defecting, as have so many others).

2:5 / The analogy calling for wholehearted devotion to service in order to "please" his Lord, calls for the companion analogy of **an athlete** (cf. 1 Tim. 1:18 and 6:12), **who . . . cannot win the prize unless he obeys the rules**. The emphasis now is on his "obeying the rules" (lit., "compete lawfully"; Gk., *nomimōs*, as in 1 Tim. 1:8), which seems to reflect a similar concern to that in verse 4. But it is not totally clear what "obeying the rules" means: either **the rules** of the contest or **the rules** of training (e.g., the Games required a ten-month period of strict discipline). It probably refers to **the rules** of the contest itself, since the concern is not with Timothy's need for discipline as such but with his taking his share "in suffering." The "noble contest" (cf. 1 Tim. 6:12), like the "noble war" (cf. 1 Tim. 1:18), requires wholehearted devotion to the task, as well as full compliance with **the rules** of the contest, which in this case includes suffering.

However, although the accent falls upon **obeys the rules**, the metaphor also reflects the eschatological emphasis recurrent in this letter (see esp. vv. 11–13; 4:6–8; cf. 1:1, 12). The athlete who **obeys the rules**, that is, "takes his part in suffering," will in fact **win the prize** (cf. 4:8). For a similar use of athletics imagery in Paul, see 1 Corinthians 9:24–27.

2:6 / With yet a further image, farming, Paul re-emphasizes, with the promise of eschatological reward, the point of wholehearted devotion, even if it calls for suffering. As with the analogy in verse 5, the emphasis here lies on **the farmer who has done the hard work**; again the point refers back to verse 3 with its sharing in suffering.

But also as in verse 5, the imagery again accents the eschatological reward; he **should have the first share of the harvest**. The point of his receiving **the first share**, therefore, is not about his making a living from the gospel (D-C, Hanson), which is totally foreign to the context, but about his final reward for **hard work**.

Thus, even though the military imagery does not precisely say so, each of the metaphors, besides calling Timothy to "take his share in suffering," looks forward to the eschatological prize. As Barrett nicely puts it: "Beyond warfare is victory, beyond athletic effort a prize, and beyond agricultural labour a crop" (p. 102).

2:7 / The compounding of metaphors in verses 4–6 has led Paul from the specific point of his imperative for Timothy to "take part in suffering" to an equal emphasis on the eschatological "prize." These two emphases form the basic point of the rest of the appeal (vv. 8–13). But in order to get to that final paragraph, Paul calls on Timothy to **think about** ("ponder," "reflect on") **what I am saying**, that is, the point of the three metaphors, which Paul has given without including explanations.

Just in case Timothy might miss the point, Paul adds that **the Lord will enable** you (not "may the Lord grant you"; cf. KJV, which is based on an inferior text) **to understand it all**. Thus everything is from **the Lord**, both the strengthening to stand in his grace (v. 1) and the ability to understand the need to share in suffering.

Additional Notes

2:2 / Those who take the "church manual" approach to these letters, and especially those who would date the letters as later pseudepigraphs, see this imperative as a key to understanding all three letters. Here is "the author" betraying his post-Pauline concerns of preserving the pure gospel through properly trained and ordained ministers. But the singularity of this verse in these letters must not be overlooked. The interpretation offered in this commentary accounts both for its singularity and its place in the context of this Epistle.

2:3 / On the use of the military and athletic metaphors in Paul, see J. N. Sevenster, *Paul and Seneca*, pp. 162–64; and V. C. Pfitzner, *Paul and the Agon Motif*, pp. 157–86. Here is a clear case of the "authentic" Paul reflecting imagery in common with such contemporaries as Seneca and Philo, yet using it in a uniquely Christian way. The usage here, as Pfitzner convincingly demonstrates, reflects Pauline usage, not Hellenism or Hellenistic Judaism. This fact should cause one to be more cautious in describing other such metaphors, unique to these Epistles, as un-Pauline.

2:5 / For the information that participants in the Olympic Games had to swear an oath to Zeus to observe strict training for the ten months prior to the competition, see Pausanius, *Descriptions of Greece* 5.24.9 (Loeb, II, p. 529). Kelly sees the point as "arduous self-discipline," but that seems to move too far afield from the thoroughgoing context of sharing in suffering.

2:6 / D-C, followed by Hanson and others who see the letter as pseudepigraphic, think the point of both the athlete and the farmer metaphors is remuneration. But this misses the clear eschatological sense of the reward (see vv. 11–13 and 4:6–8), as well as the point of the metaphors in the present context. Such an interpretation is the result of their view of authorship and their subsequent fascination with the author's "sources" (here, 1 Cor. 9:7 and 24–27) while paying little or no attention to the point of the metaphors in context. The meaning of the metaphors, they argue, is left for "the reader . . . to find out for himself," which is their interpretation of v. 7 (p. 108). It is arguable that an interpretation that makes good sense both of the details and the context is to be preferred to this procedure.

6

Basis for the Appeal

Remember Jesus Christ, who was raised from death, who was a descendant of David, as is taught in the Good News I preach. ⁹Because I preach the Good News, I suffer and I am even chained like a criminal. But the word of God is not in chains, ¹⁰and so I endure everything for the sake of God's chosen people, in order that they too may obtain the salvation that comes through Christ Jesus and brings eternal glory.

¹¹This is a true saying:
"If we have died with him,
we shall also live with him.
¹²If we continue to endure,
we shall also rule with him.
If we deny him
he also will deny us.
¹³If we are not faithful,
he remains faithful,
because he cannot be false to
himself."

With this paragraph Paul brings to a fitting conclusion his long appeal for Timothy to remain loyal—even to the point of suffering. His loyalty is to be primarily to Christ and the gospel, but it will be evidenced by his loyalty to Paul, a prisoner because of the gospel, and by faithfulness to his own ministry (1:6–14). When this appeal resumed in 2:1, it especially picked up the theme of Timothy's readiness to share in suffering for the gospel, reinforced by the promise of eschatological reward (vv. 4–6; cf. 1:12).

This present paragraph provides the theological basis for the appeal. Timothy is urged to remember Jesus Christ himself, whose resurrection and Davidic descent are to bring him confidence (v. 8). But this mention of Christ leads to yet another reminder of Paul's imprisonment and the reasons for it (vv. 9–10). He then concludes with the fifth "faithful saying," a quatrain, apparently from a hymn or poem, which both encourages endurance (line 2) and warns against its lack (line 3) but concludes on the high note of God's faithfulness (line 4).

Thus the basic themes of the whole section are reiterated: Christ and his gospel, Paul's present suffering, and an appeal, with a warning, for Timothy himself (and now including God's people) to endure despite the suffering.

2:8 / Although verse 7 was something of an afterthought to the three preceding analogies, the reminder that the Lord would enable him to understand prompts the next imperative: **Remember** ("bear in mind," Kelly) **Jesus Christ**. This picks up the "memory" motif that recurs in this letter (1:4–5, 6; 3:14–15). Just as Paul had earlier reminded him of the faith of his forebears (1:5), of his own call and empowering for ministry (1:6–7), and of the "sound teaching" he had had modeled before him in Paul (1:13; cf. 1:9–10), so now he calls him to focus his attention on **Christ** himself.

In his "bearing in mind **Jesus Christ**," Timothy is to focus on two realities: that he **was raised from death** (lit., "the dead"), and that he **was a descendant of David** (lit., "of David's seed"). The reason for the first of these two qualifiers to easy enough to discern. **Jesus Christ . . . raised** [better, "risen"] **from** "the dead" is both the prime example of eschatological victory after death (hence reflecting on vv. 5–6, and thus an encouragement to one who is also suffering) and Timothy's source of strength (i.e., he who conquered death through resurrection will "strengthen you" for your task and endurance). Furthermore, it also anticipates the exposure of the false teachers in verses 14–18, who, by arguing that the "resurrection [of believers] has already taken place," are in effect denying the eschatological future that Paul is affirming (vv. 5–6, 10).

That the focus of Timothy's **remember**ing **Jesus Christ** is on his being the Risen One is further demonstrated from the first couplet in the hymn (vv. 11–12a): "if we *have died* with him, we shall *also live* with him; if we continue to *endure*, we shall *also rule* with him." Since this is so, one wonders, then what is the point of the second qualifier, **who was a descendant of David**? Several options have been offered. On the basis of the similar combination in Romans 1:3–4, some have seen the whole as a piece of early creedal material and suggest that this phrase was included from the source, but without its having any necessary significance for the context. Others see it as reference to the Incarnation, with emphasis on Christ's humanity, over against an alleged Gnosticism on the part of the opponents (but its use in Rom. 1:3 speaks against this). Most likely, as in other such references in the NT, the point is not so much Christ's humanity as it is his being the fulfillment of God's promise and his people's expectations. If so, then it fits the theme of continuity with the past (see disc. on 1:3, 5; cf. 3:14–17), especially of Christ as the true fulfillment and visible expression of God's faithfulness.

Together these two realities, **Jesus Christ** risen **from** the dead and

Jesus Christ of the seed **of David**, form a brief epitome of **the Good News I preach** (lit., "according to my gospel"; cf. 1 Tim 1:11; Rom. 2:16; 16:25, "not invented by me but entrusted to me," Lock). It assures Timothy, and in verse 10 God's people also, that he, and they, belong to something that God has been doing in history, culminating in Christ, and that they are the heirs of final eschatological salvation, also through Christ. Thus, "Be steadfast."

2:9–10 / Having called Timothy's attention once again to Christ as the content of his gospel, Paul also once more reminds him that his (Paul's) present suffering is in the service of that gospel. **Because I preach the Good News**, Paul reminds him, **I suffer** this present evil, **even** to the point (translating the preposition *mechri*) of being **chained like a criminal**, a clear indignity for one who was both a Roman citizen and innocent. The word **criminal**, which occurs in Luke 23:32–39 for the brigands who were crucified with Jesus, is an especially strong word, used for those "who commit gross misdeeds and serious crimes" (BAGD). It is clear from this sentence, as well as from 1:8, 16, and 4:16–18, that Paul's imprisonment was a serious one, and that it was personally repugnant to him.

But his repugnance at his chains is immediately contrasted with **the word of God** that **is not in chains**. They may stop the messenger, but they cannot stop the message. As Luther sang: "The body they may kill; God's truth abideth still; His kingdom is forever." And this, of course, is Paul's concern for Timothy throughout the letter. "Take your share in suffering," he urges him, "and above all, preach the word (4:2); for it is **the word** alone, the message of the gospel, that counts. They may imprison us and chain us, but they cannot chain our message" (cf. esp. Phil. 1:12–18).

Paul's imprisonment, however, is not mentioned simply as a contrast to the unfettered **word of God**. As in Philippians 1:12–18, it is portrayed as being in behalf of that **word** and **for the sake of God's chosen people**. Thus **I endure everything**—and by implication Timothy should too (cf. v. 12a). **God's chosen people** is an excellent translation of *tous eklektous* ("the elect"). Far too much ink has been spilled on the theological implications of this term, whether it refers to the "elect" who are already saved or to the "elect" but not yet saved. Such theologizing quite misses Paul's point. Here again, as in Titus 1:1, 2:14, and many other places, Paul has appropriated OT language for **God's . . . people** and applied it to Christian believers. Furthermore, as in verse 8 above, the emphasis here falls on their continuity with the past, not their theological status.

The effect of his imprisonment **for the sake of God's chosen peo-**

ple—and the reason he is willing to **endure everything**—is that **they too** will **obtain the salvation that comes through Christ Jesus**. It is not clear, just as in Colossians 1:24 and 2 Corinthians 1:6, how Paul understands the relationship between Christ's sufferings, his own sufferings, and the people's salvation. He certainly cannot mean that his suffering **obtains salvation** for them. More likely he means that his imprisonment will somehow "help on the work of the Gospel" (Barrett), by means of which **God's people obtain** their **salvation**. But just how he understands his suffering to "help it on," we are not told. In any event it is the gospel for which he suffers, not his suffering for the gospel, that ultimately brings their salvation; for after all it **comes through Christ Jesus**, and through Paul only as secondary agent—as its messenger. As throughout these letters, and especially this one, **salvation** is primarily an eschatological reality: It **brings eternal glory**. Thus he reminds Timothy—and now the people as well—that beyond present endurance awaits the eschatological prize (see disc. on vv. 4–6).

It should not go unnoticed that with these words Paul begins temporarily to look beyond Timothy to include **God's . . . people**, the **chosen ones**, who will, with Timothy and Paul, renounce the false teachings (2:14–21) and "endure unto **eternal glory**."

2:11-13 / As a way of wrapping up this segment of the argument (appeal), and thereby reinforcing the appeal itself (which now includes **God's . . . people**), Paul "cites" a fifth (and last) **true** ("faithful") **saying**. On the formula itself, see the discussion on 1 Timothy 1:15 (cf. 1 Tim. 3:1; 4:10; Titus 3:8).

Because the **saying** in this instance begins with a connective *gar* ("for," untranslated in the GNB), some have argued that the saying is actually verse 8 or 10 or that *logos* does not mean **saying** here but refers back to the **word of God** in verse 9 or that the "for" was an original part of a borrowed saying that was thus incorporated by Paul, but without meaning for the present context. However, the rhythmic balance of the four lines that follow gives them the clear character of a "saying" (perhaps an early Christian poem or hymn, more likely from Paul himself or from his churches). The *gar* is probably explanatory—and thus intentional—but does not refer to **this is a true saying**. Rather it goes back to all of the appeal in verses 1—10. "Take your share of suffering," Paul says; "keep in mind your risen Lord," he further reminds him, "*because* if we have died with him, we shall also live with him," and so on.

The poetic nature of the **saying** can be easily seen. It is a quatrain of conditional sentences. Each protasis ("if"-clause) deals with the believers' actions (all in the first person plural, the language of confession); each apodosis ("then"-clause) gives the results in terms of Christ, with the final apodosis having an additional explanatory coda. It may be that couplets are intended, since the first two lines deal with positive actions and the second two with negative. However, there is also a progression of tenses (past, present, future) and ideas in the first three lines, whereas the final line exhibits some remarkable shifts (both verbs are present; no *also* in the apodosis; a surprising turn to the apodosis).

The most likely interpretation of the first three lines is that they progress from Christian conversion (line 1) through perseverance and its eschatological prize (line 2) to a warning about the dire consequences of apostasy (line 3). Although there are considerable differences among scholars about line 4, it probably responds to line 3 as a word of hope. Our faithfulness or disloyalty cannot alter the greater reality of Christ's faithfulness (to us, being implied).

Before examining each line, one should note that the language and thought of the whole is thoroughly Pauline—to the detail. If he did not compose it, then it was certainly composed in his churches. In the final analysis there is no reason to think that the man who wrote 1 Corinthians 13 and Romans 8:28–39 could not also have written this marvelous piece.

Line 1: **If we have died with him, we shall also live with him**. This clearly mirrors Romans 6:8 (cf. Col. 2:20; 3:1), and there is no reason to think that it means anything different here from what it does there. Using baptismal imagery, Paul is reflecting again on Christian conversion as a dying and rising with Christ. The future, **we shall also live with him**, has primarily to do with life in Christ in the present (as it does in Rom. 6:8–11), although such language always has latent in it the thought of the eschatological fulfillment yet to be realized. After all, the present life **with him** is the result of his resurrection, *the* primary eschatological event that has already set the future in motion.

In the present context, however, the language of dying and living in Christ is perhaps also to be heard with the broader implications of Christian martyrdom. What was true figuratively at one's baptism would also be true of a "baptism" of another kind. One might well guess that the implication of this was not lost on Timothy.

Line 2: **If we continue to endure, we shall also rule with him**. This line is the basic reason, along with its warning counterpart in line 3, for citing the saying. It speaks directly to the concern throughout the whole appeal (1:6–2:13) that Timothy remain loyal, even in the face of suffering. The verb **to endure**, although it clearly implies persevering, is especially used by NT writers of holding one's ground patiently in trouble or affliction (cf. Mark 13:13; Rom. 12:12). That is certainly the sense here.

The apodosis also speaks directly to the context, namely, the promise of the eschatological victory alluded to in the three analogies in verses 4–6. To **rule with** Christ is a Pauline way of expressing the "eternal glory" that awaits those who are faithful to the end (cf. 1 Cor. 4:8; cf. also Rev. 3:21).

Line 3: **If we deny** [lit., "shall deny"] **him, he also will deny us.** With this line there is a shift to negative actions of believers. The content stands in clear contrast to line 2 as its opposite. Therefore, it also almost certainly presupposes the context of suffering and persecution (i.e., "being ashamed" of Christ in the time of trial). Thus it is both warning—to Timothy and "the elect" (v. 10; hence the future tense)—and judgment—on those such as the Asians of 1:15 who have already deserted.

The language of this line precisely reflects the saying of Jesus found in Matthew 10:33 (par. Luke 12:9). Thus the subject in the apodosis changes from "we" to an emphatic **he** (Gk. demonstrative pronoun, "that one").

Lines 2 and 3 together, therefore, form the basic reason for the citation: promise and warning attached to a call for endurance in the face of suffering and hardship.

Line 4: **If we are not faithful, he remains faithful** (cf. Rom. 3:3). This line is full of surprises, and it is also the one for which sharp differences of opinion exist regarding its interpretation. Some see it as a negative, corresponding to line 3. **If we are not faithful** (i.e., if we commit apostasy), God must be **faithful** to himself and mete out judgment. Although such an understanding is possible, it seems highly improbable that this is what Paul himself intended. After all, that could have been said plainly. The lack of a future verb with the adverb "also," as well as the fact that God's faithfulness in the NT is always in behalf of his people, also tend to speak out against this view.

What seems to have happened is that, in a rather typical way (cf., e.g., 1 Cor. 8:3), Paul could not bring himself to finish a sentence as it began. It is possible for us to prove faithless; but Paul could not possibly say that God would then be faithless toward us. Indeed, quite the opposite. **If we are not faithful** (and the context demands this meaning of the verb *apistoumen*, not "unbelieving," as KJV, et al.), this does not in any way affect God's own faithfulness to his people. This can mean either that God will override our infidelity with his grace (as most commentators) or that his overall faithfulness to his gracious gift of eschatological salvation for his people is not negated by the faithlessness of some. This latter seems more in keeping with Paul and the immediate context. Some have proved faithless, but God's saving faithfulness has not been diminished thereby. So Timothy and the people should continue **to endure** that they might **also rule with him**. Thus all four lines cohere as an exposition of "the salvation that comes through Christ Jesus and brings eternal glory" (v. 10).

The final coda simply explains why the final apodosis stands as it does: **because he cannot be false to** [lit., "deny"] **himself**. To do so would mean that God had ceased to be. Hence eschatological salvation is for Paul ultimately rooted in the character of God.

With this great affirmation, in the context of equally severe warning, this first appeal to loyalty comes to a conclusion. The defections in Asia, the warnings in this text, plus the raising of his sights in verse 10 to include "the elect," all coalesce to turn Paul's attention one final time to the false teachers (see 1 Tim. 1:3–11, 18–20; 4:1–5; 6:3–10) and Timothy's responsibilities (2:14–3:9).

Additional Notes

2:8 / The unusual word order (for the PE) of **Jesus** before **Christ**, and esp. the appearance of the phrase "from David's seed" in Ignatius of Antioch (ca. A.D. 110), have also contributed to the conviction that this is a segment of creedal formulation that has been borrowed both here and in Rom. 1:3–4. Although the word order is probably irrelevant (see Titus 1:1), the creedal nature of what is said is certainly possible. But it is highly unlikely that we are dealing with a fixed creed. Rather, a "common body of doctrine . . . was beginning to crystallize into more or less conventional patterns and forms, and sometimes set types of verbal expression were becoming current, [but] the language still remained fairly fluid" (J. N. D. Kelly, *Early Christian Creeds*, pp. 23–24).

2:9–10 / For a typical example of "too much ink spilt" on "who are the elect" in this passage that rather misses Paul's point, see Hendriksen.

2:11–13 / For a rather full discussion of the issues involved in this passage (what is the **true saying**; what is its extent and structure) as well as an extensive exegesis of its details, see G. W. Knight III, *The Faithful Sayings in the Pastoral Letters*, pp. 112–37. Knight and G. R. Beasley-Murray (*Baptism in the New Testament*, pp. 207–9) both argue that it is a baptismal hymn (but see J. D. G. Dunn, *Baptism in the Holy Spirit*, pp. 169–70). Bernard probably comes closer to reality by seeing it as "a hymn on the glories of martyrdom." But if one takes seriously the thoroughly Pauline nature of the poem, neither of these options is necessary. The hymn, in all of its parts, fits the context so well, that, whatever its origins or original setting, it now *functions* to inspire loyalty to Christ.

For an interpretation that sees line 1 as essentially reflecting martyrdom, see Hendriksen. But even he recognizes the difficulties that the aorist (past tense) verb, **we have died**, presents for this view, so he spiritualizes the death as being to "worldly comfort, ease," etc.

For examples of the "negative" understanding of line 4, see the comments by Bernard and Hendriksen. See Knight, pp. 126–31, for a more detailed refutation.

7

Exhortation to Resist False Teachers

---

2 TIMOTHY 2:14–19

Remind your people of this, and give them a solemn warning in God's presence not to fight over words. It does no good, but only ruins the people who listen. [15]Do your best to win full approval in God's sight, as a worker who is not ashamed of his work, one who correctly teaches the message of God's truth. [16]Keep away from profane and foolish discussions, which only drive people farther away from God. [17]Such teaching is like an open sore that eats away the flesh. Two men who have taught such things are Hymenaeus and Philetus. [18]They have left the way of truth and are upsetting the faith of some believers by saying that our resurrection has already taken place. [19]But the solid foundation that God has laid cannot be shaken; and on it are written these words: "The Lord knows those who are his" and "Whoever says that he belongs to the Lord must turn away from wrongdoing."

The concern for the "salvation" of "God's chosen people" expressed in verse 10, plus the exhortation to perseverance, with its warning against apostasy, in verses 11–13, bring Paul—and Timothy—back to the hard realities of the situation on Ephesus, with the presence of the false teachers (cf. 1 Timothy). Apparently they continue to plague the church, as Onesiphorus had probably informed him, although clearly not all have capitulated. This concern dominates the appeal from here to 4:5. In 2:14–3:9 the focus is almost entirely on the false teachers and what Timothy is to do in light of them. Thus it has much in common with 1 Timothy 1, 4, and 6. In 3:10–4:5 the focus is almost totally on Timothy himself and his ministry, with the presence of the false teachers serving as background to the exhortations. Three concerns dominate this opening paragraph, which prepares the way for the rest: an exposure of the false teachers and their teachings, an appeal to Timothy to resist them (both the teachers and their teachings), and a concern that the rest of the church not capitulate. Thus Timothy, and those who succeed him (Tychichus? cf. 4:12), are to lead the church in resisting these errors.

This dual concern for both Timothy and the church, reflected throughout 1 Timothy, has probably led to such a long section on the false teachers in this otherwise personal letter. On the one hand, the gospel is still at stake in Ephesus and Paul feels constrained to address the situation one more time. On the other hand, Timothy, even though he must soon leave Ephesus, must also take responsibility for leading the resistance, even if it costs him suffering and hardship.

2:14 / This opening imperative picks up Paul's concern for the "salvation" of "God's chosen people" (v. 10) in light of the threat—and dire consequences—of apostasy. He urges Timothy, **remind** (cf. Titus 3:1) **your people** (this is not in the Gk. text but is implied from the context) **of this** (lit., "these things"). This is the only *tauta* ("these things") imperative in 2 Timothy (there is a *tauta* in 2:2; however, its antecedent is not what has preceded in the letter but the "what things you have heard me proclaim" in the same verse). Many see it as referring to everything that has preceded, or to the teachings alluded to in 2:2. However, what makes most sense of the context is to see it as referring specifically to the preceding "true saying" (cf. Titus 3:8). That is, in light of the spreading "gangrene" (v. 17) of the false teachings, **remind your people of** the need for perseverance and of the awful consequences of rejecting Christ.

This reminder is to be accompanied by **a solemn warning in God's presence** (cf. 1 Tim. 5:2; 2 Tim. 4:1); that is, those so warned are to recognize themselves as being called into account by God himself. The content of the **warning** is that they are **not to fight over words**, which is one of the chief characteristics of the false teachers in Ephesus (see disc. on 1 Tim. 2:8; 6:4–5; cf. Titus 3:9). Thus the **people** are warned not to engage in the empty, purposeless, speculative (cf. v. 16) disputes **over words** carried on by the false teachers, because it does no good of any kind (cf. Titus 3:8); indeed, quite the opposite, it **only ruins the people who listen**.

This first imperative, therefore, charges Timothy to fulfill his responsibilities toward the people. They are to be reminded of their need to persevere and thus solemnly warned not to get into the "word battles" of the false teachers. This warning will be elaborated in verses 16–18. But before that, in a manner in keeping with 1 Timothy, Paul addresses a personal word to Timothy.

2:15 / As with similar passages in 1 Timothy (e.g., 1:18–19; 4:6–8, 13–15; 6:11–14), this imperative sets Timothy and his ministry in sharp contrast to the false teachers. They ultimately seek human approval (for the sake of gain; 1 Tim. 6:6–10); Timothy is to **do** his **best** (Gk., *spoudason*; cf. 4:9, 21; Titus 3:12; the KJV translation, "study," has misled generations of English-speaking Christians) **to win full approval** (implying "tested and approved"; cf. 1 Cor. 11:19; 2 Cor. 10:18) **in God's sight**.

The false teachers are workers who will experience "shame" before God because of their errors and sins; Timothy is to do his best to be **a worker who is not ashamed of his work**. This could (less likely) mean "**not ashamed of** the gospel." Most likely it means "**not ashamed** because he was worked well"; that is, in contrast to the false teachers, he should work so as to have no cause to be **ashamed**.

The basis for his **not** being **ashamed**, again in contrast to the false teachers, is that he **correctly teaches the message of God's truth**. The word translated **correctly teaches**, which occurs only here in the NT (but cf. Prov. 6:3 and 11:5, LXX), is a metaphor that literally means "to cut straight." There has been considerable speculation regarding the metaphor itself, as to what kind of "cutting" (wood, stones, furrows) may have been in mind. Most likely the original sense of the metaphor has been lost, and the emphasis simply lies in doing something **correctly**. Hence the GNB is perfectly adequate. Barrett correctly notes that a similar intent, based on a completely different metaphor, is found in 2 Corinthians 2:17. Thus Paul is not urging that he correctly interpret Scripture but that he truly preach and teach the gospel, **the message of God's truth**, in contrast to the "word battles" (v. 14) and "profane and foolish discussions" (v. 16) of the others.

2:16 / With this imperative Paul moves back to those who are not "approved," because they do not "correctly teach the message of God's truth" (v. 15). As elsewhere (cf. 1 Tim. 4:7; 6:20), the imperative, in this case **keep away from** (cf. Titus 3:9), is addressed directly to Timothy, but the people are also expected to pay attention. The description **profane and foolish discussions** is identical to that in 1 Timothy 6:20 (translated there "profane talk and foolish arguments"). Both the **profane** (having nothing to do with true godliness) and the empty, purposeless nature of their teaching are being sharply criticized.

The *reason* such **foolish discussions** are to be avoided (in the Gk. this is an explanatory, not a relative, clause) is somewhat ambiguous, since the verb *prokopsousin* (lit., "shall advance" or "make progress"; cf. 3:9, 13) has no expressed subject. The GNB takes **foolish discussions** as the implied subject, suggesting that these "only advance ungodliness all the more" (**only drive people farther away from God** is a bit misleading). However, the context and the pronoun *their* (translated **such** in GNB) in verse 17, meaning the false teachers, clearly imply that these people are the subject of the verb. As noted in 1 Timothy 4:15, this word ("shall advance") is probably a slogan related to the elitist nature of their teaching. Thus, with a fine piece of irony, Paul allows that they are "advancing" all right, but their advance shall be "all the more in ungodliness" (*asebeia*; the antonym of the *eusebeia*, "godliness," that recurs in these letters; see disc. on 1 Tim. 2:2). See discussion on 3:9, where in a great burst of confidence similar to verse 19 in this paragraph, Paul asserts that "they will make no more progress."

2:17-18 / Not only do these people themselves "advance the more in *asebeia*," but *their* **teaching** (see disc. on v. 16) also spreads so as to bring about the ruin of others. **Teaching** (Gk., *logos*) here stands in contrast to the "message [*logos*] of God's truth" in verse 15.

In keeping with the medical imagery of these Epistles (see esp. disc. on 1 Tim. 1:10 and 6:4), their **teaching** is metaphorically described as "shall have pasture like gangrene." This can mean either that it spreads like sheep in a pasture, similar to the spread of gangrene, or, as the GNB, that it **is like an open sore that eats away the flesh**, implying that their teaching will feed upon, or eat way at, the life of the church. In either case it "spreads" or "eats away" like a disease, and therefore must be avoided at all costs.

Two of these teachers are now identified: **Hymenaeus and Philetus**. Since **Hymenaeus** is not a common name, this must be the same man whom Paul "handed over to the power of Satan" in 1 Timothy 1:20 but who is still at work **upsetting the faith of some**. He is now joined by a **Philetus**, of whom nothing more is known. For a conjecture about Hymenaeus' former companion Alexander (1 Tim. 1:20), see the discussion on 2 Timothy 4:14.

These two men, obviously leaders among the false teachers, are further described as having **left the way of truth** (cf. 1 Tim. 1:6 and 6:21 for this usage). In the Greek text this clause is followed by the phrase, **by saying that our resurrection has already taken place** (cf. 2 Thess. 2:2, "the Day of the Lord has come"), one of only two passages in 1 and 2 Timothy where some content of the heresy is given (cf. 1 Tim. 4:3). This is probably some form of over-realized eschatology, that is, that the fullness of the End, especially **our resurrection**, has already been realized in our spiritual dying and rising with Christ (cf. v. 11; Rom. 6:1–11; Col. 2:20–

3:4). Such an idea had been around for a long time (cf. 2 Thess. 2:2; 1 Cor. 15:12; 4:8) and was probably related to the Greek conception of the soul as immortal and released from physical existence at death. Such dualism, we have previously noted, may also lie at the root of the asceticism in 1 Timothy 4:3.

But such teaching, Paul assures Timothy, goes far beyond the bounds of legitimate differences. Indeed they are **upsetting** (better "overturning") **the faith of some believers** (cf. Titus 1:11). This is the great urgency; hence the concern in verses 10–13 for God's people's "salvation that brings eternal glory" and for their perseverance, lest they be rejected by Christ. For Paul, denial of our (future bodily) resurrection is to deny the faith itself, in that it is to deny our past (Christ's own resurrection, on which all else is predicated) and our present as well (our eschatological existence as both *already* and *not-yet*; see Introduction, pp. xxx–xxxi).

2:19 / As always in Paul, Satan does not get the last word; God does. Just as in line 4 of the hymn/poem in verse 13, so here, the final word is not the faithlessness of some (v. 18), but the abiding faithfulness of God. With a strong adversative **but**, Paul affirms that, despite some defections and falling away, **the solid foundation that God has laid cannot be shaken**.

It is not altogether certain what, if anything, Paul intended by this metaphor. In other places (see disc. on 1 Tim. 3:15) Paul uses the building metaphor for the church and makes Christ (1 Cor. 3:10–12) or the apostles and prophets (Eph. 3:20) the **foundation**. In light of the further metaphor in verses 20–21, that may be what he has in mind. But it is altogether likely that he does not "intend" some specific point of reference. The emphasis, as the rest of the verse shows, is on God's proprietary ownership, on the certainty of eschatological triumph for those **who are his**. Since the metaphor stands in sharp contrast to the fact that the faith of some is being overturned, Paul clearly intends it to affirm the opposite: What God is doing in Ephesus, saving a people of his own (cf. Titus 2:14) for eternal glory, cannot be thwarted by the activity of the false teachers. In that sense, of course, the implied "building" refers to the church in Ephesus, his chosen people (v. 10).

Those who are Christ's and cannot be overthrown are recognizable by a double inscription (**on it are written these words**). The Greek literally says, "having this seal" (on this word, see NIDNTT, vol. 3, pp. 497–501). What is intended is the "seal" of ownership that the architect or owner would have inscribed on the foundation stone (similar in some ways to our modern cornerstones).

The double inscription reads: "**The Lord knows those who are his**" (cf. Num. 16:5, LXX, from Korah's rebellion). God's building rests not on the shaky foundation that we know God but that he **knows** us (cf. 1 Cor. 8:1–3). This is the primary ground of all Christian confidence. God's action is the prior one: He **knows those who are his**.

But God's prior action demands response. Therefore the inscription also reads: "**Whoever says that he belongs to the Lord must turn away from wrongdoing**" (the language, lit., "to name the name of the Lord," comes from the LXX—Lev. 24:16; Isa. 26:13; the sentiment of the second part is found in Ps. 34:14; Prov. 3:7). Those who are known by God are in turn expected to **turn away from wrongdoing**, that is, depart from Hymenaeus and Philetus and their teaching, who are recognizably *not* God's people because they persist in wrongdoing. In their case, false teaching has led to moral corruption (cf. 1 Tim. 6:3–10).

Thus, despite the devastating inroads made by the false teachers, Timothy and the church are to be heartened by this sure word (cf. also how the next two paragraphs conclude: 2:26 and 3:9).

Additional Notes

2:14 / Some interpreters (e.g., Lock, Hendriksen), impressed by the appearance of *tauta* here and in 2:2, understand the implied "them" after **remind** to refer to "the teachers of 2:2" (Lock). This view is also partly based on the mention of those **who listen**, thus teachers and their hearers. Although that view might make sense in the overall context, it seems to overlook the immediate context, the singularity of 2:2, and the considerably different use of *tauta* in 2:2.

2:15 / For discussion or speculations as to the possible meaning of the metaphor "to cut straight," see, e.g., Bernard, Lock, Hendriksen, or Kelly.

2:17-18 / Many are perplexed by the fact that Hymenaeus is still carrying on in Ephesus after having been excommunicated by Paul. Although D-C casually dismiss such "inconsistencies," this phenomenon, plus the fact that his compatriot is now Philetus, not Alexander, puts a special burden on theories of pseudepigraphy. One who invented the settings of these three letters, with their plausible historical and chronological details, would have been expected to "clean up his act" a bit better here.

But, taken as serious history, this is precisely the kind of "problem" that historical distance from the events often gives us. Probably Kelly is right: "We cannot assume that the Apostle's ban was instantaneously effective in silencing a heretic, and indeed the fact that Hymenaeus could apparently ignore it illustrates the difficult situation in the Ephesian church" (p. 184).

For an early understanding of **our resurrection has already taken place**, see the *Acts of Paul and Thecla* 14, where it is interpreted "that it has already taken place in the children whom we have, and that we are risen again in that we have come to know the true God" (HS 2, p. 357). Irenaeus (*Against Heresies* 1.23.5) refers to a Gnostic sect who believed that disciples of their founder (Simon) would "obtain the resurrection by being baptized into him, and can die no more, but remain in the possession of immortal youth" (ANF, vol. 1, p. 348).

8

A Supporting Analogy
from Household Vessels

2 TIMOTHY 2:20–21

In a large house there are dishes and bowls of all kinds; some are made of silver and gold, others of wood and clay; some are for special occasions, others for ordinary use. ²¹If anyone makes himself clean from all those evil things, he will be used for special purposes, because he is dedicated and useful to his Master, ready to be used for every good deed.

The main point of verses 14–19 was to reassert the need for Timothy—and God's people—to "keep away from [the] profane and foolish discussions" of the false teachers (v. 16), which "do no good [but only] ruin the people who listen" (vv. 14, 18). That train of thought was broken by verse 19, which, with the metaphor of an inscription (seal of ownership) on a foundation, reaffirms the certainty of God's work, despite the "ruin" caused by the false teachers.

Paul now moves to the related but significantly different metaphor of a house with two kinds of vessels, in order to further elaborate the second part of the inscription: "Whoever says that he belongs to the Lord must turn away from wrongdoing." At the same time this new analogy functions as the lead-in for the next imperatives to Timothy about his own personal responsibilities toward both the false teachings and teachers (vv. 22–26). (Note the differences in paragraphing between the GNB [RSV, NAB] 14–19, 20–26, and the NEB [NA²⁶, Kelly] 14–21, 22–26.)

The passage is in two clear parts: Verse 20 gives the facts of the analogy itself; verse 21 makes the application. Analogies are seldom perfect; but Paul's point seems clear enough, despite some breakdowns in the application.

2:20 / The analogy itself reflects on a common phenomenon in antiquity. **In a large house**, that is, in the houses of the more well-to-do, **there are dishes and bowls** (lit., "vessels") **of all kinds**. Some of these are very expensive (**silver and gold**); some are quite inexpensive (**wood and clay**). Usually the expensive ones were used for meals or **for** other **special occasions** (lit., "for honor," i.e., for public functions such as meals); the less expensive ones were used "for dishonor" (perhaps **for ordinary use**, but more likely garbage or excrement is in view).

This particular reality, two kinds of vessels for two different uses, but both of them vessels, had already fascinated biblical writers (see Jer. 18:1–11; Wisd. of Sol. 15:7), as well as Paul himself (Rom. 9:19–24). Paul's problem in this instance, however, is that he has set up an analogy that, strictly pressed, would make a considerably different point from the one he wants to make following verse 19. Thus, as verse 21 and the context make clear, Paul's point is *neither* that of 1 Corinthians 12:21–24 (though of differing kinds and uses, *both* vessels are useful to the master of the house) *nor* that of the parable of the wheat and tares (Matt. 13:24–30, 36–43; where the church is pictured as containing both the elect and false teachers, who will be separated at the End), interpretations that are often given to this passage.

2:21 / Paul's own application of the analogy (a "therefore" tying it to v. 19, through v. 20, is left untranslated in the GNB), though it does not seem to fit very well, is precisely the one *he* wants to make. It has to do with verse 19, that those who name God's name, Timothy and the believers— those who are known by God—are to turn away from evil, especially in the form of the false teachings of such as Hymenaeus and Philetus.

Thus, **if anyone** (probably purposely ambiguous as in v. 19, but now certainly moving back to include Timothy) **makes himself clean** (lit., "cleanses himself"; using the language of the ritual cleansing of vessels) **from all those evil things** (the false teachings), **he will** become "a vessel for honor" (GNB, **be used for special purposes**). In applying the imagery, Paul has thus moved from the house that contains all sorts of vessels to the good vessels themselves and argues that only these, with their "honorable" purposes, count (although it is not the value of the vessels, but their contents, i.e., purposes, that is the reason for "cleansing oneself" of the others). In particular Paul is anticipating what he will say to Timothy in verses 22–26, in light of verses 14–19, so he must therefore "cleanse himself" **from all those evil things**.

The rest of the application, which continues to do wordplays with the imagery, supports this interpretation. Timothy **is** to be **dedicated** (Gk., *hēgiasmenon*, "sanctified"), a most appropriate double entendre. Just as the "vessels" of the Temple were "sanctified" for sacred purposes, so is

Timothy to be set apart (**dedicated**) and thus **useful to his Master** (cf. the metaphor in 2:4), which of course keeps the imagery of the **large house** with its "honorable vessels."

Such a vessel is also **ready . . . for every good deed**. This, too, reflects a skillful use of the imagery. As metaphor it means "fit for any honorable purpose" (so NEB), but as applied metaphor it reflects the urgency for correct behavior ("good deeds") that recurs in these Epistles (cf. 1 Tim. 2:10; 5:10; 6:18; and esp. Titus 1:16; 2:7, 14; 3:1, 8, 14). As such it leads directly to the imperatives that follow.

Additional Notes

2:20 / One of the common errors in interpreting this passage is the attempt to apply the analogy of v. 20 on its own merits, without letting v. 21 be the sure guide. This is probably due to the sense that it is "misapplied" in v. 21 and therefore that v. 20 can stand on its own, as having its own application—to the church as being full of all kinds of vessels. But v. 21 makes it clear that that is *not* Paul's point, and the *oun* ("therefore") in v. 21 also makes it clear that v. 20 is not intended to have its own meaning, apart from, or different from, that given in v. 21.

2:21 / A very common interpretation of the ambiguous *apo toutōn* (lit., "from these," which the GNB translates **from all those evil things**) is that Timothy is to "sternly separate himself from teachers like Philetus and Hymenaeus" (Kelly; so most commentaries), which Kelly calls "the obvious exegesis" (p. 188). Though there may be good reason to look at it this way, the context seems to demand "false teachings" as the emphasis more than the "false teachers" themselves. The imperatives in both vv. 14 and 16 have to do with the teachings, as does the **wrongdoing** (or "evil") in v. 19b. So also do the imperatives in the paragraph that follow, and in this instance Timothy is even to try to "correct his opponents" in hopes of winning them back—which is especially difficult if v. 21 is seen as a kind of excommunication of them. The full images get considerably stretched in either case.

9

Timothy's Responsibilities in Light of the False Teachers

2 TIMOTHY 2:22–26

Avoid the passions of youth, and strive for righteousness, faith, love, and peace, together with those who with a pure heart call out to the Lord for help. 23But keep away from foolish and ignorant arguments; you know that they end up in quarrels. 24The Lord's servant must not quarrel. He must be kind toward all, a good and patient teacher, 25who is gentle as he corrects his opponents, for it may be that God will give them the opportunity to repent and come to know the truth. 26And then they will come to their senses and escape from the trap of the Devil, who had caught them and made them obey his will.

The commands introducing this section flow directly from the application of the analogy of verses 20–21, but all the time in the context of the concerns that began in verse 14. In "cleansing himself from these things" (v. 21), Timothy is again urged to avoid the foolish arguments of the false teachers, which only lead to quarrels. On the contrary—and this is a new theme—he is to try to rescue people from their entrapment by error.

The entire paragraph is directed toward Timothy and his responsibilities in view of the presence of the false teaching. The dominating theme is **peace**. The false teachers revel in arguments that breed quarrels (cf. 1 Tim. 6:4); Timothy, by contrast, should pursue peace. He must not quarrel but be kind toward all, and must gently correct, with the desire that his correction and gentleness may lead some to repentance.

2:22 / These two imperatives (**avoid** and **strive for**), which are identical to those in 1 Timothy 6:11, are closely related to verses 19–21, which emphasize "turning away from wrongdoing" and "cleansing oneself of these things." But the negative imperative in this case is somewhat surprising in the context. Why *here* is Timothy told to **avoid the passions of youth**?

The answer lies basically in the meaning of the word **passions** (*epithymiai*; cf. 1 Tim. 6:9; 2 Tim. 4:3) in these letters. Rather than "lusts," it simply means "desires," especially "evil desires." Thus Paul is not so much speaking of sensual **passions** as he is those kinds of headstrong **passions of youth**, who sometimes love novelties, foolish discussions, and arguments that all too often lead to quarrels.

Instead of engaging in the pastimes of the false teachers, Timothy is to **strive for righteousness, faith, love, and peace**. For these first three items see the discussion on 1 Timothy 6:11. Just as the final items on that list were especially relevant to the context, so here Timothy must also **strive for . . . peace**, as do all those **who with a pure heart call** upon the name of **the Lord** (not **call out to the Lord for help**; cf. 1 Cor. 1:2). This last phrase is another idiom for God's people in the OT (cf. 2:10; Titus 2:14); they are those who "call upon his name," that is, worship Yahweh, the God of Israel, and none other. Along with the modifier **with a pure heart** (cf. 1 Tim. 1:5; the same root as the verb "cleanse oneself" in v. 21), this designation sets off the true people of God (who **strive for righteousness**, etc.) from the false teachers, who do not truly know God (cf. Titus 1:16) but are ensnared by Satan. Perhaps, too, as with verse 19, it is a word of encouragement to Timothy by reminding him that not all "have bowed the knee to Baal."

2:23 / Precisely because Timothy is to "strive for peace," he must **keep away from** (same verb as in 1 Tim. 4:7; 5:11) **foolish** (cf. Titus 3:9, a strong pejorative) **and ignorant** (*apaideutos*, "uninstructed, ill-informed") **arguments** (see disc. on 1 Tim. 6:4; Titus 3:9). Although *apaideutos* can mean ignorant, or "stupid" (NIV), in this context (see disc. on v. 25) it more likely refers to the fact that the perpetrators of these quibblings, who have rejected the truth, are themselves uninstructed or poorly informed (cf. 1 Tim. 1:7; "they do not understand their own words or the matters about which they speak with so much confidence").

Timothy, therefore, is to "strive for peace" (v. 22), which means to reject **foolish** debates, based on lack of instruction, because such debates only **end up in** (lit., "give birth to") **quarrels** (*machai*; cf. Titus 3:9; cf. also "word battles," *logomachiai*, 1 Tim. 6:4; 2 Tim. 2:14)—one of the serious sins of the false teachers (see esp. disc. on 1 Tim. 6:4–5).

2:24–26 / In contrast to the false teachers, whose **foolish arguments** breed **quarrels**, Timothy, as **the Lord's servant**, who wants to be "useful to his Master" (v. 21), **must not quarrel** (cf. the qualifications for overseers/

elders, 1 Tim. 3:3; Titus 1:7). The term **servant** is commonly used in Paul for those who minister in the Word (cf. Titus 1:1); the combination **Lord's servant**, which occurs only here in Paul (usually it is "servant of Christ"), is apparently a conscious attempt to reflect on the metaphor in verse 21 by using OT language (cf. similarly, 1 Tim. 6:11). Thus, even though **the Lord's servant** must "wage the noble war" (1 Tim. 1:18), he must not do so by engaging in **quarrels** with his opponents.

But **not** to **quarrel** does *not* mean that he must thereby let error go on its way. To the contrary. However, in standing against error he must exhibit a different disposition. **He must be kind toward all**—even to his opponents. The point is attitudinal and reflects the very difficult stance of Ephesians 4:15 ("speaking the truth in love"). He must also be **a good and patient teacher**. This combines two Greek words: *didaktikon*, "an able **teacher**" (cf. 1 Tim. 3:2), and *anexikakon*, literally, "ready to put up with evil," hence **patient**, or "tolerant" (NEB). Again, the requirement is attitudinal. Timothy must show himself equal to the task as a **teacher** of God's truth (2:15), but he must do so without getting heated in his response to evil. Finally, he must be **gentle** (cf. 1 Tim. 6:11; Titus 3:2) **as he corrects his opponents**. This last phrase presents some considerable difficulties. The verb (*paideuō*) can mean either "to instruct" or "to educate" (cf. *apaideutos* in v. 23; see esp. disc. on Titus 2:12), or to **correct** or "discipline" (cf. 1 Tim. 1:20). The greater difficulty is with the word translated **opponents**, an extemely rare word that can refer either to the **opponents** themselves or to "those who are adversely affected" (Bernard) by the opponents. Is Timothy to discipline his **opponents**, as 1 Timothy 1:20 might allow? Or is he to **correct** or re-educate those who have been "taken in" by the false teachers? This is not easy to determine, since both are elsewhere seen as entrapped by Satan (cf. 1 Tim. 4:1–2; 3:7; 6:9). It is probably safe to say that it at least includes the people who have been so ensnared and may also include the false teachers themselves (although 3:6, 9, 13 do not seem to be so hopeful).

In either case, Paul hopes that by pursuing the path of peace and gentleness, Timothy can be an instrument in God's hands: **It may be** (Gk., indirect question, "will God perhaps . . . ?") **that God will give them** "repentance" (although that might include **the opportunity to repent**, repentance itself is understood here to be God's gift; cf. NEB: "the Lord may grant them a change of heart"). Such a change of heart has as its goal that they will **come to know the truth**, a term that in the PE is nearly synonymous for "getting saved" (1 Tim. 2:4) or belonging to God's true people (1 Tim. 4:3). All of this implies that those who persist in their errors are in genuine danger of forfeiting salvation, as line 3 in the hymn/poem of 2:11–13 also asserts.

The remainder of the sentence further confirms such an implication (v. 26; vv. 24–26 are a single sentence in Greek; this is the second verb controlled by "it may be that"). If perhaps God grants them repentance, that also means that **they will** thus **come to their senses** (a metaphor for soberness; cf. 4:5 and also the *sōphrōn* words demanding clearheadedness or sound-mindedness, e.g., Titus 2:2). Such a metaphor emphasizes the deceitful nature of the false teaching, which here, as before, is depicted as ultimately demonic (see esp. disc. on 1 Tim. 4:1–2). To experience God-given repentance and a return to soberness means to **escape from the trap of the Devil** (cf. 1 Tim. 3:7; 6:9). Although the final description is not fully certain (see note), Satan is further portrayed as having **caught them** (lit., "having been captured alive by him") **and** thus having **made them obey his will**. As noted in the discussion on 1 Timothy 4:1–2, this is a thoroughly Pauline view of what has happened to those who oppose the gospel.

The emphasis in this sentence has been clearly redemptive. Paul wants Timothy to model a kind of teaching that will not simply refute error (Titus 1:9; 2:15) and save his hearers (1 Tim. 4:16) but that will also be used by God to rescue those who have already been entangled in the false teaching. However, Paul is also a sober realist, and the mention of those "captured alive" by Satan to do his will launches him into a final indictment of the false teacher themselves (3:1–9).

Additional Notes

2:22 / For a full presentation of the position taken here on **the passions of youth**, see W. Metzger, "Die *neōterikai epithymiai* in 2 Tim. 2,22," *ThZ* 33 (1977), pp. 129–36. Cf. Kelly.

The prepositional phrase, **together with those who . . . call** "on the name of the Lord," is ambiguously placed, so that it could mean that Timothy is to **strive for peace** only with true believers (so Barrett, Kelly). However, not only does the context of the whole paragraph suggest otherwise, but this positioning of prepositional phrases at the end of clauses, even though they modify the verb, is characteristic of these letters (see, e.g., 1 Tim. 1:14; 2:7, 10; 2 Tim. 1:12).

2:24–26 / The word translated **opponents** occurs in extant literature only in Philo (*On the Special Laws* 4.103) in the active, meaning something close to "retaliate," and, in the passive, in Pseudo-Longinus (*On the Sublime* 17). Most scholars consider it to be a Gk. middle here (thus, "oppose oneself to" or "be opposed"). However, if it is passive here, as Bernard argues, it would imply that some had been affected by the opposition of others. On the whole, this latter seems more likely, since Paul uses other words to speak specifically of his opponents (1 Tim. 5:14; Titus 1:9).

The final phrase in v. 26, **who had caught them and made them obey his will**, is especially rough in the Gk., so that some argue that it means: " 'God may grant them to escape from the snare of the devil after they have been captured by him, so as to do His will—i.e., the will of God' " (Scott, following Moffatt; cf. Bernard); or "Having been saved alive . . . by the servant of the Lord to do the Lord's will, and not the devil's" (Lock). But both of these solutions create even greater difficulties in the Gk. text. On the whole, the GNB (cf. Kelly, Spicq, D-C, Hanson) is to be preferred. For a more extensive treatment of the issue, see J. P. Wilson, "The Translation of 2 Timothy 2:26," and Hanson.

10

Final Indictment of the False Teachers

2 TIMOTHY 3:1–9

Remember that there will be difficult times in the last days. ²People will be selfish, greedy, boastful, and conceited; they will be insulting, disobedient to their parents, ungrateful, and irreligious; ³they will be unkind, merciless, slanderers, violent, and fierce; they will hate the good; ⁴they will be treacherous, reckless, and swollen with pride; they will love pleasure rather than God; ⁵they will hold to the outward form of our religion, but reject its real power. Keep away from such people. ⁶Some of them go into people's houses and gain control over weak women who are burdened by the guilt of their sins and driven by all kinds of desires, ⁷women who are always trying to learn but who can never come to know the truth. ⁸As Jannes and Jambres were opposed to Moses, so also these people are opposed to the truth—people whose minds do not function and who are failures in the faith. ⁹But they will not get very far, because everyone will see how stupid they are. That is just what happened to Jannes and Jambres.

With this paragraph Paul shifts his focus from Timothy to the false teachers themselves and sets them against the backdrop of the eschatological urgency that runs throughout the letter. The only personal word to Timothy is the reiterated imperative in verse 5—that he should keep away from such people—which functions to tie the two parts of the paragraph (vv. 1–5, 6–9) together.

Timothy is again reminded (cf. 1 Tim. 4:1) that the presence of the false teachers should come as no surprise; they belong to the theme of eschatological fulfillment, begun with the coming of Christ. But in this case Paul does an interesting turn. By including a typical vice list (vv. 2–5), he ties together the defections of the false teachers with the general increase in evil seen all about them as evidence that the final evil days have dawned.

The second part of the paragraph (vv. 6–9) makes an equally arresting correlation. By describing their activities of subverting weak women (vv. 6–7) and by comparing them with the Egyptian magicians who opposed Moses (vv. 8–9), Paul intimates what he finally asserts in verse 13, that the false teachers are nothing more than religious charlatans, comparable to the sorcerers and charlatans of all kinds of which the ancient world was full (cf., e.g., Acts 8:9; 13:6–8; 19:13–16).

Except for the passing references in verse 13 and 4:3 (and perhaps 4:14), this is the final word about the false teachers in this letter. Thus it functions very much like 1 Timothy 6:3–10, as both exposure and indictment. From here Paul will return to his personal exhortations to Timothy, but now (esp. in 3:10–4:5) with what has been said in 2:14–3:9 always hovering in the background.

3:1 / This sentence follows 2:22–26 rather abruptly. But its place in the argument is not difficult to follow. Although the letter is primarily a series of personal appeals to Timothy, the continuing influence of the false teachers and Timothy's apparent failure to stem the tide have caused Paul to address this issue in some detail, beginning at 2:14. What he does here, similarly to 1 Timothy 4:1 (which see), is to place their presence into a broader theological perspective—the eschatological reality that the time of the End, the coming of the New Age, has already been set in motion with the coming of Christ.

Thus the presence of the false teachers belongs to the well-known (**remember**, or, as the RSV, "understand this") phenomenon **that there will be difficult times in the last days**. This was a common motif in Jewish apocalyptic (cf. Dan. 12:1: "And there shall be a time of trouble, such as never has been since there was a nation till that time" [RSV]; cf. 1 Enoch 80:2–8; 100:1–3; Assumption of Moses 8:1; 4 Ezra 5:1–12; 2 Baruch 25–27; 48:32–36; 70:2–8). It was picked up by Jesus (Mark 13:3–23), and the early church saw it as evidence that the End had already begun (cf. 1 Cor. 7:26, 29–31; 1 John 2:18; 2 Pet. 3:3; Jude 17–18). For the term **the last days** as referring especially to the beginning of the Christian era, see Acts 2:16–21 and Hebrews 1:2.

3:2-4 / As evidence that **the last days** are already upon us (despite the future verb **will be**) Paul resorts to a common practice of his—a catalogue of vices (cf. 1 Tim. 1:9–10; 1 Cor. 6:9–10; Gal. 5:19–21; Rom. 1:29–31). The list itself contains eighteen items, six of which occur only here in the NT, four others are found only here and in the list in Romans 1, and five are shared vocabulary with Luke-Acts. While only five of the words occur elsewhere in the PE, the catalogue has nonetheless been tailored somewhat to fit this situation. Thus, in a way similar to 1 Timothy 1:9–10 and

Romans 1:29–31, the list especially reflects the prevailing evils of pagan society. At the same time Paul is indicting the false teachers, both by characterizing their existence as in keeping with these evils and by implying that they themselves fit many of the items in the list (pride, arrogance, greed, lack of love, slander, etc.).

The list itself doesn't seem to have any clear design to it, such as one finds in 1 Timothy 1:9–10. Some items seem to be in pairs, but that is not evident for all. It begins appropriately enough with **selfish** (lit., "love of self"; cf. Titus 1:7 where "not self-willed" tops the list), since from such misdirected love all other vices flow. "Love of self" is paired with "love of money" (**greedy**), which was one of the basic vices of the false teachers (see 1 Tim. 6:5–10; Titus 1:11). The next two, **boastful and conceited** (or "arrogant"), which also appear together in Romans 1:30, emphasize boastfulness in words and thought, respectively, and also reflect what is said elsewhere of the false teachers (1 Tim. 1:7; 6:4). The word **insulting** (*blasphēmoi*) reflects the "insults" ("malicious talk," NIV) of 1 Timothy 6:4; **disobedient to their parents** (cf. Rom. 1:30) may be reminiscent of some(one?) not caring for parents in 1 Timothy 5:8.

The next four words, all of which begin with the negative prefix *a-* (comparable to the English *un-*, *in-*, *im-*), seem to broaden the perspective. In **the last days** people will be **ungrateful** (which meaningfully follows **disobedient to parents**), **irreligious** (in the sense of "offending against the fundamental decencies of life," Barclay), **unkind** (lit., "unloving," in the sense of lacking natural affection; cf. Rom. 1:31), and **merciless** (i.e., incapable of being reconciled to a fellow human being). They will be **slanderers** (cf. 1 Tim. 3:11; Titus 2:5), **violent** (lit., "without self-control"), **and fierce** (a different word for the sentiment expressed in 1 Tim. 3:3; Titus 1:7). **They will hate the good** (cf. the opposite expected of elders in Titus 1:8), will be **treacherous, reckless** ("stops at nothing to gain his ends," Kelly), and **swollen with pride** (same word as in 1 Tim. 3:6; 6:4). The list concludes with yet another form of misdirected love, **they will love pleasure rather than God**.

As always, such lists seem to come down a bit heavily on the human race and are the object of attack by those with humanist tendencies. But unfortunately the list is only too realistic, reminding God's people over and again that these, too, are **the last days**.

3:5 / With this final description, Paul brings the eschatological motif of the increase of evil in the last days to focus on the false teachers. Their great problem, from Paul's point of view, is that they **hold to the out-**

ward form of our religion (*eusebeia*; see disc. on 1 Tim. 2:2), **but reject its real power**. They liked the visible expressions, the ascetic practices and the endless discussions of religious trivia, thinking themselves to be obviously righteous because they were obviously religious. But they thereby denied the essential **power** of the Christian *eusebeia*, since they engaged in so many of the "irreligious" attitudes and practices that characterized the pagan world. Compare the similar indictment in Titus 1:16. So one more time, Timothy is told to **keep away from such people**, the clear evidence that Paul did not have some future time in mind in verses 1–4. This imperative also serves for Paul as a transition to the final exposure of the false teachers.

3:6–7 / This sentence, which was certainly unnecessary information for Timothy himself, is probably something of a reflex action on Paul's part. Perturbed as he is by the false teachers, with their "outward form of religion" without "its real power," he reminds Timothy (and the church) of the kind of people they are dealing with—religious charlatans. Paul intends this description to be a scathing censure. It serves us, however, by filling in all kinds of blanks in 1 Timothy about the false teachers and their relationship to the women in the church.

Although our other sources date from a somewhat later period, there is plenty of evidence that religious quackery had an especially fruitful field among women. Both their less-than-satisfying social position in Greco-Roman society and their religious hunger, typical of the era, made women easy prey. With these words Paul simultaneously associates the false teachers with such quackery and condemns the women in the church who have let themselves be taken in. It is with this information in hand that one must read 1 Timothy 2:9–15; 3:11; 4:7; 5:3–16.

Thus the false teachers (**some of them** is not quite accurate; the text literally reads, "of such people [as in vv. 2–4] are those who . . . ") **go into people's houses and gain control over weak women**. The verb translated **go into** is a much stronger word than that, suggesting "creeping in" under false pretenses (cf. "worm their way in," BAGD, NIV, Moffatt; "some of that ilk sneak into," Berkeley). The verb **gain control**, when used metaphorically, as here, means to take captive by misleading or deceiving (cf. Jdth 16:9; Ignatius, *Philadelphians* 2:2). This is quite in keeping with the theme throughout these letters of the deceptive nature of these teachers (1 Tim. 2:14; 4:1–2; 2 Tim. 3:13).

The **women** themselves are designated with the Greek diminutive (lit., "little women"), which was a scornful pejorative connoting "silly" or "foolish" (intended by the GNB's **weak**, meaning "easy prey"). They are further described as **burdened by the guilt of their sins** (which could mean that they are currently full of sin, but more likely means "burdened with a sinful past," NEB) **and driven by all kinds of desires**. It is just possible that there was some sexual involvement between the false teachers and these women, which would throw light on several texts in 1 Timothy (see note). But that is not a necessary inference, and Paul does not pursue such a point. He pursues the point that **the guilt of their sins** and their having **all kinds of desires** has made them religious dilettantes, **women who are always trying to learn but who can never come to know the truth**. Thus the false teachers and these women feed on one another. The women are given "religious training"—of the worst kind, destined to feed their curiosity but not bring them to the freedom of the gospel—and they in turn undoubtedly pay the false teachers handsomely (1 Tim. 6:3–10). No wonder that Paul forbade the women to teach, encouraged submission to their husbands (1 Tim. 2:9–15), and wanted the younger widows, who had given themselves to pleasure (5:6) and had already turned away to follow Satan (5:15), to marry (5:14).

3:8–9 / Paul now turns from the women to the false teachers and by analogy places their activities in the category of the religious sorcerers. As Pharaoh's magicians used sorcery to withstand **Moses** (Exod. 7:11–12, 22; 8:7), so by implication the false teachers use deceptions to oppose **the truth** (cf. Acts 13:8). It is not certain by this whether Paul actually thought them to be using sorcery; in any case, he sees clear analogies between their deceptions and the sorceries of the magicians.

In the OT the magicians are not named, but it is a part of the religious tradition of both Judaism and Christianity to give names to the nameless. Thus by at least 150 B.C. the Egyptian magicians had been narrowed to two brothers and given the names **Jannes** (a form of Johanna, still found in some sources) **and Jambres** (or Mambres in other sources). By the time of Paul this tradition had become common stock (cf. the similar use of such tradition in 1 Cor. 10:4).

But Paul is not finished. Once more (cf. 1 Tim. 6:4–5) he describes the lack of "clear-mindedness" (see disc. on 2 Tim. 1:7; Titus 2:2) in these teachers. Their **minds do not function** (lit., "depraved in mind"; cf. 1 Tim. 4:5), and they are **failures** ("rejects"; the opposite of "approved" in 2:15) **in** ("as to") **the faith**.

As often happens (cf. 2:13 and 19), Paul cannot conclude on such a dismal note. So he returns to their theme of "making progress" (see disc.

on 1 Tim. 4:15 and 2 Tim. 2:16) and once again gives it an ironic twist. With great confidence in God's faithfulness (cf. 2:13, 19) he affirms: **They will not get** ("progress" or "advance") **very far**. The reason for this is tied back to what was just said at the end of verse 8: **because everyone will see how stupid** ("mindless") **they** really **are**. This does not mean that they will no longer be effective in their deceptions (cf. 3:13), but, for Paul, truth will win out. Thus their end, in terms of the exposure of their folly, will be **just what happened to Jannes and Jambres**. This may refer to Exodus 9:11; although it is equally possible that he is reflecting on a legend, which included their names, that is no longer available to us.

Thus the analogy has served a further useful turn. Just as the magicians were shown up for what they were, Paul cannot see the false teachers as ultimately triumphing.

Additional Notes

3:2-4 / Those rejecting Pauline authorship feel obliged to determine both the *source* and the *function* of this vice list. Hanson sees the source as Rom. 1:29–31, with most of the vices having "an exact or fairly close parallel" to that list (p. 144); he considers the function as irrelevant, "probably part of the author's source material." Again, the evidence speaks favorably for Pauline authorship. Such lists are a common feature, yet none closely resembles the others, and each is adapted to its context—as here. For an analysis of this and other vice lists, see McEleney, "The Vice Lists of the PE."

3:6-7 / For texts that reveal the susceptibility of women to religious charlatans, see Lucian, *Alexander the False Prophet* 6: "They went about the country practicing quackery and sorcery, and 'trimming the fatheads'—for so they style the public in the traditional patter of magicians. Well, among these they hit upon a rich Macedonian woman, past her prime but still eager to be charming . . . and lined their purses fairly well at her expense" (Loeb, vol. 4, p. 183); and Irenaeus, *Against Heresies* 1.13.3. Cf. also the story of the lady Paulina (Jos. *Antiquities* 18.65–80) and her readiness to please the god Anubis and, although the author did not intend such a comparison, the readiness of women to follow Paul in the *Acts of Paul and Thecla*.

D-C suggest, on the basis of 1 Tim. 1:11, "that emancipation tendencies may be present" among these women. That is altogether possible, given the similar problems in Corinth, which stemmed from some similar theological tendencies.

The possibility that sexual liaison may also be involved would make further sense of such texts as 1 Tim. 2:9–10, and the concern there for chastity; 3:2, that the overseer be "faithful to his own wife"; 5:2, that Timothy treat "the younger women as sisters, with all purity"; 5:6, 11–15, that the younger widows were giving themselves to pleasure and "becoming wanton"; and 5:22, in the context of judgment on the straying elders, that Timothy "not join in others' sins but keep himself pure." Nonetheless, it must be admitted that there is a degree of speculation involved in this suggestion.

3:8-9 / For the phenomenon of naming the nameless in early Christianity, see B. M. Metzger, "Names for the Nameless in the New Testament: A Study in the Growth of Christian Tradition," in *New Testament Studies: Philological, Versional, and Patristic* (Leiden: Brill, 1980), pp. 23–43, reprint from the Quasten *Festschrift*, 1970.

Because the names of **Jannes and Jambres** were such a widespread phenomenon in antiquity, both Jewish and pagan, the suggestion by Kelly that this may belong to the elaboration of Jewish legends about Moses makes a lot of sense. The names are mentioned in the *Damascus Document* 5:18; Targum Ps-Jonathan 1.3 (on Exod. 1:15) and 7.2 (on Exod. 7:11)—although there is some debate on the dating of this source; *Manahoth* 85a; *Midrash Rabbah Exodus* 9:7; and Pliny, *Natural History* 30.1.11. In the Targum (Ps-Jonathan 40.6) on Num. 22:21–22 they are called the sons of Balaam!

Another Appeal to Loyalty and Endurance

2 TIMOTHY 3:10–17

But you have followed my teaching, my conduct, and my purpose in life; you have observed my faith, my patience, my love, my endurance, [11]my persecutions, and my sufferings. You know all that happened to me in Antioch, Iconium, and Lystra, the terrible persecutions I endured! But the Lord rescued me from them all. [12]Everyone who wants to live a godly life in union with Christ Jesus will be persecuted; [13]and evil persons and impostors will keep on going from bad to worse, deceiving others and being deceived themselves. [14]But as for you, continue in the truths that you were taught and firmly believe.

You know who your teachers were, [15]and you remember that ever since you were a child, you have known the Holy Scriptures, which are able to give you the wisdom that leads to salvation through faith in Christ Jesus. [16]All Scripture is inspired by God and is useful[b] for teaching the truth, rebuking error, correcting faults, and giving instruction for right living, [17]so that the person who serves God may be fully qualified and equipped to do every kind of good deed.

b. All Scripture is inspired by God and is useful; *or* Every scripture inspired by God is also useful.

With this paragraph, which focuses on its single imperative in verse 14 (**continue in the truths that you were taught**), Paul renews the appeal with which the letter began. (Note how many themes from 1:3–2:13 are touched on: Timothy's long relationship to Paul [vv. 10–11, 14; cf. 1:4, 6, 13]; Paul himself as the model of loyalty [vv. 10–11; cf. 1:8, 11–12, 13; 2:9–10]; the call to suffering [vv. 11–12; cf. 1:8, 16; 2:3–6, 11–12]; the appeal itself [v. 14; cf. 1:6, 13–14]; the faith of his forebears [v. 15; cf. 1:5]; the focus on salvation [v. 15; cf. 2:10–13].) However, he does so now in full view of what has been said about the false teachers and Timothy's responsibilities regarding them (2:14–3:9).

Thus he effectively brings together the concerns of the first two sections of the letter (the appeal to loyalty to himself and his gospel—in the face of suffering—in 1:6–2:13; and the continuing threat to his gospel—in the form of the false teachers—in 2:14–3:9). At the same time the paragraph serves as preparation for the final charge in 4:1–5.

The paragraph is in two parts (vv. 10–13, 14–17), structured around two occurrences of *su de* ("but as for you," vv. 10, 14) and the central imperative of verse 14. The two parts hold the keys to Timothy's abiding loyalty: first, to recall the past, especially Paul's teaching and example, learned through long association, and second, to give heed to the Scriptures, with which he has also had long association, and which both lead to salvation through Christ and are useful for all the tasks of his ministry.

3:10-11 / This new section begins with an emphatic *su de* ("but as for **you**, you have . . .; cf. 2:1; 3:14; 4:5). After the ringing exposure and indictment of the false teachers (vv. 1–9), who not only teach falsehood but also live as reprobates, Timothy is going to be urged, in contrast to them, to abide faithfully in the truth of the gospel. The way Paul does this is to remind him of his (Paul's) own example, which **you have followed** (cf. 1 Tim. 4:6). This verb, which ordinarily means "to accompany," also came to mean "to study at close quarters" (Kelly; cf. Luke 1:3). In Stoic circles it became a technical term denoting the close relationship of a disciple to his master. Such a relationship had long before been established between Paul and Timothy, so that, when sending Timothy to Corinth some ten years earlier, Paul could entrust him to "remind you [the Corinthians] of my ways in Christ, as I teach them everywhere in every church" (1 Cor. 4:16–17). Now the reminder is to Timothy himself, who must carry on Paul's "ways" after his departure.

His "ways," in fact, is a list of virtues (comparable in some ways to 2 Cor. 6:4–6) that stands, in part at least, in sharp contrast to the vice list in verses 2–4. As usual the list has been tailored to the situation. It begins with the two urgent items in these letters, **teaching** and **conduct** (see disc. on 1 Tim. 1:10 and throughout), then moves to his **purpose in life** (i.e., Paul's resolve, his single-minded commitment to Christ). Next appear the cardinal Christian virtues (see disc. on Titus 2:2; cf. 1 Tim. 1:11), **faith** (toward God), **love** (toward all), and **endurance** (to the End), interrupted in this case with **patience** (forbearance toward others, as well as toward circumstances, in the midst of trying situations; cf. 4:2 and the attitudes called for in 2:24–25).

All of these virtues Timothy should have observed, and therefore learned as a disciple, in Paul's life. But the concern here is for Timothy to reflect them as well (v. 14: "continue in what you have learned"), especially in light of the twin realities of the false teachers and the inevitable suffering he is called upon to share. Thus the list moves from **teaching** and **conduct**, through the cardinal virtues of Christian behavior, to **endurance**. And why **endurance**? Because Paul's life in Christ—and Timothy's after him—involved him in many **persecutions . . . and sufferings**. This now becomes the heart of the present appeal and clearly recalls 1:8–2:3.

You know all that happened to me in Antioch (cf. Acts 13:50), **Iconium** (cf. Acts 14:2–6), **and Lystra** (Timothy's hometown; cf. Acts 14:19–20), **the terrible persecutions I endured!** Many have been perplexed by Paul's going so far back—even before Timothy's conversion—to make this point. Why not those instances where Timothy was present to observe—and experience—the persecution, such as at Philippi (Acts 16:19–34) or Ephesus (2 Cor. 1:1–11) or Rome [?] (Phil. 1:1, 12–18)? The answer to this lies in what we noted as early as the thanksgiving (1:3–5), namely, that part of the appeal to loyalty made in this letter is to remind Timothy of his origins. It is Paul's way of saying: "Look, you were there in Lystra when I was stoned. You recall that such sufferings were visible to you from the time you began your Christian walk. So don't bail out now in the midst of this present—and coming—distress."

Since in verse 12 Paul will apply this matter directly to Timothy, he reminds him of something else he knows about those early events in Asia Minor. In a near citation of Psalm 34:19, he encourages Timothy: **But the Lord**, as you well know, **rescued me from them all** (cf. 4:17–18)—which in this case, of course, does not mean **rescued** from the persecutions themselves but from the death that was so often at hand. "So take heart, pilgrim, because you, too," Paul assures him in the next sentence, "are due for your share of the sufferings."

3:12-13 / These two sentences, despite appearances, are companion sentences, applying what has just been said. The first word (v. 12) is another invitation for Timothy to join Paul in suffering, with the reminder that the sufferings to which he is being called are not unique to Paul and himself. "Indeed" (to translate with the RSV a *kai*, missing in the GNB), **everyone who wants to live a godly life** (*eusebōs* again; see disc. on 1 Tim. 2:2) **in union with Christ Jesus will be persecuted**. That is, those who want **to live in . . . Christ Jesus** (live a truly Christian life), and do so with true *eusebeia* ("godliness," as opposed to the *asebeia*, "ungodliness," of the false teachers), must expect as disciples to experience in some measure what Christ did. Jesus himself called for such discipleship (Mark 8:34; Matt. 5:11–12), as did Paul (1 Thess. 3:4; 2 Cor. 12:9–10; Rom. 8:17; Phil. 1:29).

227

It is otherwise with the false teachers. Not only do they *not* live godly lives, thus avoiding persecution, but they are **evil persons** (cf. the list in vv. 2–4) **and imposters** (better, "charlatans," as the NAB, a direct reference to vv. 6–9), who **will** only **keep on going** ("progressing" again; see disc. on 1 Tim. 4:15; 2 Tim. 2:16; 3:9) **from bad to worse.** Fine "progress" these charlatans will make, as they go only deeper into their sins and "sorceries"—**deceiving others and being deceived themselves** (cf. vv. 6–9; 1 Tim. 4:12)—and turn further away from **a** truly **godly life.** It may be, of course, that they are also mentioned here because they are the source of the persecution for many of the godly. In any case, the **godly**, who because of persecutions may look as if things are worse for them, are in fact in **Christ Jesus** and therefore destined for glory, while the false teachers, who may look as if "all is right with the world" for them, are in fact **going from bad to worse** and are destined for destruction.

3:14–15 / Through their interest in novelties and meaningless speculations and their foolish desires and greed, the straying elders, having been "deceived" themselves and now "deceiving" others, have abandoned the truth (2:18) and have made shipwreck of their own faith (1 Tim. 1:19). By way of contrast (**but as for you**), Timothy is urged to remain faithful to the apostolic gospel (**continue in the truths that you were taught**; lit., "in what you learned," both referring back to vv. 10–11 and anticipating what is about to be said). "What you learned," Paul hopefully affirms, is also that which you **firmly believe**.

There are two reasons for Timothy to stay by what he has learned: First, **you know who your teachers were**. This curious plural, changed to the singular in the majority of later manuscripts, may reflect the plural of 2:2 ("through many witnesses"). More likely it refers both to Paul (vv. 10–11) and to Timothy's mother and grandmother (1:5), who had taught him **the Holy Scriptures ever since** he was **a child**. Thus Paul reminds him that what he is to **continue in** has deep roots in his own past and that he can trust those, his family and his closest friend, whose legacy he is to carry on.

Second, **you have known the Holy Scriptures**. This is a first in these letters. (Elsewhere "the Word" refers to the message of the gospel; see disc. on 1 Tim. 4:5.) However, what is explicitly said here for the first time is implicit throughout. The false teachers have been using (abusing) Scripture to their own and others' detriment (cf. 1 Tim. 1:6–7). But **the Holy Scriptures** belong to us, because they point to **salvation through faith in Christ**.

It was a Jewish parent's sacred duty to instruct children in the Law from their fifth year. Thus Paul knew that Timothy, **ever since** he was **a child** (lit., "from infancy"), had **known the Holy Scriptures** (lit., "the Sacred Writings," apparently a favorite term in rabbinic Judaism, which would have been a part of Paul's own personal history). The term **are able to give you wisdom**, which probably reflects the usage of the LXX in Psalm 19:7 ("making wise the simple"), contrasts the "mindlessness" and "deceptions" of the false teachers (vv. 9, 13).

Thus Paul urges Timothy's loyalty, not only to himself and his own past, but also to the **Scriptures**, because they, too, lead to **salvation**. But **salvation** lies not in **the Scriptures** themselves, but only as they are properly understood to point to Christ. Always for Paul **salvation** is **through faith in Christ Jesus**.

3:16–17 / The reminder of Timothy's long knowledge of the Holy Scriptures causes Paul to conclude this appeal by reflecting on the divine origins of Scripture, hence their total usefulness for Timothy's ministry.

First, he affirms Scripture's divine origins: **All** (or "Every") **Scripture is inspired by God**. As the marginal reading suggests, this could be translated, "Every scripture inspired by God is also useful." If so, then it would probably be a further explanation of verse 15, meaning something like: "Scripture makes one wise unto salvation; indeed every God-inspired Scripture is also useful for instruction . . ." However, on the basis of a similar construction in 1 Timothy 4:4, and in light of the context, Paul probably intended to emphasize that the **Scripture** that gives "the wisdom that leads to salvation" is in its totality **inspired by God** (lit., "God-breathed," reflecting the creative activity of God), that is, of divine origin. (Cf. the "commandments of men" in Titus 1:14.) In so doing he is not offering a theory of inspiration; he is, rather, reflecting the common tradition of Judaism (cf. 2 Pet. 1:21).

Second, he affirms that all **Scripture is useful for** all the tasks of his ministry—and this is why the emphasis on its divine origins. The tasks outlined are a clear reflection of the historical context of the letter.

For **teaching** (the words **the truth** are not in the text, but are implied from the full context of the letter): This is Timothy's primary responsibility—to use the Scriptures to give sound instruction in the gospel to God's people (cf. 1 Tim. 4:6, 13, 16; 6:3).

For **rebuking** (see 4:2; again, **error** is not in the Gk. but is implied by the context). This is the other side of the task; he must use Scripture to expose the errors of the false teachers and their teachings.

For **correcting** (again, **faults** is a contextual addition): This word occurs only here in the NT. It is a companion of **rebuking error**, but emphasizes the behavioral, ethical side of things.

And giving instruction (*paideia*; cf. 2:25; Titus 2:12) **for right living**: This corresponds to **correcting faults**, as its positive side.

Thus **all Scripture, inspired** as it is **by God, is useful for** Timothy's twofold task of **teaching the truth** of the gospel with its right behavior and of resisting the errors and immoral behavior of the false teaching.

But Paul is not quite finished. He adds a purpose, or perhaps here a result, clause to verse 16, whose intent is not altogether clear. Such a clause should point to those receiving the instruction; thus the GNB: **so that the person who serves God** (lit., "the mån of God"; cf. 1 Tim. 6:11) **may be fully qualified and equipped to do every kind of good deed** (cf. 2:21; Titus 1:16; 3:1). However, the context, plus the use of the title "man of God" in the singular, almost demand that Paul is, rather, concerned with Timothy, as the one responsible for giving the instruction. The clause in a certain sense doesn't follow; yet Paul's concern is clear enough. By continually nurturing his own life in the Scriptures that he is to use in his ministry, Timothy will be **fully qualified** ("able to meet all demands," BAGD) **and equipped** "for every good work," which here means not only Christian behavior but the ministry of the gospel as well, and especially points forward to 4:1–5.

With these words the appeal that began in 1:6 is brought to a conclusion. Paul urges loyalty—to his (Timothy's) own calling, to himself (Paul), to Christ and his gospel, and to his ministry, including the teaching of Scripture—and to continue in loyalty despite suffering and in the face of opposition. But these words also prepare the way for what follows—a final charge that brings all these things together before he reveals to him the real reason for the letter (4:6–16).

Additional Notes

3:10–11 / Those who see these letters as inauthentic are particularly impressed that the mention of **Antioch, Iconium, and Lystra** supports their view. The real Paul would have mentioned more recent persecutions, and our author's knowledge was limited to what he could glean from Acts (see Hanson). J. D. Quinn, who believes Luke wrote these letters, also sees this as supporting evidence (see "The Last Volume of Luke: The Relation of Luke-Acts to the Pastoral Epistles," p. 66). The explanation offered in the commentary, however, is fully in keeping with the full context of the letter, if seen as coming ultimately from Paul.

3:14–15 / There is a considerable literature on the training of Jewish children during this period, of which the main component was the study of the Law (see, e.g., Jos., *Against Apion* 1.60; 2.173–78). In the Mishnah tractate *Pirke Aboth* 5:21, a rabbi from the end of the first century A.D. said, "At five years old [one is fit] for the Scripture" (Danby, p. 458). For primary sources that give much of this evidence, see Str-B, vol. 3, pp. 664–66. For a helpful survey of these data and further bibliography, see S. Safrai, "Education and the Study of the Torah."

Scholars have debated the meaning of the phrase **the Holy Scriptures** in v. 15. There is textual variation as to whether or not the article should be included (probably in this case it is not original; its addition is far easier to explain than its omission). But even without the article, the term *hiera grammata* (lit., "sacred writings") undoubtedly refers to **the Holy Scriptures** (cf. Jos. *Antiquities* 10.210; Philo, *Moses* 2.292). Philo uses similar expressions without the article and means *the* Scriptures (see *On the Posterity and Exile of Cain* 158; *Who Is the Heir* 106). The context of this passage almost demands such a meaning here, and not "religious teachings" or "sacred *writings*" (as opposed to oral traditions), possibilities suggested by Lock. Hendriksen's suggestion that vv. 15 and 16 mean different things, the one (v. 16) comprising "more than the former," is purely gratuitous.

3:16-17 / The literature and debate on v. 16 is rather extensive. The problems are three: First, does *pasa graphē* mean **all Scripture** (i.e., Scripture as a whole collectively understood) or "every Scripture" (i.e., distributively understood to mean each individual passage). This one is almost impossible to decide on grammatical grounds, and in either case the meaning comes out at the same place.

Second is the problem already discussed, where to place the understood **is**, thus making inspired by God predicative (GNB text) or attributive (GNB margin). For a more complete discussion, see the commentaries by Hanson, Kelly, and Hendriksen (for the text) and by Bernard, Spicq, and Barrett (for the margin).

Third is the problem of the meaning of *theopneustos* ("God-breathed"). For this discussion, see B. B. Warfield, *The Inspiration and Authority of the Bible* (Philadelphia: Presbyterian and Reformed, 1948), pp. 245–96.

For a brief overview of the understanding of inspiration in contemporary Judaism see Warfield, pp. 229–30, and the entry on *theopneustos* by E. Schweizer in *TDNT*, vol. 6, pp. 454.

12

Final Charge to Timothy

In the presence of God and of Christ Jesus, who will judge the living and the dead, and because he is coming to rule as King, I solemnly urge you ²to preach the message, to insist upon proclaiming it (whether the time is right or not), to convince, reproach, and encourage, as you teach with all patience. ³The time will come when people will not listen to sound doctrine, but will follow their own desires and will collect for themselves more and more teachers who will tell them what they are itching to hear. ⁴They will turn away from listening to the truth and give their attention to legends. ⁵But you must keep control of yourself in all circumstances; endure suffering, do the work of a preacher of the Good News, and perform your whole duty as a servant of God.

Paul now brings to a conclusion the long appeal that makes up the larger part of this letter. This appeal began in 1:6 and was picked up again in 3:10 after the interlude on the false teachers in 2:14–3:9; but it now takes the form of a solemn charge (v. 1), followed by nine imperatives (five in v. 2 and four in v. 5).

The first set of imperatives (v. 2) repeats the concerns about Timothy's own ministry and flows directly out of the preceding appeal. This is followed (vv. 3–4) by one more statement of the reason for it, the errors of the false teachers—although in this case it is the people themselves who are in view. The final set of imperatives (v. 5), which stands in contrast to verses 3–4, is more personal, although Timothy's ministry is still clearly in view.

Since this charge is grammatically tied to verses 6–8 ("Fulfill your ministry, *for* I am already about to be poured out as a drink offering"), those verses will give us the clue to much of this section. Paul knows he is about to die. This charge, therefore, though made against the backdrop of the situation in Ephesus, looks far beyond that. Here we have a kind of changing of the guard, the word of a dying man to his heir apparent. To use the athletic metaphor of verses 7–8, it is the passing of the baton. The whole paragraph needs to be read with this reality in view.

4:1 / The opening words of this sentence (**I solemnly urge**, or "charge"; cf. 1 Tim. 5:21; 2 Tim. 2:14) turn the preceding appeal into a final solemn charge for Timothy to stay by his ministry under any and all circumstances. The language of the charge, which has clear affinities to those in 1 Timothy 5:21 and 6:13, is given a very highly charged eschatological setting. The basis of the oath is fourfold: **God**, **Christ**, the Second Coming, and the Eternal **King**dom. That is, as one whose life is lived out **in the** very **presence of God and of Christ Jesus** (see disc. on 1 Tim. 5:21) and is accountable to them, and in light of the certainty of Christian eschatological realities, Timothy is **solemnly** charged to fulfill the responsibilities of his God-given ministry, especially that of proclaimer of the gospel. (Note the similar eschatological perspective in vv. 6–8, esp. v. 8.)

The eschatological thrust of the charge is begun by the qualifier added to **Christ Jesus**, namely, **who will judge the living and the dead**. This terminology, which was unique to Christians (cf. Acts 10:42; 1 Pet. 4:5), very soon became a semicreedal formula (*Barnabas* 7:2; Polycarp, *Philippians* 2:1; *2 Clement* 1:1; cf. the Apostle's Creed). It was based on the conviction that he who appeared once to save will appear a second time to complete that salvation and for judgment (cf. also Acts 17:31 and 2 Cor. 5:10). Thus he **will judge** both those who are alive at his **coming** and those whose death has preceded it and who will be raised for judgment.

Having mentioned the future judgment, Paul elaborates by adding (literally) "and his appearing [cf. 1 Tim. 6:14; Titus 2:13] and his Kingdom" (GNB: **and because he is coming to rule as King**). Although the Greek is rough here (Paul has mixed two constructions, a prepositional phrase and two objective modifiers, following the verb "to solemnly charge"), his intent is clear enough. In light of the reality of Christ's **coming** (cf. 4:8), followed by his eternal Kingdom (cf. 4:18)—eschatological realities related to Christ's being **the judge of the living and the dead**—Timothy should pay special heed to this final charge. After all, all of them, he himself, the false teachers, and the people, will have to give a final account at Christ's **coming**.

4:2 / The charge itself is a series of five imperatives. The first, **preach the message** (for this as the proper understanding of *logos*, "word," see disc. on 1 Tim. 4:5), is the rubric for the others. Above all else, Timothy must proclaim **the message** of the gospel, which here has the same effect as the charge to "guard the deposit" in 1 Timothy 6:20 and 2 Timothy 1:14. This is what the whole appeal from 1:6 to 3:17 is all about.

Furthermore, he is **to insist upon proclaiming it** (**whether the time is right or not**). This is the GNB's rendition of the KJV's famous, "Be instant in season, out of season." Unfortunately, what Paul intends is not all that clear. The verb is probably best translated "stand by it" (D-C) or "keep at it" (Kelly), that is, your proclaiming of **the message**. The double adverbs (*eukairōs, akairōs*) are either subjective (having to do with Timothy) or objective (having to do with his hearers). If the former, which was how Chrysostom understood it, then it means that he should stay with the task whether it is convenient or not. If the latter, then it means what the GNB intends, that he should stand by it "whether or not the preaching comes at a convenient time for the hearers." In the context, especially in light of what follows, the latter is probably intended, although it just may have to do with Timothy's reticence (cf. 1:6–7).

The final three imperatives, **convince**, **reproach**, **encourage**, are related to the various aspects of his task as proclaimer of the Word. He is to **convince** (better, "rebuke," as in 3:16; Titus 1:13; 2:15) those in error; **reproach** (perhaps, "warn") those who do not heed the rebuke; and finally "exhort" (or "urge," not **encourage**; see disc. on 1 Tim. 2:1; 5:1; 6:2) them all.

He is to do these final three tasks **with all patience, as** he **teaches** (lit., "**with all patience** and teaching"). **Patience** is required because of what will be said next—not all will give heed to him. Nonetheless he must always patiently hold forth the truth (i.e., **teach**).

4:3–4 / This sentence begins with an explanatory *gar* ("because" or "for") and gives the reasons for the nature of the charge in verse 2: "Proclaim the message; stay by it no matter what comes; in so doing, rebuke, warn, and exhort, with all patience, for the time will come . . . "

As with 3:1–5 and 1 Timothy 4:1–2, the present reality is seen as a future event as well. This is again related to the concept of the increase of evil with the approach of the End, which, as evidenced by the situation in Ephesus, has already begun. But in this case it probably also represents the passing-of-the-baton nature of this final charge. Timothy is to carry on Paul's ministry in a world in which there is no promise of eager response—even on the part of God's people.

The description is a familiar one; however, in this case it focuses on the believers themselves, rather than the false teachers, and it clearly lays some of the blame at their feet—despite the emphasis heretofore on their being deceived (cf. 1 Tim. 4:1–2; 5:15; 6:5; 2 Tim. 3:6–7, 13). The description is given in two pairs of contrasts.

First, they **will not listen to sound doctrine** (see disc. on 1 Tim. 1:10; cf. 6:3); rather, they **will follow their own desires** (cf. 3:6; 1 Tim. 6:9) **and will collect for themselves more and more teachers** (which of course is what 1 Timothy and much of 2 Timothy is all about), **who will tell them what they are itching to hear**. This latter, very pejorative, expression is a metaphor for "curiosity, that looks for interesting and spicy bits of information" (BAGD) and therefore fits the speculative, dilettantish nature of the false teachings (see disc. on 1 Tim. 1:4; 2 Tim. 3:6–7).

This is further elaborated, secondly, in what are by now familiar terms. On the one hand, **they will turn away from listening to the truth**, that is, the gospel (see 1 Tim. 6:5; Titus 1:14; 2 Tim. 2:18; 3:7–8); on the other hand, they will **give their attention to legends** (see 1 Tim. 1:4; 4:7; Titus 1:14). This is the final word in these letters about the false teachings, and it is very much like the first word (1 Tim. 1:3–7). The errorists and their followers have simply abandoned truth for a lie. And there is no promise to Timothy that things will get better after Paul's death.

4:5 / As throughout the letters, the mention of those going astray calls for a contrasting word to Timothy. With a **but you** (*su de*, "but as for you"; cf. 2:1; 3:10, 14; 1 Tim. 6:11) Paul resumes the final charge with four more imperatives.

Keep control of yourself in all circumstances. This verb literally means to "stay sober." As a metaphor it calls for Timothy to "keep his head" (Kelly). The people will go after anything because they have "itching ears." **But you must** keep on the alert so as not to be taken in.

Endure suffering brings Timothy back to a common theme in this letter (1:8; 2:2; 3:12) and prepares him for Paul's final testimony that follows. As before, it appears in the context of proclaiming the gospel.

Do the work of a preacher of the Good News. This noun, **preacher of the Good News**, is found elsewhere in the NT in Ephesians 4:11 and Acts 21:8. Here it simply recalls the imperative with which this charge began (v. 2, "preach the message").

Perform your whole duty as a servant of God. With this fitting imperative, which embraces all the preceding and beyond—Paul brings the charge to a close. Paul, as we will see, is about to leave the scene, and the mantle of his ministry is about to fall on Timothy. Therefore, this imperative takes on special urgency, as he moves to give his last will and testament (vv. 6–8). As Hendriksen nicely puts it: This set of imperatives, in serving as an introduction to verses 6–8, "draws a contrast between Timothy, still in the thick of the fight, and Paul who *has fought* the grand fight" (p. 312).

Additional Notes

4:1 / The majority of manuscripts, the earliest, however, coming from the ninth century, have specifically spelled out the intended tie of this paragraph with what has preceded by adding a "therefore."

2 / There is contemporary evidence for the verb translated **insist upon it** to be a military metaphor. Thus the NEB margin translates, "Be on duty at all times." While that is a distinct possibility, there is no need from the context itself to see the verb as a metaphor here.

13

Paul's Final Testimony

2 TIMOTHY 4:6-8

As for me, the hour has come for me to be sacrificed; the time is here for me to leave this life. ⁷I have done my best in the race. I have run the full distance, and I have kept the faith.ᶜ ⁸And now there is waiting for me the prize of victory awarded for a righteous life, the prize which the Lord, the righteous Judge, will give me on that Day—and not only to me, but to all those who wait with love for him to appear.

c. kept the faith; *or* been true to my promise.

U p to this point everything that has been said in 2 Timothy, apart from the themes of Paul's imprisonment and Timothy's taking his share in suffering, fits the concerns of 1 Timothy—and in some ways looks very much like more of the same. But this paragraph, plus what follows in verses 9–18, throws everything into a different light.

Here we learn for the first time that Paul expects his present imprisonment to result in death (v. 6); he is aware that his own ministry is now over (v. 7) and that the eschatological prize awaits him (v. 8). But as the situation in Ephesus has clearly indicated, it is a bad time for him to be leaving. The time has come when the pure gospel of Christ is being contaminated from within by foreign elements, and the people are "itchy" for more (4:3). Hence the reason for the letter, with its urgent appeals for loyalty. Paul is leaving, and Timothy is urged to carry on, faithful to the gospel that Paul—and he—have preached.

This final testimony, then, with its announcement of his impending death, serves first of all as the primary reason for the foregoing charge (vv. 1–5). At the same time, as before, it serves as one more model for Timothy to follow. (See 1:11–12; 2:9–10; 3:10–11.)

4:6 / The paragraph is closely tied to the preceding charge (esp. v. 5) with an emphatic *egō* (**as for me**) and an explanatory *gar* ("for"). "But as for you" (v. 5), Paul charges, "keep your head, . . . perform your whole duty as a servant of God; because **as for me**, I am about to depart."

The two metaphors in this verse make clear that Paul does not expect to survive this imprisonment. The first metaphor, used previously in Philippians 2:17 to refer to the possibility of his being **sacrificed** in death, is taken from the OT libations, or drink-offerings (Num. 13:5, 7, 10). Such an offering, composed of wine (probably as a replacement for the blood libations of pagans, Ps. 16:4), was poured out before the Lord in the sanctuary (Num. 28:7). Thus Paul says, "I am already being offered as a libation"; my life is being poured out before the Lord (which seems to capture the sense a little better than **the hour has come for me to be sacrificed**). The emphasis is on the "already," but it does not necessarily imply an immediate death (vv. 13 and 21 at least allow for the possibility of another winter). The metaphor implies that the whole present ordeal, culminating in death, is a libation unto the Lord.

The second metaphor, **the time is here for me to leave this life** (lit., "the time for my departure is near," cf. Phil. 1:23, where the verb form is used), images the breaking up of camp or the loosing of a ship from its moorings. It was a common euphemism for death (cf. Philo, *Flaccus* 187; Diogenes Laertius 5.71).

4:7 / With yet another change of metaphors, to the athletic metaphor common to him (2:5; cf. 1 Tim. 6:12; 1 Cor. 9:24–27; Phil. 3:12–14), Paul offers this well-known reflection on his own ministry (not his life in general, as it is so often interpreted). In three striking sentences he affirms both the finality of things and his fidelity to his calling.

I have done my best in the race (lit., "I have contested the noble contest"). This translation probably correctly sees the metaphor as a race (so Pfitzner), not wrestling or boxing (as Kelly). But it has otherwise missed the point. The word *kalon* ("good," "noble") does not imply that Paul's running was good (**my best**) but that he, as he strongly urges Timothy as well (1 Tim. 6:12), has been running in the noblest, grandest run of them all—the ministry of the gospel. This, after all, is what Paul's life is all about.

I have run the full distance (lit., "I have completed the course" or "race"; cf. Acts 20:24). The emphasis here is clearly on the fact that for Paul the race is now over, not just his life, but his ministry. But what he has finished is the *course*, the race laid out by his divine master, *not* **the full distance**. The GNB has again misplaced the emphasis, which is on the contest itself.

I have kept the faith. This may mean either that Paul, in the fulfillment of his ministry, has preserved the faith intact ("sound doctrine," 1 Tim. 1:10, or "the deposit entrusted to him," 2 Tim. 1:14) or more likely, that he has been "loyal to his trust" (Kelly; cf. GNB margin). Both the context and the fact that this is a fixed formula in antiquity for keeping one's trust seem to support this understanding. It is an especially meaningful word in light of verses 16–18, where his remaining loyal even in trial meant that all the Gentiles heard the message.

4:8 / Paul now returns to the athletic metaphor, but does so by picking up the eschatological motif from verse 1 (cf. 1 Tim. 6:12). Just as races have finishes, so victors receive **the prize of victory** (*stephanos*, the laurel wreath given to the winner; cf. 2:5; 1 Cor. 9:25). Such a **prize . . . is waiting for** Paul (safely reserved in heaven). In this case the wreath is described as "the garland of righteousness." Does this mean **the prize awarded for a righteous life** (so Bernard, Barrett, Kelly), which some argue is uncharacteristic of Paul (D-C, Hanson)? Or does it mean "one which consists of the gift of righteousness, which only the Judge, as He who alone is *dikaios* [righteous], can give" (Pfitzner, p. 184)?

The former is not as unlike Paul as is sometimes perceived. After all, it is a genitive phrase, not a clearly spelled out clause (as in the GNB), and means nothing more than the crown that the righteous will receive, but not necessarily as an award for *their* achievement. That would be to press the metaphor from verse 7 beyond recognizable Pauline bounds. Nonetheless, other uses of this kind of phrase in the NT (James 1:12; 1 Pet. 5:4) favor the second interpretation. This, too, has been objected to as un-Pauline (righteousness is received in this life); but the objection misses the already/not-yet in Paul's eschatology. One receives the final crown of righteousness precisely because one has already received righteousness in Christ.

Such a crown will be awarded by **the Lord, the righteous Judge** (cf. v. 1) **on that Day**, meaning at his coming (cf. 1:12, 18)—**and not only to me**. With this final phrase Paul redirects his concern back to Timothy. Just as he was charged in verse 1 to fulfill his ministry in light of the great Christian eschatological realities, so now he is encouraged that **the prize**, too, shall be his and **to all who wait with love for him to appear** (on this word, *epiphaneia*, see disc. on v. 1). Whether intended or not, this clause sets up a sharp contrast with Demas in verse 10, who loved this present age, rather than Christ's coming.

With this word, the main concern of the letter comes to an end. But the letter is not finished, and all that has been said thus far will need to be rethought on the basis of what is said next.

Additional Note

The very personal nature of this testimony, as well as its close affinities to Philippians, have long been arguments for authenticity. Indeed, many who cannot go that far concede that here is a genuine Pauline fragment.

But others have seen the ties to Philippians as the latter's being the "source" for the pseudepigraphic author. As is often the case, such arguments tend to be stalemated, and considerable subjectivity tends to weight the final decision. Recently, D. Cook ("2 Timothy iv. 6–8 and the Epistle to the Philippians") has argued for non-Pauline authorship on the basis of language and style. But all he has shown conclusively is that these verses are of a piece with the rest of the letter, not who actually wrote the letter itself.

4:7 / For the phrase "keep the faith" as referring to loyalty to one's trust, see such diverse authors as Polybius (6.56.13; 10.37.9) and Jos. (*Wars* 6.345). For other texts, see D-C.

See V. C. Pfitzner, *Paul and the Agon Motif*, for a thorough discussion of the athletic metaphor in Paul.

14

Personal Words and Instructions

Do your best to come to me soon. ¹⁰Demas fell in love with this present world and has deserted me, going off to Thessalonica. Crescens went to Galatia, and Titus to Dalmatia. ¹¹Only Luke is with me. Get Mark and bring him with you, because he can help me in the work. ¹²I sent Tychicus to Ephesus. ¹³When you come, bring my coat that I left in Troas with Carpus; bring the books too, and especially the ones made of parchment.

¹⁴Alexander the metalworker did me great harm; the Lord will reward him according to what he has done.

¹⁵Be on your guard against him yourself, because he was violently opposed to our message.

¹⁶No one stood by me the first time I defended myself; all deserted me. May God not count it against them! ¹⁷But the Lord stayed with me and gave me strength, so that I was able to proclaim the full message for all the Gentiles to hear; and I was rescued from being sentenced to death. ¹⁸And the Lord will rescue me from all evil and take me safely into his heavenly Kingdom. To him be the glory forever and ever! Amen.

T his section exhibits all the earmarks of a piece of private correspondence from antiquity. The author urges its recipient to come posthaste (v. 9); indicates *why* he wants him to come (he is alone, vv. 10–11a), *who* and *what* to bring (vv. 11b–13), and *whom* to watch out for along the way (vv. 14–15); and concludes with information as to how things have been going with him (vv. 16–18). On its own all of this is so ordinary as to elicit no surprise from anyone. It would be one more among thousands of letters of its kind from the Hellenistic world.

The element of surprise, of course, comes from the fact that it is not on its own. Rather, it has been preceded by a long appeal for Timothy's loyalty, which concludes with a solemn charge to keep at his task of ministry and a kind of last will and testament from Paul. But these final words give new perspective to what has preceded. The concern in the appeal was not primarily for the situation in Ephesus (as was 1 Timothy); hence only one *tauta* ("these things") imperative (2:14); hence also the reason for 2:2 ("entrust these things to others"), which is *not* suggested in 1 Timothy.

Rather, the appeal was primarily for Timothy himself to be ready to take up the reins after Paul's death, in light of *(a)* the spread of heretical/divisive teaching, *(b)* Paul's imprisonment and impending death, and *(c)* Timothy's own ministry, despite his timidity.

Now Paul returns to the second reason for the letter, first hinted at in the thanksgiving (v. 4, "I want to see you very much"). Paul is lonely in his imprisonment, and this letter is a summons to join him. Tychicus (v. 12), who carried the letter, is thereby dispatched to Ephesus, where he will probably assume Timothy's duties; and Timothy is to come as quickly as possible. The whole section breathes personal, private concerns (a first person pronoun appears in every verse). A pseudepigrapher who created this, especially in light of the other concerns of these letters, would have been an extraordinary genius.

4:9 / Immediately following the announcement of his impending death (vv. 6–8), Paul urgently requests: **Do your best** (cf. 2:14; 4:21; Titus 3:12) **to come to me soon**. Given travel conditions and the length of time involved, these (i.e., impending death and the request for Timothy to come) may seem contradictory. However, as we will note on verses 16–17, Paul has had previous experience with the Roman judicial system, and though he apparently doesn't expect to be freed, he is well aware of the delays in the system.

This request controls all that is said in the following verses. The urgency is found in the word **soon** (*tacheōs*; "quickly," "without delay") and "before winter" in verse 21, as well as in the information about his first defense in verses 16–18. Thus it has considerably different force from the similar request to Titus (3:12).

4:10–11a / Paul proceeds to give the *reason* for the request (another explanatory *gar*, "for" or "because," has been left untranslated by the GNB). All of his co-workers, except **Luke**, have left him, one dishonorably and others for various reasons.

Demas is mentioned first, perhaps because his departure was the most painful. Little is known of him—although he is well covered in the apocryphal literature—except that he was a co-worker during Paul's earlier imprisonment (Col. 4:12; Philem. 24) along with four others, including **Mark** and **Luke**.

But now he **has deserted** (the LXX word from Ps. 22:1 that Jesus cried from the cross) **me**, because he **fell in love with this present world**. This last phrase is eschatological language (cf. 1 Tim. 4:8; Titus 2:12;

Gal. 1:4; Eph. 1:21), contrasting the present with the coming age, and in this case offers a sharp contrast to Paul, Timothy, and others who "love Christ's appearing" (v. 8). Why he should go **off to Thessalonica** is unknown. It has no reputation as one of the "hot spots" of the Greco-Roman world; perhaps it was his hometown.

Mentioning Demas' **going off to Thessalonica** reminds Paul of two others who have also left: **Crescens** (of whom nothing more is known for certain) **went to Galatia** (some early MSS read *Gallia*, "Gaul," modern France; but this seems to be a corruption), **and Titus to Dalmatia**. Probably both of these had gone out on ministries. **Galatia**, in central Asia Minor, had long been the scene of a Pauline mission. **Dalmatia**, the coast of ancient Illyricum (Yugoslavia; cf. Rom. 15:19), is up the Adriatic from Nicopolis (see Titus 3:12). Perhaps Titus had gone from there, although the context implies otherwise.

That means, since Erastus stayed in Corinth, Trophimus had been left in Miletus (v. 20), and Tychicus was dispatched to Ephesus (v. 12), that of his co-workers **only Luke** (cf. Col. 4:14; Philem. 24) **is with me**. On Luke's possible role in the composition of these letters, see the Introduction, p. xxxvii.

Some have argued that the information in these verses stands in contradiction to verse 21. But not so. All of the former are Paul's co-workers, without whom he seldom ministered (cf. Acts 17:14–18:4; 1 Thess. 3:1–5, for possible exceptions). The people in verse 21 are almost certainly Roman Christians known to Timothy.

4:11b-12 / Next Paul tells Timothy whom (v. 11b) and what (v. 13) to bring along when he comes. At an earlier stage Mark had bailed out during some rough going (Acts 13:13) and had become a point of contention between Paul and Barnabas (Acts 15:36–41). But Paul's largeness of character can be seen in the fact that at a later stage Mark had once more become a co-worker (Col. 4:10; Philem. 24). Now he urges Timothy to **get Mark** (implying that he is not in Ephesus) **and bring him with you**. And the reason? **Because he can help me in the work** (lit., "he is useful to me for service"). The phrase "for service" (*diakonian*), although a favorite of Paul's for the ministry of the gospel (cf. 4:5; 1 Tim. 1:12; 2 Cor. 4:1), is ambiguous here and may refer to personal service (cf. 1 Cor. 16:15). Perhaps a little of both is intended, but the context suggests that at least ministry to his personal needs is involved (cf. 1:16–18 on Onesiphorus).

The reason for wanting **Mark** to **help me in the work** is that his former helper, **Tychicus**, had been **sent to Ephesus**—at least such is implied by the Greek *de* ("but") that joins verse 12 to verse 11 (and therefore does not go back to v. 10 as a memory lapse). **Tychicus** (cf. Titus 3:12; Col. 4:7; Eph. 6:21–22) is almost certainly the carrier of this letter (thus, **I sent** is an "epistolary aorist," meaning "I am sending," from the perspective of the writer, or "I have sent," from that of the recipient; cf. Eph. 6:22). One may assume he also was to take over Timothy's responsibilities.

4:13 / This little request for **my coat** and **the books**, which puts considerable strain on theories of pseudepigraphy, is at once full of interest and historical uncertainties. The most likely reconstruction (understanding, of course, the hypothetical nature of much that is said) is that on his way back to Ephesus, Paul had been arrested, either in Miletus (v. 20, en route from Nicopolis through Corinth?) or **Troas** itself. There, at the house of **Carpus** (presumably a believer in that city), he had left his **coat**, the heavy woolen garment used by travelers in cold or rainy weather. Now he wants Timothy to **bring** it (apparently in anticipation of winter; v. 21) and **the books**. Paul obviously expects Timothy to take the same route (Ephesus to Troas, overland across Macedonia on the Egnatian Way, by ship to Brundisium, and on to Rome).

There has been a great deal of speculation about what Paul meant by **the books, especially the ones made of parchment**. The term *biblia* (**books**) could refer to any kind of literary work, including sacred **books** (in this case the OT) or even documents of various kinds. The qualifier, **especially the ones made of parchment**, either means what is suggested by this translation (i.e., the specific narrowing down of a general group, as elsewhere in the PE; e.g., 1 Tim. 4:10) or, as T. C. Skeat has argued, it is an equating-defining term ("the books—I mean by that the parchment notebooks"). This latter is probably what is intended. What we cannot know is what they contained (although sentiment will favor OT writings of some kind) or why he made such a request.

4:14–15 / These two verses have long been puzzling—as to what they are doing here. But given that one can make good *contextual* sense of almost everything in these letters, and that the concern here is with verse 15 and Timothy himself being **on** his **guard against him**, the best contextual guess is that the **great harm** done by **Alexander the metalworker** against Paul was to have him arrested. This is further supported by the fact that the verb *endeiknymi* (lit., "show," "point out," weakly translated **did**) was often used with the legal sense of "inform against," and by the note in verse 15 that **he was violently opposed to** (same verb as in 3:8) **our message**.

If so, then who was this **Alexander the metalworker**? He was either the Alexander who, with Hymenaeus, had been excommunicated by Paul (1 Tim. 1:19–20), or the Jew of that name who tried to quell the riot in Ephesus (Acts 19:33–34)—some argue that these refer to the same person—or some other Alexander, otherwise unknown to us, whom Paul makes sure Timothy recognizes by designating him **the metalworker**. Although it is somewhat speculative, a good case can be made for the first one. After being excommunicated, he had left Ephesus (hence Hymenaeus is joined by Philetus in 2 Tim. 2:17). The mention of having had to leave his coat and books in Troas reminds Paul of the cause of his arrest, **Alexander the metalworker**, whom he now cautions Timothy also to be on his **guard against** when he goes through there. In any case, Paul has full confidence in God's justice and therefore expects **Alexander** to come under eschatological judgment: **The Lord will reward him** (the same verb as in v. 8) **according to what he has done** (words reminiscent of Pss. 28:4 and 62:12).

4:16 / Paul now turns from the request for Timothy to come to a brief explanation about his own situation, which has inherent in it the urgency noted in the request. It begins with the prepositional phrase "at my first defense" (**the first time I defended myself**), which has been the subject of some debate. However, it simply makes little or no sense for this to refer to an earlier imprisonment (e.g., Acts 28; cf. Colossians, Philemon, Philippians), as most of the early Fathers and earlier exegetes supposed (why inform Timothy of that which he would have known?). Most likely **the first time** refers to the present captivity and the Roman juridical practice of a *prima actio*, a preliminary hearing before the emperor or a magistrate, roughly comparable in purpose to a grand jury hearing. This would then be followed by the actual trial. Given the two-year delay after the preliminary hearing during his first imprisonment (Acts 24:1, 23, 27; cf. 28:16, 30), Paul had good reason to expect the same again; hence this letter and the summons for Timothy to join him.

However, on this occasion, circumstances seem to be far more serious. Paul is being kept in chains (1:16; 2:9), and despite being "rescued from the lion's mouth" (v. 17) at his preliminary hearing, he expects the final outcome to be death (vv. 6–8). Perhaps because of the seriousness of things, therefore, **no one stood by** him (implying that no one joined him or identified with him; perhaps he meant that he had had no official advocate); indeed **all deserted** him. It is simply idle speculation to ask either *what* Paul might have been expecting or *where* such friends as Tychicus or Luke were. From Paul's own perspective he had been **deserted by all**; yet like his Lord from the cross (Luke 23:34), on that matter he shows forgiveness—"**May God not count it against** them!"

4:17 / As always in Paul, however, the final word is God's. **But** (an adversative *de*, in contrast to **all** who **deserted**) **the Lord stayed with me**. As usual in Paul and these letters, **the Lord** refers to Christ. This is not necessarily the language of religious mysticism; rather, it is the language of one who has personally encountered the Living Christ, who is "in Him," and who has had his own life invaded by the power of the Holy Spirit. For Paul it would have been as natural as breathing for him to experience the presence of **the Lord** at such a time.

The Lord did two things when he stood by Paul. The first, significantly, had to do with Paul's gospel. He **gave me strength** (cf. 2:1; 1 Tim. 1:12), **so that I was able to proclaim the full message for all the Gentiles to hear**. As with the similar preliminary hearing recorded in Acts 24:1–20 (cf. 26:1–32), Paul took full advantage of the inquiry to give the "real" reason for his arrest. The first part of the Greek text literally says, "so that through me the preaching might be fulfilled." The emphasis is still on the Lord's enabling: He **gave me strength so that** *through me* (in the emphatic position) he might fulfill his own plans. "The preaching might be fulfilled" refers to the apostolic preaching of the gospel reaching the heart of the empire, and it is in that sense, Rome as "the mistress of the nations" (to use Bernard's phrase), that **all the Gentiles** were thereby able **to hear** the gospel.

Secondly, the Lord "rescued me [lit., **I was rescued**] from the mouth of the lion." This metaphor has long been the subject of debate. Satan, Nero, the empire itself, and death have all been suggested for "the lion." Most likely the clue lies in the observation of the echoes of Psalm 22 throughout the passage (vv. 9–18). Just as Paul had been **deserted** (vv. 10, 16; cf. Ps. 22:1), so he had been **rescued**—and *will be* rescued (v. 18; cf. Ps. 22:4–5)—from the mouth of the lion (cf. Ps. 22:19). If this is the proper clue, then he would be using the language of the psalm to refer to his being **rescued from** . . . **death** (but not necessarily **the sentence of death**, as the GNB).

4:18 / In typical fashion the recent rescue from immediate peril is reflected on theologically. **The Lord** who rescued me **will** always **rescue me**, not from death necessarily, but **from all evil** (cf. the final petition of the Lord's Prayer), **and will take me safely into** (better, "save me for," or "unto") **his heavenly Kingdom**. The phrase **from all evil** (lit., "every evil deed," the opposite of "every good deed," 2:21; 3:17) can scarcely mean "from the effects of every evil machination," as the eschatological conclusion of the sentence makes clear, but "from any real power of evil to destroy me." The reason is simple; **the Lord will** save **me** for **his** own **heavenly Kingdom**. Once again the focus of the letter is on eschatology, in the form of one of Paul's triumphant certainties: What God has already accomplished in Christ, he will see through to final consummation; the salvation he has begun he will indeed complete.

Such a note of eschatological triumph, not to mention past victories, calls for a doxology (cf. 1 Tim. 1:17; 6:15–16): **To him be the glory forever and ever! Amen**. Both the location and the language of this doxology are reminiscent of Philippians 4:20. What a fitting note on which to conclude, given the continuing urgencies of his and Timothy's present situation!

Additional Notes

Although is it certainly not impossible (see D-C or Hanson), the unlikelihood that a pseudepigrapher would have *created* this information, either from "whole cloth" or from sources, has caused many to opt for a theory of genuine Pauline fragments being worked into a pseudepigraphic work. For the classic presentation of this view, see P. N. Harrison, *The Problem of the Pastoral Epistles*, and *Paulines and Pastorals*, in which he reworks some things in light of subsequent criticisms. Barrett seems to favor this view.

4:9 / Many also have seen an inherent tension between vv. 9–18 and the rest of the letter. But that is due to the mistaken notions that Paul has told Timothy to stay on at Ephesus to resist the false teachers (e.g., Scott), which he has not (not in *this* letter at least) or that 2 Timothy like 1 Timothy is also a "church manual," or at least a "pastor's manual," which neither is.

4:10-11a / The notation about **Demas** is the kind of material the apocryphal Acts thrive on. See, e.g., the *Acts of Paul and Thecla* 1, 4, 12–14, 16. Some identify him with Demetrius of 3 John (Demas is short for Demetrius), but that is highly unlikely. Others argue that his action was not apostasy; but that seems to be in the interest of saving a prior theological commitment. Polycarp (*Philippians* 9:1–2) uses these words in such a way that he certainly understood "the love of the present age" to mean apostasy. The contrast, especially with v. 8, is so sharp, it is difficult to give his action a softer interpretation.

Lock (p. 116) has made an interesting correlation between all of vv. 9–18 and Psalm 22. He has perhaps carried it a bit too far, but the correlation seems to be there (see esp. note on v. 17).

4:13 / There is a rather extensive literature on this verse. For a full discussion of the meaning of *biblia*, see T. C. Skeat, "Early Christian Book Production: Papyri and Manuscripts," in *The Cambridge History of the Bible*, ed. G. W. H. Lampe (Cambridge: Cambridge University Press, 1969), vol. 2, pp. 54–79. On the qualifying phrase **especially the ones made of parchment**, see Skeat, " 'Especially the Parchments': A Note on 2 Timothy iv. 13."

4:14-15 / Lock and Bernard make the suggestion that **Alexander** opposed Paul in Rome. Thus these verses are seen to belong to vv. 16–18. But since they serve as a clear warning to Timothy, it makes more sense to locate him at the point of Paul's arrest.

4:16 / Much of the debate on this text is related to the double questions of authenticity and a second imprisonment. On these questions, see the Introduction.

4:17 / For an analysis of this passage in light of Psalm 22, see Lock (p. 116) and J. Munck, *Paul and the Salvation of Mankind* (London: SCM, 1959), pp. 331–33.

15

Final Greetings

2 TIMOTHY 4:19-22

I send greetings to Priscilla and Aquila and to the family of Onesiphorus. ²⁰Erastus stayed in Corinth, and I left Trophimus in Miletus, because he was sick. ²¹Do your best come before winter.

Eubulus, Pudens, Linus, and Claudia send their greetings, and so do all the other Christian brothers. ²²The Lord be with your spirit. God's grace be with you all.

As with Titus, but unlike 1 Timothy (see disc. on 1 Tim. 6:21), Paul concludes this letter with personal greetings, both *for* friends in Ephesus and *to* Timothy from some Roman believers. Such greetings are typical both of the Hellenistic letter and of the Apostle Paul (cf. 1 Thessalonians, 1 and 2 Corinthians, Romans, Colossians, Philippians, Philemon). Although no one of these is formally like the others, all the elements of this one are found in some form elsewhere.

There are five parts to this closing: greetings for certain people (cf. Rom. 16:3–15; Col. 4:15); personal news of friends (cf. Col. 4:13); a final request (cf. Rom. 16:17–19; 2 Cor. 13:11; Col. 4:16); greetings from specific persons (cf. Rom. 16:21–23; 1 Cor. 16:19; Col. 4:10–14); and a final benediction (cf. all the letters).

4:19 / Greetings to individuals are rare in Paul's letters. It is never done to churches where he is known to all. But in this case he makes two notable exceptions.

The **greetings** to his old friends **Priscilla and Aquila** is something of a surprise—not that Paul would greet them, but that they are back in Ephesus. Paul first met them in Corinth, where they had gone from Rome after the edict of Claudius (Acts 18:1–3). They then accompanied Paul to Ephesus, where they remained for some time (Acts 18:18–26; in 1 Cor. 16:19 a church meets in their house). A little later they are apparently in Rome, where again they have a house-church (Rom. 16:3–4); and now we find them again in Ephesus. **Aquila** himself was a Jew from Pontus; we may assume **Priscilla** was a Jew. In four of six mentions of their names, she is mentioned first, which is so highly unusual in antiquity that we may also assume that hers was a significant role in their ministry. They were such dear friends, who had worked with Paul through so many years, that he cannot refrain from greeting them.

He also sends special personal greetings **to the family of Onesiphorus**. Mentioning only the family means at least that Onesiphorus was not with them. If our interpretation of 1:16–18 is correct, that Onesiphorus has died, then this extraordinary personal greeting also makes a great deal of sense.

4:20 / This interruption of the greetings with personal news of friends also comes as a surprise—all the more so if this is pseudepigraphy! We simply cannot know the reasons for it, unless it was triggered in some way by the mention of his friends in verse 19, or the sudden remembrance that not all the co-workers Timothy knew to be with him had been mentioned in verses 10–12.

The note about **Erastus** is especially puzzling. Since he **stayed in Corinth**, was this (less likely) the city official ("director of public works," NIV) of that name mentioned in Romans 16:23, whose inscription can still be seen among the ruins of Old Corinth? Or was this (more likely) the "helper" (*diakoneō*) whom he sent with Timothy from Ephesus to Macedonia some years earlier (Acts 19:22)? And did Paul leave him **in Corinth** as they passed through the city? Or was he already in Corinth, and Timothy expected him to have joined Paul, but instead he had **stayed in Corinth**? We simply don't know. So also with **Trophimus**. Did Paul get as close as Miletus in trying to return to Ephesus (cf. 1 Tim. 3:14–15)? If so, is it possible that word about Trophimus had not reached Timothy? Or is that the wrong question, and should we look from Paul's perspective alone, who was making sure Timothy knew about **Trophimus** in the nearby city? In any case, he had to leave him **in Miletus because he was sick**—one of those rare personal touches we get quite in passing as to the tenuousness of this early ministry. How little we really know of the day-in, day-out affairs of these people's lives (cf. 2 Cor. 11:23–27)!

4:21 / The slight excursion about Erastus and Trophimus appears to trigger another reminder from verses 9–15. **Do your best to come before winter**—not only because he would need his coat (v. 13), but because the Mediterranean was closed to shipping from November to March. This probably suggests that the letter was written in late spring or early summer, and if Timothy was to get there during that year, he would need to set right out.

Finally he **sends greetings** from some friends, **Eubulus**, **Pudens**, **Linus**, **and Claudia**, and **all the other Christian brothers** and sisters. Since three of these names are Latin, one may assume that these are local Roman believers. Are they leaders, as is most likely? Or are they merely acquaintances of Timothy's from his former visit to Rome? Most likely it is both: At least they are known to Timothy; because he would also have known so many others, they are most likely also leaders. It is therefore of interest that a woman is named among them.

The only one of the four of whom there is further substantial information is **Linus**, who is mentioned as the "bishop" of Rome in tradition as early as Irenaeus (*Against Heresies* 3.3). There is no reason to doubt what for Irenaeus is bedrock fact.

4:22 / Finally, there is a benediction and grace, common to all the letters. This one is in two parts. First, there is a word for Timothy personally: **The Lord be with your spirit** (cf. Gal. 6:18; Philem. 25; Phil. 4:23). This is an expanded form of "the Lord be with you," **your spirit** in this case representing the whole person. Secondly, and interestingly, he has a word for the church: **God's grace be with you all**. Thus, even though the whole letter is a very personal word to Timothy, in much of it there is an obvious concern for the Ephesian church as well; and since he sends greetings to others besides Timothy, he therefore includes them **all** in the final **grace**.

It is altogether fitting that the very last words from Paul should be a benediction, a desire for **God's grace** to **be with all** his people.

Additional Note

For examples of these kinds of greetings from the Hellenistic letters, see F. X. J. Exler (*The Form of the Ancient Greek Letter*), pp. 69–77 and 111–13. The Pauline closings have been formally analyzed by W. G. Doty, *Letters in Primitive Christianity*, pp. 39–42, and H. Gamble, *The Textual History of the Letter to the Romans*, SD 42 (Grand Rapids: Eerdmans, 1977), pp. 56–83.

4:21 / For a full presentation of the difficulties of travel on the Mediterranean in winter, see F. Brandel, *The Mediterranean and the Mediterranean World in the Age of Philip II* (New York: Harper & Row, 1966), pp. 248–56.

Abbreviations

Commentaries are regularly cited by the author's last name (see "For Further Reading"), except for Dibelius-Conzelmann (see D-C below).

AB	Analecta Biblica (series)
ANF	*Ante-Nicene Fathers* (series)
ATR	*Anglican Theological Review*
BAGD	Bauer, Arndt, Gingrich, and Danker, *A Greek-English Lexicon of the New Testament and Other Early Christian Literature* (1979)
Berkeley	G. Verkuyl, *The Berkeley Version in Modern English*
BibSac	*Bibliotheca Sacra*
BJRL	*Bulletin of the John Ryland Library*
BT	*The Bible Translator*
BTB	*Biblical Theology Bulletin*
CBQ	*The Catholic Biblical Quarterly*
cf.	compare
CH	*Church History*
chap(s).	chapter(s)
CTJ	*Calvin Theological Journal*
Danby	H. Danby, trans., *The Mishnah* (1954)
D-C	Dibelius and Conzelmann, *The Pastoral Epistles* (1972)
disc.	discussion
DSB	The Daily Study Bible Series
EvQ	*The Evangelical Quarterly*
ExpT	*The Expository Times*
f. (ff.)	and the following verse(s) or page(s)
Gk.	Greek
GNB	The Good News Bible
Goodspeed	E. J. Goodspeed, *An American Translation*
HNTC	Harper's New Testament Commentaries
HS	Hennecke-Schneemelcher, *New Testament Apocrypha* (1963, 1965)
IB	The Interpreter's Bible
ICC	International Critical Commentary
ITQ	*Irish Theological Quarterly*
JB	The Jerusalem Bible

JBL	*The Journal of Biblical Literature*
JETS	*Journal of the Evangelical Theological Society*
Jos.	Flavius Josephus
JRelS	*Journal of Religious Studies*
JSNT	*Journal for the Study of the New Testament*
JTS	*Journal of Theological Studies*
KJV	King James Version
lit.	literally
Loeb	The Loeb Classical Library (series)
LSJ	Liddell-Scott-Jones, *Greek-English Lexicon*
LTP	*Laval théologique et philosophique*
LXX	Septuagint (pre-Christian Gk. translation of the OT)
MNTC	Moffatt New Testament Commentary
Moffatt	*The New Testament: A New Translation* (1922)
Moulton-Milligan	Moulton and Milligan, *The Vocabulary of the Greek Testament* (1930)
MS (MSS)	manuscript(s)
NA^{26}	Nestle-Aland Greek New Testament, 26th ed. (1979)
NAB	New American Bible
NASB	New American Standard Bible
NClarB	New Clarendon Bible (series)
NCBC	New Century Bible Commentary
NEB	New English Bible
NIDNTT	C. Brown, ed. *The New International Dictionary of New Testament Theology* (1975–78)
NIV	New International Version
NovT	*Novum Testamentum*
NT	New Testament
NTC	New Testament Commentary (series)
NTM	New Testament Message (series)
NTS	*New Testament Studies*
OT	Old Testament
PE	Pastoral Epistles
Phillips	*The New Testament in Modern English* (1959)
PNTC	Pelican New Testament Commentaries
RestQ	*Restoration Quarterly*
RevExp	*Review and Expositor*

RSV	Revised Standard Version
RV	Revised Version
SBT	Studies in Biblical Theology (series)
SD	Studies and Documents (series)
SNTSMS	Society of New Testament Studies Monograph Series
Str-B	Strack-Billerbeck, *Kommentar zum Neuen Testament aus Talmud und Midrasch* (1922–38)
SWJT	*Southwestern Journal of Theology*
TBC	Torch Bible Commentaries
TCGNT	B. Metzger, *A Textual Commentary on the Greek New Testament* (UBS, 1971)
TDNT	G. Kittel and G. Friedrich, eds. *Theological Dictionary of the New Testament*, trans. G. W. Bromiley (1964–72)
TrinJ	*Trinity Journal*
TS	*Theological Studies*
ThZ	*Theologische Zeitschrift*
TU	Texte und Untersuchungen (series)
UBS	United Bible Societies
v. (vv.)	verse(s)
WBC	Word Bible Commentaries
Weymouth	*The New Testament in Modern Speech* (1902)
Williams	C. B. Williams, *The New Testament, A Translation in the Language of the People* (1937)

For Further Reading

The bibliography is restricted to works available in English, except for the two particularly significant commentaries by Brox and Spicq.

Commentaries

Barclay, W. *The Letters to Timothy, Titus, and Philemon*. DSB. Rev. ed. Philadelphia: Westminster, 1975.

Barrett C. K. *The Pastoral Epistles*. NClarB. Oxford: Clarendon, 1963.

Bernard, J. H. *The Pastoral Epistles*. Cambridge: Cambridge University Press, 1899. Reprint. Grand Rapids: Baker, 1980 (Thornapple Commentaries).

Brox, N. *Die Pastoralbriefe*. Regensburger NT. 4th rev. ed. Regensburg: Pustet, 1969.

Calvin, John. *The Second Epistle of Paul to the Corinthians, and the Epistles to Timothy, Titus, and Philemon*. Translated by T. A. Smail. Grand Rapids: Eerdmans, 1964.

Dibelius, M., and H. Conzelmann. *The Pastoral Epistles*. Hermeneia. Translated by P. Buttolph and A. Yarbro. Philadelphia: Fortress, 1972.

Easton, B. S. *The Pastoral Epistles*. New York: Scribner's, 1948.

Erdman, C. R. *The Pastoral Epistles of Paul*. Philadelphia: Westminster, 1923.

Falconer, R. *The Pastoral Epistles*. Oxford: Clarendon, 1937.

Gealy, F. D. *The First and Second Epistles to Timothy and the Epistle to Titus*. IB, vol. 11. Nashville: Abingdon, 1955.

Guthrie, D. *The Pastoral Epistles: An Introduction and Commentary*. Tyndale NT Commentary. Grand Rapids: Eerdmans, 1957.

Hanson, A. T. *The Pastoral Epistles*. NCBC. Grand Rapids: Eerdmans, 1982.

Hendriksen, W. *Exposition of the Pastoral Epistles*. NTC. Grand Rapids: Baker, 1965.

Houlden, J. L. *The Pastoral Epistles: I and II Timothy, Titus*. PNTC. London: Penguin, 1976.

Karris, R. J. *The Pastoral Epistles*. NTM. Wilmington, Del.: Michael Glazier, 1979.

Kelly, J. N. D. *A Commentary on the Pastoral Epistles*. HNTC. New York: Harper, 1963. Reprint. Grand Rapids: Baker, 1981 (Thornapple Commentaries).

Kent, H. A. *The Pastoral Epistles: Studies in I and II Timothy and Titus*. Chicago: Moody, 1958.

Leaney, A. R. C. *The Epistles to Timothy, Titus and Philemon: Introduction and Commentary.* TBC. London: SCM, 1960.

Lock, W. *A Critical and Exegetical Commentary on The Pastoral Epistles.* ICC. Edinburgh: T. & T. Clark, 1924.

Moellering, H. A. *1 Timothy, 2 Timothy, Titus.* Concordia Commentary. Saint Louis: Concordia, 1970.

Parry, R. St.J. *The Pastoral Epistles with Introduction, Text and Commentary.* Cambridge: Cambridge University Press, 1920.

Ramsey, W. M. "Historical Commentary on the First Epistle to Timothy." *The Expositor,* 7th series, 7 (1909), pp. 481–94; 8 (1909), pp. 1–21, 167–85, 264–82, 339–57, 399–416, 557–68; 9 (1910), pp. 172–87, 319–33, 433—40.

Scott, E. F. *The Pastoral Epistles.* MNTC. London: Hodder & Stoughton, 1936.

Simpson, E. K. *The Pastoral Epistles: The Greek Text with Introduction and Commentary.* London: Tyndale, 1954.

Spicq, C. *Saint Paul Les Épîtres Pastorales.* Études Bibliques. 4th rev. ed. 2 vols. Paris: Gabalda, 1969.

Wilson, G. B. *The Pastoral Epistles.* Edinburgh: Banner of Truth, 1982.

Authorship

Allan, J. A. "The 'In Christ' Formula in the Pastoral Epistles." *NTS* 10 (1963/64), pp. 115–21.

Carrington, P. "The Problem of the Pastoral Epistles: Dr. Harrison's Theory Reviewed." *ATR* 21 (1939), pp. 32–39.

Ellis, E. E. "The Authorship of the Pastorals: A Resume and Assessment of Recent Trends." In *Paul and His Recent Interpreters.* Grand Rapids: Eerdmans, 1961, pp. 49–57.

Grayston, K. and G. Herndon. "The Authorship of the Pastorals in the Light of Statistical Linguistics." *NTS* 6 (1959), pp. 1–15.

Guthrie, D. *New Testament Introduction.* 3d ed. Downers Grove, Ill: Inter-varsity, 1970, pp. 584–634.

_____. *The Pastoral Epistles and the Mind of Paul.* London: Tyndale, 1956.

Harrison, P. N. "Important Hypotheses Reconsidered; III. The Authorship of the Pastoral Epistles." *ExpT* 67 (1954/55), pp. 77–81.

_____. "The Pastoral Epistles and Duncan's Ephesian Theory." *NTS* 2 (1956), pp. 250–261.

————. *Paulines and Pastorals*. London: Villiers, 1964.

————. *The Problems of the Pastoral Epistles*. Oxford: Oxford University Press, 1921.

Hitchcock, F. R. M. "Philo and the Pastorals." *Hermatheua* 56 (1940), pp. 113–35.

————. "Tests for the Pastorals." *JTS* 30 (1928–29), pp. 272–79.

James, J. D. *The Genuineness and Authorship of the Pastoral Epistles*. London: Longmans, Green, 1909.

Kümmel, W. G. *Introduction to the New Testament*. Translated by H. C. Kee. Nashville: Abingdon, 1975, pp. 366–87.

McRay, J. "The Authorship of the Pastoral Epistles." *RestQ* 7 (1963), pp. 2–18.

Metzger, B. M. "A Reconsideration of Certain Arguments Against the Pauline Authorship of the Pastoral Epistles." *ExpT* 70 (1958), pp. 91–94.

Moule, C. F. D. "The Problem of the Pastoral Epistles: A Reappraisal." *BJRL* 47 (1965), pp. 430–52. Reprint. In *Essays in New Testament Interpretation*. Cambridge: Cambridge University Press, 1982, pp. 113–32.

O'Rourke, J. J. "Some Considerations about Attempts at Statistical Analysis of the Pauline Corpus." *CBQ* 35 (1973), pp. 483–90.

Quinn, J. D. "The Last Volume of Luke: the Relation of Luke-Acts to the Pastoral Epistles." In *Perspectives on Luke-Acts*, edited by C. Talbert, pp. 62–75. Danville, Va.: Association of Baptist Professors of Religion, 1978.

Roberts, J. W. "The Genuineness of the Pastorals: Some Recent Aspects of the Question." *RestQ* 8 (1965), pp. 104–10.

Rogers, P. "The Pastoral Epistles as Deutero-Pauline." *ITQ* 45 (1978), pp. 248–60.

Simpson, E. K. "The Authenticity and Authorship of the Pastoral Epistles." *EvQ* 12 (1940), pp. 289–311.

Wilson, S. G. *Luke and the Pastoral Epistles*. London: S.P.C.K., 1979.

Background and Theology

Bourke, M. M. "Reflections on Church Order in the New Testament." *CBQ* 30 (1968), pp. 493–511.

Cranford, L. "Encountering Heresy: Insight from the Pastoral Epistles." *SWJT* 22 (1980), pp. 23–40.

Duncan, G. S. "Paul's Ministry in Asia—the Last Phase." *NTS* 3 (1957), pp. 211–18.

Dunn, J. D. G. *Jesus and the Spirit*. Philadelphia: Westminster, 1975, pp. 347–50.

Ellis, E. E. "Paul and His Opponents." In *Prophecy and Hermeneutic in Early Christianity*. Grand Rapids: Eerdmans, 1978, pp. 80–115.

Floor, L. "Church Order in the Pastoral Epistles." *Neotestamentica* 10 (1976), pp. 81–91.

Ford, J. M. "A Note on Proto-Montanism in the Pastoral Epistles." *NTS* 17 (1971), pp. 338–46.

Hanson, A. T. "The Domestication of Paul: A Study in the Development of Early Christian Theology." *BJRL* 63 (1981), pp. 402–18.

Hiebert, D. E. "Pauline Images of a Christian Leader." *BibSac* 133 (1976), pp. 213–28.

Hitchcock, F. R. M. "The Pastorals and a Second Trial of Paul." *ExpT* 41 (1929/30), pp. 20–23.

Johnson, L. T. "II Timothy and the Polemic Against False Teachers: A Re-examination." *JRelS* 6 (1978), 7 (1979), pp. 1–26.

Karris, R. J. "The Background and Significance of the Polemic of the Pastoral Epistles." *JBL* 92 (1973), pp. 549–64.

Lemaire, A. "Pastoral Epistles: Redaction and Theology." *BTB* 2 (1972), pp. 25–42.

Lightfoot, J. B. "The Date of the Pastoral Epistles." In *Biblical Essays*, pp. 397–410. London: Macmillan, 1904.

————. "Additional Note on the Heresy Combated in the Pastoral Epistles." In *Biblical Essays*, pp. 411–18. London: Macmillan, 1904.

Lightman, M., and W. Ziesel. "Univira: An Example of Continuity and Change in Roman Society." *CH* 46 (1977), pp. 19–32.

MacDonald, D. "Virgins, Widows, and Paul in Second-Century Asia Minor." In SBL Seminar Papers 1979. Edited by P. J. Achtemeier, vol. 1, pp. 169–84. Missoula, Mont.: Scholars Press, 1979.

Malherbe, A. J. "Medical Imagery in the Pastoral Epistles." In *Texts and Testaments, Critical Essays on the Bible and Early Church Fathers*, edited by W. E. March, pp. 19–35. San Antonio: Trinity University Press, 1980.

Marshall, I. H. "The Development of the Concept of Redemption in the New Testament." In *Reconciliation and Hope*, edited by R. Banks, pp. 153–69. Grand Rapids: Eerdmans, 1974.

————. *Kept by the Power of God*. Minneapolis: Bethany Fellowship, 1969, pp. 126–36.

Meier, J. B. "*Presbyteros* in the Pastoral Epistles." *CBQ* 35 (1973), pp. 323–45.

Oates, W. "The Conception of Ministry in the Pastoral Epistles." *RevExp* 56 (1959), pp. 388–410.

Quinn, J. D. "The Holy Spirit in the Pastoral Epistles." In *Sin, Salvation, and the Spirit*, edited by D. Durken, pp. 345–68. Collegeville, Minn.: Liturgical Press, 1979.

_____. "On the Terminology for Faith, Truth, Teaching, and the Spirit in the Pastoral Epistles: a summary." In *Teaching Authority and Infallibility in the Church: Lutherans and Catholics in Dialogue. VI*, edited by P. C. Empie, T. A. Murphy, and J. A. Burgess, pp. 232–37. Minneapolis: Augsburg, 1980.

_____. "Ordination in the Pastoral Epistles." *International Catholic Review/Communio* 8 (1981), pp. 358–69.

_____. "Paul's Last Captivity." In *Studia Biblica 1978 III. Papers on Paul and Other New Testament Authors*, *JSNT* Suppl. 3, edited by E. A. Livingstone, pp. 289–99. Sheffield: JSOT Press, 1980.

Ramsay, W. M. "The Church and the Empire in the First Century: The Pastoral Epistles and Tacitus." *The Expositor*, 4th series 8 (1893), pp. 110–19.

Robinson, J. A. T. *Redating the New Testament*. Philadelphia: Westminster, 1976, pp. 67–84.

Rogers, P. "How Valid is the Ecclesiology of the Pastoral Epistles?" *Milltown Studies* 3 (1979), pp. 1–20.

Safrai, S. "Education and the Study of Torah." In *The Jewish People in the First Century*, edited by S. Safrai and M. Stern, vol. 2, pp. 945–70. Philadelphia: Fortress, 1976.

Schweizer, E. *Church Order in the New Testament*. SBT 32. London: SCM, 1961, pp. 77–88.

Exegetical Studies

Austin, M. R. "How Biblical is 'The Inspiration of Scripture'?" *ExpT* 93 (1981), pp. 75–79.

Barclay, W. "Paul's Certainties VII. Our Security in God—2 Timothy i.12." *ExpT* 69 (1958), pp. 324–27.

Beasley-Murray, G. R. *Baptism in the New Testament*. Grand Rapids: Eerdmans, 1962.

Bennetch, J. H. "2 Timothy 3:16a, A Greek Study." *BibSac* 106 (1949), pp. 187–95.

Brown, R. E. "*Episkopē* and *Episkopos*: The New Testament Evidence." *TS* 41 (1980), pp. 322–38.

Cook, D. "2 Timothy iv.6–8 and the Epistle to the Philippians." *JTS* 33 (1982), pp. 168–71.

Corcoran, G. "Slavery in the New Testament I." *Milltown Studies* 5 (1980), pp. 1–40.

Dodd, C. H. "New Testament Translation Problems II." *BT* 28 (1977), pp. 101–16.

Dunn, J. D. G. *Baptism in the Holy Spirit.* SBT 2d series 15. London: SCM, 1970.

duPlessis, I. J. "The Rule of Christ and the Rule in the Church." *Neotestamentica* 10 (1976), pp. 20–30.

Ellingworth, P. "The 'True Saying' in I Timothy 3.1." *BT* 31 (1980), pp. 443–45.

Falconer, R. "I Timothy 2:14–15." *JBL* 60 (1941), pp. 375–79.

Fee, G. D. "The Majority Text and the Original Text of the New Testament." *BT* 31 (1980), pp. 107–18.

Freeborn, J. C. K. "2 Timothy 4,11: 'Only Luke Is with Me.' " In *Studia Evangelica*, vol. 6, pp. 128–39. TU 112. Berlin: Akademie-Verlag, 1973.

Fuller, J. W. "Of Elders and Triads in I Timothy 5.19–25." *NTS* 29 (1983), pp. 258–63.

Gärtner, Bertil. "Didaskalos: The Office, Man and Woman in the New Testament." *Concordia Journal* 8 (1982), pp. 52–60.

Grabbe, L. L. "The Jannes/Jambres Tradition in Targum Pseudo-Jonathan and Its Date." *JBL* 98 (1979), pp. 393–401.

Gundry, R. H. "The Form, Meaning, and Background of the Hymn Quoted in I Timothy 3:16." In *Apostolic History and the Gospel*, edited by W. W. Gasque and R. P. Martin, pp. 203–22. Grand Rapids: Eerdmans, 1970.

Hanson, A. T. *Studies in the Pastoral Epistles.* London: S.P.C.K., 1968.

Harris, J. R. "The Cretans Always Liars." *The Expositor*, 7th series, 2 (1906), pp. 305–17.

––––––. "A Further Note on the Cretans." *The Expositor*, 7th series, 3 (1907), pp. 332–37.

––––––. "St. Paul and Epimenides." *The Expositor*, 8th series, 4 (1912), pp. 348–53.

Harris, M. J. "Titus 2:13 and the Deity of Christ." In *Pauline Studies: Essays Presented to Professor F. F. Bruce on His 70th Birthday*, edited by D. Hagner and M. J. Harris, pp. 262–77. Grand Rapids: Eerdmans, 1980.

Harvey, A. E. " 'The Workman Is Worthy of His Hire': Fortunes of a Proverb in the Early Church." *NovT* 24 (1982), pp. 209–21.

Hitchcock, F. R. M. "Miscellanea—New Light on a Passage in the Pastorals (2 Tim. 2:25–26)." *Theology* 34 (1937), pp. 108–12.

Hommes, N. J. "Let Women Be Silent in the Church: A Message Concerning the Worship Service and the Decorum to Be Observed by Women." *CTJ* 4 (1969), pp. 5–22.

Jebb, S. "A Suggested Interpretation of I Tim. 2.15." *ExpT* 81 (1970), pp. 221–22.

Kirk, J. A. "Did 'Officials' in the New Testament Church Receive a Salary?" *ExpT* 84 (1972/73), pp. 105–8.

Knight, G. W. *The Faithful Sayings in the Pastoral Letters.* Kampen: J. H. Kok, 1968. Reprint. Grand Rapids: Baker, 1979.

Lane, W. L. "I Tim. iv. 1–3. An Early Instance of Over-realized Eschatology?" *NTS* 11 (1965), pp. 164–67.

Lewis, R. M. "The 'Women' of I Timothy 3:11." *BibSac* 136 (1979), pp. 167–75.

Lightfoot, N. R. "The Role of Women in Religious Services." *RestQ* 19 (1976), pp. 129–36.

McEleney, N. J. "The Vice Lists of the Pastoral Epistles." *CBQ* 36 (1974), pp. 203–19.

Moo, D. J. "I Timothy 2:11–15: Meaning and Significance." *TrinJ* 1 (1980), pp. 62–83.

Mott, S. C. "Greek Ethics and Christian Conversion: The Philonic Background of Titus ii.10–14 and iii.3–7." *NovT* 20 (1978), pp. 22–48.

Osburn, C. D. "Authenteō (1 Timothy 2:12)." *RestQ* 25 (1982), pp. 1–12.

Payne, P. B. "Libertarian Women in Ephesus: A Response to Douglas J. Moo's Article, '1 Timothy 2:11–15: Meaning and Significance.' " *TrinJ* 2 (1981), pp. 169–97.

Roberts, M. D. "Woman Shall Be Saved: A Closer Look at 1 Timothy 2:15." *TSF Bulletin* 5/2 (1981), pp. 4–7.

Saucy, R. L. "The Husband of One Wife." *BibSac* 131 (1974), pp. 229–40.

Scholer, D. M. "Women's Adornment. Some Historical and Hermeneutical Observations on the New Testament Passages." *Daughters of Sarah* 6 (1980), pp. 3–6.

Schweizer, E. "Two New Testament Creeds Compared, 1 Corinthians 15:3–5 and 1 Timothy 3:16." In *Current Issues in New Testament Interpretation*, edited by W. Klassen and G. F. Snyder, pp. 166–77. New York: Harper, 1962.

Skeat, T. C. " 'Especially the Parchments': A Note on 2 Timothy IV.13." *JTS* 30 (1979), pp. 173–77.

Spencer, A. D. B. "Eve at Ephesus (Should Women Be Ordained as Pastors according to the First Letter to Timothy 2:11–15?)." *JETS* 17 (1974), pp. 215–22.

Stenger, W. *Der Christushymnus 1 Tim. 3,16. Eine structuranalytische Untersuchung*, Regensburger Studien zur Theologie 6. Frankfurt/M: Peter Lang, 1977.

Thompson, G. H. P. "Ephesians iii.13 and 2 Timothy ii.10 in the Light of Colossians i.24." *ExpT* 71 (1960), pp. 187–89.

Wilson, J. P. "The Translation of 2 Timothy 2:26." *ExpT* 49 (1937/38), pp. 45–6.

Other Useful Books

Doty, W. G. *Letters in Primitive Christianity.* Philadelphia: Fortress, 1979.

Elliott, J. K. *The Greek Text of the Epistles to Timothy and Titus.* SD 36. Salt Lake City: University of Utah Press, 1968.

Exler, F. X. J. *The Form of the Ancient Greek Letter of the Epistolary Papyri (3rd cent. B.C.—3rd cent. A.D.)* . Chicago: Ares Publishers, 1923.

Fee, G. D., and D. Stuart. *How to Read the Bible for All Its Worth.* Grand Rapids: Zondervan, 1982.

Hill, D. *Greek Words and Hebrew Meanings: Studies in the Semantics of Soteriological Terms.* SNTSMS 5. Cambridge: Cambridge University Press, 1967.

Hort, F. J. A. *Judaistic Christianity.* London: Macmillan, 1894. Reprint. Grand Rapids: Baker, 1980.

Hurley, J. B. *Man and Woman in Biblical Perspective.* Grand Rapids: Zondervan, 1981.

Kelly, J. N. D. *Early Christian Creeds.* London: Longmans, Green, 1950.

Ladd, G. E. *A Theology of the New Testament.* Grand Rapids: Eerdmans, 1974.

Metzger, B. M. *A Textual Commentary on the Greek New Testament.* London: United Bible Societies, 1971.

Morris, L. L. *The Apostolic Preaching of the Cross.* Grand Rapids: Eerdmans, 1955.

Pfitzner, V. C. *Paul and the Agon Motif.* Leiden: Brill, 1967.

Sevenster, J. N. *Paul and Seneca.* Leiden: Brill, 1961.

Warkentin, M. *Ordination: A Biblical-Historical View.* Grand Rapids: Eerdmans, 1982.

Subject Index

Actium, 166
Acts of Paul and Thecla, 22, 209, 223, 247
Adam: Adam-Christ imagery, 29; priority in creation, 36–37
Adriatic Sea, 166
Agapētoi, 98
Age: of older people in antiquity, 139, 140; of Timothy, xvi, 68, 71; of "true" widows, 80; of "younger" men in antiquity, 71
Akairōs, 234
Alexander: companion of Hymenaeus, xvii, 13, 22–23, 206, 208, 245; the Ephesian Jew, 22, 245; the metalworker, xviii, 22, 244, 245, 248
Amanuensis, xxxvii, xl
Ambracian Gulf, 166
Amen, 19
Anakainōsis, 157
Anexikakon, 215
Angels: election of, 91; as part of heavenly tribunal, 90; as worshipers of exalted Christ, 56
Anna the prophetess, as ideal widow, 77, 80
Anthrōpos, 29
Antilytron, 30
Antitheseis, 120
Apaideutos, 214, 215
Apelipon, 130
Apistoumen, 200
Apollodorus Comicus, 106
Apollos, 166–167
Apostasia, 60
Apostasy, xxxii, 8, 22–23, 60, 99, 175, 186, 188, 199–201, 203, 204, 215–216, 242–243, 247–248
Apostle's Creed, 232
Apostolic succession, as an anachronism, 190
Apotomōs, 134
Apo toutōn, 212
Aquila, 249
Archai, 159
Aristides, on welcoming strangers, 44
Aristotle, 133
Artemas, xvi, xviii, 165, 166
Artemis (Diana), 5, 34, 99, 112
Asceticism, xxii, 10, 26, 44, 71, 88, 92, 114–115, 134–137, 207
Asebeia, 70, 147, 206, 227
Asia, province of, 5
Athens, 166
Athletic metaphors, Paul's use of, 11, 22, 65–67, 71, 108–109, 113, 189,192, 193–194, 232, 238–239
Atonement, Christ's, 29–30, 110, 149–150
Augustine, on foot-washing, 85
Augustus, 166
Autarkeia, 102, 105
Autarkēs, 151
Authenticity, xv, xvii–xviii, xix–xx, xxiv, xxvi, xxvii–xxviii, xxx, xxxi, xxxiv–xxxvii, xxxviii–xl, 3, 13, 20, 24, 47, 72, 85, 93, 94, 113, 120, 124, 129, 137, 151, 159, 160, 166, 174, 184, 187–188, 193, 194, 208, 223, 230, 239, 240, 242, 244, 247–248, 250

BAGD, 13, 88, 98, 101, 113, 119, 130, 197, 221, 230, 235
Bahr, G. J., xl
Balaam, 224
Balsdon, J. P. V. D., 85
Baptism: Christian, 157–158, 160; Timothy's, 109, 113
Baptismal imagery, 157–158, 199
Barclay, W., 120, 184, 220
Barnabas, Paul's companion, 243
Barrett, C. K., xl, 60, 66, 71, 85, 86, 98, 105, 113, 128, 135, 137, 151, 160, 170, 183, 188, 193, 198, 205, 216, 231, 239, 246
Bauernfeind, O., 24
Baur, F. C., 120
Bdelyktos, 136
Beasley-Murray, G. R., 160, 201
Benedictions, Pauline, 119–120, 168, 251
Berkeley (translation), 180, 221
Bernard, J. H., xl, 13, 18, 31, 57, 61, 71, 85, 91, 93, 94, 105, 144, 145, 184, 186, 201, 202, 208, 215, 216, 217, 231, 239, 246, 248
Biblia, 244, 245
Bishop. *See* Overseer.
Blasphēmein, 155
Blasphēmoi, 220
Book of Common Prayer, 17
Brandel, F., 251
Brox, N., 102
Büchsel, F., 13

Caiaphas, 133
Callimachus, 133
Calvin, J., 71
Carpus, 244
Carr, W., 160
Chapman, J. Wilbur, 55
Charisma, 176
Chiasmus, in the PE, 57, 79, 161
Children, religious training of, 230–231
Chloe, 84
Christ: ascension of, 56; atoning death of, xxix, 28–30, 110, 149–150; birth of, 38; as the Christian's hope, 2; Davidic descent of, 195–196; glorification of, 56; his "confession" before Pilate, 110; his forbearance, 19; incarnation of,18, 55–56, 180, 196; as Mediator, 28–29; as member of heavenly tribunal, 91, 110, 233; as the one who empowers, 16; parousia of, xxx–xxxi, xxxv, 111, 146, 148–149, 187, 233, 239; as Redeemer, 18, 150; resurrection of, 56, 180, 195, 196–197; as Savior, 3, 124, 149, 158, 180; teaching of, 89, 93, 100, 103, 106, 115, 116, 134–135, 158,

263

Scripture Index

APOCRYPHA